White Siberia

White Siberia

The Politics of Civil War

N.G.O. PEREIRA

McGill-Queen's University Press
Montreal & Kingston • London • Buffalo

Legal deposit first quarter 1996
Bibliothèque nationale du Québec

Printed in Canada on acid-free paper

This book has been published with the help of a grant
from the Social Science Federation of Canada, using
funds provided by the Social Sciences and Humanities
Research Council of Canada.

McGill-Queen's University Press is grateful to the Canada
Council for support of its publishing program.

Canadian Cataloguing in Publication Data

Pereira, N.G.O. (Norman G.O.), 1942–
White Siberia: the politics of civil war

Includes bibliographical references and index.
ISBN 0-7735-1349-3

1. Siberia (Russia) – History – Revolution, 1917–1921.
2. Siberia (Russia) – Politics and government. 3. Anti-
communist movements – Russia (Federation) – Siberia.
4. Russia (Federation) – History – Revolution, 1917–
1921. I. Title.

DK265.8.S5P47 1995   957'.08'41   C95-900686-9

Typeset in New Baskerville 10/12
by Caractéra inc., Quebec City

For Linda

Contents

Maps

All maps by Paul Duffy

Preface

With the opening up of the former Soviet archives a great deal of new material has become available for scholarly research. The present study is based in part on the fonds of the Central State Archive of the October Revolution (*TsGAOR*), recently renamed the State Archive of the Russian Federation, especially the so-called Prague Archive containing documents drawn from both Red and White sources that were taken out of Russia temporarily by the evacuating Czechoslovak Legion in 1920 and returned under the supervision of Academician I.I. Mints in late 1945 to *TsGAOR* in Moscow. Use also has been made of selected materials at the Archives du Quai d'Orsay's Ministère des Affaires étrangères (Direction des Affaires politiques et commerciales, "Russie d'Asie") in Paris; the Public Records Office in London and Kew; the Hoover Institution Archives in Stanford, California; the Bakhmeteff Archives at Columbia University in New York; and the National Archives and Records Service in Washington, D.C.

I am grateful for the assistance I received from several other institutions and their staffs: the New York Public and Columbia University libraries during my tenure as a senior fellow at the Harriman Institute for the academic year 1987–88; the Library of Congress during two sojourns at the Kennan Institute; the Russian State Library (formerly the Lenin State Library) in Moscow and the Library of the Academy of Sciences in St Petersburg; the State Museum of the Political History of Russia in St Petersburg; the Bancroft Library of the University of California in Berkeley; the Bibliothèque Nationale in Paris; the School of Slavonic and East European Studies Library in London; and most of all the Killam Library at Dalhousie University and its interlibrary loan and reference specialists (Gwyn Pace, Oriel MacLennan, and Paul Duffy) who were always willing to trace obscure references and help locate much-needed titles.

This work has benefited greatly from critical readings and technical assistance by kind colleagues and friends: Peter Kenez, Elizabeth Haigh, M.P. Iroshnikov, Alan Wood, and especially Olga M. Verbitskaia, and my editors, Joan McGilvray and Henri Pilon. Andrea Chandler and Yanni Kotsonis helped with research at Dalhousie University and Columbia University, respectively. In addition, David R. Jones allowed generous access to his private collection of rare Sibirica and J.D. Smele shared some of the British research materials from his Ph D dissertation. I have been fortunate to receive the continuing support of the Social Sciences and Humanities Research Council of Canada, which has funded this project since its inception ten years ago. My wife, Linda, has read the manuscript at three very different and difficult stages from cover to cover with painstaking care. She has contributed a great deal to its organization and clarity.

Russian words and names have been transliterated according to the modified Library of Congress system (with diacritical marks omitted), except for those, like Kerensky, Guins, and Trotsky, which have established English spellings. Dates are given in the Old Style or Julian calendar until 1/14 February 1918 when Russia adopted the Gregorian standard used in the West, thereby eliminating the thirteen-day gap that separated the two in the twentieth century.

NGOP
Halifax, Nova Scotia

Members of the Provisional Siberian Government, formed in June, 1918. Unknown source

The supreme ruler and supreme military commander, Admiral Aleksandr Vasil'evich Kolchak. Unknown source

A.V. Kolchak, General Alfred Knox, and officers from the British military mission. Environs of Omsk, 1919. Illustration courtesy of the State Museum of the Political History of Russia in St Petersburg

"The House of Freedom." Building which served as seat of Kolchak's government in Omsk during 1918–19. Illustration courtesy of the State Museum of the Political History of Russia in St Petersburg

Kolchakovite "Building." The illustration shows Kolchak sitting on the shoulders of a priest, who in turn is on top of a kulak (rich peasant). The caption reads: "Comrade! Strike at the foundation." Unknown artist and source

The Great Siberian [Rail]way. Tunnel no. 18 (circling
Lake Baikal). Postcard

Великій Сибирскій путь.—Grand Chemin de la Sibérie. № 19.
Сторожевой домъ на 643 верстѣ.

The Great Siberian [Rail]way, No. 19. Sentry outpost at verst 643. Postcard

View of Omsk. Kennan, *Siberia: Natural Scenery*, plate 28

A group of Kolchak's shock troops under the command of General Pepeliaev, 1919.
Illustration courtesy of the State Museum of the Political History of Russia in
St Petersburg

Arrested ministers of the Kolchak Government, Omsk, 1920. Illustration courtesy of the State Museum of the Political History of Russia in St Petersburg

Anti-Kolchak "Green" Partisan Detachment, 1919. Illustration courtesy of the State Museum of the Political History of Russia in St Petersburg

White Siberia

Introduction

For seventy years Civil War scholarship in the USSR was a thriving industry that produced an overwhelming number of tediously tendentious monographs as well as several invaluable sources of detailed information, the latter published, for the most part, in the relatively free 1920s.[1] As might be expected, the triumphs of Bolshevism were at the centre of virtually all these studies, but a suprisingly large amount of attention was given to Siberia. Indeed, since the beginning of the Khrushchev period more source materials on Siberia have been published than on any other region in Russia.

Soviet historiography on the Civil War in Siberia may be subdivided into a number of related fields and topics. Among the most important are 1) works detailing the Allied intervention, in combination with the "counter-revolutionary" activity of Czechoslovak prisoners of war; 2) attempts to explain away the fall of Soviet power in Siberia (which coincided with the Czechoslovak evacuation) during the late spring and early summer of 1918; 3) explanations of how and why cooperative, regionalist, and other "bourgeois" organizations threw their support to anti-Bolshevik governments that formed in several Siberian locations; 4) descriptions of the major White parties and personalities with a view to showing the fundamental similarities among the enemies of Bolshevism, from Kolchak and the Cossack atamans (chieftains) on the right to parliamentary liberals and moderate socialists on the left; and 5) analyses of the social question which seek to demonstrate that only the Bolsheviks represented the true interests of workers, peasants, and soldiers, and that the partisans also followed their lead.[2]

Both before and after 1917 the flow of information from Russia to the West was controlled and filtered by both sides. The dominant Western view was defined by Russian belles-lettres and fiction, as well as by socio-political criticism, with a strong urban, liberal bias. Western perceptions and predispositions were also reinforced by the major Russian emigration, immediately following the Civil War, that brought thousands of the most articulate and cosmopolitan members of educated society to the West, where several of their leaders took up teaching posts and helped form the outlooks of the first generation of academic Russianists. Their intellectual offspring into the third generation are currently spread across the universities and colleges of North America and Western Europe.

Émigré historiography – beginning with the work of the first wave of refugees who were actively involved in the revolutionary events they subsequently described – has been characterized by a natural desire to recast the past in the most favourable light for the foes of Bolshevism while simultaneously settling old scores with personal enemies.[3] Nevertheless, it remains an invaluable resource and one that is still not very well known, mainly because only a small portion of the corpus has been translated and published in any Western language. With the current renewed interest in all things White within the former Soviet Union, moreover, many long-neglected memoirs, accounts by eyewitnesses, and other primary documents that were previously either unavailable or printed in very small editions abroad are now appearing in the pages of major periodicals in Moscow and St Petersburg, as well as in Novosibirsk, Tomsk, Irkutsk, and other provincial centres.[4]

Mainstream Western scholarship, to the limited extent that it has taken an interest in the Siberian theatre of the Russian Civil War, has also been one-sided: it has concentrated almost exclusively on questions related to the Allied interventions and to the larger conflict with Germany. In the United States, Great Britain, France, and Canada the focus has been on the respective roles of the intervening powers in Russia, their mutual antagonisms and competition, and, only marginally, their relations with the local populations.[5] Even the most current scholarship is Eurocentric and pays scant attention to Siberia or other peripheral areas.[6] Moreover, the rare exceptions to this general pattern allot much more attention to the Bolshevik winners than to the White losers.[7] Apart from a few popular and partial treatments, there has been no serious study of the history of the Whites during 1917–22 in Siberia.[8]

It is only during the past decade or so that Civil War and (to a lesser extent) Siberian studies in the West have come into their own. The British Universities Siberian Studies Seminar was founded at Lancaster

University in 1981 by Alan Wood. While there was important work being done in the 1970s by Peter Kenez, and even earlier by David Footman, in the last few years a number of Anglo-American scholars have brought increased attention to both subjects.[9] But apart from some émigré memoirs,[10] this work is the first monograph in English to concentrate on the domestic politics of Siberia during the Civil War period, in contrast to the approach adopted by previous Western scholarship, which has treated the events in the region as no more than a sideshow to the main drama in central Russia and the international conflict between the allies and Germany.

With the recent greatly increased access to the main archival collections in Russia – especially in combination with émigré and other holdings in the United States, Great Britain, and France – a general reassessment of the Russian Civil War has become possible and is indeed underway. There have already been several important contributions by the younger generation of Anglo-American historians.[11] They are now being joined by a wave of newly mobile Russian scholars who are able to take research and teaching positions in the West.[12] An added benefit of these developments is the attendant shift of focus from an almost exclusively centralist historiography to the neglected outlying regions of the southern, north-western, and eastern parts of the former Soviet Union.

The present volume is not the definitive or comprehensive narrative history of the Russian Civil War in Siberia. Rather it is a detailed analysis of the White movement in Siberia, its internal struggles no less than its contest with the Reds, and the reasons for and the consequences of its defeat. The term "White," generically associated with the *ancien régime* and derived from the colours of the Bourbon dynasty, is used in a broadly political sense to contrast with the "Red" Bolsheviks and to encompass all those forces in Russian society – from monarchists on the right to moderate socialists on the left – whose opposition to V.I. Lenin's ascension to power in the fall of 1917 led them subsequently to take up arms against the Soviet government.

As the breadth of this definition suggests, it was not merely a matter of Whites against Reds. In many ways the conflicts within the White camp were no less serious than those that separated them from the common enemy. Elements within the left wings of both the Mensheviks and the Socialist Revolutionaries (SRs) – not to mention groups such as the Menshevik Internationalists and the Left SRs which split formally from their parent parties – stood very close to and in several instances crossed over to the Reds.[13] If such divisions did not exist within Lenin's organization, nevertheless many of the Siberian Bolsheviks did continue to cooperate with their moderate socialist allies even after the October Revolution in Petrograd (the name St Petersburg was given between 1914 and 1924). This was a logical and necessary response to the power balance in Siberia where the soviets remained under SR and Menshevik leadership long after they had come under Bolshevik ascendancy elsewhere.

The approach followed here can fairly be described as political history, but it also takes into account institutions and ideas as well as parties and policies. Moreover, comparative aspects of social history are addressed insofar as they bear directly upon the progress and outcome of the Civil War. One obvious example of that linkage was the mentality of the Siberian peasantry relative to that of its counterparts in European Russia and how it was affected by the nature and significance of Siberia's regional economy, which by Russian standards had always been more capitalist and less feudal than the rest of the country.

Given the partisan and unforgiving nature of all civil wars, the remoteness and insularity of this one in particular, the unfavourable treatment generally accorded counter-revolutions by the dominant liberal historiography in the West (not to mention the former Soviet Union), and the fate of historical records after seventy-five years of Communist rule, many questions are likely to remain. How, for instance, are we to assess the respective mandates of the nineteen White governments in the region; who empowered them and to what extent did they represent the popular will of Siberians? Even if all the public and private archives with relevant data were suddenly open and accessible to researchers – and we are still far from that – so much has already been lost through a combination of time and faulty memory, selective destruction, and purposeful obfuscation that at least parts of the puzzle will never quite fit. Thus the historian's task continues to require imaginative reconstruction, with all the challenges and foibles which that process implies.

To summarize, this book is about the nature and the causes of the failure of the White counter-revolutionaries ("democratic" or otherwise) in Siberia. The argument is that their defeat was the result of a combination of objective geographic, historical, and demographic circumstances together with critically inadequate political leadership. In assessing the relative importance of these factors, the role and attitudes of the Siberian peasantry towards the contending White and Red authorities that tried to control their destiny are obviously crucial. The condition of the peasantry, in turn, raises the difficult but vital questions of the connection between public support and success in a civil war situation, the relationship between town and country, and the concurrent phenomenon of the Green partisan movements which from the second half of 1918 became increasingly active in Siberia.

The constitutional programs and ideologies of the main White governments that vied for power in Siberia will be examined in detail with a view to establishing their differences and similarities. Did parliamentary democracy stand any real chance under the circumstances, or was it, as alleged by the Bolsheviks and other critics, merely window-dressing for the benefit of Western consumption while the real agenda was to bring about counter-revolution through military means and to restore the *ancien régime* or something very close to it?

The role of Siberian regionalism is described and evaluated. What were its purposes and goals, how broad or narrow was its support, and was it viable as a political alternative? How to account for its initial successes yet quick absorption by the centralist statism of the larger White movement?

The interventions by foreign (especially Allied) powers are reviewed, together with the presence of Czechoslovak prisoners of war on the strategic Trans-Siberian Railway. Both the quality and the quantity of the expeditionary forces, as well as their relationship to the Whites, are examined against the background of the differing and at times conflicting agendas of their respective governments; in the case of Britain and especially France, anti-Bolshevik feelings were exacerbated greatly by the Treaty of Brest-Litovsk and concerns over the issue of reopening the eastern front with Germany.

Finally, an overview and assessment is provided of the specific political and military features of the Kolchak government in its role as the chief counter-revolutionary force in the region during the period of the Civil War, as well as an explanation for the renewed resistance to Soviet authority in Siberia after the Whites ceased to be a threat.

For the sake of perspective, selective comparisons are drawn with reference to developments in other provincial centres such as Samara and Saratov that were located much closer to the seat of Bolshevik power. One obvious and key contrast was that Lenin's government did not gain full control in Siberia until after 1921; in this, at least, the political pattern in Siberia was very different than in the Volga region where the struggle was between the dominant Bolsheviks and their critics on the left – notably Left SRs and smaller splinter groups – and more like the southern and (to a lesser extent) north-western parts of Russia where White governments also existed during most of the Civil War.

A final word on periodization and historical methodology: it is much easier to see events in context when they are framed within discrete times rather than in the chaotic sequence in which they actually occurred. The historian's task invariably involves a measure of telescoping (to borrow from Trotsky and Parvus), since the evidence is dynamic rather than static and always incomplete. There will always be some, often important, pieces missing from almost any interpretation – more so for Russia than elsewhere. Nevertheless, the goal is to produce a picture that faithfully represents and explains the essential elements of the story. The inductive methodology acts as a reminder of the dangers of venturing beyond the evidence to an artificial order which may exist only in the historian's mind. Yet only through such acts of reconstructive imagination can a pattern or shape emerge from the chaos of raw "facts and events."

The period under review covers five and a half years (1917–22), but the focus is on 1918 and 1919 in Western Siberia when prospects for viable alternatives to Bolshevik rule appeared at their brightest. The year 1918 was the time of the so-called Democratic Counter-Revolution associated with the Siberian Regional Duma, which in Tomsk had ties with the government in Samara; the latter was composed largely of members of the Party of the Socialist Revolutionaries (PSR) and was made up of former delegates to the recently dispersed All-Russian Constituent Assembly. Already during the summer and fall of that year, however, political power in Western Siberia was shifting increasingly toward the more conservative and militaristic leadership in Omsk. This trend culminated in the accession of Admiral A.V. Kolchak (1873–1920) as supreme ruler in November 1918 (with at least tacit support from British and other Allied representatives) over an area Lenin referred to as "Kolchakia," which at its zenith included not only Siberia but also contiguous parts of the Volga-Kama basin and the Urals in European Russia. The admiral's initial military successes brought his administration to the verge of international recognition as the legitimate government of all Russia, but it then suffered a series of disastrous political and military reversals. Kolchak's forces spent the latter half of 1919 in a general retreat eastward to Irkutsk, where their unstable coalition came apart.

For the general population, the worst chaos of the entire Civil War in Siberia occurred during the next two and a half years, between the admiral's execution in February 1920 and the Japanese evacuation from the Russian Far East in the autumn of 1922. This was the time of the most destructive *atamanshchina* (petty war-lordism) and peasant insurrections that threatened to dismember the region and overthrow Soviet authority altogether.

The organization of this volume is chronological rather than thematic. Each of these formats presents advantages as well as problems.

A chronological approach benefits from narrative continuity but often involves going over the same topic at subsequent stages of the story. Indeed, whether involving peasant insurrection, regional consciousness, or political differences within the White coalition, many issues did recur throughout the Civil War period in Siberia. On the other hand, repetition is almost as likely if several overlapping themes are divided into separate chapters. The topical approach, however, is more disruptive of narrative flow and rather less conducive to producing an overview.

The history of the Revolution and Civil War in Siberia may be subdivided in several ways. The periodization used here has four parts: 1) from February (Old Style) 1917 to the end of the year, that is, the term of the Provisional Government and the interregnum between the October Revolution in Petrograd and the extension of its authority to Siberia; 2) from January to November 1918 – the early months of Soviet rule and the Democratic Counter-Revolution in Siberia; 3) from November 1918 to January/February 1920 – the Kolchak regime in Siberia; and 4) from February 1920 to October 1922 – the end of the White movement, the removal of all foreign forces, and the reimposition of Soviet authority throughout Siberia against the background of strong peasant resistance.[14]

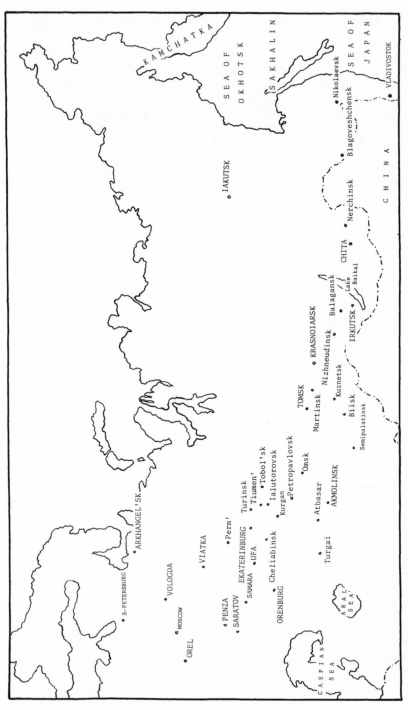

Siberia (1898) by Paul Duffy.
Source: *Entsiklopedicheskii slovar'*, 29A:740-1.

1 Physical Setting, Background, and Regional Development

From west to east Siberia extends nearly 4,000 miles between the Ural Mountains and the Pacific Ocean, and from north to south approximately 1,750 miles between the Arctic Ocean and the borders of central Asia and China. With a total area of just under five million square miles (more than 30 per cent greater than all of Canada), it is the second largest territorial unit in the world.

The expanse of Siberia traditionally has been divided into three parts – Western, between the Urals and the Enisei River and composed of Tomsk and Tobol'sk provinces (*gubernii*); Eastern, from the Enisei River to the mountain ranges near the Pacific coast, with Eniseisk and Irkutsk *gubernii* as well as Iakutsk and Transbaikal districts (*oblasty*); and the Russian Far East, from the Amur and Maritime *gubernii* to the Kamchatka Peninsula and Sakhalin Island.[1] Western Siberia is quite flat, while Eastern Siberia is hilly, rough, and thickly forested. The Western Siberian Lowland is an enormous plain, running 1,500 miles from north to south and 1,000 miles from east to west. Because of excessive surface moisture, 100,000 square miles of it is marshland. Permafrost causes a variety of problems, both for agriculture and for building construction. Only the southernmost part of Western Siberia is free of these natural impediments. A comparison of sowing seasons shows that in Siberia as a whole the frost-free period is only about half that of European Russia; similarly, shipping access through its great rivers (four of the world's ten largest) is frozen from November through May. The intense cold and minimal precipitation, especially in Eastern Siberia, is not conducive for the growth of most forms of vegetation. Instead of the mixed forest of European Russia, much of the region is taiga, a vast northern coniferous forest.[2]

Russian colonization of Siberia is dated from 1581–82 when a small band of Cossack soldiers of fortune under Ermak Timofeevich made the first incursions into Western Siberia.[3] In the following years several fortified outposts were established – Tiumen' in 1585, Tobol'sk in 1587, Tomsk in 1604, Kuznetsk in 1617, Krasnoiarsk in 1628, Iakutsk in 1632, Okhotsk on the Pacific coast in 1649, the Amur basin in 1651, and Irkutsk in 1652. Their main purpose was to project a military presence, facilitate trade (especially in furs), and collect tribute (iasak) for the Great White Tsar of Muscovy from the native peoples (inorodtsy), who at the time of the Russian incursion could be divided into at least 120 indigenous linguistic groupings. Among the most important of these were the Eskimos (known as Inuits in Canada) and the related Chukchis, Koriaks, Itelmens, and Iukagirs, all of whom used so-called Palaeoasiatic languages; the Tatar-Turkic speaking Iakuts (Sakha); the Tungus Evenks and Evens; the Mongol Buriats; and the Nentsy (Samoeds) and Kets.[4] It is estimated that at the beginning of the nineteenth century the total number of inorodtsy in Siberia proper remained under a million, but that figure does not include the neighbouring and far more populous Kazakhs and Kirghiz.[5]

Despite bouts of resistance to the Russian incursion from the Chinese along the Amur, the Treaty of Nerchinsk in 1689 recorded major gains for Moscow as it established the border along the Argun and Gorbitsa rivers and the Stanovoi mountains. In practice, however, much of the disputed area remained beyond the administrative control of both Russians and Chinese. Distant Kamchatka was annexed in the name of the tsar in 1699, but it was not until the Aigun and Peking treaties of 1858 and 1860, respectively, that China formally renounced all claims to the Amur basin and the Pacific coast between the mouth of the Amur and Korea. In south-western Siberia, the Kazakh region came under Russian dominion in 1740, with the Altai following suit in 1756. At the end of the seventeenth century there were still only about 11,400 Russian peasant households (including 27,000 adult males) in Siberia, and nearly all of these belonged to the freer and generally more prosperous state peasant – rather than serf – category.[6]

Russian administration of Siberia was directed by the Siberian office (Sibirskii prikaz) until 1763, first in Moscow and then in St Petersburg. It was not a happy arrangement for the Siberians in general and for the native peoples in particular. The adminstrative system concentrated all power in the hands of quasi-colonial officials (voevody) who were encouraged to "feed off the land" since they did not receive state salaries for their services. Given their remoteness from St Petersburg, they inevitably aquired "broader powers than their colleagues in the European part of the country," and this led to extraordinary abuses.[7]

As a result of the administrative rationalization introduced by Mikhail Speranskii in 1822, however, there were major improvements in the life of the region. His Special Statute on the Siberian Native Tribes provided some protections and improvements for the *inorodtsy* and was especially far-sighted for the time and place. Other aspects of his reforms included setting limits on the arbitrary rule of the governors, easing the lot of the exiles, raising the level of culture and science and of the general educational system, and introducing measures to facilitate the development of free enterprise.[8] To make matters more manageable, two governors-general were appointed, one for Eastern Siberia in Irkutsk, the other for Western Siberia, first in Tobol'sk and then (after 1838) in Omsk.[9] In 1882 the Western Siberian provinces of Tobol'sk and Tomsk were exempted from the jurisdiction of the governor-general in Omsk, who thereafter retained authority only over the Kazakh steppe. Finally, in 1884 a viceroy was appointed for the newly acquired territories in the Far East together with the old Russian possessions on the Pacific coast.

The main development that marked the transition of Siberia from a traditional resource-laden but undeveloped economy into a more modern one was the building of the Trans-Siberian Railway. Not everyone welcomed the coming of the railway as a panacea for all of Siberia's problems, however. Some regionalists believed that it was better for Siberia to develop its own local industry and infrastructure rather than become more closely tied to the centre in an unequal relationship. They also correctly anticipated a great influx of Russian peasants with no ties to the region, which would not bode well for the cause of self-determination and autonomy. But these reservations could hardly influence the course of events once the imperial government in St Petersburg had committed itself to this major initiative. Construction of the railway began in 1891 simultaneously in Cheliabinsk at the western extremity and Vladivostok at the eastern and was completed in 1905. It served as the decisive catalyst in the industrialization of Russia and opened the floodgates of immigration into Siberia.[10] In the year 1908 alone, 758,812 people came from European Russia, many of them illegally and without government subsidies.[11]

The opening of the Trans-Siberian Railway marked a major new phase in the attitude of the Russian imperial government towards Siberia. It ended many decades of not-so-benign neglect and, for the first time, brought the Siberian question to public attention in a positive light. After some eleventh-hour misgivings at the highest levels,

St Petersburg adopted an unambiguous position in favour of encouraging Russian peasant migration to Siberia; the deciding factors appear to have been a desire to reduce rural over-population in European Russia and simultaneously to garrison the Asian frontier.[12] This reversed earlier policy (especially in the years immediately following the Emancipation of 1861) when the official line had been to discourage out-migration, in part because of concern lest the supply of cheap peasant labour for the large landowners in central Russia be put in jeopardy.[13] From the perspective of the common man, the railway removed the chief obstacle to resettlement and opened up unparalleled opportunities for a new and better life. Siberia appealed especially to people looking to start afresh in surroundings unhampered by social impediments such as the traditions of serfdom and manorialism that characterized the European part of the country. At the time of the Emancipation, there were only about 4,000 serfs in all of Siberia.[14]

The new arrivals (*novosely*, also called *pereselentsy*), like the old inhabitants (*starozhily*) whose presence dated back to the end of the sixteenth and beginning of the seventeenth century, were almost all peasants of ethnic Slavic origins – Russians mostly, but also a fair number of Ukrainians and Belorussians. They were both free and indentured, and came mainly from either the central agricultural region of European Russia – the *gubernii* of Kursk, Tambov, Voronezh, and the fringes surrounding them, as well as Ukraine – or the middle Volga areas around Perm, Viatka, and Samara *gubernii*.

Until late in the seventeenth century, the Siberian economy was largely dominated by the fur trade. Thereafter the mining industry became more important, especially for silver and copper in the Altai and silver and lead in the Nerchinsk area of the Transbaikal. Initially mining was largely in the hands of the state and the imperial household, which routinely made use of bonded labour and convicts, but after the discovery of gold during the first third of the nineteenth century private enterprise and free labour became more important.[15]

There were not many industrial workers among the *novosely*. In the twenty years between 1897 and 1917 the population of the working-class neighborhoods of Siberian towns grew from around 328,000 to 767,000. But, because a quarter to a half of the urban population worked in government institutions there did not exist the sort of proletarian base which was already evident west of the Urals. During the same period, moreover, better than four million peasants came to Siberia via the railway, about half of them former state peasants. The new settlers congregated mainly in the fertile south-western part of the region where they continued their customary farming practices.

In the vicinity of Omsk and Petropavlovsk they not only produced a wide variety of vegetables but even melons and tobacco.[16]

Government policy subsidizing eastward migration generated a disproportionate growth of the ethnic Russian population by comparison to *inorodtsy*. The idea was to provide manpower for the creation of an agricultural base in Siberia while simultaneously securing the vast region as an integral part of the Russian empire. Under these increasing demographic pressures, the "smaller nations" (as Russian administrators often referred to the aboriginal peoples) could put off total subjugation and assimilation only by escaping into the interior, as far away as possible from the European settlements. That strategy worked reasonably well throughout the seventeenth century and into the eighteenth. But Russian government policies, technology, consumer goods, and alcohol combined to rob the *inorodtsy* of their independence, separate culture, and capacity to resist, though some Chukchi warriors continued to resist Soviet administration into the 1930s, when like everyone else they too succumbed to Stalin's control.[17] The sharpest decline in aboriginal self-sufficiency and morale occurred in and around the main urban centres, which saw the greatest rise in Russian immigration and impact upon traditional native mores.

In the middle of the nineteenth century the native population of Siberia amounted to about 648,000; at the time of the 1897 census it had risen to 870,536, and in 1911 it was estimated at 972,866. By contrast, the immigrant population was 2,288,036 in 1858, 4,889,633 in 1897, and 8,393,469 in 1911.[18] Thus, while the natives increased by about a third, the Slavic (mainly Russian) immigrants experienced a growth rate of more than three and a half times.[19] A breakdown of the figures for the *inorodtsy* shows that from 1897 to 1911 the Buriats increased from 289,480 to 332,656, the Iakuts from 221,467 to 246,405, and the Tungus from 62,068 to 75,204. The smaller groups of native peoples grew at a slower rate or, in some instances, actually decreased in number. At the same time, tens of thousands of Poles, Latvians, Armenians, Georgians, Gypsies, Jews, Koreans, Chinese, and Japanese were arriving on the scene.[20] Overall in Siberia at the beginning of the twentieth century, the inhabitants divided along the following lines: Slavic (Russian, Ukrainian, Belorussian) peasants – concentrated in the south-western region and along the railway line – constituted about 70 per cent of the population, Cossacks were another 4.5 per cent, urban dwellers were 5.5 per cent, and the *inorodtsy* were about 15 per cent. The remaining 5 per cent included convicts, exiled political dissidents, and religious sectarians. For the sake of comparison, in Russia as a whole, peasants made up about 87 per cent of the population.

Another distinct feature of the Siberian situation was that, in addition to ethnic tensions, there was increasing conflict between different categories of Russian peasants, specifically between *starozhily* and *novosely*, with the former trying to hold on to a disproportionate amount of the best agricultural land against the claims of the new settlers. With the Cossacks, the more established *starozhily* resisted any change to the existing terms of landholding and, not surprisingly, developed an appropriately conservative world-view to go along with their socio-economic interests. Cossacks had the largest holdings, totalling about thirteen million acres of the best land. Per capita, their average was 50 *desiatins* (135 acres), compared to 30 for the *starozhily* and under 20 for the *pereselentsy*. The wealthiest Cossacks owned up to 1,000 *desiatins*.[21]

On balance, the impact of the rising influx of Russian peasants and Cossacks upon the *inorodtsy* was distinctly negative. Smaller and weaker tribes especially succumbed to exploitation by merchants and corrupt officials, as well as to poverty and to diseases imported by the Russian colonists. Among the more numerous peoples, the Iakuts, Buriats, and Kazakhs were best able to adjust themselves to the new situation, and in some cases even profited from contact with the Russians that enabled them to get certain material goods and technology which were otherwise unavailable to them. But in all cases the price paid was very dear, both in terms of actual cost or value exchanged and because of the loss and degradation of aboriginal cultural identity.

On the positive side, tsarist officialdom, while hardly responsive to local needs and interests, generally steered clear of interference with native customs and rituals. Thus, Islam, Buddhism, Shamanism, and other non-European religions were usually permitted to exist side-by-side with Russian Orthodoxy as long as the latter's position as the state religion was not challenged overtly. Indeed, many outside observers noted that in Siberia even the official church tended to be more tolerant, independent-minded, and less subject to regulation by the St Petersburg hierarchy.[22] The freer atmosphere of Siberia was also a major reason in its attracting numerous communities of Old Believers (*Starobriadtsy*) and other active religious dissenters.

While the Russians did bring with them new strains of wheat and other grains, farm and draught animals, as well as agricultural machinery and techniques that could contribute to higher levels of economic productivity and living standards, not everything they brought was equally suited to the different regions of Siberia.[23] Eastern Siberia and the Russian Far East remained relatively backward and neglected into the twentieth century. By 1916 somewhat less than three million acres of land were cultivated, with nearly half of that in Transbaikal. The staple crops were wheat, oats, barley, rye, and millet. Agricultural production in the Russian Far East was not adequate to feed the local population, and so the shortfall was made up by imports from neighbouring areas, especially Manchuria on the other side of the Chinese frontier. Within the Russian Far East the chief activities were bee-keeping, lumbering, mining, and fishing (salmon and herring). The total number of cattle raised in Eastern Siberia was estimated at under five million head in the year before the revolutions of 1917. Among the indigenous peoples, only the Buriats kept many horned cattle, goats, and sheep.[24]

The railway made much more of a positive difference for the Western Siberian economy, as it reduced transport costs to the main cities of European Russia by as much as ninety per cent. Thus, that part of Siberia underwent a fundamental reorientation towards agricultural activity.[25] By the peak year of 1913 large grain surpluses were available for export. But the most impressive development was in the butter industry, which, under the leadership of the cooperative movement, increased to 102 tons in that year from a mere seven in 1894; with a value of 60 million rubles (about U.S. $30 million), it accounted for over 40 per cent of total Siberian exports.[26] The other leading exports, with their ruble values in millions, were gold (28), furs (24), wheat (21), meat (11), and fish (4).[27] Between 1901 and 1910 the amount of Siberian grain exported to Russia and Europe increased from 110,000 tons to over a million. During the course of the next three years the rise was even more dramatic. In Tomsk *guberniia*, for example, wheat production doubled. Nevertheless, the value of commodities imported into Siberia (especially its eastern portion) was far greater than what was exported; even regionalists had to concede that "altogether the central government spent more than it received from Eastern Siberia ... In 1911 its revenue ... amounted to 27 million rubles, but it spent nearly 140 million."[28] The principal imported items were manufactured goods, machinery, metals, textiles, glass, sugar, tea, and tobacco.[29]

By 1917 the Siberian grain harvest is estimated to have reached over 18 million tons, or about 17 per cent of the total for all of Russia.[30] Because the rate of increase in the cultivated area was higher than the rate of the growth of population, Siberian peasants had more to eat and more grain to sell than their brethren in Europe. In the western part of the region the soil was especially fertile; indeed, in many instances it did not require manuring – though it used less seed grain Western Siberia nevertheless produced per *desiatina* more than any area in European Russia. The local peasants also had between two and three times more horses, cattle, sheep, and pigs per capita, as well as

50 per cent more farm machinery. Prosperous (so-called kulak) households were 50 per cent more prevalent in Siberia.[31]

As long as the Ukrainian and central agricultural bread baskets were available to satisfy domestic Russian consumption, Siberian wheat and other grains – mainly from Eniseisk, Tobol'sk, and Tomsk *gubernii* – were still too far from the big markets to make their production as profitable as other commodities. Siberian grain did not have the advantages in transportation and export enjoyed by butter and meat; it was a commodity with a low value per unit weight and thus transportation costs made up a large share of its delivered price in European Russian markets (and still more abroad), especially with the addition of the Cheliabinsk "break" (a tariff to protect European Russian producers from Siberian competition) which raised grain transport costs per *pood* (1 *pood* or *pud* equals 36 lbs.) by 8 to 10 kopeks above the rate that would have been in effect without the tariff.[32] But the First World War would introduce several new elements into these relationships.

EMERGENCE OF SIBERIAN REGIONALISM

The reign of Tsar Alexander II (1855–81) marked, in its early years, a general turning point in the intellectual and political climate of Russia. For the first time a full civil society emerged as large numbers of commoners (*raznochintsy*), including Siberians, streamed to the capitals of St Petersburg and Moscow in search of higher education and careers. The defeat of Russia in the Crimean War, combined with the accession of a reform-minded tsar, seemed to herald an era of dramatic new opportunities for the country and its different regions and peoples.

The combination of a local class of merchants and industrialists and of a revolutionary intelligentsia drawn from exiled Decembrists and Polish rebels in 1825 and 1830–31 respectively provided the background for the emergence in the 1860s of a small but vocal group of Siberians with a federalist and regionalist perspective. They were inspired by the lectures and writings of A.P. Shchapov (1830–76), a professor of Russian history at Kazan University who issued the first protest from the periphery "against Muscovite violence, centralization, and the gathering of the Russian lands."[33]

The main regionalist agenda was to raise local consciousness and focus attention upon the distinctness of Siberian society as an argument in favour of eventual self-government. The Siberians pointed to the injustices and exploitative nature of their "colonial status" under the dominion of metropolitan European Russia, the administrative abuses compounded by a criminal exile system that gave all their region an unsavoury reputation, and the wretched plight of their *inorodtsy*.[34] What most alarmed the regionalists was not merely the extent of the immigration – by the end of the nineteenth century more than 80 per cent of the population of Siberia consisted of first and second generation settlers – but that so many of these people (approximately 6 per cent) were political and criminal exiles, especially in the eastern reaches of Siberia.[35]

To be sure, in addition to the exiles there were at least four other recognizable groups of settlers: free peasants and escaped serfs, Cossack hosts (*voiska*), military and civil bureaucrats, and religious fundamentalists, especially *Starobriadtsy*. It must also be noted that despite all this immigration Siberia's population density was only 3 per cent that of European Russia, with most of it concentrated in a fertile strip about 400 miles wide in western and central Siberia. The northern four-fifths of the region had only 7.5 per cent of the inhabitants overall.[36]

Some young men from Siberia – notably G.N. Potanin (1835–1920) and N.M. Iadrintsev (1842–94) – struggled to find a place for themselves and their "native land."[37] As with provincials in other times and places, the exciting process of burgeoning self-consciousness also stimulated disturbing new views and invidious comparisons with the outside world. The more educated Siberians soon came face to face with how others perceived them and their region. It was not altogether a happy or flattering picture: at best benevolently dismissive, at worst hostile and misinformed. The common impression of Siberia in St Petersburg society was of a frozen waste land inhabited by diseased and drunken oriental natives of small stature and commensurate intelligence.[38] A more positive view, ironically but not unreasonably, was held by the poorest peasants and miscreants – they saw the region as a remote refuge and haven from the misery of their own daily existence in congested European Russia. This sentiment was evident in the common saying, "Siberia is terrible, but life there is better than life in Russia."[39]

For the young Siberian patriots, the challenging experience of student life in the élite institutions of St Petersburg and Moscow, where they were obliged to come to terms with the dominant European side of Russian imperial culture and its demeaning stereotypes of them and their region, was an intellectual trial by fire. Teased and ridiculed for their provincialism, they responded by banding together in a Siberian self-help group (*zemliachestvo*). They were also moved by the idealism of the period and the notion of public service. In the words of Iadrintsev, "The idea of conscious service to the region, at a moment when social consciousness was also awakening in European Russia ... lay at the basis of our coming together."[40] Forced to think about who they were and how their region differed from the metropolis, these young men tried to develop a sense of what it meant to be Siberian as distinct from metropolitan. It was with some difficulty and confusion that they staked out an identity that was necessarily more territorial and cultural than conventionally ethnic – after all, they too were Russian.

Russian intellectual history offered the Siberian regionalists no obvious models. Thus they had to look elsewhere, and it was only natural that the young United States of America, with its frontier parallels, vigorous democracy, and federalist structure appeared particularly appealing. Such was the enthusiasm of the Siberians that some went so far as to suggest a political union between the two regions. The idea was first mooted as early as 1845 when the Decembrist I.I. Pushchin wrote: "I can think of Siberia only in terms of the United States. It could at once separate from the mother country and it would not be in need of anything."[41] Similar ideas were the subject of heated and serious discussion during the 1850s in the small circle of advisers around the eccentric N.N. Murav'ev-Amurskii, governor-general of Eastern Siberia.[42]

Comparisons with the United States appealed not least because they permitted the Siberians – following Alexander Herzen's famous dictum that history favoured the younger nations that, like grandchildren, appeared late on the scene – to imagine themselves jumping over the experience of Russia and even Western Europe all the way to the unspoiled splendour of the New World.[43] Siberian federalism did not operate in a North American political environment, however, and from the beginning it took on a very different configuration, developing as it did against a background of the St Petersburg Juridical School's centralist and statist traditions. Thus, a Right Hegelian and specifically Russian nationalist perspective marked the intellectual limits of Siberian regionalism and restrained its mainstream from becoming too radical or "too American."[44]

In any case, what the Siberian patriots really wanted was not a separate country but a proper appreciation for their region's contribution to the state and a place as a full partner in a Russian federal union. For them, this political solution constituted the ideal reconciliation of local rights with the broader state-consciousness (*gosudarstvennost'*) that was at the centre of the prevailing intellectual orthodoxy in St Petersburg. Moreover, they continued to believe that the central authorities would eventually acknowledge and appreciate the importance of Siberia, as well as its resources and materials, for the overall welfare of the country. That recognition would in turn lead to the repudiation of all government policies that discriminated against Siberia and kept the region in a subordinate and exploited position.

The continuing failure of the central government to accommodate these more hopeful views was a major factor in precipitating the first political crisis of Siberian regionalism and the emergence of a more radical approach, the 1865 Omsk proclamation "To Siberian patriots," which appealed for rebellion and immediate secession. The proclamation followed on the heels of St Petersburg's decision to exclude or at least delay the extension of the 1864 Zemstvo Reform to Siberia because of the not altogether unfounded perception that to do otherwise would be dangerous: "If there was to be a Siberian zemstvo, the government must either create a Siberian gentry artificially or accept local peasant self-government."[45] A second manifesto soon appeared in Irkutsk under the slogan "Long live the Republic of the United States of Siberia! Long live Siberian freedom – from the Urals to the shores of the Pacific Ocean."[46] The Irkutsk manifesto concluded with words that reverberated ominously all the way to St Petersburg: "We must have faith that in Siberia – a country populated by descendants of exiles, of the rebellious *streltsy* [fusiliers], of the banished *raskolniki* [religious schismatics] ... the sacred banner of independence, freedom, and progress will be easy to raise! Remember that Siberia may be the first Slavic nation to achieve the great popular deed – a democratic republic."[47]

At about the same time student radicals and populist intelligentsia – frustrated by what they believed were the unrealized promises of the reforming tsar – circulated in the streets of the capital their own proclamation, *Velikoruss* (*Great Russia*), which called for a federation of Russia, Ukraine, *and* Siberia. This eruption at the imperial centre greatly alarmed the authorities because it coincided with the peasant Emancipation decree of 1861, which was neither popular nor clearly understood in the countryside. There was also violent opposition among other volatile constituencies, most notably the nationalist Poles who rose in revolt in 1863. As a result of these events, Siberia gained several thousand new exiles from the Russian capital as well as from "the Vistula Region."[48]

It is worth repeating that the main regionalist program stopped well short of separatism. As developed over the course of the latter part of the nineteenth century, it consisted of five specific demands: 1) ending the system of criminal exile to Siberia; 2) eliminating restrictive and discriminatory barriers (such as the infamous Cheliabinsk Tariff) and other impediments to the economic and commercial development of Siberia in its own right; 3) developing an indigenous Siberian intelligentsia through the founding of a university and of a local press dedicated to regional issues; 4) subsidizing the immigration of free peasants from European Russia by providing them with access to state and crown (*kabinet*) lands; and 5) ameliorating the condition of the *inorodtsy* and minority populations of the region.[49]

It is significant that Potanin, as co-author of this program, did not choose to have it or himself described as regionalist; he preferred the term "local Siberian patriotism," which he believed better captured the spirit of his proposals and ideas. He made this distinction partly, at least, in order to reconcile his program with the dominant political culture of St Petersburg and Moscow. Potanin believed that Siberian patriotism was consistent with the idea of *gosudarstvennost'*, while the term regionalism suggested local particularism (if not separatism) and the dissolution of Great Russia. From his pragmatic, "small-deeds," and liberal perspective, there was no need to repudiate the principle of statehood, but the priorities in its order of development should be reversed: "Centralized government brings more harm than good. In building a state one must proceed from the periphery toward the center, not vice-versa. First the regions must be organized, then the state composed of them will be based on law, justice, and real freedom."[50]

Having thus made his peace with the existing order, Potanin was then free to champion local self-determination, which he flavoured with an element of the credo of the *Starobriadtsy*. "We [in Siberia]," he wrote, "want to live and develop independently, to have our own mores and laws, to read and to write whatever we wish rather than what Russia ordains, to rear our children as we see fit, to collect taxes on our own, and to spend them only on ourselves."[51] At least implicitly, as well, there was the assumption that Siberian peasants were more hard-working, self-sufficient, individualistic, and property-minded than their European counterparts. The latter, by contrast, were notorious for resenting individual entrepreneurial activity among their fellows and for preferring a common penury to the responsibility and challenge of personal initiative. Both the terms and the practices associated with the Russian peasant commune, such as equalizing the redistribution of the land and other restrictive regulations, were seen to be less characteristic of Siberia.[52]

As a reformist *intelligent* Potanin accepted the moral obligation to serve "the people," but with this difference: for him Siberians of all social ranks had fundamentally the same interests, which were defined by their unique regional location and circumstances.[53] Siberians, he maintained, had more in common with each other than with their class or social equivalents in Moscow or St Petersburg. In addition, according to another regionalist, "the Siberian intelligentsia was closer to the popular masses than was its Russian counterpart because it emerged from the people themselves."[54] Taken together, these views explicitly contradicted not only the traditional Marxist analysis but also, by implication, the moderate and liberal premise by Westerners that there was one universal model for social development and that it could be applied outside Europe, with minor variations to take into account differing historical circumstances.[55]

Given this supra-class, ethical, and territorial orientation rather than emphasis on economic and social issues, Siberian regionalism was vulnerable to criticism from the dominant "progressive" intelligentsia for ignoring the institutional structure which retarded the development of all of late imperial Russia.[56] To use the "civic" vocabulary of the day, the movement smacked of bourgeois-liberal idealism, with its characteristic stress upon "superstucture" over "substructure" – politics over social and economic issues. Even staunch regionalists like I.I. Serebrennikov had to concede that the program of Siberian regionalism "did not include any social reforms."[57]

Nevertheless, by the 1870s, through his major role in founding newspaper journalism in Siberia, Iadrintsev was promoting views that combined a unique blend of federalism, Russian populism (including faith in the peasant commune), and a lively admiration for the achievements of Western civilization.[58] He supported industrial free enterprise for Siberia, but always mitigated by ethical considerations, specifically social welfare measures.[59] He remained deeply suspicious of the motives and goals of the metropolitan centre, and was convinced that Siberia would gain little from mere substitution of revolutionary agitators for tsarist bureaucrats: their priorities would remain equally Eurocentric and untouched by local interests. As early as the 1870s he observed that "the tendency to view the life of the people from a centralistic perspective ... [has become a part] of liberal ... populist, and revolutionary theories. The centralist bureaucrats have been replaced by centralist culture-bearers, centralist 'goers to the people,' Jacobin centralists, and the like."[60] The regionalist argument went against the overwhelming intellectual tide and fashion of the day. It could not even win over a majority of the young Siberian intelligentsia that, like its central counterpart, continued to be influenced more by the exciting ideologies of the Left Hegelianism of Russian revolutionary democracy than by regionalist sentiments and concerns.

Iadrintsev understood that the critical issues for Siberia would continue to be decided in European Russia for the foreseeable future, but he hoped to appeal to the conscience of educated society in St Petersburg and Moscow. This was his main motivation in writing his *magnum opus*, *Sibir' kak koloniia* (*Siberia as a Colony*), which appeared in 1882.

The book's provocative title conveyed its thesis: central Russia behaved toward Siberia much the way other European powers treated their overseas colonies. Iadrintsev hoped to counter this "internal colonialism" by convincing his readers that Siberia deserved better and that the widespread image of the region as a waste land that had no alternative to being a dumping ground for the metropolitan centre was both unwarranted and uncharitable. European Russians must come to see Siberia as something more than a contiguous, land-locked, and frozen "Australia" – a refuge for misfits and criminals, and a source of cheap resources and produce.[61]

To strengthen the forces promoting a positive view of Siberia, as well as to raise the level of local consciousness, Iadrintsev founded *Vostochnoe obozrenie* (*Eastern Review*) in 1882 and served as its editor-in-chief and publisher until his death in 1894.[62] The first issue contained a clear statement of its perspective and purpose: "Wishing to represent the needs and requirements of Russian society in the outlying regions, we have undertaken a publication which acquaints European Russia with Asia and Siberia, and conversely, the inhabitants of the regions with [European] Russia's life and development."[63]

Iadrintsev's arguments drew a storm of condemnation from the central press. "Siberia," inveighed a typical rejoinder, "is not a colony of Russia, but Russia proper, not a Russian America, but a Russian province and must develop in the same way as have done the other outlying regions of 'the Russian state.'"[64] Comparisons with North America, where contemporary movements for independence or at least autonomy were well established, might be useful for rhetorical purposes, but Iadrintsev recognized the critical differences in their economic history and geopolitics. For better or worse, Siberia's relationship to Russia was closer to Canada's with Great Britain than the break-away United States;[65] the region's prospects for development and prosperity in the first instance were also more heavily dependent upon the central government as well as other external agencies than was the American frontier. According to the subsequent testimony of the Siberian scholar and White government official G.K. Guins (Gins), "Siberia needed capital, various investments for its economic development ... a considerable increase in the population for a labor supply ... an organization for administration and cultural needs ... [and] scientists and professors for the research and educative work. And finally, it had to be well-protected."[66]

Under the circumstances, that assistance realistically could only come from continuing close ties with European Russia. The reaction of Siberian patriots, however, was to stress the benefits going the other way in the relationship: the many (putative) contributions from their region to the centre. In addition to enormous material resources, these included intangibles such as social egalitarianism, which the Siberians believed was their special characteristic and a great advance over the servile atmosphere that prevailed in European Russia. As noted on the pages of *Sibir'*, "the absence of ... large estates is one of the guarantees of [Siberia's] great future, through the possibility of an even distribution of prosperity and of the development of the chief industry – agriculture."[67] In sum, thanks to its unique historical, ethnic, and geographic circumstances, Siberia enjoyed an altogether more wholesome and freer environment than European Russia and did not have its rigid social categories and conflicts. "In Siberia there is no class that monopolizes cultural life by itself, and therefore the Siberian peasant and the middle class of the population act unconstrained, in a free and easy manner. The Siberian peasant feels equal in rights ... [and] Siberian society, undivided by any restrictions, constitutes a homogeneous mass, where life and its interchange are free."[68]

The course of economic development, in particular, continued to bring Siberia ever closer to European Russia. By 1905 the region was well on its way to becoming an integrated part of the greater Russian system. The opening of the Tiumen'–Omsk railway branch-line in 1913 consolidated this process, making it much easier to move Siberian grain, among other goods, westward. The distance and transport time to the European capitals was reduced by hundreds of miles and several days, with commensurate savings in rail charges which minimized the Cheliabinsk Tariff differential. New industrial growth was further boosted by the development of coal mining in several key locations along the railway line, as well as by strategically located engineering plants for repairing rail-stock. All this contributed to making Siberia an integral part of the national and world economy to a degree which would have been impossible just a few years earlier. Moreover, the tsarist government committed itself to active encouragement of grain production in Siberia for the sake of export. In the peak year of 1913 about 85 per cent of the region's grain (mostly wheat) was going abroad.[69] Still, not everything was changing for the better, and many of the old problems were simply taking new forms. "[W]hat Siberia lacks," wrote a French official, "is, on the one hand, the necessary capital for using its natural wealth, and on the other hand, the transportation making it possible to export its raw material and to import the manufactured objects and machines which it needs ... It is therefore, forced to have recourse to foreign cooperation in economic as well as in military affairs."[70]

Increasingly it was clear to Siberians that the region's geographic isolation and remoteness, combined with sparse population, made economic coordination a matter of the utmost urgency. This was the impetus behind the startling growth of the cooperative movement. Starting with the butter manufacturers, but soon spreading to other industries and including a vast network of consumer purchasing and distribution agencies, the cooperatives assumed the leading economic coordinating role throughout Siberia. Members sold their dairy products to, and bought commodities from, an integrated network of cooperative societies known from 1908 as the Union of Siberian Creamery Associations. The process culminated with the formation in 1916 of the Union of Siberian Co-operative Unions (*Zakupsbyt*) – which immediately became the most important force in the entire regional economy. By that time the overall membership numbered well over one million people.[71] Bernard Pares was moved to comment that "Nothing was more impressive than the part which Co-operation then played in the life of Siberia. They ran about half the newspapers and about three-quarters of the magazines. Many of the theatres and even the circuses were their property. All this machinery they utilized for educational purposes; for instance, they kept a staff of playwrights. Whatever little was done ... in primary education was mostly their work."[72]

By 1917 there were nearly 40,000 cooperative unions throughout Russia, which was greater than the combined totals of England, Germany, Japan, France, and Italy, and the number continued to grow in Siberia despite the revolutions.[73] Cooperatives ranged across a broad variety of functions serving both consumer and producers, and provided dynamic examples for the Russian peasantry of the benefits of modern capitalism when combined with local initiative and mutual assistance. The other side of the Siberian economy, however, was essentially non-productive. It was concentrated in the main towns, where a very large portion – perhaps as much as half – of the work force were civil servants and white-collar clerks, while industrial proletarians were few and far between except in the immediate vicinity of the rail lines. This description was particularly true for Omsk (with its long tradition as an administrative centre), but it also applied to Irkutsk, Novonikolaevsk, Tomsk, and Tobol'sk.

The urban demography together with the absence of serfdom in the countryside contributed to the region's relative social stability and political tranquility, notwithstanding anarchic episodes of violent confrontation between roaming bands of desperadoes and the more settled population.[74] By contrast with European Russia, in Siberia it was not the towns but (for reasons which will be described below) the villages which experienced the greatest revolutionary turmoil.[75] Altogether, Siberian towns and cities at the beginning of the twentieth century were flourishing and enjoyed a remarkably high level of the latest technology: electrification, telephone and telegraph service, stock exchanges, restaurants, theatres, public libraries, book stores, and cultural societies. Local philanthropists – notably P.I. Makushin – did a great deal to overcome the central government's not-so-benign neglect. Two of the most important examples of Makushin's combination of business enterprise and social conscience were his pioneering academic bookstore and the Society for the Promotion of Primary Education, founded in Tomsk in 1873 and 1882 respectively. Both reflected the liberal view that access to the most up-to-date information and education were the keys to Siberia's growth and development.[76]

In the critical period from 1897 to 1917, the population of Siberia's main cities grew in spectacular fashion: Omsk from 36,000 to 114,000, Tomsk from 52,000 to 101,000, Barnaul from 21,000 to 56,000, Novonikolaevsk from 8,000 to 70,000, Krasnoiarsk from 27,000 to 70,000, Irkutsk from 51,000 to 90,000, Verkhneudinsk from 7,000 to 30,000, and Chita from 30,000 to 70,000. On the other hand, the 1897 census reveals that only 10 per cent of the Siberian population lived in cities and that there were just 6,000 primary schools and fewer than 600 hospitals, with under 1,000 doctors in attendance.

It was against this background that the distant but turbulent events of the 1905 Revolution in St Petersburg resounded in Siberia. Local regionalists saw an opportunity for the first time to establish legally an organization which might openly promote the political interests of the region. In August 1905 their newly formed Siberian Regional Union sponsored a conference in Tomsk under Potanin's presidency which announced "Basic Statutes" calling for Siberian autonomy while still opposing separation. A Siberian Regional Duma was to be convened with a mandate to deal with questions concerning public education, health, security, communications and transportion, the right to use and dispose of lands in the region (as a means of mitigating the immigration problem), and the degradation of the native peoples. Though the Union did not survive the 1905 Revolution, its ideals continued to inform the regionalist movement.[77]

In summary, Siberian society was seen by most Russian and foreign observers as being significantly *sui generis* in 1917. Both the peasant commune and seigneurial ownership of land were significantly less entrenched there than west of the Urals, while a frontier egalitarianism also kept status differences to a minimum, with the result that social tensions were substantially lower. This was consistent with the general pattern throughout the empire, whereby regions which had the greatest social polarization – as, for instance, Saratov with over 80 per cent of its population from serf backgrounds – experienced the greatest immediate revolutionary upsurge.[78] With the vast majority of Siberians from non-servile backgrounds and relatively well off, the region was not an early hotbed of insurrectionary activity.

As the revolutionary year of 1917 began, Siberia appeared in many ways to be better off than the rest of Russia. It remained relatively unscathed by the ravages of the First World War, especially in comparison to the country's western and central provinces. There finally seemed to be some hope that the imperial government would get around to completing the process of extending the long-awaited Great Reforms into Asiatic Russia. But before that could happen, the streets of Petrograd exploded with popular discontent that swept away the Romanov dynasty, leaving many issues – including those most dear to Siberia – unresolved.

2 Revolution in Siberia – Similarities and Differences with European Russia

February to December 1917

The February-March Revolution of 1917 was a distinctly capital affair. Most outlying areas of the Russian empire were neither actively involved in nor even immediately aware of the unfolding drama in Petrograd. Siberia in particular appeared to be peripheral to the whole process of the downfall of the Romanov dynasty. This was hardly surprising given the region's remoteness from the centre of events and its relative social stability and prosperity. Nevertheless, the February Revolution signalled a sharp increase in regionalist activity in Western Siberia, especially Tomsk *guberniia*, as it did in other parts of the Russian empire, notably the other multi-ethnic borderlands. The heightened desire and new opportunity for greater self-determination were felt especially keenly among those peoples of Ukraine, the Caucasus, the Baltics, Poland, and Finland who had traditionally shown the strongest national consciousness.

In Siberia, regionalist sentiment had been building underground for years and it now could finally come out into the open, but its free expression in 1917 did not precipitate a mass movement. Indeed, regionalist agitation remained limited to the relatively small educated circles around Tomsk University. A vague, general sentiment in favour of self-government and control over local affairs, however, had become more widespread and had the potential, with appropriate leadership, to be politically significant on a far wider scale. Throughout the spring and summer of 1917 different groups, including at least one peasant congress, called for broad measures of autonomy – that is, not political separation from European Russia but equal status within a federated state.[1] According to local activist M.P. Golovachev, "throughout Siberia all social and political organizations began to discuss the question of the forms and means of realizing the idea of Siberian Regionalism."[2]

The Russian state began to unravel during the last part of World War I and this made possible unprecedented varieties of local initiative. The central government could no longer effectively control Petrograd, much less places thousands of miles to the east. By March 1917 the major cities of Siberia were in the hands of Committees of Public Safety (or Public Organizations, as they were often called) led by executives that were in most cases amalgams of the peasant-oriented Party of the Socialist Revolutionaries (PSR) and Marxist Social Democrats and that included both Bolsheviks and Mensheviks, with the latter generally in control.[3] It was explicit Menshevik policy to ally with the PSR in an electoral bloc whenever there was "the danger of the predominance of the bourgeois [that is non-socialist] parties."[4]

The Committees of Public Safety were effective organs of local self-government, closely allied with municipal dumas and acting to coordinate the programs of various public organizations and democratic parties.[5] They often overlapped with both the local soviets and the authority of the new Provisional Government in Petrograd. John Keep suggests that the provinces in this way reflected some of the political divisions and tensions of the capital: "The relationship between the municipal authorities (or 'committees of public organizations') and these unofficial bodies [factory committees, trade unions, and urban and city-district soviets] reproduced in microcosm the so-called 'dual power,' the uneasy coexistence between the Provisional Government and the Petrograd soviet."[6]

The initial response in Siberia to the events in Petrograd, though somewhat more muted than elsewhere in Russia, appears to have been overwhelmingly against the Romanovs. The Omsk soviet met on the evening of 3 March, endorsed the revolution in Petrograd, and promptly ordered the arrest of the imperial governor-general. In Tobol'sk *guberniia* about 600 delegates to a peasant congress declared themselves in favour of the new regime; they also approved the idea of a Russian democratic republic, a call for the quick convocation of an all-party Constituent Assembly chosen by universal suffrage, and even the continuation of the war against Germany to a victorious conclusion.[7] On 20 April in Akmolinsk *oblast'*, peasants who had moved spontaneously to expropriate local estates, were reprimanded by the Executive Committee of the West-Siberian Council of Peasants' Deputies, which ordered that until the Constituent Assembly met there should be no more unilateral changes made in the ownership of land. Only in "Red" Krasnoiarsk – and then largely because of pressure from

Bolshevik demobilized soldiers just back from the front (*frontoviki*) – did a peasant congress pass a resolution at the end of April calling for the immediate confiscation of private property instead of waiting for the Constituent Assembly to resolve the land question. It was not until September, however, that a majority at the First Congress of Soviets of Central Siberia, also meeting in the radical atmosphere of Krasnoiarsk, finally demanded an end to the policy of "accommodation [*soglasha-tel'stvo*] with the bourgeoisie" and the transfer of "the plenitude of state power ... to ... the soviets, both at the centre and locally."[8]

On balance, the soviet apparatus appeared later in Siberia and played a less assertive role than in many other areas of provincial Russia.[9] Moreover, Siberian soviets were perceived as workers' organizations rather than as alternatives to such existing government institutions as the zemstvos and municipal boards, and they were generally prepared to subordinate themselves to the Provisional Government in preparation for the full convocation of the Constituent Assembly.[10] To be sure, the nature and configuration of the soviets varied considerably from place to place. Those in Omsk, Barnaul, Tomsk, Verkhneudinsk, and especially Krasnoiarsk were militant from the start, with a leadership that included Menshevik Internationalists and Bolsheviks;[11] however, most of the others, like those in European Russia, were willing to cooperate with the Provisional Government – overtly in terms of its war policy, and tacitly on social issues such as that of postponing the controversial and divisive land question until after the end of international hostilities. In Novonikolaevsk, Irkutsk, and Chita, the Bolsheviks and smaller radical parties were hardly a factor at all.[12]

While the left was organizing itself into soviets, the right was also busy. In Omsk, for instance, the business classes created their own local "organizational bureau" (*org bureau*) to represent their interests, and on 2 March a coalition committee was elected at a meeting of the town duma. Similar committees subsequently formed in almost all the Siberian towns. Members included former tsarist bureaucrats and others from the local establishments. In Omsk the key figures were the president of the Stock Market Committee, the local Kadet leader, and a prominent industrialist.[13]

What emerged was a Siberian version of "dual power" – in this case, the soviet versus the Coalition Committee. But the Omsk organization was so moderate that rather than call itself the soviet of workers' and *soldiers'* deputies, it preferred to be known as the soviet of workers and *military* lest the officers feel excluded. On 22 March it also pledged unqualified support to the Provisional Government. Even the Bolsheviks in Omsk were known for their willingness to cooperate with and deference to the Mensheviks.[14] This was all the more significant because, after Krasnoiarsk, Omsk had the largest and most influential Social Democratic organization in Siberia. An informal coalition of left-wing Mensheviks and right-wing Bolsheviks united informally around an anti-war platform of Zimmerwald Internationalism and pan-socialist cooperation. Siberian Zimmerwaldism occupied a middle position between the dominant SR-Menshevik "defensism" – defending the country against German aggression, but without "annexations or compensations,"[15] – and Bolshevik "defeatism," which openly advocated the defeat of Russia as a means of triggering class warfare and the socialist revolution at home and then throughout Europe. Zimmerwaldism permitted good socialists to remain true to their traditional internationalism without being unpatriotic, and it also represented the best hope for reunifying Russian Social Democracy, which had been so deeply divided by the issue of whether or not and in what measure to support the war.[16] The influence of Zimmerwaldism upon Siberian Bolsheviks was an obvious point of concern for Moscow. Apart from the so-called Leninist-Pravdists (who, as their name suggests, adhered closely to the line taken by the central party organ), most of the local cadres continued to ignore the injunctions of their own Central Committee against political cooperation with Mensheviks and SRs well into the autumn of 1917.[17]

In any case, anti-war sentiment among the peasantry was much less important in Siberia than in European Russia, and the same could be said of the land issue. Thus, the Bolsheviks were deprived of their two main appeals. But if the Siberian countryside was resistant to Bolshevik propaganda, it was not much more receptive to the agrarian policies of the Provisional Government. This was quite evident in the popular response to its decree of 25 March on the Transfer of Grain into the Jurisdiction of the State, which made trading in grain a state monopoly as part of a larger effort to increase and control agrarian production and distribution. The official rationale for the new law appealed to the populations of the cities of European Russia, and at the same time it reassured the peasants that there would be reciprocity in meeting their urgent need for essential consumer goods:

The difficult situation regarding food and the need to provide grain for the army and the population as soon as possible forces the Provisional Government to resort to the most urgent measures in the region of food. Henceforth all surplus grain reserves must be turned over to the state ... In accepting grain at new fixed prices in order to achieve a uniform and equitable distribution of food, the government at the same time considers that its first duty is to proceed at once to the establishment of fixed prices on articles of prime necessity (iron, textiles, kerosene, leather, etc.) and to make these available to the population at the lowest possible prices.[18]

The Provisional Government's intention was to gain control over all food and grain surplus through local committees designated by the government for that purpose. The plan did not work, however, because the government was never able to ensure an adequate supply of necessary goods to the countryside in exchange. Peasants were thus unwilling to surrender their grain and the local food committees usually lacked the power to take it by force. By late spring hoarding was causing a steady decline in food supplies, accompanied by prices that at first rose gradually but then climbed more dramatically. During the summer the increases became hyper-inflationary, and over the last four months of 1917 they rose by more than 500 per cent.[19] A clear gulf was developing between the villages, which were still viable, and the cities, which were bankrupt, as well as between Siberia, which was relatively prosperous and the central industrial zones, which were rapidly collapsing.

While economic conditions deteriorated precipitously everywhere, political and civil freedoms flourished as never before. In the liberated atmosphere that followed the overthrow of the Romanovs, the time seemed ideal for raising the issue of Siberian autonomy. Even the Kadets, with their aggressive Great Russian orientation, initially seemed well disposed to the idea.[20] Tomsk, as the birthplace of Siberian regionalism, was the logical place to begin the debate. There, in early May 1917, the first meeting of an openly regionalist All-Siberian Provincial Assembly, under the leadership of the venerable eighty-two-year-old G.N. Potanin, issued a call for "wide self-government."[21] After lengthy discussions and many meetings spanning several weeks, a follow up All-Siberian Regional Congress called in August for the formation of an autonomous government for Siberia. A white and green Siberian regionalist flag was unveiled with the inscription "Long Live Autonomous Siberia." Radical activists – against the strong objections of Potanin and other moderates – set the tone by unilaterally claiming supreme legislative power for a Siberian Regional Duma. This body was to assume political sovereignty in Siberia until the meeting of a Siberian Constituent Assembly and was to be elected by universal suffrage but with only the active political participation of "the Democracy" (that is, only the socialist parties, including the Bolsheviks if they could be prevailed upon to participate), while excluding the "bourgeois" propertied elements, such as the Kadets and their allies.[22]

Despite numerically unimpressive turnouts of not more than a hundred delegates for the regional convocations and the presence of precious few representatives of the "common people" among them, there were grounds for optimism that the regionalist movement would succeed. Thus, *Vol'naia Sibir'* (*Free Siberia*), a weekly newspaper published in Petrograd by the Union of Siberian Regionalists, celebrated the regionalist cause: "Only autonomy guarantees for Siberia a more complete and multifaceted development of its cultural creative forces and a more intensive development of the husbandry [*khoziatsvennoe*] activities of the population in the use of the natural resources of Siberia."[23] There was less evidence, however, that regional consciousness had spread beyond a literate minority. Even during the liberal euphoria of spring 1917 in Siberia the movement was limited to a few specific places and groups and other issues attracted much wider support in the general population. For example, just as the Tomsk meetings were passing their autonomist resolutions, a congress of peasant deputies in Altai *guberniia* was implicitly moving in the other direction by voting to endorse the majority SR position in favour of an all-socialist coalition government responsible to the Central Executive Committee of the Soviet of Workers', Soldiers', and Peasants' Deputies (*VTsIK*) in Petrograd.

Nevertheless, the activity of the Tomsk intelligentsia was not without results: an Extraordinary All-Siberian Assembly met in December despite a boycott by the Bolsheviks and other far-left groups which denounced it as bourgeois. The meeting was the crucial penultimate step in convening a Siberian Constituent Assembly for early 1918; until then interim multi-party democratic government would be provided by the Siberian Regional Duma, which would serve as an alternative to the Bolsheviks' Council of People's Commissars (*Sovnarkom*) in Petrograd. But it is a moot point just how broad the popular mandate was for these regionalist initiatives, or even how much was known about them outside the environs of Tomsk.[24] One important indication of the lack of political consensus for the future configuration of Siberia was the difficulty in building an anti-Bolshevik coalition. At Omsk and other key locations within Western Siberia, there was a variety of forces at work that were often mutually antagonistic and that, while opposed to rule by soviets, were also hostile to political and (especially) social democracy.

For transplanted imperial military officers, retired civil servants, conservative businessmen, and *gosudarstvennye* intellectuals, Petrograd and Moscow remained their spiritual home and Siberia represented a temporary exile at best. They could hardly be expected to find the ideals of regionalism attractive. On the contrary, they had a vision of a centralized and all-powerful Great Russian state that was fundamentally threatened by any such ideas. Finally, there was, as the Russians say, a "psychological moment": accustomed to thinking of themselves as the uniquely qualified leaders of society, these metropolitan leaders in exile tended to regard Siberian patriots as *déclassé* upstarts with no qualifications or aptitude for governing.

Local Siberian conservatives were also concerned about the "anti-state" implications of regionalism, such as the encouragement it gave to the growth of national consciousness among the *inorodtsy*, as was evident in their burgeoning demands for greater self-determination. In July in Orenburg, at the Convention of Kirghiz Representatives of Siberia, the Steppe Country and Turkestan, delegates voted over-whelmingly in favour of national-territorial autonomy. Subsequently, similar resolutions were passed by the All-Siberian Moslem Congress in Tomsk and by the Buriat National Congress in Irkutsk. By the end of 1917 a Kirghiz Congress voted to establish its own national government under the name of Alash-Orda at Semipalatinsk.[25]

REGIONAL PARTY POLITICS

The political atmosphere of Siberia throughout 1917 remained calmer and certainly more tractable than in many other places in the country. In Petrograd, Moscow, and other major urban centres of European Russia mounting tensions and conflicts between the workers' and soldiers' soviets and the Provisional Government were palpable, but in Siberia their respective local agents cooperated on most routine matters of government, with several instances of soviet officials even serving on Committees of Public Safety and zemstvos with formal links to the Provisional Government. This contrasted with other provincial areas: "If the Saratov example is at all representative ... the [Provisional Government's] edicts on an array of important issues merely sanctioned what local administrations had already done. Other directives went ignored ... In Saratov as elsewhere the Soviet stepped into the political vacuum and soon generated tremendous political power."[26]

The relative social calm and high level of support for the Provisional Government in Siberia was in part a reflection of the general popularity in the region of the SRs – who, as members of A.F. Kerensky's cabinet, received principal credit for the Provisional Government's decision in June to extend the zemstvos to Siberia. These institutions of rural self-government were also given greater powers than their pre-revolutionary counterparts, with enhanced jurisdiction over the police, questions of elementary education, and medical and veterinary services, among other welfare functions. Ironically, just as the zemstvos were making their way into Siberia, elsewhere in the country they were being undercut from below: "Literally hundreds of different peasant committees and executives were set up in the villages and volost' [small rural districts] townships during the spring [of 1917] ... They sabotaged the work of the district *zemstva* which were dominated by hostile gentry interests. They transformed themselves into autonomous local 'governments.'"[27]

The contrast with European Russia extended to the urban areas of Siberia as well. Again with the exception of Krasnoiarsk – where they took over almost all public organizations, the Bolsheviks exerted considerable influence upon the trade unions and the garrisons in particular in the great majority of Siberian towns, but they did not gain control of local soviets from the Mensheviks and the SRS. Their failure to do so was attributed by the Leninists to the local cadres conforming "with the line taken by [L.B.] Kamenev and other 'soft' members of the Central Committee, who sought to combine elements of 'soviet' and 'bourgeois' democracy."[28]

There were reasons for these regional differences. Issues that stymied the Provisional Government in Petrograd, such as grain supplies and land redistribution, were simply not major factors in Siberia, thanks in large part to a surplus of grain and virtually unlimited expanses of land for new settlement. Apart from Siberia, however, the land question was critical, and it was handled poorly by the Provisional Government. A declaration on 5 May 1917 was an obvious delaying tactic that did nothing to reassure poor peasants hungry for *chernyi peredel* [black repartition]: "Leaving it to the Constituent Assembly to decide the question of the transfer of land into the hands of the workers, and carrying out the preparatory work for this, the Provisional Government will take all necessary measures to ensure the greatest production of grain to satisfy the needs of the country, and to regulate the utilisation of land in the interests of the national economy and the working population."[29]

While Siberia largely escaped the social and political consequences of the Provisional Government's short-sighted land policy, regions in Russia where a higher proportion of real property was owned by classes above the peasantry witnessed dramatic increases in revolutionary turmoil: "All the *gubernii* in which the peasants owned more than 80 percent of the land, with the exception of Riazan, were characterised by comparatively low levels of unrest, while those in which peasant ownership was at a lower level generally experienced higher levels of disturbances."[30] In the main Siberian cities the authority of such populist organizations as factory committees, soviets, soldier committees, and *volost'* and village executive committees remained either relatively undeveloped or assumed less confrontational forms.[31] Nevertheless, change was in the air, and by mid-1917 the Siberian countryside was also witnessing a growing polarization between land-hungry *novosely* on the one hand, and Cossacks and *starozhily* on the other.

Many of the newcomers naturally gravitated to the Bolshevik agenda for radical social and economic levelling, including a form of land redistribution that at least tacitly recognized the rights of the poorer peasants to a greater use of both private and state lands. Inevitably, this led to violent conflicts with the *starozhily*. According to reliable estimates, there were 956 instances of peasant disturbances in Siberia during the period from March to October 1917, with twice as many occurring in the weeks immediately after the February Revolution as in September and October. Western Siberia, with its large number of *novosely* – particularly in Tomsk and Tobol'sk *gubernii* and in the Omsk district – experienced the most turbulent activity.[32] The alignment of political parties in Siberia during 1917 naturally reflected the divisions between the village haves and have-nots as well as the equally significant gulf between countryside and city. These patterns existed elsewhere in Russia but the Siberian political spectrum had its own peculiarities and differences. One important distinction was the relative weakness of the Constitutional Democrats or Kadets, even in the larger Siberian cities where, following the pattern in European Russia, they were expected to have significant support.

The Kadets, as representatives of the urban professional classes – the dominant group within that self-conscious upper 10 per cent that constituted the only truly modern portion of Russian society – saw themselves as the logical leaders of a liberal and Westernized post-tsarist Russia and the only viable alternative to the chaos and tyranny threatening from both right and left. Eurocentric gentlemen and cosmopolitans, they were at the same time politically tough-minded; in this respect they resembled the Bolsheviks much more than either the SRs or the Mensheviks. In addition, their ideology was statist, centralist, and imperialist. The Kadets never doubted that only they had the necessary combination of political culture and experience to lead the country out of its backwardness and towards a deserved place at the side of the other great powers of Europe.

In fairness, there was some basis for the elevated view the Kadets had of themselves. Many of the best minds in the academic establishment as well as the most progressive lawyers and entrepreneurs in the country as a whole were among their senior members. Moreover, it was the Kadet program that had defined the goals of the 1905 Revolution, provided much of the rhetoric surrounding Russia's involvement on the side of the allies in the Great War, and even set the opening agenda for 1917. But at the same time, the Kadets had to bear the terrible responsibility – second only to the imperial regime itself – for ignoring public opinion in continuing the war. In addition, it was Kadet legalism (or perhaps class interest) in combination with a fear of the army disintegrating and heading home that prevented the Provisional Government from taking decisive action on land redistribution, the one issue that could have won over the peasantry *en masse*.

In Siberia, with its weaker bureaucratic infrastructure and loose ties to the imperial centre, a party like the Kadets could enjoy only limited appeal, and most of that was restricted to the administrative capital of Omsk. The regionalist orientation of the Siberian intelligentsia was quite antithetical to the core beliefs of the Kadets, which stressed the central and progressive role of the Great Russian state. Thus, despite active support in Omsk from one of Siberia's most respected newspapers, *Sibirskaia rech'* and the adherence of influential business and industrial leaders as well as many leading public figures, the Kadets were never able to compete effectively for support among the Siberian middle classes, much less the workers and especially peasants, among whom the SRs enjoyed overwhelming popularity. Another problem for the Siberian Kadets was that their natural constituency was pre-empted by the regionalist movement: "They [the regionalists] drew their support from the same intellectual and professional strata as did the Kadets, but [had the advantage of not being] regarded as outsiders."[33] As in Ukraine at this time, Kadet state-centralism and opposition to all forms of regional autonomy alienated the urban professionals who otherwise would have been attracted by the liberal economic and political aspects of their program.

The Kadet leadership was neither unaware nor indifferent to the problem of the party's declining prestige and to the need for a radical resolution. But unless it redefined itself, the party had poor prospects for achieving greater popular support in the short-term. Given the increasing narrowness of its electoral base, the only way out of the dilemma was to co-opt the PSR, the party that enjoyed the widest following in Siberia and Russia and that simultaneously was the most open to its influence. Thus, following the Bolshevik take-over in October, leading Kadets purposefully drew closer and gradually infiltrated the right wing of the PSR. This was in some sense a continuation of a trend, already evident in the later stages of the life of the Provisional Government, that culminated in the amalgamation of all the duma, or parliamentary, parties under the leadership of the Kadets against the Bolshevik dictatorship.

If, as already noted, the Kadets suffered from too narrow a base of support, paradoxically the SRs had the opposite problem: their party membership was too diverse and amorphous. Socialist Revolutionaries in Siberia, as in European Russia, were a hodgepodge of interest groups with no agreed agenda or leadership. It was no secret that the PSR was less a single party than a loose collection of factions that adhered (in varying degrees) to the ideology and traditions of Russian revolutionary populism. When it came down to making specific policy decisions, however, these factions more often than not disagreed with each other and felt no obligation to abide by party decisions or discipline. The left wing of the PSR was inclined to cooperate with the Mensheviks and even the Bolsheviks against what they regarded as the greater threat from the right, specifically military dictatorship, pointing to the September events in Petrograd, when General L.G. Kornilov very nearly toppled the beleaguered Kerensky government. For this group of SRs the Bolshevik seizure of power was clearly the lesser evil, especially because any Soviet government – even one which unfortunately did not include all the socialist parties – stood a better chance of resisting the imminent counter-revolution: "Against Lenin [we] must fight with strength of words and organization; against [the Cossack leader] Kaledin, with strength of arms."[34] This distinction was at the heart of the left-centrist politics of the PSR leader, Victor Chernov, and virtually made it impossible for the PSR to function as a united movement, given that the party's right wing regarded Lenin as the chief enemy and increasingly was prepared to ally with anyone against him.

The idea of regionalism, on the other hand, at least in principle, was not incompatible with the federalism of most SRs, in contrast to the extreme centralism of the Bolsheviks and the Kadets. Indeed, some Siberian SRs alerted the party leadership to the utility of the issue as a potential means for broadening the anti-Bolshevik coalition in Siberia.[35] But of course there was also countervailing fears that it might further diffuse and fragment the already chaotic membership. This lack of a clearly defined and approved agenda was precisely what made the party, and especially its left and right wings, so susceptible to co-optation by the Bolsheviks and Kadets respectively. There were, moreover, telling signs of the underlying political centralism of the majority SRs; during the night of 26 October 1917 former members of the Fourth Duma formed an All-Russian Committee for the Salvation of the Motherland and the Revolution and called upon citizens to ignore the "anti-state" edicts of the new Soviet government and to work in restoring the Provisional Government. The Committee was led (as might be expected) by Kadets, but it also included several prominent SRs.[36]

Critics of the majority SRs, especially from the left, were quick to point out that their program was becoming virtually indistinguishable from that of the Kadets on such critical issues as social policy, relations with the allies, and the central role of the state. In any case, the deepening polarization of Russian society forced many moderate socialists to ally themselves with either the Bolsheviks or the Kadets as the leaders of the two main camps contesting for power. The main loser in this process was the PSR and its genuinely democratic "third path."[37] The doyen of SR studies in the West, O.H. Radkey, concludes unequivocally that the majority SRs were a "nonrevolutionary party after February and, in effect, a counterrevolutionary one after October [1917]." They underwent a metamorphosis "from insurrectionists in 1905 to jaded democrats in the period between the revolutions and then to fervent patriots, partisans of the Entente, and devotees of the cult of the state with the coming of war ... [A] large segment ... had become Kadets without admitting it."[38] Contemporary Soviet writers made a still harsher indictment, repeating the original Bolshevik argument based on rigid class distinctions:

[The PSR was] the party of the bourgeois intelligentsia ... the privileged section of the [secondary school] teachers, the cooperative white-collar workers and bank clerks, bureaucrats; in a word – that part of the petty bourgeoisie which in bourgeois-monarchical society enjoyed a series of material and work benefits, as well as the village kulaks ... They were interested in preserving privileges that were only possible in a bourgeois society. Therefore they were separated from the workers and the peasants by the most basic [consideration] – their economic self-interest.[39]

At the end of October, with the emergence of the Left SRs, a formal schism occurred within the PSR, although it was not felt as deeply in Siberia as in European Russia. Even in Tomsk, with its rich tradition of SR diversity and considerable sympathy for the frustration felt by the schismatics, the vast majority of rank and file members remained in the main party. But the Left SRs did have a profound effect upon events in Siberia on at least two counts. Firstly, as elsewhere in Russia, by allying with the Bolsheviks they provided the latter with entrée and credibility in the countryside, and especially among the middle and poorer peasants. Secondly, perhaps even more than the Bolsheviks, they had a radicalizing effect upon soldiers returning from the front.[40] Even before the *frontoviki* began coming home in large numbers in late summer 1917 as the Great War wound down, revolutionary seeds were sprouting in the Siberian countryside – surprisingly, more so than in the towns and cities. This was evident in the growing difficulty of the central government – whether imperial, Provisional, or Soviet – to enforce its writ with each passing month. The radicalizing process among the peasants, moreover, was occurring almost as much within the village proper as in relation to the outside world: they were rejecting all the traditional sources of authority, including the elders (*starosty*) who were unsympathetic to their rising anti-war and anti-government mood.

Spontaneous peasant radicalism was fed by an absence of political leadership in the region. Not even the soviets, much less the Provisional Government, could implement a consistent social policy, especially when it came to the land hunger of the peasants. A good example of this inability occurred in the obscure settlement of Kruglovka, some thirty miles from Omsk, where in May 1917 local peasants petitioned the SR-dominated soviet in Omsk to give them some surplus state land for their use. The soviet responded, following the lead of the *VTsIK* in Petrograd, by advising the petitioners that they would have to wait for the meeting of the Constituent Assembly. Other provincial soviets that were dominated by non-party radicals and anarchists rather than SRs and Mensheviks were willing to go against the guidelines from the centre, however, and simply took matters into their own hands; in many cases, the official representatives of the central government appeared helpless. In Tobol'sk *guberniia* land summarily changed hands to benefit *frontoviki* and others who needed it, but without the formal approval from either the soviet or the Provisional Government.[41]

Not surprisingly, the radical *frontoviki* were only too happy to aid such spontaneous local initiatives. As the summer of 1917 turned into fall, the number of war veterans swelled, and so did their militancy and influence. They were rapidly moving to the left of the majority SRs, and were even outpacing their Bolshevik mentors. The impact of these tough, armed, young men upon isolated rural gatherings may be imagined; it was enough to cause grave concern to any government. Although relatively few in number in Siberia, the *frontoviki* were usually able to carry the day against the combined authority of the *starosty* and parish priests, not to mention any Provisional Government official who dared to show his face. Their forcefulness and cockiness quickly intimidated the pro-SR village schoolteachers, clerks, and civil servants who had been the mainstay of the Provisional Government's local infrastructure. From the ranks of the *frontoviki* also emerged almost all the leaders of the spontaneous peasant movement in Siberia, as well as of the subsequent partisan armies.

The situation in urban Siberia was not nearly as volatile as in the countryside. In the main towns political cooperation, at least among the socialist parties, continued throughout most of 1917. Only the Leninist-Pravdists as early as March disavowed the "Menshevik" accommodations of the majority of their Siberian comrades and called unequivocally for the overthrow of the Provisional Government. Following directives received from Lenin via Iakov Sverdlov, they set up a Central Siberian Regional Bureau of Bolsheviks separate from the United Krasnoiarsk Social Democratic organization, which was still dominated by the Mensheviks.[42] Of fifteen Bolshevik urban committees (*gorkomy*) in the region, eight refused to follow Lenin's militant line in setting up a separate administration until after the Sixth Party Congress, which took place at the end of July, and five held out until October or later. Indeed, at a conference in Irkutsk during 20–21 July Bolsheviks joined Mensheviks in calling for the reunification of the two wings of the Social Democratic Party.[43] It was even agreed that the Mensheviks would play the leading role since they were more numerous and more experienced in local affairs. Only in Krasnoiarsk was there an effective purely Bolshevik apparatus; elsewhere in Siberia, not only did the two Marxist parties routinely work together but they did so often in collaboration with other socialist partners as well.[44]

In May the Transbaikal Bolsheviks and Mensheviks had joined with the PSR on a single, united ticket for elections to the local Committee of Public Safety. As late as July there were still meetings in Chita of all Social Democrats to define and prepare a common program. It was only in the days before the Bolsheviks came to power in Petrograd that a majority of Siberian comrades fell into line with the directive of their own Central Committee to break with the Mensheviks.[45] At the same time, an All-Siberian Executive Bureau of the Russian Social Democratic Workers' Party, Bolshevik (RSDRP(b)), finally established itself in Irkutsk.[46]

Throughout 1917 Bolshevism remained marginal as a political force in much of the region, certainly by comparison to the far more numerous and entrenched representatives of the moderate socialists, especially of the PSR. In the words of John Keep, "This organizational weakness explains why many local [Bolsheviks and their sympathizers] were not adequately informed about the [October] insurrection in Petrograd and as a consequence were ill prepared to take similar action themselves."[47] The relative weakness of Bolshevism in Siberia reflected, in part, the special circumstances of the region. Local society contrasted in at least two important ways with European Russia: the industrial working class was less numerous (constituting only one-third of the urban population of Siberia), and the middle classes – including industrialists, manufacturers, merchants, traders, civil servants, professionals, and clerks – were a higher proportion of the population of the towns and cities. The total Siberian proletariat, not including the small number of poor peasants who worked on other people's land, did not exceed 300,000, and of these only about one-sixth were actually located in the large cities; the rest lived and worked along the railway line.[48] Before the February Revolution Siberia had few trade unions, but by July, according to one estimate, the number had grown to over 170 organizations with a membership of approximately 66,000.[49]

Another problem impeding Bolshevik growth in Siberia was the lack of local roots, an obstacle similar in many respects to that facing the Kadets, though the latter had connections to the PSR intelligentsia and the regionalists. Also, with few exceptions the Bolshevik leaders, like the Kadets, were Eurocentric intellectuals who tended to regard Siberia as peripheral and only a stepping-stone to the real action at the metropolitan centre. This provided the immediate background to the abiding mutual suspicion between the Siberian muzhik and the citified party worker who was sent out in the early days of soviet rule to organize the collection of grain and other food supplies for transfer to the starving cities of European Russia. If at first explicitly anti-Bolshevik feelings were less evident in Siberia than in many parts of Russia closer to the centre of Soviet authority, it was not long before passive suspicion turned into alarm amid complaints like the one made by a Menshevik member of the Petrograd Duma that "language is inadequate to describe the chaos, the anarchy perpetrated by bands of cutthroats, branded criminals, and ex-convicts, now calling themselves Bolsheviks."[50]

This theme, with embellishments, was taken up eagerly by the Kadet establishment: "to understand Bolshevism, one must bear in mind that the Bolsheviks deny all moral standards."[51] The point was that Lenin's party categorically stood apart from all others because it alone dismissed all traditional values and common rules as bourgeois while sanctioning any means to achieve victory for itself. This was more than mere political opportunism; it represented a new and terrible nihilism that threatened the foundations and achievements of Western and Russian history. "Bolshevism consists just in the organisation and gathering of these barbarian forces existing inside contemporary society, hostile to culture and civilisation."[52]

OCTOBER IN SIBERIA

During the weeks and days preceding the October 1917 Revolution the Bolsheviks may have been misled by the revolutionary turmoil evident in the Siberian countryside to believe that things were going their way. For instance, on 26 September in Akmolinsk *oblast'* a district congress of peasant deputies called for all crown, church, and other private land to be made available for everyone's use; henceforth, hired labour was to be "forbidden forever" and "all factories, plants, and mines ... should become the property of the people without compensation." The peasant deputies denounced all manner of speculation and middle-man activity at the expense of the consumer, demanded free schools and libraries, and declared that henceforth Russia should be "a republic with a president."[53]

Just prior to the October Revolution there was some evidence of an upturn in Bolshevik organizational performance. At the important First All-Siberian Congress of Soviets in Irkutsk, the Krasnoiarsk Pravdists managed to orchestrate an ideological majority: of the 184 delegates, sixty-four were Bolsheviks, while another thirty-five were Left SRs and ten were Menshevik-Internationalists, both allies of the Bolsheviks; on the other side were fifty regular SRs, eleven Menshevik-Defensists, and fourteen others.[54] A reliable Central Executive Committee (*Tsentrosibir'*) was thus elected under the chairmanship of Boris Shumiatskii, who, as it happened, was a leader of the Krasnoiarsk group.[55]

At the same time, however, the results of the October elections to the town duma of Tomsk were less gratifying for the Bolsheviks, or at least for the Pravdist wing. Out of 102 places, the Bolsheviks and Menshevik-Internationalists jointly won thirty-four, the SRs twenty-four, the Kadets seventeen, the conservative Union of Householders ten, and the Menshevik-Defensists six.[56] But perhaps most significant was the outcome of the subsequent elections to the All-Russian Constituent Assembly which involved the broadest cross-section of the population. Here the SRs got nearly fifty per cent of the total Siberian vote, about five times more than the Bolsheviks.[57]

The overall disparity throughout Russia may have been more apparent than real, according to Lenin. His argument was that the PSR's percentages were misleadingly high because they did not make allowance for Left SR supporters, who were subsumed in the majority party's electoral list, and because many of the more radical soldiers did not get an opportunity to vote. Moreover, even among those who consciously cast their ballots for the PSR were some tactical allies whose true allegiances lay elsewhere, such as to their own minority nationality, religion, or region.[58] Lenin's argument, of course, did not stop there. Parliamentary elections were too easily subject to manipulation by the upper classes and their hired opinion-makers, and therefore should be discounted. He denounced the moderate socialists as advocates of "compromise with the malignant bourgeoisie" and for their adherence to an empty political democracy that permitted power to be vested in a Constituent Assembly elected by universal suffrage where the workers' representatives would not be in a majority. The Bolsheviks, he added, were not afraid of "civil war ... as we will not give up Soviet power for anything in the world."[59] Almost all the other political parties – the PSR in particular, for obvious reasons – took the opposite view, arguing that the elections to the Constituent Assembly accurately and properly reflected the minority status of the Bolsheviks, who therefore had no legitimate claim to power. Under the circumstances, Lenin's decision to disband the Constituent Assembly in January 1918 in the name of the higher authority of the soviets was virtually certain to bring on the civil war he had predicted.

With one or two exceptions, the reactions in Siberian cities to the Bolsheviks' seizure of power in Petrograd were not positive and varied from indifference to outright resistance. In the regional capital of Omsk, during the evening and night of November 1–2 hundreds of residents took to the streets, and similar protests occurred in Irkutsk, Novonikolaevsk, and several smaller towns. More commonly, however, there was no reaction at all; indeed, the news took several days to reach the more remote eastern parts of the region.[60] The quick passing of these uncoordinated and unfocused protests in Siberia was not the result of Bolshevik strength so much as a reflection of widespread popular exhaustion and ennui. Despite the absence of general support for, or even an understanding of what had transpired in Petrograd, on 30 November a new Omsk soviet elected its Executive Committee made up of eleven Bolsheviks, three Mensheviks, and two SRs, which then proceeded to declare the establishment of Soviet authority in Omsk. Tomsk and Novonikolaevsk followed in due course. It was several weeks before the new order was established as far east as Irkutsk, and beyond that there were additional delays. In Chita the local soviet did not became Bolshevik until February.[61] As usual, Vladivostok was the exception: there was a Bolshevik majority in its soviet's Executive Committee already on 19 November.[62]

Most pre-existing public organizations were vociferously condemnatory of the Bolshevik coup but, with the demise of the Provisional Government, could offer no alternatives.[63] The reaction of the Omsk town duma – still dominated by SRs and Mensheviks – was typical in decrying the "anarcho-Bolshevik *démarche* in Petrograd." Even the local soviet initially was opposed on the grounds that the coup interfered with all "all power going to the Constituent Assembly." Siberian business and civic leaders gathered together in a Union for the Salvation of the Motherland, Freedom, and Order, and promised to subsidize armed resistance to the "Bolshevik usurpers."[64]

The less than enthusiastic response in much of Siberia to his revolution came as no great surprise to Lenin. He acknowledged that the October Revolution had much less to offer the Siberian muzhiks than to their central Russian counterparts. The latter, acting on their own initiative even before the famous edict proclaimed by the Second Soviet Congress in Petrograd during the night of 26 October 1917, took over both public and private property, that is, state, appanage, monastic, and church lands, as well as big landowners' estates, and subsequently even some holdings of more affluent fellow peasants. Bowing to the inevitable, Lenin made sure that the Soviet government would receive credit among the poor peasants for what in any case it was powerless to prevent. A supplemental decree of 19 February 1918 incorporated three elements: the levelling of land holding and farming, the important Bolshevik principle calling for the nationalization of all the land with legal title kept in the name of the state,[65] and the reorganization of land tenure and use into larger social units. While *de jure* these arrangements placed the confiscated tracts at the disposal of cantonal land committees and the district soviet of peasants, these bodies were in many cases simply too weak to do anything about the peasants' spontaneous "personal" appropriations.

Questions about how much the Soviet land decrees owed to the PSR and to peasant socialism generally, and about who gained the most from them have been highly controversial. Western sources tend to see the populist debt as great, whereas Soviet scholars have argued the opposite.[66] In any case, almost three million formerly propertyless peasants did receive new holdings.[67] The big winners from the Soviet decrees were undoubtedly the poor peasants of the central agricultural zones, but in Siberia the land legislation remained largely a symbolic gesture: there by 1917 the state held 35.5 per cent of the land, peasants 49 per cent, the Cossacks 8 per cent, the crown 7 per cent, and private landlords only .5 per cent.[68]

Nevertheless, the political and symbolic impact of the land decrees was enormous throughout the former Russian empire, and they were all the more remarkable in view of Lenin's own negative feelings about petty peasant proprietorship. To be sure, he left the details of ownership purposefully vague in order to avoid any permanent entrenchment of petty proprietorship in the countryside. Moreover, his long-term goal continued to be the introduction of large farms operated collectively and with a high level of mechanical sophistication – factories in the field with an industrialized work force. A certain vagueness or imprecision in the agrarian program at this stage was useful, lest the peasants turn against the new regime. Similar considerations caused Lenin to refrain from alienating property belonging to enlisted Cossack soldiers or to middle (as opposed to affluent) peasants.

The Siberian countryside was even less disposed than other rural areas to welcome the new agrarian initiatives emanating from Soviet Petrograd. Moreover, Bolshevik decrees in the first days after October that called for increasing the supply of grain to the cities of European Russia could go unheeded with little fear of retribution. Many Siberians firmly believed that the socialist government would soon follow its immediate predecessor into oblivion.[69] Local authorities (including most incumbent municipal officials), with their institutional ties to the Provisional Government, saw little reason to cooperate with the soviets even after the Bolshevik coup. Thus, the Kurgan town duma passed a resolution on 28 October condemning the events in Petrograd as an infringement on "the sovereign authority of the Constituent Assembly." Similar resolutions were passed by the municipal dumas in Tiumen', Omsk, Tomsk, and elsewhere.[70] In its declaration of 22 December 1917 the Novonikolaevsk (Novosibirsk) town duma reasserted "the authority of the *guberniia*, district, and town administrations and reject[ed] in principle the transition of local power to the soviets."[71] The Tomsk Mensheviks were almost alone in advocating some accommodation with the new regime, but they too insisted that the Bolsheviks would have to agree on an all-socialist coalition government responsible to *VTsIK*: "The Tomsk organization of United Mensheviks recognizes the necessity for unity of all revolutionary forces and organizations in the decisive struggle with bourgeois counter-revolution and for the defence of the gains of the revolution ... [and calls] for the creation of an authoritative ... [not merely Bolshevik] socialist ministry of representatives from all the socialist parties."[72]

Of course, the Bolsheviks were not in fact distracted or swayed by these debates from pressing on with their own political agenda, which consisted of consolidating their exclusive power. By the end of December the agencies of the Provisional Government were forced to withdraw or go underground, while Bolshevik-controlled soviets (often with the help of local Red Guards) imposed their authority in most towns in Siberia. The SRs in Omsk, Tomsk, and Irkutsk tried to resist but failed, even when they had the support of some sympathetic military forces. Opposition was more effective in Siberian villages where armed resistance to the central government combined with traditional hostility toward outsiders to create a strongly anti-Bolshevik atmosphere.[73] Many peasants regarded the political developments of 1917 as alien and unrepresentative of their interests or values:

The whole revolution was manufactured in the towns, and it is as flimsy as other town productions ... They say, "This is a democracy. We speak for all the people." But how can they claim to speak for us when we have never heard of them? What right have they to speak in our names and say that the peasants want this and that, when we have not yet opened our mouths? That is damnable trickery! Between them and us there is the same gap as between a man who drives a sledge and another man who rides on a train.[74]

Popular opposition to Bolshevism, however, should not be construed as endorsement of any other political option, including regionalism. For example, at the end of December in Tomsk, SRs, Mensheviks, Popular Socialists,[75] regionalists, and unaffiliated individuals making up the All-Siberian Extraordinary Congress of Delegates from Public Organizations finally appointed a temporary government known as the Provisional Siberian Regional Council, which in turn undertook to convene the Siberian Regional Duma as an alternative to illegal Soviet power in Siberia; these events all went virtually unnoticed outside a narrow circle of local intellectuals. In its political makeup and purpose, the Siberian Regional Duma was most reminiscent of the ill-fated Constituent Assembly in Petrograd. Like it, the Duma was broadly based and democratic in the political and parliamentary, if not social and economic, senses. In both assemblies the PSR was the dominant party, and both convened under the shadow of imminent Bolshevik sanction. The main difference was that, by contrast to the centrally located Constituent Assembly, the Tomsk-based Siberian Regional Duma had an explicitly regional focus. Even so, it was separatist only to the extent that it wanted more autonomy for Siberia within a reconstituted federalist Russian union, and its regionalism was always mitigated by other considerations, notably the PSR's preoccupation with power politics and statist "defensism."[76] In a vain attempt to broaden its mandate, the Duma appealed to all "democratic" (that is socialist) political parties to participate. Predictably, the Bolsheviks were sharply critical of the proceedings, while the propertied classes resented their arbitrary exclusion.[77]

But it was the mass apathy towards the Duma that left a gaping political vacuum which undoubtedly encouraged local Soviet authorities to believe that things were going their way. They were mistaken, however, in equating popular indifference to the niceties of parliamentary democracy, or regional self-determination with passivity in the face of onerous Soviet edicts like the immensely unpopular grain requisitions. Quite the contrary proved to be the case: during December only half the assigned norm, about 16,000 tons of grain, could be extracted from Siberia; in January 1918, because of even greater resistance, the amount shipped westward decreased to 10,500. Only the use of bloody strong-arm measures by the Cheka security police and by the army would reverse the trend and enforce the will of the centre. February deliveries went back up to 33,000, and in March the figure was an impressive 55,000 tons.[78]

As 1917 came to a close Soviet policies generated strong popular opposition throughout Siberia and talk of counter-revolution and civil war became widespread. The success of any effort to combat Lenin's government, however, had to be predicated on an effective use of force (almost certainly involving foreign troops) *plus* a social and economic program that could offer the broad mass of the people an alternative to Bolshevism. As will become more evident in the following chapters, that was a good deal easier said than done.

3 Early Resistance to Bolshevik Rule, Contending White Governments, and the Rise of Omsk

January to July 1918

In Siberia opposition to the new Soviet government did not assume the immediate or extensive forms that were apparent in parts of European Russia. The reaction to the Bolshevik coup was more muted and isolated: there was no immediate equivalent to the counter-revolutionary Volunteer Army and its Cossack allies that appeared in the south.[1] Instead, local resistance was at first limited to such episodic occurrences as the mutiny of officer cadets in Omsk and in Irkutsk. Somewhat more significant, but still relatively small in scale, was the effort at the very end of 1917 by a Captain Kirilov to organize some former tsarist officers into his "White Legion." At about the same time, local Cossacks revolted against Soviet authority in Orenburg, parts of Western Siberia, and the Transbaikal.[2]

Opposition that was formal and politically more respectable had become apparent at the end of January 1918 with the convening in Tomsk of the Siberian Regional Duma dominated by followers of the leader of the Party of the Socialist Revolutionaries (PSR), Victor Chernov. The Duma offered itself as the regional equivalent of the democratic principle most clearly expressed by the Constituent Assembly. As such, it claimed to be the legitimate alternative both to the Second All-Russian Soviet Congress dominated by the Bolsheviks which sanctioned the October coup and to the new central government Council of People's Commissars (*Sovnarkom*) in Petrograd. From the beginning, however, the Siberian Regional Duma's mandate and make-up were quite restricted. By excluding the propertied classes ("census society" – *tsenzovoe obshchestvo*)[3] in the hopes of appeasing the Bolsheviks and other radicals, the Duma only succeeded in further isolating itself. The net result of its machinations was a narrowing of the political base to members of the PSR and a few non-party regionalists. The Bolsheviks were in any case not appeased and they refused to participate or even to recognize the Duma's legitimacy, while the Kadets denounced the disenfranchisement of the middle and upper classes as a gross violation of political democracy.[4]

Nevertheless, there was some initial support for the Siberian Regional Duma among the *frontoviki* returning from the front lines as Russian participation in the war drew to a close. In the reserve units stationed near Tomsk, "the majority is sympathetic to the Regional Duma and even the 12th Army, known for its Bolshevism, is 2/3 for the autonomy of Siberia."[5] A leading regionalist warned, however, that the SRs were using the Duma as a tool in their own larger struggle for power in Russia and that they were out of touch with local interests and needs: "To say that the Duma represents the Siberian population is impossible."[6] As with so many other institutions at this time, assessments of the Duma tended to reflect the ideological loyalties of the observers rather than any measure of clear and objective criteria. Federalist-minded SRs and their regionalist allies found themselves opposed on the role of the Duma by a curious combination of Bolsheviks and equally centralist Kadets-cum-monarchists. These strange political bedfellows rarely agreed, and so their common hostility to the Duma was particularly significant and did not augur well for its prospects.

It was thus something of an accomplishment when forty leading activists of the Siberian Regional Duma managed to form an executive under the chairmanship of a young PSR lawyer, P.Ia. Derber. As a recent arrival from European Russia, with no claim on local loyalties or any expertise to qualify him for the job of heading a vast regional government, his sudden prominence can only be explained by his shrewdness in positioning himself close to the party's left-centre under Victor Chernov. That no one more senior or widely respected in the PSR came forward at this time to assume the leadership role was a clear indication of the Duma's isolation and essential weakness.

Paradoxically, there were almost no limits on Derber's political aspirations. In the temporary absence of serious countervailing claims and encouraged by the free air of Siberia, he gave his little group the high-sounding title of the Provisional Government of Autonomous Siberia (PGAS).[7] The power vacuum in the region during the early months of 1918 encouraged far-reaching pretensions and a sense of unreality. Even so, the lack of support for the PGAS and its parent Duma became all too obvious when the Bolshevik-dominated Central

Executive Committee of the Soviets of Siberia (*Tsentrosibir'*) quickly ordered its Soviet affiliate in Tomsk on 26 January to disperse the Siberian Regional Duma and arrest any recalcitrant members. *Tsentrosibir'*, founded with the goal of bringing together the forces of revolutionary democracy, was made up of a majority of five Bolsheviks with four Left SRs and Mensheviks, and of a minority of four Right SRs and Menshevik-Defensists. The decision to act against the Duma was thus by no means unanimous and was made under the influence of militant appeals and pressures from local trade unionists and soldiers' deputies who denounced it as counter-revolutionary.[8] With the political situation deteriorating rapidly and fearing for their personal safety, a majority of the delegates to the Duma decided to go underground, while most of the PGAS followed Derber in hurried escape (just ahead of the advancing Red Army) to the safe havens of the Far East.

As with the case of disbanding of the Constituent Assembly in Petrograd, there was no widespread public outcry. P.V. Vologodskii, who was destined to play a major role in Siberian politics in the period that followed, provided an explanation. Though not entirely unbiased, it contained more than an element of truth: "I cannot say that the Siberian population was particularly sympathetic to this convocation [of the Duma]. No. It accepted it rather indifferently."[9] Nevertheless, according to one account in a sympathetic local PSR newspaper, delegates at an Extraordinary All-Siberian Peasant Congress in early February overwhelmingly endorsed the Siberian Regional Duma as the legitimate government authority until the convening of the All-Siberian Constituent Assembly and condemned the Soviet action against it.[10] The same Congress voted a strong condemnation of both the Bolsheviks and the SR-Maximalists for their role in the October "experiment upon the living flesh of Russia," and reiterated that only the Constituent Assembly had legitimate claim to "all political authority in the country." The meeting closed with a call for the convocation of an all-Russian congress of peasant deputies, with mandatory representation exclusively from the local districts as the only way to establish "the true will of all the working peasantry."[11] For the next several months Western Siberia continued in a state of political dormancy. Neither the clandestine representatives of the anti-Bolshevik PGAS (operating increasingly without the "Autonomous" part of the original title) nor *Tsentrosibir'* exercised effective control over the vast region. Farther to the east there was still less Soviet presence and more confusion among contending "White" forces, as the enemies of Bolshevism were starting to be called.

Even before the arrival of Derber and company in the Russian Far East, there already existed – in addition to a variety of local soviets –

several independent regional "governments" and autonomous Cossack fiefdoms, such as the Transbaikal domain of the notorious Ataman G.M. Semenov.[12] For Russia's Maritime Province, the overwhelming fact of life was the proximity of Tokyo, separated from Vladivostok only by open sea. The Japanese were not shy about taking an active role in Siberian affairs, and they were known to be opposed to the formation of any strong (and especially socialist) Russian government that could resist their expansionist designs in the region. Any limits on Japanese policy in Eastern Siberia were set by Tokyo's extreme sensitivity to American opinion rather than by concern with local Soviet authorities.[13] President Woodrow Wilson's objections were the chief reason for Japan's decision to put off massive intervention until there was Allied agreement on a coordinated plan. This, however, did not prevent Tokyo from acting unilaterally in response to an incident that occurred during the evening of 4 April 1918 in Vladivostok: the Japanese landed less than seven hours after three Japanese store clerks were killed in the course of a robbery. To ensure against Tokyo stealing a march, the British followed the next day.[14]

The best measure of the weakened state of political authority in the region was that the strongest Russian "government" was not even located on Russian territory but rather just across the border in Manchuria. With headquarters in Harbin, General D.L. Khorvat, imperial governor of the Chinese-Eastern Railway and the last official representative of the Provisional Government in the Far East, saw himself as the sole legitimate representative of Russian political authority in the region, despite the anomaly of his extraterritoriality.[15] In his role as director of the railway in Manchuria, Khorvat alone had an established administrative apparatus, the experience of having governed, and some armed force at his disposal. Moreover, he spoke for Harbin's conservative Far Eastern Committee for the Defence of Fatherland and Constituent Assembly, and was able to co-opt its members into his "Business Cabinet," which then included such prominent national figures as arms manufacturer A.I. Putilov, right-wing Kadet and former tsarist ambassador to Peking Prince N.A. Kudashev, and Vice-Admiral A.V. Kolchak, recently of the Russian Black Sea Fleet.[16] With two prominent Kadets, two Popular Socialists, and three non-party conservatives, the Business Cabinet was clearly to the right of Derber's PSR politics.[17]

At a minimum, the Business Cabinet saw itself as the guardian in the Far East of the interests of the Russian state, even if its claim, based on its formal connection with the deposed Provisional Government, was tenuous on both political and legal grounds.[18] Khorvat was encouraged in these pretensions by the Japanese, who favoured his government as the most congenial to and compatible with their own interests in Manchuria and Eastern Siberia.[19] It was no secret, moreover, that Khorvat and his associates were anathema in the eyes of Derber's group of moderate socialists, and they fully reciprocated the sentiment.[20] In fact, none of the contending parties in the region was disposed to recognize the authority of the diminutive Jewish "Prime-Minister" of the PGAS and his odd assortment of "European intellectuals" who claimed to represent the Siberian Regional Duma, about which no one in Vladivostok or Harbin knew anything. As the acerbic contemporary observer Baron A.P. Budberg commented, "Some new Siberian Government ... emerged, made up of persons of very low caliber who are totally unknown in the Far East."[21]

Derber, therefore, found himself in the unenviable position of having a formal mandate from the Siberian Regional Duma but little else in the way of either economic resources or political power. His only hope was to play on the presumed preference of the allies for democratic government. But the U.S. mission in Vladivostok, which was in the best position to help PGAS, was at all times limited by President Wilson's instructions to avoid interference in Russia's domestic affairs and to stick strictly to the business of guarding the Allied war supplies (that had originally been intended for the Provisional Government). Nevertheless, Derber continued to talk and behave as though Allied intervention was imminent and would be on his behalf. He argued that because it was essential for the allies to control the main means of communication in order to protect against the danger of the war *matériel* ending up in the hands of the German enemy, cooperation with a like-minded and loyal Russian partner, such as his government, was their only possible choice. Derber appealed to the United States in particular and attempted to link recognition for his government (as at least the regional authority) with a role in administering the Trans-Siberian and the Chinese-Eastern railways. But the transparently desperate nature of these tactics only served to underscore the PGAS's evident lack of legitimacy and viability.[22] All the high-sounding rhetoric and claims contrasted with the sorry reality of the Derber government, stuck near Harbin in railway cars and giving new and comic meaning to the notion of seat of government.[23]

While the PGAS technically had the best connections with the Siberian Regional Duma and therefore some measure of legal sanction, its only real hope for attaining power in the Russian Far East was through foreign intervention. Indeed, it was only *after* 29 June 1918 – when the fragile Soviet system in the Pacific Maritime Region crumbled under minimal external pressure from Czechoslovak prisoners of war in transit to their homeland – that Derber and his ministers fortuitously were able to make their way to Vladivostok and stake their claim from Russian, as opposed to Manchurian, soil.[24]

The PGAS's brief window of opportunity, however, amounted to nothing. Allied recognition, and effective government were effectively blocked by the opposition of local interest groups intensely jealous of their own turf and prerogatives. Civil administration existed only in the limited form of municipal institutions left over from the Provisional Government, while military control passed into the hands of the Czechoslovaks.[25] Even the Vladivostok Zemstvo Board under A.S. Medvedev, which was reasonably close to Derber's strongly pro-Western and mildly socialist position, was unwilling to surrender any power to the PGAS. Thus the U.S. consular representative in Vladivostok came to the inescapable conclusion on 5 July 1918 that Derber "has no authority for claiming to be the government of Siberia."[26]

Despite the PGAS's continued insistence on its legal authority and its denunciations of General Khorvat's pretensions, his prestige actually increased. This was probably less a tribute to the general's leadership than the absence of any serious alternatives in the White ranks. Nevertheless, to many observers Khorvat seemed the most qualified candidate for the job of political command in the Russian Far East at this time.[27] If he happened to be an uninspired administrator and anathema to the democrats, that did not count against him with either of the two groups that really mattered, the local White military and the Japanese. The general's chief disadvantage, however, remained his physical location in remote Harbin and his evident inability to move his base of operations onto Russian territory.

Another independent and totally unpredictable variable in the politics of White Siberia was the activity of the wild Cossack atamans, notably G.M. Semenov, R.F. Ungern-Sternberg, I.P. Kalmykov, I.M. Gamov, and B.V. Annenkov. The names of these men became synonymous with the worst atrocities of the Civil War, at the same time that they represented the most active anti-Bolshevik forces in the region.[28] Their behaviour was so utterly disreputable and wantonly predatory that they probably brought more harm to their allies than to their enemies. The Maritime Regional Zemstvo Board – no hotbed of radicalism – complained of arbitrary actions taken by Cossack bands against political offenders, especially Bolsheviks, an open-ended category which could include virtually anyone who stood in their way or was in possession of something they coveted. Cossack marauders dispensed equally harsh and random punishments to villagers without regard to the gravity of their alleged offences, which might range from serious matters such as hiding arms and munitions to the most trivial issues.[29]

Ataman Kalmykov in Khabarovsk district was notorious for his especially severe measures, which included killing a twelve-year-old boy and
an assortment of elders for not knowing the whereabouts of some local
Bolsheviks. On several occasions Kalmykov's men, in the company of
Japanese officers, beat up on peasants. The Khabarovsk District Zemstvo Board reported that the "whole population [was] in a panic, with
women and children completely terrified ... [and that] in the absence
of the appropriate apparatus, [they were] utterly powerless to do
anything about it."[30] At the other end of Siberia, a similar pattern
existed. The Semipalatinsk Cooperative Union issued several formal
protests against the actions of Ataman Annenkov, warning that they
damaged the reputation of the Omsk government and constituted a
threat to the overall goal of reconstructing the Russian state.[31]

The atamans did not need any additional encouragement for their
total disregard for the rights of the civilian population, but got some
anyway. The Japanese secretly, and right-wing Russian political circles
more openly, saw the activity of the atamans as a major destabilizing
force, one which could create such chaos in Russia that foreign intervention would be seen as a lesser evil even by those who presently
opposed it. Moreover, the Japanese knew that in the remote outposts
of the Transbaikal, especially, decisive advantage could be achieved
with relatively few well-armed, well-supplied, and mobile men. A small
number of Cossacks could terrorize, if not always effectively control,
a territory larger than all of Europe or Japan. It mattered little to the
Japanese that these desperadoes were far more likely to despoil
defenceless Russian peasants than to take on armed Soviet forces.
Tokyo harboured no illusions about winning a popularity contest in
Siberia and saw regional turmoil there as its natural ally. Indeed, for
the Japanese, part of the appeal of the atamans was their refreshing
disregard for all the civil libertarian niceties so dear to the Derbers
and other westernizing Russians who modelled themselves on the
principles of Paris, London, and especially Washington.[32]

Yet it would be an oversimplification to regard these steppe warlords
as simple tools of Tokyo or any other foreign power. Fiercely anti-
Bolshevik, anti-intellectual, anti-Semitic, and proudly jealous of their
prerogatives, the Cossack atamans were deeply patriotic according to
their own lights. In many cases they were strong champions of Russian
Orthodoxy and nationalism, even when they themselves (as in the
case of the half-Buriat Semenov) and their followers were multi-
ethnic.[33] Nevertheless, their negative impact upon the destiny of
Siberia and the Russian Far East during 1918 and 1919 was great,
perhaps decisive.

GROWING IMPORTANCE OF OMSK

Western Siberia in the first half of 1918 was undergoing a somewhat different experience. The emergence of Omsk as the main centre of the anti-Bolshevik movement in the region was no accident. While lacking the relative cosmopolitanism and commercial activity of Vladivostok and Irkutsk, with their large Oriental and Jewish communities, or of Tomsk, with its university and cultural consciousness, Omsk had served for years as the imperial administrative centre for Western Siberia and was located closest to the country's European capitals. Consequently, it had bigger buildings, wider streets, better lighting and sewage systems, and many of the other amenities of a provincial administrative centre. The ambience was characterized by a militarism and a bureaucracy more reminiscent of European Russia than Siberia.

More than half the town's population consisted of government employees and pensioners, every fourth man was in uniform, and one in ten was a member of the gentry. Many retired officers and civil servants came to Omsk because it was a relatively cheap place to live out their lives. This pattern was already evident in the third quarter of the nineteenth century. Industry, on the other hand, was minimally developed, and even in the town duma, normally the bastion of liberals and the Third Element, about half the members were military men and civil servants.[34]

At the end of the nineteenth century, visitors from the West were not favourably impressed with Omsk. George Kennan provided this drab description: "The largest building is a military academy and the most picturesque building a police station ... There is neither a newspaper nor a public library, and ... one half the population wears the Tsar's uniforms and makes a business of governing the other half."[35] Even among Siberians the main attraction of Omsk was its material benefits rather than any aesthetic or cultural qualities. With characteristic generosity, G.N. Potanin tried to paint a balanced picture: "[T]here was the lowest cost of living of any place between Petersburg and Irkutsk, and at the same time thanks to the fact that it was the governor-general's residency, life was more animated here than in any other provincial town; there were concerts here, shows, balls, and fireworks ... [From] the other cities of Siberia, even from Irkutsk and Orenburg, retired civil servants congregated here to live out their lives as pensioners."[36] By the early years of the twentieth century Omsk had acquired a reputation as the place in Western Siberia for good restaurants and lively entertainment. It reminded visitors of Harbin, with much the same combination of late-starting days filled with political gossip and epicurean evenings that lasted into the wee hours.[37] But it was the Civil War which gave the town added prominence, first in the spring of 1918 as the capital of the regional Provisional Siberian Government (PSG), then the All-Russian Directory in September-October, and finally Admiral Kolchak's administration after November.

Already towards the end of 1917 assorted refugees from European Russia, ranging from aristocrats and the old intelligentsia to petty criminals, began arriving by the thousands. Judging from the first-hand account of Bernard Pares, despite obvious class and cultural differences these people shared a common antipathy to the Soviet order that had taken over in Moscow as well as a remarkable lack of interest in their new eastern surroundings.

Omsk is less normal than any other place in Siberia ... This is largely due to the mass of emigrants of the higher classes from European Russia and the dominance of a military atmosphere. These people have hardly learned anything at all, and try to live as much as possible as they did before the revolution. They are really living in a kind of oasis which has nothing in common with Siberia, consisting of the Aquarium Garden [a famous night spot] and other places of entertainment, where they spend extravagant sums derived from unknown sources on luxuries or absurdities ... The military are in this the worst offenders, especially the juniors of them.[38]

The usual tensions that arise with the arrival of large numbers of refugees were exacerbated in Omsk by the unsettled political situation and the struggle for power among the different anti-Bolshevik forces.[39] Not only were rowdy young men in resplendent uniforms making their presence felt at all hours of the day and night, but they were doing so on the streets and in public places, as well as on the dance floors of the Evropa, Apollo, and Rossiia restaurants, which they clearly prefered to the front line.[40] Moreover, like their counterparts in other White enclaves of the former Russian empire, they combined a "lack of the most elementary understanding of politics [with a] distrust of politicians – that is, of [democratic] intellectuals."[41] Fortunately for the White cause, Omsk society had at its core much more substantial and productive people. Chief among these were financially solvent and powerful members of the Siberian producers' and consumers' cooperatives. These cooperatives, led by the politically conscious dairy industry, combined the resources and the will to bankroll alternatives to the Soviet government.

As early as February 1918 the All-Siberian Congress of Cooperatives meeting in Novonikolaevsk passed a resolution overwhelmingly rejecting the authority of Lenin's *Sovnarkom*, and it also called for complete Siberian autonomy and granted a sizeable loan to the PSG (as the PGAS affiliate was known in Western Siberia).[42] Bolshevik agitators, as well as some Siberian peasants, countered with charges that these actions were clear indications of the class nature of the cooperatives which, after all, were organizations of the well-to-do. "They have sugar, tea, white flour, beautiful things [*krasnyi tovar*], while we have nothing!"[43] It was clear that the cooperatives were not only economic bulwarks of the most dynamic form of capitalism in Siberia, but were also politically committed to liberal government.

Nevertheless, throughout the first half of 1918 most of the region remained beyond anyone's effective control.[44] The chief local alternative to Soviet power was the so-called West-Siberian Commissariat of the PSG, in the persons of four obscure SRs in Tomsk, P. Mikhailov, B. Markov, M. Lindberg, and P. Sidorov.[45] While adopting a conciliatory tone on social issues, the West-Siberian Commissariat was quick to announce that it would not permit any organizations of a divisive "class and party" nature lest they interfere with or challenge the governmental authority of the PSG.[46] But the Commissariat was also careful not to infringe upon the gains of the February Revolution, particularly in the areas of labour legislation and land usage.[47] On the latter point, it left vague the legal status of private property while confirming the use of land by all.[48] Most of its energies, however, were concentrated on restoring civil liberties, freedom of the press, municipal and zemstvo self-rule, and economic rights originally granted by the Provisional Government.[49]

At about the same time, anti-Bolshevik military groups were organizing in several key West Siberian locations. They were undermanned, lacked a common program, and had only the vaguest ties to each other or to the West-Siberian Commissariat and the Siberian Regional Duma. The most important among them was the Organization of the Thirteen in Omsk under the ataman of the Siberian Cossacks, P.P. Ivanov-Rinov, and it had a membership of 3,000 men; in Tomsk there were another 1,500 under A.N. Pepeliaev, and Novonikolaevsk had 600. By late spring 1918 these groups, together with a few smaller ones, accounted for some 7,000 men under arms. By the standards in the area west of the Urals this was a very modest number, but at that time and in that region it constituted a serious threat to Soviet authority.[50]

As in Eastern Siberia, the power vacuum also encouraged armed bands of strategically located Cossacks to intimidate the surrounding rural population.[51] This had the effect, at least temporarily, of driving the peasants towards the soviets, which were already at odds with the

Cossacks following Sovnarkom's decision of 13 December 1917 to abolish traditional Cossack privileges. The Western Siberian peasantry had particularly bad experiences at the hands of atamans A.I. Dutov and B.V. Annenkov, both infamous for their unquenchable thirst for booty and blood as well as utter contempt for civil authority and due process of law.

If *atamanshchina* was clearly a major disruptive factor and one that became identified with right-wing forces in Siberia at this time, there was also, in the so-called Czechoslovak Legion, a countervailing pro-Western element. As World War I drew to its protracted conclusion on the eastern front, the approximately 50,000 battle-tested, estranged, Austro-Hungarian prisoners of war who made up the Legion found themselves on Russian and Ukrainian soil in the midst of the great revolutionary transition between the Provisional Government and Lenin's *Sovnarkom*. While this group contained diverse elements, there is general agreement that overall their sympathies were very much with Russia's moderate socialist parties, in particular the PSR.[52] Under almost any circumstances, several thousand armed and disciplined men would constitute a dangerous and formidable force. But in the chaos of Russia in 1918, the Czechs were much more than that, they were potentially the decisive military and political arbiters, especially in remote places where the Red Army was less present or effective. Moreover, these men were not derelicts or bandits but soldiers and officers of relatively high professional standards; they were "reported to be as good as French troops by the French officers who were with them. Fifty per cent of the men had received a higher and another 80 per cent a middle education, whilst there was not an illiterate man among them."[53] For the defeated and scattered enemies of Bolshevism – and the PSR first of all – the Legion was nothing less than a godsend, a second chance at power.[51]

While there remains some question about the good faith on both sides in the negotiations between the Czechs and the new government in Moscow, initially it appeared that a quick evacuation was what both wanted. For their part, the men in the Legion were anxious to return to their homeland as soon as possible in order to assist in fighting the Germans and participate in the setting up of their newly independent state. But great power politics intervened, with far-reaching consequences for all parties involved. The French, in particular, seemed to change their mind about the desirability of a speedy removal of the Legion and, as the chief patrons of Thomas Masaryk's nationalist campaign for an independent Czechoslovak state, their views were decisive.[55]

The Czechs thus remained on Russian territory and continued to be a major strategic force. Moreover, because they could not pass through hostile Austro-German territory, even if agreement on their evacuation could be reached they were obliged to take the long way around by sea through either Murmansk or Vladivostok. To reach the latter destination meant an extremely arduous and dangerous trek along the Trans-Siberian Railway into the politically volatile Russian hinterland, and naturally it also raised serious misgivings among the soviets. The French volte-face further delayed the process. The reasoning in Paris was never entirely clear or consistent; however, it appears to have been influenced by the expectation that the Czechs' continued presence in Russia would constitute a mini-eastern front, thereby relieving German pressure on France while simultaneously deterring the new Soviet leadership in Moscow from pursuing a pro-Berlin foreign policy.[56]

If Paris wished to register strong opposition to any separate Russo-German peace initiative, delaying the Legion's evacuation certainly did that; it also helped to destabilize further the Soviet rear. The change in French policy from favouring the immediate departure of the Czechs, so that they could help out on the western front, to virtually its opposite very likely reflected increased alarm at the Quai d'Orsay over the Bolshevik menace.[57] Paradoxically, the Soviet government also saw some advantages in a policy of delay. Trotsky initially favoured the idea of collaborating with the allies against Germany and only decided on evacuating the Legion when it became clear that he was not going to be able to strike a deal with the western powers and therefore that the armed Czechs represented a major threat to Moscow.[58] Sending the Czechs out through Siberia had the added appeal of potentially pitting them against the Japanese, who were becoming increasingly more aggressive in the area.

Such was the background then for the Legion's transmigration across Siberia. While relatively minor players in the arena of international diplomacy, the role of the legionnaires in Russia during 1918 was nothing less than critical. Whatever their original intentions – and Ambassador Kennan probably comes closest to the truth with his suggestion that they wanted to score points with the allies but had no long-term interests in domestic Russian politics or territory[59] – their progress along the Trans-Siberian Railway had major consequences because it brought them into direct conflict with soviet authorities. If the latter regarded them with ever-growing suspicion as counter-revolutionaries and foreign agents, the Czechs reciprocated by subscribing to a view of the soviets as potential collaborators with the Germans.

Negotiations between the Legion and the soviets stalled in the middle of May when the Czechs were broken up by Trotsky into several contingents and ordered to disarm in preparation for final evacuation through ports of departure at opposite ends of Russia. According to one source, when they began to mutiny on 25 May the westernmost group at Penza consisted of about 8,000 troops under Colonel S. Čéček, at Cheliabinsk there were about an equal number under General S.N. Voitsekhovskii, in central Siberia there were some 4,500 commanded by R. Gajda, and at Vladivostok under General M.K. Diterikhs there were between 12,000 and 14,000 men.[60] If the Soviet authorities saw the disarming as simply a measure to reduce the security risk, to the Czechs it appeared a deliberate attempt to reduce their capacity to defend themselves. This atmosphere of mutual suspicion and hostility was compounded by the Czechs' obvious sympathy for the programs and "legitimate role of the SRs as leaders of the Russian Democracy."

Trotsky had not helped his own situation by issuing an unenforceable order to arrest legionnaires who refused to surrender their arms during the evacuation. It was a bluff, and a bad one, because it pushed the Czechs into open revolt. The precipitating incident was an unfortunate confrontation at Cheliabinsk station between the legionnaires and a group of pro-Soviet Hungarian prisoners of war. With the local authorities taking the side of the Hungarians but unable to disarm the rebellious Czechs, the mutiny spread rapidly along the length of the Trans-Siberian Railway. What followed was a close approximation of Trotsky's worst nightmare. The advance by the rebellious Czechs along the railway line served as a catalyst and rallying point for all varieties of anti-Bolshevik forces to emerge from underground, including former officials and agents of the Provisional Government as well as representatives of the dispersed Constituent Assembly. A majority belonged to one or another branch of the PSR, but there were also Kadets, Popular Socialists, Mensheviks, minority ethnic groups, nonparty regionalists, and assorted monarchists.

The Soviet view of the Czech mutiny as an Allied conspiracy against the new regime contrasts with the scholarly consensus in the West, which has emphasized instead the spontaneous initiative of rank-and-file legionnaires:[61] "It must be attributed to the Czechs on the spot. It was a revolt by resolute young men against their timid local leaders, who can also be absolved of responsibility for its preparation ... The revolt was a sudden and spontaneous affair, which surprised everybody, foe and friend alike. It caught the allies utterly unprepared, and although it provided them with the pretext they had been seeking for so long, they were very slow to exploit it."[62] It has also been suggested that the timing of the revolt had much to do with the growing fear among the legionnaires that the Bolsheviks were about to turn them over to the Germans, who would treat them as deserters and execute them all.[63]

While the role of the Czechs is well documented, much less is known about other prisoners of war and foreigners in Russia who took the Red side at this critical time. It is not surprising that over the years (for patriotic and other ideological reasons) Soviet sources have sought to play down their contribution while exaggerating the negative impact of the interventionists and the "White Czechs." Yet, by the spring of 1918 there existed more than a dozen such "internationalist" detachments that brought tens of thousands of additional foreign sympathizers to the Communist side.[64]

Nevertheless, Moscow had reason to be alarmed by the ease with which the Czechs occupied key points along the railway line and quickly overran everything in their path. Even reluctant Soviet authorities conceded that the rapidity of this advance was at the very least an indication of the relative weakness of the Bolshevik party infrastructure in Siberia.[65] By the end of May undermanned Red positions collapsed in Penza and Syzran. There was little resistance to the legionnaires because the bulk of Moscow's forces – which still numbered only about 300,000 men, drawn mostly from the urban proletariat – was concentrated in the south, fighting the more immediate threat of Denikin's Volunteer Army several hundred miles from the Siberian theatre.[66] Cheliabinsk itself fell to the Czechs on 27 May. In June, together with their resurgent White Russian allies and with financial assistance from the Siberian cooperatives, they captured Kurgan, Omsk, Barnaul, Achinsk, Krasnoiarsk, Semipalatinsk, Biisk, Buzuluk, and Ufa. Thus, the full length of the Trans-Siberian Railway, from the Urals to the Pacific coast, came under the control of the Czechs, though they were in no position to administer these vast territories. Nevertheless, by mid-summer 1918 in much of Siberia "the deciding word in everything belonged to the Czechs."[67]

While the PSR and its allies in the cooperative movement were the chief beneficiaries of the Legion's activities, several other groups also welcomed the overthrow of Soviet power, and some of them, as we shall see, were in a better position to take advantage of it. Moreover, despite the obvious benefits, the Czech role was not seen by even the most anti-Bolshevik Russians in an entirely favourable light. In fact, bad feelings came to the surface almost immediately. The legionnaires tended to look down upon their eastern Slavic cousins as culturally inferior, and they did not hesitate to assert their privileges in obvious and petty ways, whatever the cost to local pride and feelings. Russian soldiers routinely complained that all their best girls were taken by the Czechs and that they could not compete with the largesse of the foreigners. Many shopkeepers and merchants felt powerless in the face of Czech demands and requisitions. And several of the Czech officers were known to have engaged in unseemly business practices, exploiting the competitive advantage they enjoyed by virtue of their control of more than 1,200 miles of the Trans-Siberian Railway, as well as some of its best rolling-stock.

If a majority of Siberian society looked upon the presence of the Czechs as a mixed blessing, members of the cooperative movement were much less equivocal. For them, as for the PSR, the Czechs represented a second chance – specifically, a second chance to do their own thing economically. Soviet rule, needless to say, had interrupted their flourishing entrepreneurial capitalism. In addition, the arrival of the Czechs freed the cooperatives from constraints in pursuing not only their economic interests but also their political power. In the words of one of their leaders, N. Fomin, with the help of the legionnaires "authority in Siberia had passed" to his organization. It should be noted, however, that Fomin did not regard this as a return to the old pre-revolutionary order. On the contrary, he and other cooperative activists were among the chief champions of the SR-Chernovite notion of a democratic "third path" between the reactionary "Bolshevism of the right," represented by Omsk, which acted as a magnet for the militarism and ultra-nationalism of ex-imperial officers and likeminded civil servants of the old regime, and the harsh "Bolshevism of the left" in Lenin's *Sovnarkom*. Because of the expansive nature of their economic activities, the perspective of the cooperatives tended to be national (indeed even international) rather than regional. Their leaders looked beyond Siberia. Fomin urged his organization "to declare that the [new White] government ought to be 1) national, directed toward the national resurrection and the national defence of the country; 2) all-state, representing the interests of the whole and not a part [of society]; 3) democratic, based upon the participation of the majority of the country in recognition of the one path to the salvation of the country, the path that leads to democracy through popular authority."[68]

DEMOCRATIC COUNTER-REVOLUTION

The net effect of the Czech uprising, in combination with anti-Bolshevik insurrections in the south and north of Russia, was the reduction of Soviet power to the territorial limits of medieval Muscovy, and even within those borders it was not secure because of the activity of such "counter-revolutionary" organizations as the multi-party Union of Regeneration (*Soiuz vozrozhdeniia*), the Kadets' National Centre, and the more conservative Right Centre.[69]

The Union of Regeneration was founded in the Russian capital in April 1918 as an underground coordinating agency for "democratic resistance" to the Bolshevik dictatorship. It grew out of a decision by the Kadet Central Committee to reach out beyond its own party organizations to unite (*ob"edinit'*) "all healthy social forces" in the task of national renaissance. The goal was to form "a wide inter-party social and political front, whose duty would be to prop up the anti-Bolshevik fighting force, to give a focal point for Allied aid, and to facilitate the formation of the Russian state system."[70] The Union was to provide coordination and leadership for all those who shared a common set of principles which included "state-consciousness, patriotism, and civil liberties." It had "personal" representatives from the Kadets as well as from the right wing of the PSR, and it included the entire membership of the Central Committee of the Popular Socialists. Somewhat later, a few Mensheviks and several cooperative leaders joined. On 8 May 1918 the Eighth Party Council of the PSR took an overtly anti-Soviet stand and tacitly acknowledged the leading role of the Union.

The main Union goals were 1) to liberate Russia from her foreign enemy, Germany, and her domestic one, Bolshevism; 2) create an effective army for that purpose; 3) organize an all-Russian authority that would unite all the parts of Russia and take the lead in the process of regeneration; 4) set aside party and class differences in the name of national salvation; 5) base the regenerated Russian state on the principle of comprehensive civil liberties for all citizens; 6) establish organs of local elected self-government with real authority and responsibility; 7) restore order and productivity in the domestic economy; and 8) lead the country to the All-Russian Constituent Assembly to be convened on the basis of universal, direct, equal, and secret franchise, but only after the liberation from the "Germano-Bolshevik yoke."[71] A Siberian branch of the Union was formed in Omsk in July.[72]

The National Centre, on the other hand, reflected the views of the Kadet party in favouring strong political leadership to restore a centralized and indivisible Russian state, capable of continuing the struggle against Germany. It was founded in Moscow in June 1918 and some of its members were also active in the Union, but it viewed the alternative of a three- or five-man directory as much less desirable than a one-man military dictatorship; it was also strongly opposed to compromising with the PSR or the regionalists on any decentralizing initiatives. The program of the National Centre included the following main points: war against Germany and Bolshevism; restoration of a unified and undivided Russia; loyalty towards the allies; support for the Volunteer Army in the south as the basis for a forceful restoration

of Russia; formation of an all-Russian government in close concert
with the Volunteer Army; and a constitutional order to be determined
by a freely elected popular assembly at some future date. The Centre's
agents in Siberia, notably V.N. Pepeliaev, N.A. Borodin, and A.K.
Klafton, all on the right wing of the party, were particularly outspoken
in their preference for a military dictatorship in the short term under
someone like General Khorvat:

The National Centre believes that under the present condition of extreme
disorganization, only a military dictatorship of a single person, firm in his
decision, can bring the country to that state of organization and pacification
under which it would be possible to transfer the authority to a permanent
government, legally established and recognized by all the nation ... The
building of the Russian state on the principles of federation is inconsistent
with and dangerous to the unity of Russia ... The right of private ownership,
which is a fundamental principle of the life of contemporary civilized nations,
must be restored.[73]

Despite these differences among the parties of the centre and the
moderate left – the Kadets, the Popular Socialists, the PSR, and the
Mensheviks – the political logic of multilateral cooperation against the
Soviet regime was compelling, especially in light of their individually
uncertain popular support and prospects. "In the very beginning of
1918," noted one of the key participants, "among the Kadets active in
the Right Centre there arose the idea of attempting union in a multi-
party organization with some representatives of the [moderate] socialist parties. The same idea occurred among the Popular Socialists."[74]

The Kadets were prominently targeted for Soviet repression. A
Sovnarkom proclamation on 11 December 1917 declared their party
to be the "headquarters of all counter-revolutionary forces in the
country ... and the [main] enemy of the people." [75] Following this
decree, a number of leading Kadets were arrested: Countess C.V.
Panina, A.I. Shingarev, F.F. Kokoshkin, Prince P.D. Dolgorukov, N.N.
Kutler, M.M. Vinaver, and F.I. Rodichev. A few days later orders went
out for the arrest as well of several SRs and Mensheviks: I.G. Tsereteli,
V.M. Chernov, F.I. Dan-Gurevich, M.M. Bramson, M.I. Skobelev, A.R.
Gotz, V.N. Rozanov, M. Binasik, G. Vengerov, V.V. Ivanovskii, P. Gam-
burov, and V. Herman-Kamenskii.

The opposition parties responded to these arrests with varying
degrees of alarm and resistance. The *Upolnomochennye* (empowering)
Movement was organized in Petrograd at the Menshevik Club on 13
March 1918 to appeal to the non-party working class in an attempt
to mobilize the majority of the industrial proletariat against the

Bolsheviks' growing authoritarianism.[76] The Kadets, at their May 1918 party conference in Moscow, endorsed the policy of all-party unity against Bolshevism, but again insisted on a single unlimited ruler and a reconstituted Constituent Assembly.[77] Neither the Mensheviks nor the PSR was prepared to go so far, but the latter did call for the transfer of Soviet functions to municipal, zemstvo, and parliamentary organizations, and it also sanctioned limited foreign intervention.[78] Siberian SRs were heartened by evidence that public opinion continued to move in their direction and they believed that the trend would only accelerate as people learned of the undemocratic nature of Bolshevism. Thus, they encouraged publicity (*glasnost'*) for any instances of soviet repression of local government, such as when the Tomsk zemstvo was abolished by order of the Second Provincial Congress of the Soviets of Peasant Deputies in March 1918.[79] But, as elsewhere in provincial Russia, popular reaction tended towards indifference rather than indignation.[80]

The Bolsheviks attempted to turn this apathy to their own advantage. From March to July 1918 the soviets, recognizing their extreme vulnerability both at home and abroad, were careful not to pursue an aggressive social and political agenda. In particular, *Sovnarkom* did not engage in a radical nationalization of industry. Even the banks were left alone until they refused to cooperate with the new government on the transfer of operating funds. Nevertheless, even the moderate socialists would not be appeased as long as the Bolsheviks refused to surrender their monopoly on political power. In Samara, the Committee of Members of the Constituent Assembly (*Komuch*), with the strongest lawful claim to power as the political successor of the disbanded All-Russian Constituent Assembly, set the tone for the centre-left democrats by cancelling all Soviet decrees, denationalizing banks and many other public sector enterprises, and, most signficantly, restoring free trade. This latter measure was immensely popular among the rich and middle peasants who had surplus grain for the market. "The people want free trade all over the country, without fixed prices on food items in light of the fact that in the present circumstances it is difficult to get consumer and other goods at low prices."[81]

Komuch's order no. 1, issued on 8 June 1918, stressed the removal of Bolshevik political restrictions: "In the name of the Constituent Assembly we hereby declare the Bolshevik Government ... has been removed. All commissars are dismissed from their posts. All organs of local self-government abolished by the soviet government are reinstated to full powers ... All restrictions on freedom and repressive measures introduced by the Bolsheviks are declared void. Freedom of speech, of the press, and of assembly is reinstated."[82] At the same time,

Komuch was careful not to reverse the main popular gains of the February Revolution, such as the eight-hour workday (introduced in the spring of 1917), or the Constituent Assembly's land law of 5 January 1918. A *Komuch* declaration of 24 July gave assurance that "the land has irrevocably become the property of the people and the Committee will not sanction any attempt to return it to the land-lords."[83] Samara's politics were closest to those of the West-Siberian Commissariat in Tomsk, except for the more regional orientation of the latter, as was evident in its white and green (rather than Samara's red) flag symbolizing Siberia's snows and forests. Both believed in local self-government, in particular that zemstvos were more democratic and better suited than soviets to meet the needs of the people of their region. But, as noted by a White official, many zemstvos in Siberia lacked sufficient funds to carry out their duties, and those that did have the means put a heavy burden on the local peasant population to feed and house their functionaries.[84] In the words of a local informant, "The population was especially hostile to zemstvos in those rural districts and villages where there were no schools, or where there were schools but no teachers. 'Why do we need zemstvos,' said the peasants of these settlements, 'when they take our taxes and levies but leave our children the same ignorant [people] that we are.'"[85]

The problem for both the West-Siberian Commissariat and *Komuch* throughout their existence, however, was not merely administrative, it was also their lack of credibility. Despite their claims that they "alone can save the country through the route of unifying all the forces of revolutionary democracy,"[86] they never had sufficient military power at their disposal to enforce their authority among their own constituents, much less against Soviet belligerents. A good indication of the true state of affairs was the offer on 10 June 1918 by representatives of the West-Siberian Commissariat to send food to the hungry cities of European Russia in return for guarantees that the forces of *Sovnarkom* would not attempt to reassert Soviet power east of the Urals.[87] The sorry fact was that the Commissariat – as only a temporary agent of a provisional local government – never had a military force of its own. At the same time, Samara's optimistically named People's Army was undermanned and undoubtedly weaker than any of the other armies in the region: the friendly Czechs who were nearby, the rather less benign White Siberian Army that was operating from Omsk, and the openly hostile Third and Fifth Red Armies that were approaching from the west.[88]

The military situation at the end of June, in turn, caused a general rightward turn in Siberian politics. The rump of the original PGAS, which remained behind in Omsk and, known as the Cabinet of Five, was made up of I.A. Mikhailov, G.B. Patushinskii, M.B. Shatilov, V.M. Krutovskii, and P.V. Vologodskii, ordered the moderate West-Siberian Commissariat to cease its activities. In a confidential memo dated 29 June to Vologodskii, Mikhailov described the transfer of power from the Commissariat to their inner circle as both a matter of course and of increasing urgency because it had become clear that the latter "had no authority among the Siberian population and none in the eyes of foreigners."[89]

In its Charter (*Gramota*) of 30 June 1918, the reconstituted PSG then called upon "all state-conscious elements [*gosudarstvenno-mysliashchie*], for whom is dear the resurrection of Russia and the freedom of Siberia, to unite around the Government in its state-building [effort] on the principles of popular rights as articulated by the Siberian Regional Duma."[90] Initially there appeared to be a genuine political consensus when even the president of the Duma, I.A. Iakushev, who was known to have misgivings about the rightward orientation of the Cabinet of Five, vigorously endorsed the re-emergence of the PSG and pledged his support for the new government based upon the principle of popular sovereignty (*narodopravstvo*). He also affirmed that "Siberia [was] as an inseparable [*nerazdel'naia*] part of the great all-Russian democratic republic."[91] Iakushev's enthusiasm for the PSG, however, was not unqualified; it was more of a reflection on the relative decline in the fortunes of the alternative, namely *Komuch*, which was proving itself unable to attract either extensive political support or recruits to its army even in its own backyard. This was evident in the Samara municipal elections of August and September 1918 when only about one-third of the eligible voters bothered to exercise the franchise and fewer than half of them cast their ballots for the combined PSR-Menshevik list.[92]

Not even the fact that *Komuch*'s People's Army offered its recruits more democratic working conditions – such as equal pay of fifteen rubles per month for all soldiers regardless of rank; a ban on saluting while both soldiers and officers were to be addressed as "citizen"; and the elimination of epaulettes from the uniforms – seemed to add much to its popular appeal.[93] If anything, these measures affected morale adversely; the one striking exception to the pattern was the largely working class Izhevsk and Votkinsk contingent which, under the inspired command of V.O. Kappel', more than held its own against the best Red units.[94]

Samara's PSR leadership quickly became the object of open derision in military and conservative circles throughout Siberia. As the acerbic Baron A.P. Budberg observed, "It is too bad ... there has emerged a SR-ism that is in a class by itself when it comes to undermining and

overthrowing governments, but is hopeless in terms of healthy construction; it means that once again there will be endless discussions
and various democratic posturings, [including] vague attempts to
create the socialist paradise on earth."[95]

Not surprisingly, the general populace continued to view all these
developments with unsympathetic suspicion. The chief lesson once
again was that outsiders (*chuzhye liudi*) making empty promises with
big words were seeking to gain advantage for themselves, given that
what they really wanted was to take provisions for their cities and
recruits for their armies. Moreover, adding to the confusion, not only
did Samara and Omsk each have their own military forces that
regarded the other with antagonism, but also the Reds, who opposed
both, were making similar claims for a democratic base. Whom was
the simple peasant to trust and what did it all mean anyway? Many
villagers believed that the apocalypse was near at hand: "Such times!
One is a People's Army and the other is also a People's Army, and
they fight each other! Oh, Lord, we can't begin to make it out. Is this
perchance the end of the world, as the Scripture says that in the last
days brother will rise against brother and son against father?"[96]

In this frenetic atmosphere, even the most reasoned and eloquent
appeals to the peasantry fell on deaf ears. Still, it did not prevent some
patriotic regionalists from trying. The difficulty of their task – in terms
both of the balance of the ideological message and of finding the right
language for communication – was formidable, as may be seen in the
address "To All Citizens," drafted by a group of Siberian officers:

We joined the ranks of the army not at all in order to restore the old,
universally hated times; we have no intention of taking away from the working
people their civil liberties, any more than of taking away from the peasantry
their right to the land or from workers the 8-hour workday ... The will of the
working people of Siberia, as expressed through the All-Russian and All-
Siberian Constituent Assemblies, will be sacred for us. Working people should
not be alarmed by our military association. Time and the facts will demonstrate the truth of our words. We are not part of any White Guards ... but
wear ribbons [that are] white and green ... [denoting] the national colours
of Siberia.[97]

Siberian peasants, nevertheless, remained skeptical about "pretty
words" from above and continued to resist the recruiters, passively
when possible, actively when necessary. As a result, Samara's People's
Army probably never had more than 35,000 troops and was constantly
troubled by desertions. This voting with the feet (to borrow from
Lenin) reflected a long-standing and widespread opposition in the

villages to any "Government [that] will take our sons, moreover the young ones, with the idea of training them and then sending them against us if we express unwillingness to go to war."[98] While these peasant attitudes existed throughout Russia and were applied to all the combatant armies, their negative impact was much greater on Samara than on Omsk. With its haphazard drafts and general lack of military professionalism, *Komuch*'s army was clearly no match for the army of the PSG, much less that of the Reds.

If relations between Samara and Omsk were never very good, they became worse as many of the best fighting men in the People's Army defected to the service of the PSG.[99] The main attraction seemed to be the traditional (and considerably less egalitarian) military regimen, as well as the more dependable pay. Even *Komuch*'s senior military staff was rumoured to be on the verge of transferring *en masse*; as one officer remarked in explaining the non-monetary appeals of Omsk, "The ultra-democratic principles of [Samara's] People's Army did not exist in the Siberian Army. [Omsk Minister of War] Grishin[-Almazov] ... declared that the army should be created 'on the basis of strict military discipline, without any committees, conferences, or meetings whatsoever and without limiting the prerogatives of commanders.'"[100]

Outside forces also played into the hands of the Omsk military and Siberian conservatives by underscoring the political weakness of the *Komuch*-PSR position in the international arena. It was no secret that the closely related politics of PGAS had been unable to do anything to prevent the Japanese from intervening in Vladivostok, and that only the American army prevented further occupation of Eastern Siberia. Indeed, the official communiqué from Tokyo stressed the Japanese intention "to fall in with the desires of the American government and also to act in harmony with the allies ... [in] maintain[ing] order along the Siberian railway."[101]

The tone and comportment of the Japanese soldiers on Russian soil did little to assuage or reassure Russian patriotic sensibilities. The Japanese commander, General Fuji, issued an extraordinary public warning that was more appropriate for conquerors than for allies:

It may be said that the Japanese army is the real savior of the Russian nation, but if anyone resists our army or puts any obstacle in the way of our sacred purpose, our army will adopt severe measures and persecute him *without making any discrimination as to his nationality*, and in this way will remove all the obstacles which might prevent the solutions of the problems of our army. As I desire to bring real happiness to the Russian people, I advise you to live peacefully and work for yourselves and your own social welfare and not become agitated by false ideas which will bring you complete destruction.[102]

Even in Western Siberia the Japanese move was welcomed to the extent that it was thought to signal the beginning of the long-awaited Allied push to oust the Bolshevik usurpers. Optimism soared in White circles with the landing of the American expeditionary force in August in Vladivostok and of smaller contingents of British, French, and other allies (there and in Murmansk and Arkhangel'sk). There was talk of the imminent fall of Moscow: Vologodskii declared that "the time may be near when we meet in the walls of the Holy Kremlin, on the square where the 'Tsar-Bell' and the 'Tsar-Cannon' stand, those historical symbols of Russia's might."[103]

The truth, however, was that the Allied interventions had several different and even contradictory purposes and that they were not generally effective. There were, of course, military and strategic considerations, with each intervening power hoping to gain some advantage for itself. Specifically, the British had major interests in Siberian industry and banking, and coveted the region's raw materials and markets; the French also had capital investments, especially in the railways; the Americans wanted an "open door" in the Far East and limits placed on Japanese expansion; and Tokyo hoped to get Allied approval for control, if not annexation, of at least part of the Russian Far East and Manchuria. Only the Americans (and not all of them) appeared to believe their own official pronouncements – that they were there to protect Allied munitions in Vladivostok and to facilitate the evacuation of the Czechs: "Whether from Vladivostok or from Murmansk and Archangel, the only legitimate object for which American or Allied troops can be employed ... is to guard military stores which may subsequently be needed by Russian forces and to render such aid as may be acceptable to the Russians in the organization of their own self-defense. For helping the Czecho-Slovaks there is immediate necessity and sufficient justification."[104]

Some resident American officials – such as Consul General E. Harris in Irkutsk – acting on their own initiative but with tacit support from the State Department, worked at cross-purposes with representatives of the Department of War and actually encouraged the Czechs to delay their departure until the political situation in Siberia and Russia was stabilized.[105] While the political message was always left vague and ambiguous, the Czechs naturally assumed that American diplomats like Harris reflected their government's true position. They could not know that a battle was going on behind closed doors in both Washington and London to determine whether the interventionists of the State Department, in alliance with their British counterparts (notably Winston Churchill), would be able to convince President Wilson and Prime Minister David Lloyd George to act more aggressively.[106]

In the meantime, the commander of the American Expeditionary Force in Siberia, General W.S. Graves, put a strict construction on his orders from the president to keep U.S. forces away from any direct involvement in Russian domestic affairs. From the beginning of his mission in Vladivostok Graves thereby found himself in conflict with U.S. consular officials who, he concluded, were guilty of leading "the Czechs [and the Whites] ... to believe the United States and the Allies were going to intervene in Siberia. As a result of this belief, the Czechs willingly remained in Western Siberia, always hoping and expecting that United States and Allied troops would soon come to their assistance."[107] The truth was that Wilson and Lloyd George were less likely to take such steps with each passing month. Official British pronouncements took on an increasingly defensive tone as Whitehall stressed that the intervention had as its sole purpose to guard the territorial integrity of Russia against Germany and "is not, as seems to be commonly supposed, an attempt on the part of His Majesty's Government to carry out a campaign against Bolshevism."[108] The French, after a brief initial flirtation with the Soviet government, became the most hostile of the three Western powers, but dared not diverge significantly from the Anglo-American policy on the limits of intervention.[109]

RIGHTWARD TURN IN OMSK

Within days of reasserting its authority at the end of June 1918 in Omsk the Provisional Siberian Government began moving away from positions taken by its two affiliates, the West-Siberian Commissariat in Tomsk and the Provisional Government of Autonomous Siberia in Vladivostok, not to mention those by the overtly socialist *Komuch* in Samara and the Siberian Regional Duma, also in Tomsk.[110] A leading SR participant and observer of these events noted in his memoirs that "members of the Siberian government in Omsk did not wish, under any circumstances, to unite with the other members of the Siberian government, who had been elected at the same time as they by the Oblast Duma but who [now] ... found themselves in the Far East."[111] For their part, Derber and his associates in the PGAS in Vladivostok continued to insist on their coequal status with the Omsk government, but this only had the effect of convincing Omsk that it was preferable to deal with the pro-Japanese Khorvat than with its own embarrassing PGAS affiliate.

Still overtly regionalist in orientation and with an eye to American history, the PSG chose July to announce the independence of Siberia. In retrospect, the declaration was meant more as a rejection of Soviet authority than as an affirmation of separate sovereignty or a repudiation of a great and united Russian state. Indeed, the PSG statement was carefully qualified by the caveat that the region was not going to be "permanently cut off from those territories that in their totality constituted the Russian state ... [and would] direct all its strength to the restoration of Russian statehood."[112] On social and economic matters the PSG immediately took positions that were meant to reassure the census society, even if that meant antagonizing the democrats and the peasants. Going much further than the West-Siberian Commissariat or Komuch, the new Omsk leadership summarily annulled all Soviet decrees and banned the soviets themselves, imposed strict guidelines for political meetings, abolished factory committees and severely restricted trade unions, and restored all industries and confiscated lands to their former owners.[113]

For Siberia proper the latter decree represented more of a symbolic gesture than substantive revision since very little land had changed hands in the first place. Nevertheless, the point was made that the new authorities in Omsk were in favour of the landlord and would safeguard the interests of the upper classes. The response to these edicts in Siberian villages, even according to Omsk's own agents, was not positive, with only a third of the population willing to express itself in support of the government and no more than 10 per cent prepared to join its army.[114] Vologodskii's belated attempt to explain Omsk's policy on legalistic grounds sounded both unconvincing and strongly reminiscent of Provisional Government pronouncements on the subject: "[Any] radical resolution of the land question, in the view of the Siberian Government, is the business of the Constituent Assembly. That is why the Government has not taken it upon itself to decide the root problem of the nationalization of the land and has limited itself to partial solutions ... in the context of the urgent demands of the existing situation."[115]

Meanwhile, however, prices were allowed to rise on all items of consumption, including staples like bread and meat, which respectively immediately tripled and doubled in cost.[116] On the other hand, the eight-hour workday was confirmed by the awkwardly entitled "Statute regarding measures for the restoration of the normal development of the work of industrial enterprises and the increase in the productivity of labour" of 31 July, though there were immediate instances of individual enterprises getting their workers to work for as many as ten hours. The statute also prohibited trade unions from getting involved in the hiring and firing of workers, abolished the committees of workers' control, and freed employers from having to make contributions to trade union funds and to hospitalization and social insurance.[117]

The real assault on the eight-hour day, however, came in the fall of 1918 with the introduction of piece (*sdel'naia*) wages, which were a major precipitating factor for railway strikes in October. The PSG responded harshly to the labour unrest. "[A]t this moment every railway strike is a treason to our country ... [We will] take resolute steps in order to stop the strike, including military execution of agitators on the spot, and of persons who hinder the re-establishment of work."[118] Following the crushing of the malefactors, the normal workday rose to over ten hours. The response to the strike was part of a larger government policy for treating labour demands: they were to be put down by force, if necessary through the agency of punitive Cossack expeditions. Ostensibly the tactics were directed against the Bolsheviks, but in practice no distinctions were made among militant workers organized in trade unions, as was evident in Tomsk during August and in Omsk the following month.[119]

The social policies of the government in Omsk exacerbated its already strained relations with the Siberian Regional Duma. Mutual antipathy deepened throughout July and soon overshadowed even their common hostility to Bolshevism. For several weeks the PSG purposefully delayed reconvening the Duma in order to avoid what everyone anticipated would be a major confrontation over programs and political power.[120] Within Omsk itself the growing military presence accelerated the turn rightward of the political balance. This could be seen in the increasingly influential role of the conservative Omsk Bloc, made up of big merchants and industrialists, civil servants, senior officers, and community leaders. Sensing that power was shifting in its favour, the Omsk Bloc did not bother to hide either its distrust and contempt for parliamentary democracy or its preference for undivided political authority in the person of a military dictator. Some elements within the Bloc would not even acknowledge the legitimacy of the PSG. The Siberian Kadet leader, V.A. Zhardetskii, refused to participate in the Omsk government because it was too narrowly regionalist and did not adequately address larger national issues.

Regionalism was unceremoniously abandoned when the statist views of the Kadets took precedence at the Commercial-Industrial Congress held in Omsk in July 1918. Zhardetskii set the tone when he stated aggressively that "it is essential to bring in strong unipersonal authority" in order to restore Russia's position as a whole, not merely Siberia's.[121] The notion of military dictatorship increasingly appealed even to those whose political loyalties lay somewhere closer to the centre of the political spectrum. In Omsk itself newspaper editorials came out strongly in support of the idea, with additional comments to the effect that General L.G. Kornilov had been on the right track in August–September 1917 when he tried to restore order and prevent further drift to the left.[122] In any case, by early July the PSG removed all doubts about its priorities when it announced that "everything [should be] for the army, [and] politics should be kept out of it."[123]

In point of fact, Omsk was anything but free of politics. Gossip and intrigue were the order of the day and involved virtually everyone, from the lowest *dvornik* (yard-keeper) to the highest government minister. It was no secret that among those championing the military ideal most vigorously were profiteers. The Wild East atmosphere encouraged political opportunism and naked self-promotion. It also made possible the meteoric rise of political fortunes. No better example of this can be found than I.A. Mikhailov (born in 1895 in Irkutsk prison to populist revolutionary Adriana Mikhailova), whose career is worth following in some detail because of its intimate connections with the fate of the White movement in Siberia. He was a young man of unlimited ambition and extraordinary capacity for political in-fighting who, at the tender age of twenty-three, talked himself into the key job of minister of finance in the PSG. His dramatic rise to power was all the more remarkable because it occurred despite an absence of formal education and his only experience was limited to being personal secretary to A.I. Shingarev, a Kadet minister in the Provisional Government. Nevertheless, Mikhailov may have been the most powerful individual behind the scenes in Omsk and throughout White Siberia during the critical periods of the Civil War.[124] Hegel once observed that the impact of historical figures has much to do with timing and location. Mikhailov's quick and easy ascendancy can partly be explained by the relative weakness of the other members of the PSG and by the contrasts in their characters. Among the more senior leaders, P.V. Vologodskii suffered from a hypochondria that frequently prevented him from doing anything more taxing than pursuing his passion for playing cards, while I.I. Serebrennikov had neither the motivation nor the refined capacity of Mikhailov for political intrigue.[125]

In the cacophony of clashing ambitions, corruption, speculation, and back-room politics in Omsk in 1918, it was no easy task for the assorted opponents of Bolshevism to organize themselves into an effective fighting unit. Indeed, a contemporary French observer remained sceptical that battling the Bolsheviks ever was anyone's top priority and remarked that "For the most part, they only thought about how to line their pockets."[126] Whatever the complex of motivations, the political climate in Omsk increasingly coincided with the position of the Kadet party, which heretofore had not been strongly represented in Siberia.

Moreover, the imperatives of civil war and of fighting the Bolsheviks were overwhelming all earlier loyalties and considerations, including liberalism, democracy, and regionalism. The process blurred many of the distinctions between traditional positions on the left and the right of the political spectrum for the sake of two main principles, the overthrow of Soviet rule and the restoration of the unified Russian state.

By mid-summer 1918 a clear trend had become evident: the centralist statism of the Kadets was pushing aside the earlier autonomism that had peaked with the 4 July declaration of Siberian independence by the PSG. Later that month, events overtook regional ideals when all attention focused on stopping the eastward advance of the Red Army. To that end, groups ranging from conservatives to Mensheviks agreed on the necessity of "the establishment, first of all, of a temporary all-Russian [anti-Bolshevik] central authority."[127]

An additional factor in the changing ideology of the PSG was internal to its nature. While outwardly Socialist Revolutionary and regionalist, its most important figures – Mikhailov, Guins, and Vologodskii – were essentially pragmatic careerists. What attracted them increasingly to the Kadet approach was its hard-headed *Realpolitik* that gave priority to the military victory over the Bolsheviks. N.V. Ustrialov, later an important adviser to Admiral Kolchak, confirmed that "although the Omsk ministers were not part of the ... Kadet [Party], in essence they were Kadets, as were the ideology and program of the government ... [Thus] our Civil War [was throughout] 'a war between the Bolsheviks and the Kadets.'"[128]

The phenomenon of the growing influence of the Kadets and of their centralist and statist Great Russian ideology upon high politics in Omsk requires additional comment because of its broader implications for the intellectual history of this period. The Kadets were the party of the 1905 Revolution and, to a lesser degree, of the Constitutional Experiment that followed. From 1905 to 1914 and increasingly thereafter, however, they and their constituents grew disenchanted with each other. The Kadets' dilemma deepened when their initial political advantage in February 1917 dissipated in favour of the Petrograd soviet, which was at that time dominated by the PSR and by Mensheviks. The clear choice facing the traditional party of liberalism was either political marginalization or making common cause (preferably as the senior partner) with the moderate socialists. Even the second option did not guarantee success because by fall 1917 Bolshevik majorities emerged in the soviets of both Petrograd and Moscow, as well as in several strategically-located military garrisons. The final blow to the Kadet scheme of things came with the elections to the Constituent Assembly in the fall of 1917 which produced a feeble 8 per cent vote

for the party.[129] The theories of liberal democracy and political pluralism did not provide any satisfactory rationalizations for this massive
repudiation in the freest election in Russian history. Finding someone
to blame, in good Russian fashion, was no way out of the dilemma
either. What was needed was some creative new thinking and a refash-
ioning of the Kadet program.

Of the two issues for which the party was most severely criticized
during its tenure in the Provisional Government – continuation of the
war and inaction on the land question – the former appeared easier
to modify. Paul Miliukov and some other senior Kadets had already
suggested a fundamental reorientation of Russian foreign policy.[130] In
Siberia (by contrast to Ukraine and the south), however, there was
little support for their idea of a separate peace, much less a general
tilt in favour of Germany. The question of land redistribution
remained too controversial and divisive to broach during civil war.[131]
Nothing was left but to move away from the party's traditional parliamentary focus toward a more controlled and indirect political model.
In the Kadet world-view, after all, liberalism had always been less
important than Russian *gosudarstvennost*; prior to 1917, however, there
had been few occasions for the two principles to oppose each other.[132]

The other side of the Kadets' belief in the centrality of the state was
a deep suspicion – which they shared with the Bolsheviks and, it is
worth noting, the old imperial regime – of rebellious peasant spontaneity, especially in the form of the violent mass anarchism of *pugachevshchina* (mass peasant rebellion of the sort that was led by E. Pugachev
against Empress Catherine ii). The danger of this became especially
acute during 1917–18 and served to deepen the existential malaise of
the Kadet leadership to the point that it effectively abandoned the
party's long-standing commitment to liberal democracy. At the very
least, there had to be some redefinition of the party's traditional terms
of reference in order to account for the fact that the vast majority of
the people chose freely not to vote for the Kadets. An internally
consistent, if not entirely convincing, explanation was that the peasants remained an unconscious and dangerously nihilistic mass, whose
blatant disregard for property rights and laws in general demonstrated
that they were too ignorant, depraved, and irresponsible to understand even their own best interests, much less the greater issues con-
fronting the Russian state.

Within weeks of the October Revolution the Kadet leadership developed a new formula that treated the large peasant vote for the PSR –
the majority party in the Constituent Assembly, with overwhelming
support in virtually every election in Siberia in 1917 and 1918 – as
an indirect mandate for themselves. The argument was based on an

ingenious theory that the SRs were the Kadets' immediate constituency as well as their intermediary (or leftward bridge) to the people: "The liberals had no troops of their own ... and, most important, no mass following. If they wanted an army, they had to turn to others."[133] The new formula allowed the Kadets to discount the disappointing percentages of their recent electoral record and to reiterate their claim to be the true, if once removed, representatives of both the statist and the national principles. They could find corroboration of this view in the report of P.D. Iakovlev, a regional administrator for the Omsk government. It demonstrated that the Irkutsk duma, while formally overwhelmingly PSR, was dominated politically by the Kadets, and that even the Social Democrats (presumably Mensheviks) could be expected to follow the Kadet lead.[134]

However ingenious the new theory of the Kadets, it could not have worked in a political vacuum. Specifically, it needed a large, divided, and accessible PSR on the immediate left of the Kadets. Fortunately for this strategy, the PSR was less a party in the traditional sense than a collection of loosely affiliated dissenters who were loath to accept any party discipline whatsoever. In the words of a close observer of the political scene in Siberia, "the SR party began to resemble an army staffed exclusively by officers."[135] Many SRs, especially on the fringes, were very susceptible to co-option from both left and right, that is, from both the Bolsheviks and the Kadets. As Radkey and others have shown this was facilitated by such serious internal divisions that by 1917 it was impossible for the PSR to agree on a party platform or program.[136]

Even apart from the extreme left of the PSR, which split off after the October Revolution to form the Left Socialist Revolutionary Party that allied briefly with the Bolsheviks, there still remained two other subgroups: the left-centre, under Chernov, and the pro-Kadet right, led by A.R. Gotz, N.D. Avksent'ev, and V.M. Zenzinov. The latter "was small in numbers but large in influence, and clung to [its liberal] partners in coalition as a protection against all ... evils."[137] In fairness, the Bolsheviks also had a hand in forging the Kadet–Right SR entente. Lenin's abrupt dissolution of the Constituent Assembly on 7 January 1918 was the final straw for the majority of the PSR who had been hoping for a compromise that would resurrect the old dream of a democratic, all-socialist government. After that day, therefore, the Avksent'evs and Zenzinovs, if not the party's Central Committee, felt fully justified in cooperating with other "democrats" against the Bolsheviks. Indeed, for these Right SRs the main lesson of the preceding three months was that the Chernovite leadership had been profoundly mistaken in its *soglashenie* (accommodation) policy of "no enemies to the left."

For many Right SRs an alliance with the Kadets provided the best antidote to the self-destructive romantic populism that had clouded the judgement and interfered with the effectiveness of the later cabinets of the Provisional Government. Moreover, after their humiliation in October 1917 and January 1918 at the hands of the Bolsheviks, followed by the banning of their party and its expulsion from the Soviet executive, they were prepared to ally with the devil if that would bring about the overthrow of the Leninist dictatorship and the recall of the Constituent Assembly. On 8 May 1918, at the PSR's Eighth Party Council, the following resolution was passed: "The fundamental task of the party is the struggle for the restoration of the independence of Russia [by nullifying the Treaty of Brest-Litovsk] and for ... her national-state unity ... The main obstacle in the way of realizing these tasks is Bolshevik power. Therefore liquidation of [that power] is the immediate and urgent task of all democracy."[138]

Implicit in this statement was a recognition that the Kadets and their philosophy represented the only viable alternative to Bolshevism in Russia and Siberia.[139] For Siberia that meant turning away from the more democratic tendency represented by the Siberian Regional Duma in Tomsk. Its juridical claim to sovereignty, as the most representative freely elected body in the region, was thus summarily set aside in favour of the undisguised militarism of Omsk. On 18 July, the Omsk Trade–Industry Conference called for abolishing the Duma altogether for the sake of strong, unified government under the PSG. When the Duma was permitted to meet again on 15 August, out of ninety-two delegates in attendance, exactly half still identified themselves as members of the PSR while no other party could claim more than seven representatives. Hardly anyone bothered to notice that there were precious few workers or peasants in that number.[140] The Duma's sitting was interrupted after just five days and closed down by order of the Omsk Council of Ministers. The pretext given for the decision was the "divisiveness" of the Duma, but the real reason, as everyone understood, was that the PSG no longer recognized its constitutional subordination to the Duma and wished to be rid of it once and for all.

[T]he socialist groups stood for the strengthening of the Siberian Regional Duma ... and for the quick summoning of the Constituent Assembly ... [But the members of the PSG] were enthusiastic about ... the notion of a military dictatorship. For them the dispersed Constituent Assembly ceased to exist ... Their chief concern was organizing a military force capable of continuing the war with Soviet power and the Communists. From this point of view the role of the Siberian Regional Duma had to be reduced to the minimum ... [in favour] of the Provisional Siberian Government.[141]

The power brokers in Omsk had become totally disenchanted with the Duma as well as the social democracy it represented; V.V. Kulikov of the Omsk branch of the Union of Regeneration noted that "at the present time it is impossible to establish parliamentarism, [while] essential to introduce state dictatorship and to dismiss the Duma."[142] That, of course, had for some time been the view of the Kadets.

4 Democratic Counter-Revolution and White Union

Spring to Fall 1918

In spite of agreement in Siberia on the evils of Bolshevism (fuelled by more than a tinge of anti-Semitism) and vigorous common opposition to the Treaty of Brest-Litovsk, the early months of 1918 witnessed little unity or coordination among the assortment of political parties and groups that came to be known as the Whites.

There was certainly no consensus on either domestic political or social policy. On the left of the White spectrum, *Komuch*, the West-Siberian Commissariat, and the Siberian Regional Duma all stood for a mildly socialist agenda: civil liberties, local government (zemstvos and municipal dumas), minority rights, collective bargaining, and social welfare.[1] By mid-year, however, a rightward shift was evident with the re-emergence of the Provisional Siberian Government (PSG) in Omsk and of its regional allies in Ekaterinburg and elsewhere; their emphasis was on a free-market economy, the restoration of property rights to former landowners, and the denationalization of industries and enterprises taken over by the Bolsheviks.[2]

Not everyone accepted or appreciated the differences that existed among the Whites. The Bolsheviks, in particular, gained political advantage from arguing that both groups were counter-revolutionary and, if anything, those who called themselves socialists were more dangerous than those who openly called for restoration of the old order. Regionalists, Kadets, Socialist Revolutionaries (SRs), and Mensheviks – in whatever combination or location – all accepted the precepts of Western parliamentary democracy, while the Bolsheviks regarded these principles as bourgeois deceptions meant to confound the working classes and contribute to their false consciousness.[3]

To be sure, the Siberian peasantry were not concerned so much with Bolshevik rhetoric or analysis as with specific Soviet policies that affected them directly. Measures limiting their freedom of movement and trade, attempts to requisition their grain at less than market value, and efforts to interfere with their local self-government were all extremely unpopular. Despite being far enough away from the centre of Soviet power to escape the harshest aspects of the government's new agrarian programs, many Siberian peasants concluded that Bolshevism did not represent their interests and that other parties, with stronger local connections, at least might be more responsive. The residents of Bashorskii settlement in Akmolinsk district on 8 August 1918 approved a resolution that stated in part: "[We] decided that Bolshevik authority did not justify the hopes and desires of the majority of the population of the Russian state … Before convocating the All-Siberian Constituent Assembly, the legislative and executive authority should be placed in the hands of the democratic Siberian Regional Duma."[4] While this should not be taken to mean that Siberian peasants had suddenly become great champions of parliamentarism or regionalism, it suggested that they were at least unhappy with Bolshevik policy pronouncements, and that they preferred what was closer and more familiar to them. East of the Urals the new Soviet government's land policy was largely irrelevant, but its initiatives directed at grain requisitioning were bound to be resisted vigorously.

From the perspective of *Sovnarkom*, however, there really was little choice: whatever the political differences between it and its predecessors, the Russian central government had to secure a guaranteed supply of food for the cities and the army at the lowest possible cost. The feelings of the peasantry could not be permitted to interfere with this priority. Indeed, many elements of the Bolsheviks' plan for a full state grain monopoly were remarkably similar to the wartime programs of their immediate predecessors in the tsarist and provisional governments.[5]

Bolshevik agrarian policies undoubtedly presented the Whites with an opportunity to gain political capital among the peasants, but for a variety of reasons they failed to do so. In large measure this was because the Whites could not agree among themselves on a common land program or, for that matter, a general political platform. Their evident vagueness, however, was necessary protective covering, designed to paper over ideological differences until after the main threat of Bolshevism had been defeated. The White coalition included diverse and often contradictory positions that could not easily have been reconciled under the best of circumstances, much less under the conditions of civil war. Thus, while the *Komuch* in Samara accepted the 1917 agrarian revolution in full – that is, the nationalization of land by the sole session of the Constituent Assembly on 5 January 1918 – the same could not be said for the psg in Omsk or for many of the Cossacks and other regional authorities in Western Siberia.

These variations reflected differences between moderate socialists and Kadets, with the latter becoming daily more conservative as their ranks were supplemented by a wide range of people from the political right who had no place else to go. The land question also divided the Party of the Socialist Revolutionaries (psr) internally. Even after the split that resulted in a separate Left sr party, the remaining left-centre was in many ways closer to the Soviet position than to its own right wing. As a result, while both Samara and Omsk had governments run by men who at one time or another called themselves srs, the differences between them were substantial, extending beyond considerations of turf, personality, and political ambition. The Samara government tried to appeal both to the poor peasant beneficiaries of the land transfers and to the more affluent middle and upper peasants who wanted assurances that there would be no more such activity. Thus, *Komuch* order no. 124, issued on 22 July, sanctioned the status quo in property use, while allowing former owners to gather the crops they had planted before the land was alienated. This measure satisfied neither side, and only added to the general confusion about the true intention of the government.

In its effort to steer a middle course to reassure the business interests and political conservatives (who might otherwise transfer their allegiance and their resources to Omsk), while not abandoning the welfare programs with which the psr was identified traditionally, *Komuch* issued a series of decrees that were not entirely consistent. Thus, banks were denationalized on 12 June, but lockouts were declared illegal by order no. 88 on 7 July and collective bargaining was reaffirmed, as were several progressive labour laws. Even so, a distinct drift to the right could be detected.[6] By 14 August 1918 V.K. Volskii, who represented the extreme left wing of the psr and served as president of *Komuch*, felt obliged to make a public statement affirming the stability of the existing capitalist order. In an obvious appeal to the apprehensive middle classes, he promised that the Samara government would not threaten their economic and social interests. "There should not even be any talk about different sorts of socialist experiments. The capitalist system cannot be liquidated at the present time."[7]

Ironically, while White governments in Siberia and the Urals were busy appeasing forces on their right, in Moscow the Bolshevik Central Committee was being challenged from the opposite direction by Left Communists, Workers' Oppositionists, and Democratic Centralists.[8] It particularly alarmed the Central Committee that this new thrust coincided with the return of the armed and dangerous ultra-democratic *frontoviki*, who espoused their own distinct brand of Leninist Bolshevism as "a spontaneous and unconscious protest against all forms of inequality, and not merely against economic inequality."[9] From Moscow's point of view, the *frontoviki* had been welcome revolutionary allies in the countryside during the build-up to October, but shortly thereafter they became a serious negative factor representing alternatives to Bolshevik leadership in many parts of Russia and Siberia. Even Soviet agents in Siberia conceded that this was especially the case because "the Siberian peasantry's economic position [made them] indifferent to the socialist revolution." Indeed their overtly anti-Bolshevik nature brought several peasant assemblies into violent conflict with local Soviet authorities during the spring of 1918 in Siberia.[10]

Even in the absence or relative insignificance of coercive grain-requisitioning by Committees of the Peasant Poor (*Kombedy*) – often staffed or led by urban workers from European Russia – Bolshevism's hostility to the type of independent petty farming that characterized much of Siberia was no secret.[11] The instructions received by a *Kombed* in European Russia read in part: "Announce to your citizens that [they have] three days to supply 10,000 *poods* of bread ... The authorized agent[s] ... [are] empowered, at non-compliance, to shoot."[12] And shoot they did. It was no easy task to seize Siberian grain during the early months of 1918, even before there was an organized opposition to Soviet rule. Moscow's procurement campaign during the winter of 1917–18 was supposed to be preceded by the delivery from European Russia of a substantial amount of manufactured goods as a quid pro quo, but because of technical difficulties and unforeseen demands on limited supplies this never occurred.

These circumstances help explain why Siberian peasants delivered far less than the planned 43 million *poods* of grain they were supposed to provide by 1 May; in fact, only about 3 million *poods* were transferred from the beginning of February to the middle of April.[13] L.M. Spirin concludes that this was a traditional form of peasant passive resistance, and that the bread issue was critical in determining rural political loyalties: "The vast majority of the Siberian peasantry did not support soviet power. The kulaks, the wealthy peasants, and a significant portion of the middle peasants followed the SRs who promised [them] free trade in bread; the rest of the middle peasants adopted a neutral position. There spoke the 100 million poods of surplus bread located in Siberia [in the spring of 1918]."[14] Better-off peasants in Siberia – those who, with some property and livestock, managed to live above the poverty line – constituted about 60 per cent of the population, and had obvious reasons for resisting the levelling social policies of the Bolsheviks.[15] More often than not they were also joined by significant numbers of poorer villagers in a show of rural solidarity against the food-grabbing urbanites, including representatives of the working class. The picture bore a striking resemblance to 1916–17, the last winter of the old regime:

There were fights between hoarders and government agencies, attacks on estates to force them to cultivate land or give up their grain, attacks by food-collecting gangs on villages, fights between army and civilian grain purchasers, fights between grain purchasers from different gubernias and uezds, etc. None of this constituted a struggle of poor vs. rich, nor did it constitute a peasant 'movement.' The capital cities were attacking farmers of all sorts, and farmers were trying to hide their harvests.[16]

Apart from some important instances in the central agricultural zone of European Russia, there was not much evidence (and least of all in Siberia) of villages dividing into the three major Leninist categories of poor, middle, and rich peasants, with the first two falling in behind the militant proletariat.[17] In truth, the poor and middle peasantry were not generally revolutionary; if anything, their natural instinct was to follow the lead of the kulaks. As in the pre-revolutionary past, the dominant sentiment in the village was fear of the outsider, even from neighbouring districts. All strangers (*neznakomye*), whether new settler, urban worker, Red commissar, White general, Cossack, or Kirghiz, were regarded with the deepest misgivings, but no one more so than those *intelligenty* and political workers from the big cities of European Russia, who took from the peasants the hard-earned product of their toil.[18] In the face of these requisitions there was almost total social solidarity in the villages.[19]

Spontaneous reactions against Bolshevik policies increasingly assumed violent form in "mass manifestations of dissatisfaction." The new Soviet laws curtailing free trade in grain were deeply resented; they were seen as unfairly depriving the peasants of their livelihood. A common response was to hide all surpluses and to refuse to take any grain to market. New taxes on horses and cattle that were ostensibly aimed at the rich were also seen to affect a high proportion of all Siberians.[20] Resentment ran especially deep in those village households that had managed through hard labour to better themselves.

The opinion was widespread that Soviet agrarian policy was meant to divide the peasants while appealing to the worst criminal elements in their midst. The more cynical came to an obvious conclusion: "Why should we sow? Better to remain without grain, and to be classed as the poor, when we can take it away from others without doing any work."[21]

Siberia was spared the worst of *Sovnarkom*'s ministrations because Moscow was too busy fending off threats closer at hand to be able to pay much attention to Asiatic Russia. Nevertheless, the situation was steadily deteriorating there as elsewhere. A Soviet official in Irkutsk warned Lenin himself of the political consequences at the end of April 1918, after several earlier pleas for relief for the growing number of urban homeless and poor had gone unheeded: "The most opportune time for neutralizing [*rassosat'*] the largest part of the unemployed, who otherwise are capable of devouring Siberia and Russia, is slipping by." In the same report he characterized the government's high-handed treatment of Siberia as similar to a fiefdom (*votchina*) administered under the medieval practice of feeding (*kormlenie*), whereby a region was stripped of its resources while nothing was given in return. Because of this short-sighted policy, the author concluded, "Siberia is no longer capable of providing Russia with that which would have been possible under the right set-up."[22]

With expenditures far outpacing revenues, however, *Sovnarkom* was simply unable to respond to the impassioned appeals from all sides for urgent assistance. To take just one example, the Tobol'sk soviet in early June sent an urgent telegram to Moscow stating that it had received "not one cent from anywhere" over the past two months and that it would have to suspend its activities *as well as support for the Red Army* if 300,000 rubles were not forthcoming from Moscow immediately.[23] Such dire warnings had to be taken seriously, yet resources were so strained that it was a matter of making some very difficult and harsh choices in order to satisfy at least the key constituencies. Thus, strategically located railway workers, proletarian shock troops in the *kombedy*, and especially party cadres and Red Army men were given preferential rations in addition to other special benefits; in an economy of severe deprivation this inevitably meant that many others, ranging from "bourgeois class enemies" to just plain folks, got less than they needed to survive.[24] This policy of overtly preferential treatment for the urban workers and the military – largely at the expense of the peasantry – was dictated not only by circumstances but equally by the ideological predisposition of the Bolsheviks.[25] Needless to say, it exacerbated existing points of friction, notably over the terms of the Treaty of Brest-Litovsk and over restrictions on the activities of all other political parties, even including such allies as the Menshevik Internationalists and the Left SRs.

Despite the fact that the peace treaty with the Germans was unpopular both within the Central Committee of his own party and outside (some Bolsheviks and virtually all other socialists regarded it as nothing less than a betrayal of revolutionary ideals, as well as an enormous loss of territory, resources, and prestige), Lenin remained adamant on the issue. He was confident that he could ignore the views of the politicians because the popular mood was on his side; if ever there had been any enthusiasm for the war, it had dissipated long ago. In the words of a Siberian peasant, "We will not go to war; let them shoot us at home."[26] Nevertheless, at major Soviet meetings, such as the Second All-Siberian Congress held in February 1918 that was attended by 202 delegates, including 123 Bolsheviks and 53 Left SRs, resolutions against the treaty passed by overwhelming votes. No democratic parliamentary government could have survived such a crisis of confidence.

For the Left SRs, the only (and temporary) allies of the Bolsheviks, the combination of Brest-Litovsk with the onerous agrarian policy of *razverstka* (grain tax) was just too much. Emergency food requisitions in time of war were one thing, but a shameful peace that simultaneously institutionalized draconian confiscations under the wider campaign of "War Communism" convinced them that the Bolsheviks had conclusively turned against the Left SR constituency of middle peasants who produced the bulk of the grain in the countryside: "Until now the party of the Bolsheviks was the party of genuine revolutionary socialism. But now it has turned away from this path."[27] Their worst fears and suspicions were confirmed by the decree on grain of the Central Executive Committee of Soviets (*VTsIK*) that was printed in the government newspaper *Izvestiia* on 14 May 1918:

There must be an end of this stubbornness of the greedy village kulaks and rich [peasants]. Experience with the food problem in preceding years has shown that the breakdown of fixed prices for grain and the abolition of the grain monopoly, while it would make it possible for a handful of our capitalists to feast, would place grain absolutely out of reach for millions of the workers and would condemn them to an unavoidable death from hunger. To the violence of the owners of the grain against the starving poor the answer must be violence against the bourgeoisie.[28]

It should be noted that this *VTsIK* decree could only be applied to the Volga region, as the other main grain-producing areas (including Western Siberia, the northern Caucasus, the Don and Kuban' valleys, and Ukraine) were all under White control. But the message was clear:

Peasant non-compliance with *razverstka* would not be tolerated, and if the Left SRs refused to accept his policies Lenin was prepared to govern without them and even against them.

That had quickly become a certainty when in March Lenin forced through both his own Central Committee and the Soviet government the fatal decision to sign a separate peace with Germany. There could be no question in his mind about the negative consequences of the Treaty of Brest-Litovsk for the already fragile Soviet coalition government. Whether or not Lenin wanted civil war, there may have been no better alternative if he wished to stay in power. Under the circumstances, a rump state surrounded by external enemies and crisscrossed by internal ones was still preferable to German occupation and the restoration of the Romanovs. Nevertheless, Lenin may have been surprised by the ferocity of the public outcry, especially among the Left SRs. In the event, they promptly withdrew from the ruling coalition and began to wage "revolutionary war" on both the Germans and on the Bolsheviks.

Adding to the Soviet government's vulnerability, several of its former Left SR allies were well situated to do real damage from strategic posts within the Cheka and the military leadership. Lenin himself was gravely wounded in an attack on 30 August by Fania Kaplan and other prominent officials, notably M.S. Uritskii, fell to the bullets and bombs of Left SR assassins, as did the German ambassador in Moscow, Count Mirbach, a few weeks earlier, on 6 July. To make matters worse, this campaign (depicted in the Bolshevik press as a full-scale Left SR uprising in Moscow) grew in intensity as spring passed into summer, and coincided with Right SR insurrections in more than a dozen Russian provincial centres, notably in Iaroslavl under Boris Savinkov with French backing, and with Allied landings at Arkhangel'sk and Vladivostok.[29]

In addition to these already serious complications, there were critical mutinies within the Soviet front lines. The most damaging of the latter occurred in Simbirsk on 10 July 1918 when M.A. Murav'ev, the Left SR Red Army commander on the Siberian front, crossed over to the White side with 10,000 of his best men. This was just days after Savinkov's *démarche* north of Moscow and it also coincided with the fall of Ekaterinburg to the Czechs, the execution of Nicholas II and his family, and anti-Soviet workers' risings in the industrial towns of Izhevsk and Votkinsk along the Kama. Of these developments, the last proved to be the most consequential for the government in Moscow. Its inability to deal effectively and expeditiously with that rebellion continued to be a major impediment to the success of the Red Army on the eastern front throughout the Civil War. Moreover, the very

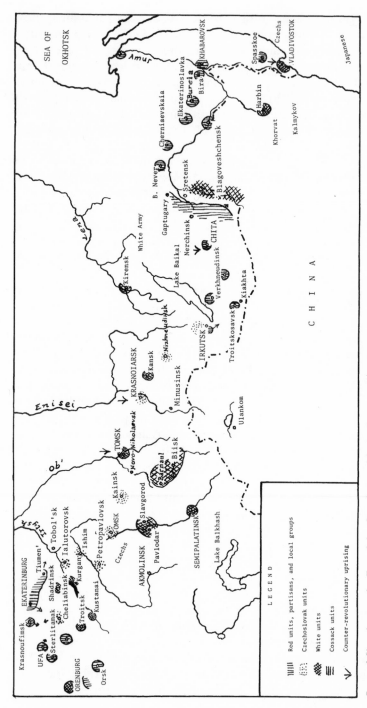

General Situation on the Eve of the Overthrow of Soviet Power in Siberia (7/1918) by Paul Duffy.
Source: Kakurin, *Kak srazhalas' revoliutsiia*, 1:208ff.

existence of a Izhevsk-Votkinsk army within the White ranks called into question basic Soviet premises about the loyalties and interests of working-class men: drawn largely from the proletariat of these two towns, the units, under General V.O. Kappel', were by far the best Russian fighting force in White Siberia.[30] In late July, thanks in large part to the successes of the "Kappelites," a decisive military breakthrough by the Whites seemed imminent. The entire eastern (Siberian) front was in shambles, with the Red Army deeply demoralized. Kappel's stunning victory in Simbirsk was followed in early August by his capture of Kazan and the great unexpected prize of the imperial gold reserve – over 750 million rubles worth of precious metals – that subsequently served as the main White war chest.[31]

At this critical moment, Trotsky intervened personally with the full backing of Lenin to restore discipline and to redeploy to Siberia the forces he needed from the southern and western fronts and from the centre. Lenin identified Siberia as the main and critical theatre of the Civil War, warning his followers that the socialist revolution was imperilled by the progress there of the White armies and their Czech allies. He called upon all good proletarians and Communists to throw themselves into the fray: "It is essential to move the maximum number of workers from Petrograd. Otherwise we shall fall, for the situation ... is as bad as could be."[32]

The problem for the Bolsheviks, however, was that they still had very limited local infrastructure or organizational support in Siberia.[33] Moscow's chief agency in the region, the *Tsentrosibir'*, was for the most part unable to enforce its directives; its many calls to the peasants and workers of Siberia to come to the defence of Soviet power, to organize partisan detachments, and to provision the latter with bread, feed, and horses were widely ignored.[34] The relative disposition of forces only began to shift with the appointments of I.I. Vatsetis in September and later of M.V. Frunze as commanders of the main Red armies in the region. These personnel changes and the massive reinforcements from working-class districts of European Russia on the Soviet side, as opposed to the lack of coordination and leadership among the innumerable White parties and governments, turned the military tide back in favour of the soviets in Siberia. This strategic improvement also owed a great deal to new diplomatic agreements with Germany that removed the immediate danger of German attack and freed the Red army to concentrate its forces on the eastern front.[35]

Despite the obvious military necessity to coordinate their efforts, it is doubtful whether the Whites would ever have come together to form a united movement without strong outside pressure from their foreign friends. Against the background of the Omsk leadership's open contempt for civil rights and Siberian Regional Duma parliamentarism, only the concerted pressure of the allies was capable of overcoming all the petty jealousies and territorial disputes that throughout the summer of 1918 stood in the way of any effective anti-Bolshevik coalition. But the Allied role itself was neither clearly nor consistently defined. In part this was because serious tensions existed between London and Paris as well as between their representatives in the region. The British General, Alfred Knox, had little use for his French counterpart, General P.T.C.M. Janin, who nominally was his superior as supreme commander of all troops – Allied, Russian or other – in east Russia and Siberia west of Lake Baikal.[36] In turn, Janin resented the Englishman's evident influence in the highest quarters in Omsk.[37] While the French and the British were equally anxious to see "their" Russians united, each wanted its own main man to have the lead role in the process, not so much out of concern for the local populations as to safeguard its own strategic and economic interests in the area. Thus, although they urged cooperation on the Whites, the two European powers shamelessly jockeyed with each other to gain advantage and influence: "The outlook and actions of the French government in regard to Siberia during the summer of 1918 highlight a burgeoning rivalry with Britain and the other intervening Allies in Russia. The Quai d'Orsay's efforts to create an Allied high commission were intended to preserve political and economic influence for France vis-a-vis its more powerful allies."[38]

Largely to please Paris and London, as well as with a sideward glance to Washington and Tokyo, the PSG and *Komuch*, the leaders of the two main antagonists in the anti-Bolshevik movement of eastern Russia, finally agreed to seek an accommodation between themselves. Even so, relations continued to be very strained between Omsk and Samara as demands, reproaches, and territorial jurisdictional claims (over such prizes as the semi-autonomous Ural Regional Government in Ekaterinburg) went back and forth. It would not be easy to find common ground: "The politics of Samara and Omsk sharply differed one from the other ... In a word, Samara wanted to keep the revolution at the limits of the SR programs, while Omsk strived to move back from the revolution, even to the extent of resuming certain old external forms."[39]

Neither side was prepared to compromise on the basic questions, and particularly not on the leadership of the White movement. Matters very nearly came to open warfare between the PSG and *Komuch* when they set up mutual tariff barriers against each other during the summer of 1918: "one region did not allow passage of bread to the other, while the latter refused to send any of its goods to the former."[40]

When negotiations began at two meetings during July and August in Cheliabinsk they only served to raise the level of mutual antipathy without bringing the sides any closer to an agreement. The common gossip was that the Omsk delegation came under instructions not to reach any agreement since, with the deteriorating military situation, further delay could only strengthen the bargaining position of the PSG relative to both the Samara *Komuch* and the Siberian Regional Duma. With its own army and administrative apparatus firmly in place, Omsk clearly had the least to gain and the most to lose from the creation of a superordinate central government, especially one with SRs in positions of leadership.[41]

Nevertheless, great pressure from representatives of the allies persuaded both the PSG and *Komuch* to make another attempt to come to an agreement at Ufa in September. This proved to be the most comprehensive of the conferences, with participants from not only all the parliamentary democratic parties (though not the Bolsheviks, Left SRs, Menshevik Internationalists, or anarchists), but also most of the national minorities and the Cossacks. The Kadets immediately took upon themselves the role of defining the agenda for the proceedings: "The first task ... [must be] the reestablishment of a great, united, and undivided Russia ... [We believe] that the best form of government is a one-man government. But if we have to settle for a directory, then it ought not to be responsible to anyone ... [We] advocate a government which stands outside any control."[42]

The Omsk contingent arrived late and its members conducted themselves throughout with the arrogance of people who knew that they had the strongest Russian military force in the region at their disposal and thus were much less dependent on the goodwill of the Czechs or the allies. They were led by the mild regionalist I.I. Serebrennikov who was, however, in constant touch by telegraph with the much tougher-minded Mikhailov and who did nothing without the latter's approval. Serebrennikov was further influenced in a conservative direction by the presence of such fellow delegates as P.P. Ivanov-Rinov, the powerful Cossack general and newly-appointed war minister, and the right Kadet leader V.N. Pepeliaev, both of whom were such Great Russian chauvinists that they objected to the representation of the Siberian minority nationalities at the Ufa State Conference on the grounds that these people were not sufficiently "state-conscious."[43]

As the delegations jockeyed for position, the failure of Samara's military estabishment to stem the eastward advance of the Red Army (Kazan and Simbirsk fell during the second week of September) undermined the credibility of *Komuch* and so demoralized its People's Army that several dozen senior officers were reported to have removed their uniforms and donned those of Omsk.[44] Mikhailov was quick to instruct his representatives to play the situation for maximum political advantage and to be firm, "not to make any concessions ... even at the risk of a rupture [of the negotiations]."[45] The aggressive attitude of the Omsk group did not surprise observers like Baron Budberg, who concluded that one could hardly expect more from such a "greedy, stupid, and dishonest camarilla."[46] What Mikhailov wanted was nothing less than the transfer of all governmental authority to the existing apparatus in Omsk. By September he had already managed effectively to wrest day-to-day decision-making from the Council of Ministers and put it into the hands of the Administrative Council that, while ostensibly chaired by Serebrennikov and answerable to the Council of Ministers, was really his personal instrument.

Founded on 24 August 1918, the Administrative Council contained the heads and deputy heads of each ministry of the PSG. Its official duty was to assist with the administrative functions of the Council of Ministers, but in fact it was used by Mikhailov to further his own political ambitions and to undermine the power of the socialists in the government and in the Siberian Regional Duma. Moreover, on 7 September 1918 the Administrative Council's powers were broadened so that, in the absence of a majority of the Council of Ministers, it would assume full governmental authority. The following day a decree (of dubious constitutional validity) gave it complete jurisdiction over the Duma, up to and including authority to dissolve that body.[47] The power of the Administrative Council and its rightward bent became obvious with the removal of the moderate A.N. Grishin-Almazov and his replacement by Ivanov-Rinov as minister of war in the first days of September.[48] The precipitating event in Grishin-Almazov's disgrace had occurred on 23 August at Cheliabinsk when he committed a serious breach of diplomatic protocol by loudly questioning the benefits of Allied support. This caused an uproar and demands for his resignation, probably orchestrated by Mikhailov. The personal animus was widely believed to be generated by Mikhailov's scandalous romantic liaison with the very beautiful Mme Grishin-Almazov.[49]

In the event, Ivanov-Rinov immediately restored epaulettes and other traditional military insignia, reinstated the old ranks and formal address, and gave commanders in the field summary powers to impose discipline as they saw fit. These changes were not merely cosmetic: the importance of symbols of rank and other icons for both ordinary peasants and for more sophisticated officers should not be underestimated. The sight again of "brilliant epaulettes" signified for many people the return of the old order, including the twin evils of renewed recruiting and tax collecting.[50] There was no mistaking that the change in Omsk was not merely superficial. New directives from Ivanov-Rinov reflected a much less democratic military philosophy which gave the army virtually a free hand to deal with the civilian population as it pleased, and which removed even the semblance of civil controls over the Omsk generals.

These developments and their implications were brought to a head by the notorious "Novoselov Incident" that unfolded in the midst of the Ufa negotiations. At the time, only one member, I.A. Mikhailov, of the six-man Council of Ministers (the other members were P.V. Vologodskii, I.I. Serebrennikov, M.B. Shatilov, G.B. Patushinskii, and V.M. Krutovskii) was definitely present in Omsk: Vologodskii was on his way to the Far East, Serebrennikov was in Ufa, and Patushinskii was in Irkutsk; there is some question on the whereabouts of Krutovskii and Shatilov. On 19 September the president of the Siberian Regional Duma, I.A. Iakushev, probably in the company of Krutovskii and Shatilov and certainly with their consent, attempted to use the temporary absence of Mikhailov's allies to effect the liberalization of the Council of Ministers by forcing the co-option of the recent arrival of the Provisional Government of Autonomous Siberia minister, A.E. Novoselov, which would give the progressive forces on the Council of Ministers at least a temporary majority.[51]

Needless to say, Mikhailov was not slow to understand the implications of Iakushev's stratagem or to respond. With the addition of Novoselov to Krutovskii and Shatilov, the Council of Ministers would have a quorum and it would be one that Mikhailov could not control. The Council of Ministers could then reassert its executive prerogative over or even disband the Administrative Council. In any case, it was quite clear that Iakushev's intention was to use this oppportunity to re-establish the constitutional and political primacy of the Siberian Regional Duma. Iakushev's cleverness backfired, however, as he and his allies proved to be no match for the quick-witted Mikhailov, who had all four men arrested. The subsequent murder of Novoselov (on 22 September, just as the Ufa Conference was concluding) by Cossacks under the command of Colonel V.I. Volkov and Captain I. Krasil'nikov shocked polite society and brought home the harsh reality of the true balance of power in Siberia. Despite protestations by Iakushev, assorted SRs, and several Czechs and Allied representatives, nothing was done to punish the perpetrators even though their identity was no secret.[52]

The whole Novoselov affair brought discredit upon all parties involved and added to the sense that what was going on in Ufa was a sideshow or window-dressing for the benefit mainly of foreigners.[53]

The incident, however, did much to polarize and entrench the mutual hostility between the militarists of Omsk and the members of the PSR, while exposing to full public view the latter's weakness. Even when, in late September, the sympathetic Czechs offered to intervene on behalf of the "progressive forces" to remove Mikhailov and his ally A.A. Gratsianov (assistant minister of internal affairs in the PSG) by force and to bring them to justice, no Russian authority, including the vociferous leaders of the Duma and the PSR, was prepared to take responsibility for such action. Whether this was out of simple fear or the result of poor political judgement is difficult to say, but it certainly added to the general impression of the debility of "the democracy."

Fifteen difficult days of negotiations in Ufa did finally produce an agreement that set up an All-Russian Provisional Government (ARPG) with a Directory of Five that consisted of two moderate SRs (N.D. Avksent'ev and V.M. Zenzinov), one former SR turned Kadet fellow-traveller (P.V. Vologodskii), one Kadet in good standing (V.A. Vinogradov), and one non-partisan representative of the Union of Regeneration (*Soiuz vozrozhdeniia*) (General V.G. Boldyrev). Altogether it was a respectable, moderate, and markedly pro-Western group, although not one that commanded wide recognition or enthusiasm. Despite the presence of Avksent'ev and Zenzinov, who were in any case identified with the right wing of the PSR, the political momentum of the ARPG was much more in the direction of capitalist Omsk than of socialist Tomsk or Samara.

Without heavy pressure from Major Guinet of France in particular, even this measure of unity would not have been achieved by the Ufa Conference. Only the threat of an Allied boycott forced the acceptance of the two SR directors, who otherwise almost certainly would have been vetoed by Omsk. Guinet was abetted in these efforts by Bogdan Pavlu, the main representative of the Czechoslovak Legion at the meetings.[54] Allied pressure also was necessary to achieve the main terms of the Ufa agreement, which provided that the Directory was to act as a provisional government until 1 January 1919 when power would revert back to the Constituent Assembly, assuming that 250 of its members had been assembled by then. If the first deadline was not met, the transfer of power would occur on 1 February, but again only with the participation of at least 170 members.

In the meantime, those members of the disbanded Constituent Assembly who were already present, together with most of the *Komuch* leadership, gathered in Ekaterinburg as a quasi-official assembly, the Congress of Members of the Constituent Assembly (CMCA). The one hundred or so members of this body considered the outcome of the Ufa meeting to be unacceptable, and on 13 September issued a statement claiming to be "above and independent of the provisional government [the Directory] and its organs."[55] The CMCA saw itself as the legitimate extension of the one true Constituent Assembly and therefore at least temporarily as the body where sovereignty resided, while the Directory "regarded itself as the reborn Provisional Government."[56] To add further to the confusion, the so-called Council of Directors of Departments remained behind in Ufa and continued to function as a branch of *Komuch*.[57] All these claims and counter-claims were made with the deadliest earnestness, despite the fact that they represented little more than fanciful wishful thinking with little and diminishing relationship to the surrounding realities.

The action and exercise of real power was in fact elsewhere, as was evident in P.Ia. Derber's and D.L. Khorvat's formal subordination to the PSG in late September, and by the Directory's reluctant decision on 9 October 1918 to move its base of operations from Ufa to Omsk, rather than to Ekaterinburg, which was the original preference of its SR members, given that the Ural city housed the CMCA as well as the Czechoslovak National Council and a good number of friendly Czech troops. In the end, Omsk was selected as the home of the Directory, ostensibly because it was more secure and further from the front lines which were being pushed eastward by the advancing Red Army. In fact, during the first week of October Syzran and then Samara itself were taken by the enemy. The fall of the latter thoroughly undermined what was left of *Komuch*'s and the PSR's authority and conversely strengthened the appeal of Omsk's established administrative apparatus and powerful military machine without which, it was becoming clear, no White government had any chance of succeeding against Trotsky's rampant forces.

Once in Omsk, the members of the Directory found themselves in a very delicate and undignified position, reminiscent of Derber's experience in the Far East. They were totally dependent upon the good will of the PSG's Council of Ministers and its omnipresent Administrative Council. What followed was not the expected co-option of the PSG by the Directory, but almost exactly the opposite, disguised by a name change that did not affect the existing balance of power in Omsk. The combination of Mikhailov and the military in such close and intimidating proximity proved too much for the politically isolated Directory whose authority was marginal "long before Kolchak put an end to the game of SR-Menshevik 'democracy' in Siberia."[58] Lacking their own bureaucratic apparatus, the members of the Directory were obliged to accept the existing PSG structure and attach themselves to it as best they could. A true measure of their weakness was the unseemly haste with which they agreed to co-opt the entire PSG Council of Ministers; each Omsk official simply assumed the identical post in the new government. P.V. Vologodskii served as chairman in both, and I.A. Mikhailov, P.P. Gudkov, N.I. Petrov, I.I. Serebrennikov, N.S. Zefirov, L.I. Shumilovskii, V.V. Sapozhnikov, and G.K. Guins did the same in their key posts at the ministries of finance, trade and industry, agriculture, supply, food, labour, public education, and administrative secretary respectively. This meant that the Council of Ministers of the Directory, the executive arm of the multi-party all-Russian coalition that had been negotiated with such difficulty at Ufa, was now constituted without a single socialist.[59] Moreover, the central and superordinate role of Mikhailov's Administrative Council was also accepted without qualification.[60]

If, in terms of personnel and power, the Directory was absorbed by the PSG, the paradox was that in the process, the political orientation of Omsk changed dramatically in the direction of the all-Russian character of the ARPG. Henceforward, the focus would be not merely on Siberia but on the whole country: "Let everyone unite around one slogan, precious to every Russian citizen: 'Hail to the United, Independent, Great [and] Free Russia.'"[61] This was the major alteration to the politics of Omsk, and it proved to be irreversible. Indeed, there were signs of the change even before the formal transfer of power to the coalition government established during the Ufa meeting, with leaders of the PSG abandoning their autonomist rhetoric in favour of a modified federalism that sounded more and more like the mainstream statism of the Kadets: "Without a Great Russia, Siberia cannot exist. In the hour of extreme danger all forces and all means should be made to serve one main purpose, namely the regeneration of one united and strong All-Russian State ... [while] the principles of Siberian autonomy would be acknowledged and affirmed, after the solution of the political difficulties in Russia."[62] Tactically this abandonment of the regional orientation may have been a critical error: "The turning point in the sympathies of the local population was reached when the Omsk government, which was a local organisation, became 'All-Russian.'"[63] It was also far from certain that maintaining a more regional focus would have made much difference in broadening the appeal of the anti-Bolshevik coalition in Siberia, but it would certainly have alienated key elements of the White Russian officer corps.

The centralist consensus was growing stronger by the day. Even the Siberian Regional Duma announced that it "unconditionally recognize[d] the Central All-Russian Government [i.e., the Directory] and would obey its orders";[64] similar statements followed from the smaller regional governments. As a gesture of good faith directed at the

Mikhailov clique, the Directory accomplished what had frustrated the PSG by getting the Duma to dissolve itself on 10 November.[65] Notwithstanding these efforts and its grandiloquent all-Russian title, the ARPG remained isolated and without a power base in Siberia; as one of its own alternate directors was obliged to admit, it "did not have ... [support] even in left circles, not to mention the right."[66] Fearful of antagonizing the conservative Omsk establishment, the Directory followed the failed path of its spiritual predecessor, the Provisional Government, and put off addressing controversial political and social issues. Once again, popular demands for freedoms, equality, and fair treatment at the hands of government could not, or would not, be satisfied, despite vocal entreaties from the villages. In a petition to the Directory, peasants asked it "to pass a law so that the freedoms of speech and press and all civil liberties generally will become real freedoms, and not just on paper. When the army and the people know that [these] freedoms are being trampled underfoot, then they will rise up immediately and without mercy strike down those who have strangled popular freedoms and the individuals in power who have allowed such disgraceful behaviour."[67] What was requested was very close to the program of the Directory and it should have been implemented forthwith. After all, the directors were on record as favouring several similar principles: self-determination for national minorities in cultural, educational, and language areas; restoration of the powers and functions of zemstvos and town dumas as organs of local self-government; and full civil liberties for all Russian citizens regardless of class, gender, religion, or national origin. But the truth was that all these civil concerns were secondary to the ARPG's military priorities of liberating Russia, and not merely Siberia, from Soviet power, reuniting the separated parts of the whole country, repudiating the Treaty of Brest-Litovsk, and continuing the war against Germany.

In the sphere of economics the Directory's announced goals were to attract domestic and foreign capital investment for industrial development, and to encourage private initiative and enterprise. Some government regulation of industry and commerce, however, was deemed to be necessary. As well, there was to be legislation to protect workers against unfair labour practices. The principle of the bread monopoly and fixed prices in grain was repudiated, but allowance was made for maintaining fixed rates for certain food items in short supply. While expressing their general sympathy for the land-hungry peasants, the directors were unwilling to take actions that might prejudice the final resolution of the land question by the Constituent Assembly.[68]

This balanced and moderate combination of policies predictably pleased almost no one.[69] Yet, if the main point was to reassure and encourage the business and industrial classes, the interests of the peasants were not abandoned either. Thus, nothing was said about restoring expropriated land to former owners; on the contrary, the transfer of land that had already occurred was tacitly confirmed:

the All-Russian Provisional Government [intends] to develop the productive forces of the country with the help of private Russian and foreign capital, and to stimulate private initiative and enterprise. [It] will refrain from introducing such changes in the existing system of land tenure as would interfere with the subsequent and final solution of the land question by the Constituent Assembly. The land will, therefore, be left for the time being in the hands of its de facto holders.[70]

As if the Directory's position in Omsk was not already problematic, it was further undermined by the actions of the SR Central Committee. In a document issued on 24 October, which came to be known as the Chernov *Gramota* (Manifesto), after its main author, the SR leaders harshly criticized the Ufa agreement as a betrayal of the democratic February Revolution and the party's program, stopping just short of urging the overthrow of the new government. It called upon all SRs to rally around the old Constituent Assembly and to organize the people as "a third force" for struggle on two fronts: against the Bolsheviks in the west and the counter-revolution in the east. In an explanatory memorandum, Chernov implied that his original draft was made more radical by unnamed colleagues. As published, however, the manifesto condemned the Bolsheviks and the Whites equally and in very intemperate language.[71] Only the forceful intervention of the Czechs spared Chernov and his entourage from the wrath of Cossacks in Ekaterinburg. On 26 October 1918 in Omsk, SR leader B.N. Moiseenko was not so fortunate and was murdered by Krasil'nikov's men.

Not surprisingly, the meaning of these events, and the question of who was responsible for what, produced still more controversy. Chernov's assessment, as usual, was self-serving but not without a measure of truth. "The principle of the Constituent Assembly was not salvaged but abandoned without a fight. After the Ufa Conference there could be no further talk of the 'fully-empowered Constituent Assembly' that the [SR] party had always defended."[72] On the other hand, the U.S. Consul General at Irkutsk, Ernest Harris, drew the exact opposite conclusion: "The [Ufa] convention was dominated by the Social Revolutionary Party of Samara and the difference between it and the Bolsheviks is in name only."[73] Whatever the merit of Chernov's argument, it ignored the circumstantial weakness of the PSR and attributed all the recent political failures to the misbehaviour of certain right-wing members. In fact, it was quite unreasonable to expect that the Ufa (or any other) meeting could somehow reverse the unfortunate "correspondence of forces outside the conference that did not favour *Komuch*." What really mattered was that Omsk had the strongest army around, and that the allies and the Czechs were still unwilling to become more deeply involved on the White side.[74]

In his anger at what he deemed to be the pusillanimous accommodation by his comrades Zenzinov and Avksent'ev of the Omsk camarilla, Chernov had overreacted so badly that he ended up doing grave damage to his own prestige and that of his party within moderate left circles. He also added fuel to the fire of conservative misgivings about the possibility of coexistence with "the democracy" under any circumstances. Chernov's intemperate actions had the predictable effect of reinforcing the view of the right that SRs were not much better than Bolsheviks and that their presence on the Directory compromised it categorically. No less a figure than General Alfred Knox was quoted to the effect that the SR leader and all like-minded members of his party ought to be shot for treason.[75] All differences between Zenzinov and Avksent'ev, on the one side, and the Chernovite leftist majority, on the other, were ignored, depite the fact that the two SR directors vehemently denounced the October 24th Manifesto and joined in calling for the arrest and prosecution of its authors.[76]

The net effect of all this was a further polarization of political positions. V.N. Pepeliaev, at a gathering of Omsk Kadets in late October, vigorously attacked the Ufa Conference as "a victory for the anti-state elements." The delegates then voted overwhelmingly in favour of a resolution calling for a "unipersonal [*edinolichnyi*] dictatorship."[77] A month earlier in Omsk, at a meeting of merchant-industrialists, the monarchist Prince A.A. Kropotkin had made a similar statement to enthusiastic applause: "We have seen all the parties in power but they have only destroyed Russia ... In order to preserve Russia a strong authority is needed, with a stone heart and tough intelligence. In as much as Russia is at war ... she cannot afford two sources of authority – there must be unitary power – [i.e.] military."[78] By the end of October 1918, in Omsk virtually everyone anticipated an imminent *coup d'état*. According to Guins, "the idea of a dictatorship was ... in the air";[79] educated society (*obshchestvo*) and public opinion had reluctantly come to the conclusion that there was no viable alternative if law, order, and the state were to be preserved. Unfortunately, Guins continued, the notion that "everything [should be] for the army, [and] that politics should be kept out of it,"[80] seemed to operate in only one direction, with officers and Cossacks becoming completely shameless in ugly public displays of drunken chauvinism. Their overbearing behaviour came to a head at a celebratory dinner in the middle of October for the newly arrived British colonel, John Ward, and the Middlesex Regiment, when Krasil'nikov and his Cossacks forced the orchestra at gunpoint to play "God Save The Tsar," causing Ward and his company to walk out in protest.[81]

Ironically, and rather comically, it was at this precise time, when the fortunes of the Directory were reaching their nadir in Siberia, that Great Britain, and possibly France as well, were coming around to granting diplomatic recognition to the ARPG. It may, however, have been more than mere coincidence that the British War Cabinet's fateful decision of 14 November 1918 was overtaken by the events three days later (during the night of 17–18) in Omsk which brought Admiral A.V. Kolchak to power as supreme ruler of Russia: the architects of the coup would have had every reason to make their move against the Directory before rather than after it gained formal international status.[82] While all the details are still not clear, it is possible to reconstruct the essence of the story. A secret meeting was held on 17 November at the headquarters of the Omsk Military-Industrial Committee, probably at the initiative of Mikhailov but involving also such other key figures of the conservative Omsk establishment as the Kadet leaders V.N. Pepeliaev and Zhardetskii, General Syromiatnikov of the *Stavka* (General Headquarters), and several Cossack officers. Following it, the decision was taken to replace the Directory with a military dictatorship headed by Kolchak.

There have been suggestions from several sources of some British complicity in the *coup d'état*, most likely in the persons of Lieutenant Colonel J.F. Nielson and Captain L. Steveni, but no conclusive evidence has been adduced.[83] All that can be said with certainty is that the Allied representatives and soldiers on the scene did not interfere on 18 November when the Council of Ministers hastily convened and proceeded to order the dissolution of the Directory, to arrest its two socialist members, Avksent'ev and Zenzinov, on the dubious grounds that they "were preparing a traitorous agreement with the Bolsheviks," and to transfer all power to the supreme governorship of Kolchak.[84]

The coup was bloodless; at the critical moment there was no one to defend the Directory. Subsequently, in the official Omsk account the events of 17–18 November were justified on the grounds that "to all state-minded elements" it would be obvious that the issue had been forced by the Central Committee of the PSR, "led by its antigovernment group – the very same group that disrupted, disarmed, and led the Provisional Government of Kerensky to its death."[85] In any case, the nature of the *démarche* reflected public apathy and disillusionment, as was evident in the words of a local worker: "What Directory, what Kolchak – one and the same devil. Are we to bust our heads for the sake of Avksent'ev?"[86] The message of the moderate socialists, with their precious distinctions from the Bolsheviks on the left and the White military on the right, was still not getting through to a wide audience.

5 Kolchak's Regime in Ascendancy

18 November 1918 to Spring 1919

What happened in Omsk during the night of 17–18 November 1918 is still not known in all details. For instance, what were the degree and the nature of Allied, in particular British, involvement in the coup, the precise role of I.A. Mikhailov and other members of the Council of Ministers, and the advance knowledge and attitude of Admiral A.V. Kolchak.

We can at best provide only tentative answers to these questions: Colonel Ward and his men, by choosing not to take sides, at the very least tacitly tolerated the move against the duly constituted Directory, even though General Alfred Knox categorically denied their involvement, noting that the "coup d'etat which placed Kolchak in power ... was carried out by the Siberian Government without the previous knowledge, and without in any sense the connivance of Great Britain." On the other hand, a well-informed (if no less biased) French observer was convinced that "the *coup d'état* was certainly effected with the support of English military representatives."[1]

Quite apart from the question of direct involvement, it was no secret that the Allied representatives in Siberia generally favoured a military dictatorship. This was not only true of the British, French, and Japanese, all deeply engaged in internecine intrigues with rightward-leaning White Russian clients, but also of the American diplomats, who often appeared to be acting on their own discretion and at some variance with the stated intentions of their president. Ernest Harris, U.S. consul general in Irkutsk, was an early and strong supporter of Kolchak; he stated flatly that "a military dictatorship should be established in Siberia and Russia during the time of war [so that] the Russian people will have an opportunity to find themselves politically,"[2] a view he repeated on several occasions.

The one obvious exception was General W.S. Graves, commander of the American Expeditionary Forces in Siberia. He fastidiously limited his role to guarding the Allied supplies stored in Vladivostok and to help expedite the repatriation of the Czechoslovak prisoners of war through that city. Graves's admirably strict adherence to orders against interfering in domestic Russian affairs, however, only succeeded in antagonizing virtually everyone, without achieving the desired results. The Bolsheviks remained deeply suspicious of American motives, while their enemies saw the general as a dupe of his staff and of certain "Russophobic elements" – often an anti-Semitic code for Jews. The French representatives in Vladivostok seemed to believe that the Americans favoured the Bolsheviks and were prejudiced against the Russian Whites,[3] while the British privately concurred that Graves and his party were "plainly influenced by their interpreters who for the most part are Russian Jews, with strong sympathies for the Bolshevists."[4]

The chief beneficiaries of these mutual antagonisms and suspicions in the short-term were the Japanese, who relished the growing American isolation and did nothing to discourage anti-Graves sentiments among the Russian leadership or the other allies. For Japan, the major ongoing obstacle to achieving its expansionist designs in Siberia was not so much the Russian armies, Red or White, but the American general and his moralistic commander-in-chief in Washington. With far and away the largest contingent – over 70,000 men, many more than were necessary to rescue any Japanese citizens stranded in the Russian Far East – Tokyo was not bothering to disguise its larger agenda. A comparison with the other major Allied forces in the region reveals quite different levels of commitment. There were only 9,000 Americans, 1,600 British, and 700 French, as well as the 50,000 Czechoslovak prisoners of war and about 27,000 assorted Poles, Serbs, Romanians, Italians, and Chinese, not to mention 4,000 Canadians. Despite its small contingent of troops, however, Britain was spending the most money, about £100 million, the bulk of which went to Kolchak. In addition, between October 1918 and October 1919 British ordnance at Vladivostok included 600,000 rifles, 346 million rounds of small-arms ammunition, 6,831 machine-guns, 192 field guns, 300,000 rounds of artillery ammunition, 435,000 blankets, 210,000 sets of uniforms, 400,000 sets of underclothing, and one million hand-grenades.[5]

Nevertheless, as we have seen, the evidence for Allied, or even British, involvement cannot be described as conclusive. All that can be said with certainty is that on that night the Directory's Council of Ministers met in emergency session, relieved the directors of their powers (arresting the two SR members, N.D. Avksent'ev and V.M. Zenzinov), and set up Kolchak, its own recently appointed minister of war and marine, as supreme ruler.[6] Mikhailov himself was almost certainly party to the plot, if not its chief architect; all the key military players in Omsk – the commander of the garrison, Colonel V.I. Volkov, Captain I. Krasil'nikov, and the city commandant, Major G. Katanaev – were his close associates. In a revealing letter dated five months later, another participant congratulated Mikhailov on the centrality of his role and outlined the terms of their conspiracy:

If it were not for you, the Council of Ministers would never have decided to give full authority to Admiral Kolchak ... [And] various political groups would not have responded with such sympathy to the overturn, and, possibly, Volkov might not have agreed to arrest the members of the Directory, since, [he] demanded ... four preconditions: 1) assurance from leaders of the main political parties that the coup had their support; 2) your participation in the coup; 3) assurances from the allies that they would not oppose the coup; 4) [his own] promotion to general.[7]

Admiral Kolchak purposefully absented himself from Omsk that night in order to avoid any suggestion of personal impropriety. In addition, G.K. Guins, the administrative secretary, always insisted that he and those closest to him in the government did not know of the planned coup in advance.[8] But even apart from contrary testimony as cited above, the attitude of those around the admiral may be inferred from the subsequent failure to prosecute the perpetrators even though the illegality of their action was formally recognized. Indeed, they were all promoted, Volkov (his fourth condition) to general, and Krasil'nikov and Katanaev to colonel.[9]

It is worth noting that the transfer of power, *sensu strictu*, was not to the person of Kolchak but to the new All-Russian Supreme Governorship that included the Council of Ministers (rather like the British situation of King in Parliament, according to one participant).[10] A more credible reading of the transfer of power, however, was expressed by a Czech soldier who voiced the concern of many of his confrères: "Brothers, this is nothing very fine. I heard that in Omsk many members of the Constituent Assembly have been arrested by Kolchak ... Does the whole thing simply mean, then, that Kolchak, a former Admiral of the Tsar, is trying to restore monarchy in Russia?"[11] While the coup came as no surprise, reactions nevertheless ranged across a wide spectrum, from outright disapproval and outrage (by most, but by no means all, SRs and Mensheviks, the Czechs as a group, the British prime minister, and the American president), to watchful scepticism (by regionalists, Ataman G.M. Semenov and his allies, and the Japanese),[12] indifference (by the bulk of the peasantry), and finally enthusiastic support (by Kadets and all parties to their right, Russian officers, several British and American officials in Siberia, and Omsk business circles).

By an Act of Provisional Governmental Organization in Russia the defunct Directory's Council of Ministers gave unlimited and exclusive authority for the conduct of the war to the supreme ruler. Civil matters, however, continued to require confirmation by the Council. In practice, because of Kolchak's dislike of politics and administrative details, the Council of the Supreme Ruler, an inner cabinet of five comprising A.N. Gattenberger, interior, Iu.V. Kliuchnikov, foreign affairs, G.G. Tel'berg, administrative secretary, P.V. Vologodskii, chairman, and, of course, I.A. Mikhailov, finance, immediately took charge of day-to-day government.[13] With the partial exception of Tel'berg, all had served in the same positions in the Directory. Moreover, the first three were formally members of the Kadet party, as were the other two in all but name. The same political orientation applied to the rest of Kolchak's top aides and confidants, G.K. Guins, V.N. Pepeliaev, I.I. Sukin, and S.G. Feodos'ev.[14]

"The democracy," and SRs in particular, objected in the strongest terms to the coup and the arrests through their numerous newspapers, and the Czechs registered their disapproval, though in more muted tones. Most of educated Russian society and the chief Allied representatives in Omsk said little or nothing, however, leaving the impression that they were secretly pleased or at least not unhappy with the turn of events. On 19 December 1918 Kolchak received the strong endorsement of the Omsk Bloc, the influential umbrella group that represented eleven different organizations, spanning the political spectrum from moderate socialist to right of centre.[15] The Kolchak coup was also vigorously defended in émigré publications, especially those that all along had been critical of the leftist leanings of the Chernov leadership of the Party of the Socialist Revolutionaries (PSR):

It was but a very small fraction of the Constituent Assembly that took part in the election of the Directorate ... [and] during the six weeks of their existence they did not show the necessary qualities for a successful struggle against the Bolsheviki. The intrigues of Chernov with the Social-Revolutionary members of the Directorate made the formation of a strong, well disciplined army almost impossible, and the coup d'etat by which Kolchak came into power was the inevitable result of the failure of the Directorate. To compare his action with the dissolution of the Constituent Assembly by the Bolsheviki is manifestly absurd.[16]

Initially there was hope even among those who normally might have been expected to oppose military dictatorship that the chivalrous admiral would be above petty and partisan politics, and thus make the ideal national saviour. The Kadets, ever pragmatic and quick to claim any Napoleon as their own, called for a "dictatorship in the name of democracy."[17] But many ordinary Russians also responded to Kolchak as the knight errant *sans peur et sans reproche* who could unite the people in the sacred task of national reconstruction. This appealed to the admiral's vanity, as did comparisons with the symbolic role of the British constitutional monarchy, which probably came closest to his own political values. Kolchak immediately announced his intention to concentrate on doing military battle with the Bolsheviks while avoiding taking sides on controversial political issues that might further divide his unwieldy constituency. "I will not go down the path of reaction, nor the ruinous path of party politics. The main goal I will set myself is the creation of a battleworthy army, victory over Bolshevism, and the establishment of law and order, so that the people may without prejudice choose for themselves the manner of government which they prefer, and realize the great ideas of freedom which are currently being proclaimed across the entire [civilized] world."[18] Apart from his own generally conservative nature, there was at least one other consideration that must have disposed Kolchak to avoid taking a clear stand on the major social issues. The fragility of his immediate political coalition, spanning moderate socialists on the left to monarchists on the right, was such that delay and vagueness might well have appeared necessary in order to keep it together and to give it a chance of defeating the Bolsheviks militarily.

By most standards, nevertheless, Kolchak was an unlikely candidate for the job. Baron A.P. Budberg described him as "absolutely unfamiliar with military matters and with administration," adding that his most positive qualities, "sincerity, dedication to the idea of fighting for Russia, crystal honesty, hatred of illegality – all this [amounted to] very little for the wielder of supreme power in times like these."[19] By his own admission, Kolchak was not a statesman or a civic leader but a traditional officer, with old-fashioned notions about the superiority of apolitical soldiery virtues at a time when all around him everything and everyone were being politicized and vulgarized. Writing in January 1918, Kolchak observed that "the only form of state administration which corresponds to the very notion of the state is that which has come to be called militarism."[20]

For the admiral, war specifically represented purifying catharsis. "War is beautiful even though it is tied to many negative manifestations; still it is everywhere and always good ... I put the war [even] higher than my homeland, higher than everything."[21] It followed that service in the army was the highest human calling and should take priority over everything else, especially during the present conflict which threatened the very existence of the Russian state. "Without the army there can be no state; without the army there is no way to preserve the dignity and the honour of the homeland."[22] Unadulterated Western democracy, in his view, was not suitable for Russia precisely because, as a political system, it denied the necessity of war-making. By disposition, as we have seen, a constitutional monarchist and admirer of the British tradition, he had reluctantly come around to the view that in Russia the Romanov dynasty was bankrupt and that therefore the authority of the Provisional Government should be accepted in good faith and indeed defended.[23]

For Kolchak, however, democracy was inextricably tied to pacifism, socialism, and internationalism, all of which were counterpoised to the chief human virtues of nationalism and militarism. He was unalterably committed to continuing and winning the struggle against Germany, from which the anti-state Bolshevik usurpers had so dishonourably withdrawn Russia. He regarded the terms agreed to by Lenin at the Treaty of Brest-Litovsk as a national disgrace and a catastrophe of unprecedented dimensions. "We shall lose our political independence, our borderlands, and shall finally be reduced to a 'Muscovy,' an inland state, forced to do whatever [the Germans] please; all that has stood back of our political independence and freedom will be taken from us. This was the essence of the matter."[24]

In the Omsk of 1918 the supreme ruler's politics actually appeared centrist, especially by comparison to the overt monarchism of certain business and military circles around Prince A.A. Kropotkin.[25] Both ideologically and personally, Kolchak was closest to the right (and increasingly dominant) wing of the Constitutional Democrats, in Siberia, although he would never permit his office to be associated formally with any political party. Nevertheless, the Omsk Kadets, representing the party of lawful order within a Great Russian state, saw Kolchak as very much their man and his program as a close corollary of their own. The 1 June 1919 edition of the *New York Times* contained the text of an open telegram they addressed to Kolchak that was also intended for Western consumption: "The Constitutional Democratic Party shares fully your views that the Government must be above all parties and classes, that order must be established upon *law* and *liberty*, and that the future of Russia shall be established upon the

free will of the Russian people."[26] Kolchak's minister of information,
N.V. Ustrialov, was also very clear about the Kadet connection: "The
Kadet milieu, such as it was, served as the base of Kolchak's power.
Although the Omsk ministers were not part of the [Eastern] Committee of the Kadet [Party], in essence they were Kadets, as were the
ideology and program of the government ... [Thus the Kadet spokes-
man] Novogorodtsev was right when he characterized our Civil War
as 'a war between the Bolsheviks and the Kadets.'"[27]

From Kolchak's perspective the Kadets recommended themselves in
two very important ways: they shared his devotion to the ideal of a
great Russian state, and their affinity for politics made up for his own
inexperience in that arena. But the real irony was that Kolchak was
not at all suited temperamentally for the role of military dictator.
Despite a notoriously violent temper, he was in fact a lax disciplinarian
who could not control his own staff. The admiral's bark was well
known to be worse than his bite, and he was terribly thin-skinned
about any criticism. Often ill-informed and intellectually lazy, he made
a habit of delegating details of routine management and even major
decisions to others. Moreover, Kolchak was a notoriously bad judge of
character, surrounding himself with men who were not worthy of his
trust or very good at their jobs. "Unreservedly brave, direct and
sincere, of crystalline honesty and nobility, Kolchak lacked the one
quality essential for a dictator – a strong will ... It was not Kolchak
who led the government, but a crowd of intriguers and politicos who
controlled Kolchak. He was only the screen behind which ... hid these
petty egoists."[28]

From the outset, moreover, the admiral's authority was constitution-
ally limited by the necessity of getting prior approval for any action
from the Council of Ministers, and he never was able to implement
fully even those orders that were properly sanctioned. The army, while
nominally under Kolchak's leadership, operated with a great degree
of autonomy and internal divisions among rival commanders, and he
frequently saw his orders ignored or reversed in the field. He could
not always effectively curtail instances of flagrantly insubordinate
behaviour in the environs of Omsk, much less in remote areas of
Eastern Siberia, which experienced the most predatory forms of *atamanshchina*.[29] An American military observer reported that Kolchak
"has not the power to enforce his will. For instance, the Cossack
Atamans, such as Semenoff [Semenov], Dytoff [Dutov] and Ivanoff
[Ivanov] cannot be controlled by Kolchak, as facts have indicated on
many different occasions ... [E]very Ataman is in reality a monarchist
... Should [Kolchak] attempt to oppose the Cossacks openly he would
imperil the existence of his Government."[30]

It was no accident that the most belligerent and unsavoury of the Cossack fiefdoms were located in those areas of Eastern Siberia farthest away from the centralizing authority of Omsk and nearest not only to their Japanese benefactors but also to a country like China, where the phenomenon of warlordism had so many of the same features.[31] Kolchak's failure to control the behaviour of these wild men of the steppes seriously damaged his authority and reputation, both at home and abroad.[32] Such blatant flaunting of law and order, as well as of property and civil rights, could only have the most serious consequences for the credibility of the supreme ruler's oft-stated commitment to *pravoporiadok* (law and order). Indeed, the fact that the Cossack atamans continued their pillaging and brigandage, even in Western Siberia, without effective intervention from Omsk led many people to conclude that these activities enjoyed tacit sanction.[33] Whether or not that was actually the case, the inaction of the Kolchak administration served to underline its own internal weakness and disorganization, while doing nothing to dissociate it in the public mind from the worst abuses of the *atamanshchina*. In the words of one eyewitness, "even the Bolsheviks did not behave in this way."[34]

Unquestionably these were among the main concerns that delayed the formation of a common Allied policy toward Omsk, with the British and French generally disposed to recognition, and the Americans and Japanese (for different reasons) more hesitant. Throughout the spring there were rumours that Allied recognition was going to occur any day. On 26 May 1919 the *Herald* in England announced, "Allies to Recognise Kolchak," and on the next day the *Times* bore the headline, "Kolchak Regime Recognised." But for a number of reasons having more to do with domestic politics in Britain and the United States than foreign policy issues and despite the obvious urgency, it did not happen. Kolchak and his supporters believed that a strong and united Allied endorsement at this time might well have made the crucial difference.[35]

The delay in international recognition naturally added to Kolchak's domestic problems. But it also seemed that the supreme ruler and his advisers had learned nothing – or perhaps the wrong things – from the mistakes of their predecessors in the Provisional Government. With familiar promises to address all outstanding national issues as soon as the Bolsheviks and their German allies were defeated, Omsk called once again upon the people of Russia to sacrifice their narrow self-interests for the greater good of the state, with no regard, moreover, for the particular needs of its immediate Siberian constituency. The wishful assumption was that the Provisional Government in Petrograd had failed because it lacked the proper leadership and state-consciousness, not because of its policies. Now, with a proper military dictatorship in charge, instead of the proto-Bolshevik SRs and Mensheviks, Russia had a real chance to defeat both her domestic and foreign enemies.[36]

The official Omsk rhetoric echoed imperial and PG wartime slogans in an endless and unconvincing stream. Once again, there was an unhappy attempt to achieve a balance between, on the one hand, the political pluralism so dear to the "Russian Democracy" and to influential Western allies and their Czech protégés, and, on the other hand, the militarism and patriotism of Kolchak's main supporters in the army and in business circles.[37] Despite profound misgivings about the motives of the moderate socialist parties (especially the Chernovites), Kolchak recognized the importance of at least appearing to cooperate with them for the sake of international public opinion and benefit of the strongly pro-PSR Czechs in Siberia. Specifically, Kolchak wanted to demonstrate the falseness of allegations circulated by disgruntled socialist émigrés like Kerensky, now joined by Avksent'ev and Zenzinov.

"We have no political tendencies, and therefore charges that we are reactionary are unjust," Kolchak insisted to the New York Times on 2 August 1919. He even tried to turn things around on his critics by insisting that he was observing constitutional limits in not usurping the issues that fell beyond his government's mandate. Omsk was "not entitled to decide many pending questions concerning territory and nationality, since to do so would be to exercise autocratic powers."[38] The question of Kolchak's true feelings on many of these issues remains controversial. One thing is certain: he was not going to repeat what he believed to be the Provisional Government's greatest political mistake, its futile and self-defeating attempt to please all segments of public opinion, including the extreme left. Moreover, the admiral would not allow parliamentary politics to interfere with the paramount goal of waging effective war against Bolshevism and the other enemies of the Great Russian state.[39] As Kolchak's minister Tel'berg put it, "we are for democracy, but our only [true] task is the restoration of the state."[40]

For Kolchak qua officer, the chief objective was always to uphold the honour of his country, especially in the eyes of the Western allies with whom Russia shared the bloody bond of the Great War for four years. That was why some of his first decrees announced his government's sacred ties to the allies and its solemn intention to repay the burdensome national war debt in full. As early as 2 December 1918 the Manchester Guardian had printed a proclamation signed by the supreme ruler and his Council of Ministers that recognized all Russian foreign debts and obligations and all internal loans except those incurred by the Bolsheviks. For Kolchak as head of state and of the legitimate government, moreover, a restored Russia meant a great and united empire, which was why, like Nicholas II, he could not make any separate deals or give up any part of the country's historical territory, even if that meant risking defeat and disaster. From a strategic standpoint, nothing would have been easier or more cost-effective than to have given the Poles, the Ukrainians, and especially the Finns their independence in exchange for help against the Bolsheviks. In June 1919 the Finnish General Mannerheim offered Kolchak a force of 100,000 men to help take Petrograd in return for recognition of the independence of Finland. Without a moment's hesitation, Kolchak defiantly (and perhaps stupidly) rejected the offer.[41]

The political atmosphere in Omsk had become belligerently and urealistically chauvinistic. Already by nature strongly inclined to a course of intransigence, Kolchak surrounded himself with similarly minded people, such as the industrialist S.G. Feodos'ev and the leader of the Siberian Kadets, V.A. Zhardetskii. While neither man had an official position, both were powerful local personalities, known for their advocacy of a firm governing hand that would tolerate no territorial or other concessions to "anti-state elements."[42] The grandiose sense of mission and exaggerated self-confidence in Omsk was fostered by early White military successes against the undermanned Red Army in Siberia. Moreover, from May 1918 to about the same time in 1919 it was undeniably the main theatre of the whole Russian Civil War, first, because it was the battleground where the largest number of White troops were supplemented by the Czechoslovak Legion and the potentially vast resources of the Allied interventionary forces,[43] and secondly, because Western Siberia was the crucial source of the surplus grain that the populations of the central industrial regions of the country under Soviet control depended on for survival. *Sovnarkom* explicitly recognized the priority of the Siberian front when it ordered the bulk of its Red Army regulars (105,000 out of a total of 213,000 in September 1918) to be concentrated there.[44]

Despite the refusal of Semenov and some other renegades to accept the overall authority of Omsk, all the main White armies fell into line. These included the forces fighting under generals A.I. Denikin in the south (Ukraine), E.K. Miller in the north (White Sea), and N.N. Iudenich in the north-west (Baltic), as well as most of the Cossack and ethnic groups in the non-Russian parts of Siberia and central Asia. The tide really seemed to be flowing in Kolchak's direction when, on 26 May 1919, he was notified that the Allied and associated powers were willing to provide arms, supplies, and food and help establish him as the official ruler of Russia if he, in turn, promised that he would abide by specified guidelines for political pluralism and civil liberties. Kolchak accepted all the more important conditions and sent back an answer that seemed to satisfy the Allied leaders on 12 June. Whatever his true feelings, the volatile military situation in Siberia and the vulnerability of his armies forced his hand. In the words of one of the admiral's top aides, "[T]o get the support of the Allies – which was as necessary for the White government as air – required masquerading as a civil democratic regime."[45]

CIVIL LIBERTIES AND SOCIAL POLICIES

In times of civil war, press liberties are restricted and suspended even in free societies. It was hardly surprising then that this should have been the case in Russia and Siberia. The record of the Omsk governments in this respect was certainly no worse than the Soviet one. For instance, it was not until 5 April 1919 that the pro-Bolshevik *Rabochii put'* was suppressed in Siberia, well after Soviet censorship had closed down all non-socialist (and most SR and Menshevik) newspapers in Petrograd and Moscow. In the period immediately preceding, however, between 157 and 201 periodicals appeared in 42 different Siberian towns and cities. These included 24 that were Bolshevik, another 28 that were SR-Menshevik, and 8 that were Kadet, as well as over 100 affiliated with such organizations as the cooperatives, zemstvos, and free trade unions. To be sure, by September 1919 even the pro-government *Zaria* was shut down because it published an article suggesting that Bolshevik sympathies seemed to be on the rise in Siberia.[46]

Freedom of the press naturally has been less important for peasants than unlimited access to the land or unregulated trading in grain, and Lenin fully understood that distinction. Almost alone among his fellow Russian Marxists, he had the political judgement and will to satisfy village priorities, even if that meant temporarily adopting the PSR program. While retaining his belief in the superiority of land nationalization and large-scale collective farming (to both of which he fully intended to return), Lenin recognized the political expediency of bowing to peasant spontaneity in the interim. However, the land taken by the peasantry was to be transferred to the jurisdiction of local soviets and communes rather than to individual households, even if in practice the distinction was not always meaningful.[47] The land question was another example of Lenin's pragmatism coming into conflict with the ideology of more orthodox Marxist colleagues, even within his own party. Years of viewing the rural masses as "petty-bourgeois and counter-revolutionary" disposed most Bolsheviks to treat not just the kulaks but also the middle peasants as class enemies who should be squeezed rather than encouraged. But this approach was particularly problematic in Siberia where the remaining "rural proletariat" (poor peasants) consitituted less than half of all village households, a fact that left the party with, at best, a small potential constituency.[48]

In any case, Bolshevik policies did not recommend themselves to the Siberian peasantry. While restrictions on such practices as the employment of wage-labour and the private enclosure of communal land did not reach the region until somewhat later, rumours detailing requisitions and government excesses in European Russia abounded and were circulated actively through the White press. But even in remote Siberia it was not difficult to see that the trend of Soviet legislation was increasingly against private farming. On 14 February 1919 regulations on socialist land measures were introduced in Moscow; these declared all agriculture based on peasant family farms to be "transitional and obsolescent" and called for the development of state and collective farms. From the middle of 1918 until the beginning of 1921 this policy was supplemented by a ruthless campaign to confiscate surplus grain from the peasantry under the banner of War Communism. In the summer of 1918, in the areas which they controlled, the Bolsheviks had already begun to limit further the freedom of the peasantry by requiring them to have written permission from their *volost'* authorities to leave their village, even to travel to the next town on routine business. The purpose was to prevent the peasants from engaging in free trade by taking their produce to the market. But, though this did indeed limit the mobility of the peasants, it did not prevent bagmen (*meshechniki*) from coming to them. So in the end, the policy did not work and encouraged more imaginative marketing and hoarding techniques in the countryside. Voluntary cooperation with grasping Soviet officials was out of the question since "to each peasant all that is his, however petty, is precious."[49]

In contrast with European Russia, where the Bolsheviks' social revolution brought on a major levelling of land holdings (and therefore, at least in theory, benefited the poor peasants), not much land actually changed hands in Siberia.[50] As noted above, there was much less "land hunger," even among the *novosely* who initially might be obliged to hire themselves out as wage farmers. Everyone was better off than in "the mainland" because of the tight labour market in Siberia, especially in Tomsk and Eniseisk *gubernii*. Moreover, while many Siberian peasants also lived on communes, it was much easier to get out and set up individual households.[51]

In general, the Siberian peasantry had a less collectivist mentality and were less bound by communal regulations than their brethren in

European Russia. Their local organizations were freer on all counts: villagers usually did not work in common fields or have to satisfy their needs from common storehouses. By contrast to the situation west of the Urals, Siberian peasants had considerable mobility and could engage in a far wider range of business initiatives.[52] But arguably the most important reason for the greater well-being of Siberian villages was the absence of serfdom – according to one estimate, there were never more than 3,700 serfs in the whole region – with its attendant bad habits of dependence and passivity.[53]

A relatively free economy without servile labour, remoteness from the centre, traditions of rural autonomy, suspicion of outsiders, all combined to make Siberian society particularly resistant to Bolshevism. Moreover, except in small proletarian communities such as the workers along the railway, there was almost no grass-roots support for the party, even in the towns. The upper layers of urban society, including the important group of service personnel, middle management, and petty bureaucrats that, elsewhere in Russia, made significant contributions to consolidating Soviet power, were put off by what was seen as Bolshevik intransigence and arbitrariness in dealing with fraternal socialist parties and representative institutions like the Siberian Regional Duma and the Constituent Assembly.[54] While our judgement must remain impressionistic in the absence of more comprehensive statistical data, the Whites were apparently getting a more sympathetic hearing than the Bolsheviks from the Siberian peasantry during the summer of 1918. If so, it was, at least in part because of the local influence of village intelligentsia, who were members of the very active and popular Siberian branch of the PSR and therefore highly critical of the new Soviet government. These men understood the village mentality and made every effort to appeal to it by scaring the peasants with the threat that the Soviet government would prevent them from freely marketing their grain as they saw fit.[55] It was no secret that the Siberian muzhik wanted most of all to be left alone: "We need a government which allows us to sow, reap, and sell [our produce] so that in our old age there will be something with which to wash away [zamalivat'] our sins."[56]

The truth of the matter, however, was that under the circumstances of a war economy any government, whether tsarist, liberal, or Soviet, would have resorted to many of the same unpopular and coercive tactics, including military recruiting, agrarian taxes, fixed grain prices, and other centralizing administrative measures, to mobilize and control those precious resources that were in the possession of the peasantry. In this critical regard ideology was less important than administrative necessity, as may be seen in the short duration of the

White honeymoon in Siberia. The imperatives of governing and making war caused the authorities in Omsk to resort to many harsh measures against the peasantry similar to those used during the "old Romanov times."[57] Indeed, punitive recruiting expeditions were being launched by the Provisional Siberian Government (PSG) shortly after it reorganized itself in July, and they intensified with each passing month. This was undoubtedly the main reason why "a widespread peasant movement began already in September, that is before the [pro-Kolchak] coup of 18 November and even before the formation of the Directory."[58]

The wholesale application of brute force to villages that refused to cooperate in surrendering their young men to military service was a key element in defining the negative public image of the government in Omsk well before Kolchak came to power. One of the worst incidents occurred in September when Ataman B.V. Annenkov's Cossacks, acting in the name of the PSG, slaughtered hundreds of resisting peasants in the Slavgorod district of Altai *guberniia*.[59] Playing on the cruel logic of the village aphorism, "People die, the road is made smooth for us," Annenkov rewarded those who identified the hiding places of their neighbours or turned them over to his recruiters.[60]

For most of the Siberian peasants, the advent of the supreme ruler was a non-event that may have seemed as remote as Soviet power. They did not know who Kolchak was or what he stood for; some believed he was somehow tied to Lenin and Trotsky, others that he was the agent of the tsar's brother, Grand Duke Michael, and still others that he was a British officer. G.K. Guins recounted a revealing episode where this last view of Kolchak was expressed with absolute conviction by a village elder just outside Omsk months after the admiral had come to power. In fact, the connection was not so far-fetched: the British had donated surplus army uniforms to the Whites, and in due course they made their way through desertions and the black market from the backs of soldiers in Kolchak's Siberian Army to Red Army men. It was not only Siberian peasants who must have found it confusing to see Russians fighting Russians with some of the combatants on both sides wearing British uniforms.[61]

In any case, there was no reason to believe that Kolchak's ascension to power would lead to a better life in the Siberian countryside. If anything, there would be greater demands on the villages, both in terms of recruits and produce. Already in October violent uprisings occurred against the White draft and food levies in eighteen districts. Morale among White troops was so bad that desertions were commonplace: "Order is maintained only by the Czechs and the Cossacks."[62] By November these mutinies had grown and spread to the Minusinsk district of Eniseisk *guberniia* and the Mariinsk district of Tomsk *guberniia*. There was also an unsuccessful workers' uprising at the beginning of October in Novonikolaevsk. Some 500 participants were arrested. Similar disturbances took place in Krasnoiarsk, and in Omsk a well-organized strike committee demanded overtime pay or threatened to strike immediately.[63] Not that the Bolsheviks were having much better luck with their recruiting efforts. But their chief advantage was that they drew from constituencies – *frontoviki*, workers, and religious schismatics – who had regarded the old regime with utmost hostility and for whom the Whites, as its successors, seemed to offer little improvement.[64]

Even in Omsk, however, where the workers were better organized and more politically conscious than elsewhere in Siberia, Bolshevik support was a mere fraction of that found in the large urban centres of Petrograd and Moscow. This was all the more significant because the total working-class population of Siberia was only about three-quarters of a million people who were easily outnumbered, even in the towns, by middle-class professionals, merchants, and craftsmen.[65] The social balance, moreover, continued to shift towards the middle classes as Omsk became a magnet for all manner of refugees, including the malcontented "former people" of European Russia: "Here appeared uprooted landowners still clinging to the idea of revenge, representatives of industry anxious for restoration [of their factories] ... former Petersburg civil servants."[66]

The original Bolshevik idea was to promote urban unrest in Siberia following the pattern that had proved so effective west of the Urals, thereby demonstrating to peasants and workers alike their common interest in establishing Soviet power. In fact, living conditions for the urban proletariat were deteriorating toward the end of 1918. But a Bolshevik-led uprising of radical railwaymen on 20–22 December 1918 in Kulomzino, a working-class suburb of Omsk, failed badly from poor planning and execution. Among the main reasons for the fiasco were a weak local Bolshevik organization and Moscow's inexplicably cavalier approach, reflected in the very limited resources and personnel of the recently created Siberian bureau of the party, which was supposed to act as the coordinating agency.

At about the same time, P.P. Ivanov-Rinov and his Siberian Cossacks were suppressing a major railway strike with characteristic exuberance and excessive force – *pour décourager les autres* – causing up to 500 civilian deaths and seriously alienating large sections of urban society from the Kolchak government. Even some of its own ministers (Serebrennikov, as well as Guins in retrospect) saw this as a turning-point in public opinion; after this "the government of Admiral Kolchak did

not enjoy the sympathy of the broad masses of the urban population."[67] Few of these victims were actually Bolsheviks, but it was convenient to treat them as such anyway. Genuine party members, on the
other hand, were singled out for particularly savage attention. There
were wholesale arrests and executions of underground cadres across
Kolchakia, from Khabarovsk to Omsk and Ekaterinburg.[68] Among
them were active trade unionists and community leaders who at one
time or another had been critical of the Omsk regime and the strong-
arm tactics of some of its agents. Unfortunately, it did not end there.
Another sickening display of barbaric blood vengeance followed in
late December. Several political prisoners, mainly PSR and other moderate leftists, released by insurgents were foolish enough to return
voluntarily to jail on the explicit promise from the Omsk authorities
that they would not be harmed. Instead, armed and drunken Cossacks
dragged the unfortunates out of their cells in the dead of night and
shot them for "trying to escape." While no conclusive evidence of
direct government complicity has been established, suspiciously little
effort was made to punish the malefactors. The message was clear: in
the eyes of Omsk (no less than of Moscow), those who were not fully
with us were against us, and would be treated as enemies of the state.

This experience reinforced the view of Chernovite SRs as well as
most Mensheviks that the greater threat still came from the right and
that "the revolution had to be saved from the bourgeoisie, not from
the Bolsheviks."[69] For one group in particular, the December outrage
in Omsk constituted the final provocation. These radical veterans of
Komuch, calling themselves the narod faction under V.K. Volskii, crossed
over to the Soviet side at Ufa in early January 1919 and issued the
following statement: "The delegation of members of the PSR and the
presidium of the Congress of Members of the All-Russian Constituent
Assembly calls upon all the soldiers of the People's Army to stop the
Civil War against Soviet power ... and to turn their arms against the
dictatorship of Kolchak."[70] The numbers involved were not great, but
the symbolic significance of this action should not be ignored; it
completed the process of political polarization, eliminating Chernov's
"third course" and reinforcing hard-liners at both extremes who
wanted the choice to be narrowed to the dictatorships of the left and
of the right. The big losers, once again, were the parties of "the
democracy" – especially the majority PSR – as well as the institutional
integrity of the original Constituent Assembly.[71] Indeed, it was now
much easier for Kolchak to dismiss that body as "an artificial and
partisan assembly," adding that "even though the Bolsheviks had few
worthy traits, by dispersing [it] ... they performed a service and this
act should be counted to their credit."[72]

Believing that they had successfully intimidated the peasantry and "the democracy" in Siberia and that Moscow's military position in the east was deteriorating, Omsk became overly optimistic, even arrogant, at the beginning of 1919. So convinced were the men around Kolchak that things were going their way that they summarily rejected an Allied invitation to participate in peace parleys with all the combatant Russian factions at Prince's (Prinkipo) Island in the Sea of Marmara. By contrast, the soviets were quick to accept, even though they never received a formal invitation. Moscow's public statement of 4 February 1919 was a measure of Lenin's and Trotsky's grave concerns about the unfavourable combination of circumstances and forces facing their young Soviet state. While appealing to pacifist sentiments in the West, the statement promised major and unprecedented concessions in return for guaranteed (if greatly reduced) boundaries:

The Soviet Government is so anxious to secure an agreement that would put an end to hostilities, that it is ready to enter at once into negotiations to this end, and ... is even willing in order to obtain such an agreement to make serious concessions, provided they will not menace the future development of Soviet Russia ... [With regard to the outstanding] Russian loans, the Soviet Government first of all declares its readiness to make concessions in this matter ... [It also will] guarantee the payment of interest on its [future] loans by a certain amount of raw materials ... [grant] concessions in mines, forests, and other resources ... [and give] consideration to the question of *annexation of Russian territories by the Entente Powers.*[73]

The contrast between the conciliatory Soviet position and Omsk's intransigence at this time could hardly have been greater. At the height of its (transitory) military success, the White government believed itself to be in the driver's seat and saw no advantage in sitting at the same negotiating table with the Bolshevik "usurpers," as though the claims of the latter to represent Russia were equally legitimate.

These heady illusions in Omsk were also encouraged to some extent by the rise of interventionist sentiments among the Tories in Britain. It will be remembered that the White cause was championed by no less a figure than the secretary of state for war, Winston Churchill, who argued in 1918 that the moment for overthrowing Bolshevism and reopening the eastern front against Germany would never be as opportune.[74] The Omsk leadership, however, had no way of knowing or understanding that Britain's cabinet politics had little in common with Russia's manner of making decisions, and that even the persuasive Churchill might not be able to impose his will upon a majority of his colleagues.

The French were another matter; they were not led by a prime minister or a president troubled by non-interventionist scruples. But their chief military representative in Siberia, General Janin, did not get off to a good start with Kolchak and remained on bad terms with him. This was not merely a matter of personality conflict, but had rather more to do with the nature of the Frenchman's assignment. Janin had been sent to Siberia in August 1918 (arriving just ahead of Kolchak) to assume supreme command of all Allied armed forces in Western Siberia, including the White Russians and the Czechs. It really should not have surprised anyone that this would be offensive to patriotic Russians, especially someone as thin-skinned as the admiral. The government in Omsk therefore ignored the French general (as well as his Czech subalterns) and dealt with the allies as much as possible through his British rival, General Alfred Knox.[75]

But the key to Allied involvement in the Russian Civil War was not to be found in Paris or London; it was in Washington. Only Woodrow Wilson had the resources and the prestige to expand the intervention, and he was unlikely to do so. It was clear that without the American's approval and support, nothing could be done to enlarge the relatively minor Allied contingents already there; indeed, given Wilson's stubborn adherence to principle, there was a good chance that he would insist that they all be withdrawn.

Omsk's best hope for assistance from the outside, therefore, remained with the Czechoslovak Legion, now under the command of Janin. This was hardly a viable option, not only because of wounded Russian pride and Kolchak's personal objections, but also because the Czechs, like their French mentors, were very astute about knowing which way the political wind was blowing and were not disposed to waste their precious capital on the "bankrupt eastern cousins." Without an explicit quid pro quo from the allies, they saw less and less reason to continue to risk their lives on behalf of a military government that could not even carry its own weight on the battlefield, looked increasingly like the old tsarist regime, and was hostile to them and their French commander. Many White Russian officers in Siberia, as well as members of both local officialdom and the intelligentsia, on the other hand, came to feel like second-class citizens in their own country. Naturally this caused a great deal of resentment and xenophobia. "The Russian population," in the words of one contemporary, "during the intervention had to suffer a lot from different foreigners who came to Russia as new rulers, [thus] the ignorant population began to think that better to be under our own tyrants, than to suffer the tyranny of different foreigners, whom they do not even understand."[76] The Czechs came in for particular criticism in this regard.

Several senior White officers commented on their "highhanded treat-ment of Russian troops on Russian soil."[77] And since it was known that the Czech commander, General J. Syrovy, answered directly to Janin, there was also growing anti-French sentiment.[78] Franco-Czech ties, it must be remembered, were a major factor in making Siberia the major beneficiary of French investments during the Civil War. These grew out of the July 1918 agreement to maintain the Czech Legion in Russia, followed in early 1919 by a commitment to provide Omsk with a monthly credit of 18 million francs. Together this amounted to 700 million francs annually. For a variety of reasons, including the pro-British bias of Omsk's policies and Russian resistance to some highly speculative French financial initiatives, Paris became thoroughly dis-enchanted, and the decision was made to send the Czechs home and to end all subsidies to Kolchak.[79]

From the fall of 1918, as it became clear that the Russian Civil War would be a protracted and terribly costly affair and that their own evacuation would be neither speedy nor uneventful, the Czechs tacitly removed themselves from the conflict. They concluded that their own interests would be served best by staying out of the way of the Red Army and by retaining control of the Trans-Siberian Railway, which still represented their only way home. Needless to say, this did nothing to endear them to their White Russian allies. From the perspective of the Whites, the railway clearly ought to be under the jurisdiction of the Russian national government, that is, Omsk. It was one thing for the Czechs to fill temporarily a power vacuum left by the overthrow of Soviet authority in the region, but quite another for foreigners, even the allies, to act as if they owned the place.[80]

Russian sensibilities over how the railway should be run were taken into account by the American engineer, J.F. Stevens, and his Commis-sion, but less so than the political and military realities. The plan of the Commission for the Allied administration of the Trans-Siberian Railway called for setting up an Inter-Allied Railway Committee with a Russian chairman and representatives from the United States, Japan, China, Britain, France, Italy, and Czechoslovakia. The countries on the Committee were assigned responsibility for guarding individual sec-tions of the line, with each agreeing to provide security for its zone. The Americans took charge of the area around Vladivostok; the Japanese covered the distance from Khabarovsk to Chita and then Verkhneudinsk, including the Amur Railway; the Czechs were respon-sible for the territory west of Irkutsk to Omsk. Overall, positions west of Lake Baikal answered to General Janin; those to the east were under the Japanese commander. General Graves did not recognize any Allied authority over his command, however, and Kolchak never approved of the whole arrangement. Still, U.S. troops did their part in keeping the track open, and Omsk was not about to object too strongly since the railway was its lifeline.

Nevertheless, Kolchak's lack of confidence in the support of the allies, and even more of the Czechs, was evident in his rash decision at the end of 1918 to strike without consulting any of them. He did so with three main armies which, in ascending order of importance, were the Southern (or Orenburg), under Cossack Ataman A.I. Dutov, the Western, under M.V. Khanzhin, and the Northern (also referred to as the Siberian), under the renegade Czech Rudolf Gajda. The strongest of the three, with approximately 60,000 combatants, was Gajda's and it also faced the least effective resistance from the Red Army. This, as well as the appeal of linking up with the small Anglo-Russian forces descending from the north-west under the command of the British general, Edmund Ironside, proved decisive in Kolchak's decision to give priority to the northern campaign despite the contrary advice of several more seasoned military strategists who argued that efforts should be concentrated in the southern part of European Russia, where General A.I. Denikin's White Volunteer Army was enjoying significant successes.

To be sure, Gajda's Northern Army made major initial advances, all the more striking in view of the fact that these were achieved without Czech participation, the latter having ceased playing an active role after November 1918.[81] Perm fell to the Northern Army on 24 December, and with it came 31,000 prisoners of war and large amounts of munitions. But a disturbing pattern of behaviour by the victors immediately became evident as they engaged in random violence against the civilian population. A "thousand and five hundred workmen ... were thrown in the river Kama. The motive given for this, was, that these men were Bolsheviki. No attempt was ever made to investigate and establish the truth if these men really were Bolsheviki."[82] The victory, moreover, was not all that it appeared at first glance. It was greatly facilitated by a decision of the Soviet high command to withdraw several divisions from Siberia to reinforce the southern front against Denikin. Thus, it was a weakened and exhausted Third (Red) Army that collapsed under Gajda's offensive. The White advance quickly spanned more than 200 miles and exposed the road to Viatka and Arkhangel'sk.[83] It continued to Glazov, stalling just short of General Ironside's forces, which were *en route* from Arkhangel'sk along the rivers Dvina and Pinega. But it went no further; the critical link between the Russians and the British was never achieved.

Kolchak's decision to give priority to the northern theatre may have been his basic strategic error, but at the time it seemed reasonable enough. On military grounds alone, the decision could be defended as the best way to stretch and disperse the Red Army along the widest possible front.[84] It has also been suggested, however, that personal considerations may have been more important: in particular, that Chief of Staff D.A. Lebedev and his coterie of aides – by one estimate, as many as 2,000 officers were occupied in staff work in Omsk – wanted to achieve victory in the north independently of the southern Volunteer Army lest they be obliged to share the glory of defeating the Bolsheviks with Denikin or anyone else.[85] In the event, Khanzhin's Western Army, formed from the nucleus of *Komuch*'s People's Army and numbering about 40,000, and Gajda's army were supposed to cover each other's flank. However, at the critical point, after Khanzhin's quick advance to the Volga in April 1919 had left his army vulnerable to counter-attack, Gajda refused to be diverted from his own campaign and move his forces southward to bolster the central front.[86] Instead he continued to advance until his southern flank became exposed by Khanzhin's retreat. When Gajda finally recognized his tactical error, it was too late; the Siberian Army had to give up all the ground it had conquered and fall back.[87] If Kolchak disagreed with his northern commander, he took no action when it might have made a difference.

Meanwhile, further to the south, Ataman Dutov's forces of 33,000 men, mainly Cossack combatants, made only modest advances. Moreover, there was a clear pattern to their successes and failures: "[W]here the battle lines never crossed the Cossack homeland, the Cossacks were not eager to fight. This explains why the Don, Orenburg, and Ural Cossacks fought so doggedly for the Whites; the front swayed back and forth across the frontiers of these three regions."[88] The first half of April saw the White armies, now totalling between 130,000 and 140,000 men against approximately 100,000 in the Red Army, advancing along three fronts stretching over 700 miles from the Caspian Sea in the south to the Kama River in the north. The front line ran west of Glazov, Urzhum, and Malmyzh, and eighty miles east of Kazan. In the centre it followed the Viatka River; in the south it curved down from Samara to Krasnyi Iar on the Caspian Sea.[89]

The White advance halted as abruptly as it had begun. A major contributing factor in this dramatic reversal was the reinvigoration of the Fifth Red Army under its capable new commander, M.V. Frunze. The Soviet forces held their ground at the end of April and then counter-attacked, blowing a gaping hole in the Western Army's left flank at Buzuluk. To the north, the Siberian Army refused to turn around and come to their comrades' assistance. Thus, in early June Ufa was retaken by the Reds under V.I. Chapaev. Because Gajda stubbornly continued his offensive, this created a situation where both the Siberian and Western armies were fighting with badly exposed flanks. Further White advance became impossible, at least for a time, and Moscow got breathing space to redeploy its forces to the south where they were desperately needed.[90]

The White military success during the early spring of 1919 masked fundamental problems in Kolchak's "hands-off" management style: ineffective mobilization of men and resources compounded by venality and corruption (especially in the war-related industries), a pattern of amateurish staff and personnel decisions that resulted in inexperienced and incompetent men being given many of the top military appointments, and a lack of coordination, even outright conflicts, in the chain of command itself. Symptomatic of these problems was Kolchak's selection as chief of staff of the 36-year-old Lebedev, who had only arrived in Omsk in October 1918 without the benefit of any command experience. Kolchak's choice was all the more inexplicable since there were several more qualified candidates close at hand; perhaps the most obvious was the eccentric but capable M.K. Diterikhs (Dieterichs), who had already served as a general in the imperial army, but there were several other candidates as well. Instead the supreme ruler picked a nonentity whose appointment was certain to fan existing internal jealousies among senior commanders, as well as between the field and *stavka*. It was difficult to understand "what got into the admiral to take on this accidental [*sluchainyi*] youth without any status or experience as his aide."[91]

Within a matter of weeks, a serious breach of military discipline occurred as the fiery and perpetually ambitious Gajda ceased altogether to accept orders from headquarters. Moreover, in the middle of the spring 1919 offensive he demanded that Lebedev be fired and even threatened to shoot him personally. Kolchak could not bring himself to part with either his young chief of staff or his most successful general. He attempted to placate Gajda – by adding the command of the Western Army to his existing responsibilities – while reaffirming Lebedev in his place.[92] This, of course, made no one happy. What finally decided the issue were not military considerations, but once again the personalities in play: the Czech's lack of tact in dealing with the supreme ruler and Lebedev's refined capacities for intrigue and character assassination. In June it was Gajda who lost out, relieved of his duties by Kolchak.

The impact of all these developments upon civil government could hardly have been beneficial. This was doubly unfortunate because initial victories on the battlefield seemed to encourage Kolchak to be more forthcoming with policies designed to satisfy the crucial demands of the peasantry. Major land reforms were being considered in Omsk during the late winter and early spring of 1919, just prior to and during the first successful stages of Kolchak's new offensive. These popular initiatives, however, could not be pursued if the White military position in Siberia deteriorated, and that, of course, is exactly what happened. But if we may judge by Kolchak's strongly pro-peasant speech in Ekaterinburg on 16 February 1919, the rightward turn in Omsk politics two and a half months later, when several moderate ministers were replaced by more conservative ones, was neither inevitable nor a true reflection of his social agenda.[93] Nevertheless, an American diplomat was not far from the truth when he noted that these "ministerial changes undoubtedly had for their object the limitation of the influence of the Zemstvos and municipal Dumas whose representatives were nearly all social[ist] revolutionaries many of whom belonged to the left wing of that party."[94]

As a consequence of the combination of these circumstances and forces, the Omsk regime lost the support of the Siberian peasantry at the most critical stage of its military campaign against the Reds. Arbitrary and roughly applied instances of "barracks' justice" were becoming so commonplace that even hardened White bureaucrats resigned their posts in protest. In explaining his decision – taken precisely during the month of April when the tide of battle was turning against Kolchak at the front – one such official described some of the excesses practised by the military against the civilian population:

Legal irregularities, reprisal without trial, the flogging even of women, the death of those arrested "while trying to escape," arrests solely on the basis of accusations, the transfer of civil legal cases to military authorities, prosecution that can be explained only by slander and intrigue – when this is inflicted on the civilian population, the territorial administrator can only be a witness of what is taking place. I am not aware of a single case when a military official, guilty of anything listed above, has been called to account ... I can no longer administer a hungry territory held by bayonets in a state of dissembled calm.[95]

These were the desperate devices of a losing army and government in disarray taking out their frustrations on civil society just before their own rendezvous with disaster in the next phase of the Civil War in Siberia.

6 Kolchak's Regime in Decline

Spring 1919 to February 1920

There are many theories and explanations for the White military débâcle on the eastern front in the Russian Civil War that occurred during the late spring and early summer of 1919, but none is entirely satisfactory. Graves, the American general, suggested that Kolchak's recruiting techniques were in large part to blame. These methods were so brutal and unpopular that the new recruits were "embittered by fear, not of the enemy, but of their own forces. The result was, as soon as they were armed and equipped they deserted by regiments, battalions, and individually to the Bolsheviks."[1]

It has been suggested also that Kolchak's inability to hold the loyalty of his troops could be traced to his failure to provide the mobilized peasants who made up his army adequate incentive for fighting on the White side.[2] By comparison, the Bolsheviks seemed preferable. As one popular formulation put it, "the Bolsheviks fight for the people so that there shall be no Tsar any more and so that the land shall be taken from the lords and given to the peasants ... [while] the White Army ... is the army made up mostly of people from the well-to-do class, who want everything in Russia to remain as it used to be under the Tsar."[3] Similar sentiments were commonly expressed in many of the places subject to the rule of Omsk: "So this is how things stand; for nothing at all they will arrest muzhiks and take them away, God knows where, and then they say that they will recruit village people for Kolchak, and it is his epaulets the soldiers wear, and I'm telling you there won't be any more epaulettes on us. We have had enough of that. You just wait till the Bolsheviks come, and we'll see

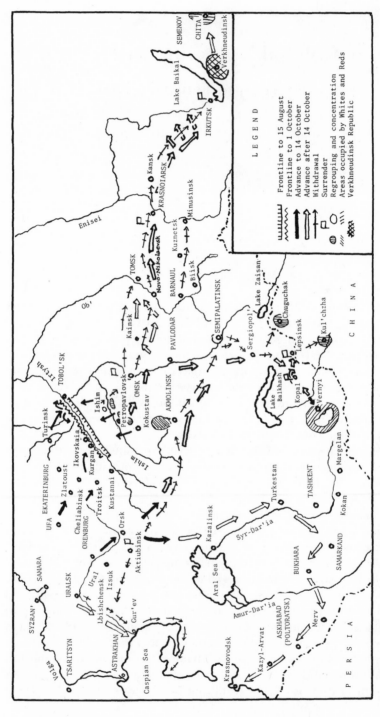

Liquidation of the Eastern Front (8/1919–4/1920) by Paul Duffy.
Source: Kakurin, *Kak srazhalas' revoliutsiia*, 2:288ff.

who is the strongest ... It seems that there is more justice on the Bolshevik side."[4]

Even if this is taken to be representative of an overall attitude or trend, it says nothing about why the turning point occurred when it did. Certainly the renewed strength of the Soviet side, in particular the reorganized Fifth Red Army, was a major factor in the White defeat, as was the infusion of strategically placed Bolshevik cadres. Still, at the end of 1918 the condition of the Red Army in Siberia was far from ideal; official Soviet reports described the morale among soldiers there to be unsatisfactory (*nevazhnoe*) because many of them were without proper clothing and footwear. Moreover, their level of political education was very low or non-existent, and drunkenness was commonplace.[5] Things only began to change for the better in the spring of 1919 when large numbers of party-conscious (*partiinye*) workers raised discipline and morale where it was most needed by going to the front lines. According to one source, "from April to July 1919, the party mobilization [in central Russia] gave the Red Army 20 thousand Communists, of which the major portion was sent to the Eastern Front."[6] Trotsky himself believed that these were the men who turned the tide of battle in Siberia. "We owe these victories, first and foremost, to the soviets of Petrograd and Moscow, in the shape of the proletarians they hurled into battle on the Eastern Front."[7]

Lenin's decision to soften his grain requisitioning policy as part of an effort to win over the middle peasants was also an important ameliorating factor. At his urging, the Eighth Party Congress in Moscow on 22 March 1919 passed a resolution calling off the war against the rural majority and appealing to it for support. "The middle peasantry does not belong to the exploiters, because it does not extract profit from the labour of others. Such a class of small producers cannot suffer from socialism, but, on the contrary, will gain very much from the overthrow of the yoke of capital, which, even in the most democratic republic, exploits it by thousands of means."[8] This change in party policy reflected a tacit recognition that the initial Bolshevik effort to divide the villages while forging an alliance between the predatory *kombedy* and the rural lumpenproletariat was a failure. Still, it was not easy to abandon the idea that had for so long been central to Lenin's world-view: "The organization of the rural poor is the most important problem of our internal development and even the most important problem of our revolution ... [It] separates the bourgeois from the socialist revolution."[9] The decision was, therefore, all the more a measure of Lenin's realism and tactical flexibility. In the event, by December 1918 the *kombedy* themselves were disbanded and some of the worst discriminatory taxes removed from the middle peasantry. There was a growing recognition in Moscow that at the very least a tactical readjustment of the government's social policy in favour of the peasant majority was unavoidable because the "attitude and the behaviour of the middle peasantry had a decisive significance for the outcome of the Civil War."[10]

On the other side, there were specific negative features of the Kolchak administration that also contributed to its military reversal. To begin with, the rapid advances of Kolchak's armies in March and April masked disarray, cynicism, and rampant corruption in Omsk. An American observer commented that "All official reports of strength are false. Kolchak was supposed to have ten army corps, but each corps did not number more than 2,000 bayonets. Desertions are constant and unpunished. There is no discipline. A commander makes a return for 20,000 troops and considers himself fortunate if he receives rations and pay for 5,000. As a matter of fact he will have 2,000 bayonets and will pocket the extra pay."[11] Moreover, many of the 100,000 uniforms provided by the British ended up on the black market and subsequently on the backs of Red Army men. For some regiments as much as 85 per cent of their allotments of food, clothing, tobacco, and other necessities were similarly siphoned off.[12] There was serious social unrest in several key locations along the railway, fueled by the failure of the Omsk government to provide the workers with desired social guarantees. An illegal strike of 2,000 coalminers in strategically located Suchan near Vladivostok was so badly mishandled by the local authorities that in July 1919 Cossacks had to be called in, with predictable mayhem, bloodshed, and disruption of important railway services.[13]

It was not only the Siberian working class, however, that proved resistant to the political authority of Omsk. Too often Kolchak's government had great difficulty finding a credible public voice and identity, appearing mainly to be concerned with the sensibilities of Allied capitals and content to leave the Russian masses in the dark. This could only add to the general confusion, trepidation, and misinformation. Making intelligent choices under the circumstances was difficult for educated society; for illiterate peasants it was almost impossible. Moreover, their ignorance and anxiety disposed them to fanciful conspiracy theories, which nevertheless often contained more than a grain of truth. An anti-Kolchak Siberian partisan leader provided the following revealing account, via Maxim Gorky, of the popular state of mind:

Our people are not ready for events. They flounder about blindly ... [M]y lads asked me: don't you think that Kolchak's right? Aren't we fighting our own? And some days I myself feel like a sheep, I don't understand anything

... A wounded Kolchak marine ... proved to us that Lenin was playing into the hands of the Germans. He had documents and they showed that Lenin had been corresponding with German generals about money. I had him shot so he wouldn't bother our people, but all the same I was long troubled in my heart. Nothing is straightforward, who are you to believe? Everybody is against everyone else. You're frightened even to believe yourself.[14]

The decisive consideration for most peasants in Siberia during 1919 was the identity of their immediate tormentor, usually either a representative of the Kolchak government or someone associated with it. Thus they rose up throughout Eniseisk *guberniia* against White recruiting agents, and in Tiumen' and Tomsk workers and peasants also resisted mobilization and were only overcome at the cost of over 500 fatalities, including 36 Bolshevik agitators. The critical railway lines, despite Allied guards and heavy government subsidies, were so susceptible to sabotage by Red sympathizers, partisans, and the railwaymen themselves that Kolchak was obliged to declare martial law and order his troops to shoot striking workers on sight.[15]

An additional factor in undermining morale and confidence in the Omsk government was Finance Minister Mikhailov's ill-advised and drastic currency reform of April 1919 that was meant to be a quick fix for the unhappy situation in Siberia whereby, apart from actually printing bills, the only significant source of income was the government monopoly on alcohol and sugar. Instead of the intended results, by the end of the month the value of the new Omsk ruble declined by 50 per cent against the Japanese yen and the U.S. dollar, and the people who had been forced to exchange their imperial and Provisional Government currency felt victimized and cheated.[16] The timing of Mikhailov's monetary reform was in response to the escalating costs of the spring military campaign, but it only made matters worse. Widespread loss of confidence in the government fuelled a speculative panic that "inflicted great hardships on the population of Siberia and caused popular discontent."[17] The immediate impact of the Omsk currency legislation was to shoot prices up by 25 per cent, and within a few days by another 50 per cent.[18]

Official figures in Omsk indicated that 1.8 billion rubles were issued from May 1918 to May 1919; another 500 million were produced by the various regional governments, and Omsk was printing an average 400 million or so every month.[19] An unofficial calculation concluded that "throughout the existence of the Omsk State the amount of actual currency issued reached a total of almost 15 billion rubles and in addition to this sum, more than one billion rubles in certificates ... continued ... to flood the money market for as long as a month and a half after the fall of Admiral Kolchak's government."[20] Soviet agents purposefully contributed to the financial havoc and consequent social turmoil by printing and distributing large amounts of forged bank notes, especially the Provisional Government's issue. In the second quarter of 1919 there were at least six currencies circulating side by side in Siberia: three foreign ones (the U.S. dollar, the Japanese yen, and the British pound), and the three main Russian issues, in descending order of value, the imperial, the Provisional Government "green" (also known as *kerenki*), and the Omsk "yellow." But increasingly it was the dollar and to a lesser extent the yen that became the standard of exchange.[21]

Controlling as it did the imperial gold reserve captured in Kazan, the government of Omsk could have forestalled the deepening fiscal crisis. Its most obvious recourse was to make use of the reserve to back the Siberian currency with gold. Instead, under the growing deluge of forged bank notes coming from European Russia, Mikhailov issued a decree invalidating the most widely transacted of these bills, the twenty- and forty-ruble *kerenki*, and replaced them with new issues of unsupported Siberian money. The result, as noted above, was a speculative panic: merchants would only accept *kerenki* at half their face value, and Omsk notes at still steeper discounts, further fuelling inflation.[22] Because the replacement bills were of such poor quality and could not be brought into circulation before the beginning of the summer, precisely when military reverses caused confidence in the Kolchak government to reach an all-time low, the new currency dropped precipitously in value as the quantity increased in a disastrous spiral that Omsk was powerless to check.[23]

Another coincident negative factor for the Whites was the breakdown of a critical ethnic alliance within their coalition. In the early days of the civil conflict, Cossacks and Bashkirs had been among the best Siberian troops because they fought fiercely to protect their homes and privileges against what they perceived to be the levelling, anti-nationalist policies of the Red intruders. They were a Turkic people who were disposed to ally with the Whites. Living between the middle Volga and the Urals, they were astride the battle lines of the Civil War and initially were strongly opposed to Bolshevism.[24] However, they turned against Kolchak because of his nationalist stand, and specifically because of his order to dissolve the separate Bashkir corps and to incorporate its units into the regular Siberian army. After the Bashkir leaders had gained a commitment from the Reds for an autonomous Bashkir republic, in February 1919 some 2,000 of their best troops defected from the White army and crossed over the lines to join the other side. This *démarche* had a devastating effect on the stability of Kolchak's already shaky command.[25] Some observers believed that it was a critical moment for the military campaign in the region.[26]

The volatility and changing make-up of the White armies in Siberia were evident in other important ways as well. From élite volunteer forces at the outset, made up largely of Cossacks, officers, and non-commissioned officers, they were becoming of necessity mass-based. On 18 June 1918 more than half of Omsk's small army of 6,000 men were officers; by the end of the summer the overall number had already risen to 40,000, of whom half were Cossacks and a quarter were ex-officers, perhaps 5,000 were military cadets, and peasants constituted the remainder, only about 12 per cent. These proportions were completely reversed, however, by the spring of 1919, thereby changing the social and psychological base of the army, making it much more broadly representative of the peasant population and much less voluntary.[27] There was a sharp decrease in morale and preparedness, with unwilling peasant recruits by the tens of thousands, for the most part inadequately clothed and supplied, forced to serve under increasingly onerous conditions. According to a British report, "The men at the front were marched to a standstill, without drafts to replace casualties. They were without the smallest comforts such as tea, sugar and tobacco. Their winter felt boots had not been replaced by leather boots and fell to pieces in the spring slush."[28] The stronger men deserted, and those who stayed behind often did so not out of loyalty or discipline, but because they saw army service as a convenient way to plunder the surrounding civilian population. Kolchak was not unaware of the problem, and attempted to do something about it; he issued a stream of instructions, noble in sentiment but ineffective and unenforceable: "It is imperative that the troops respond with consideration to the needs of the peasants and of the population in general … that nothing should be arbitrarily destroyed, that nothing should be taken without remuneration, and even more, that there should be no violation of civil rights."[29]

In fairness, most of the abuses were not unique to Kolchak's armies or to Siberia. Lenin and Trotsky also had their hands full with desertions, insubordination, plunder, rape, pillage, and generalized exploitation of the civilian population.[30] But a comparison reveals important differences that favoured the Reds. Chief among them was that Moscow drew its recruits as much as possible from among the industrial working class, a constituency that could not as readily switch sides because of both practical and political obstacles. A decree on compulsory military training, adopted by the All-Russian Soviet Central Executive Committee on 22 April 1918, specified limits on the class make-up of the Red Army: "military training and the arming of the people in the coming transitional epoch will be extended only to the workers and to the peasants who do not exploit hired labour."[31] Although this definition had to be expanded to satisfy Trotsky's growing demands for men, a critical core remained proletarian.

Morale in the Red Army by the middle of 1919 was improving while the opposite trend was evident in Kolchak's ranks. Whether this was the result of victories on the battlefield or the other way around, the contrast was increasing and undeniable:

The regular Red soldiers showed themselves in the summer and fall of 1919 to be more disciplined than the White soldiers ... [The latter] and especially the[ir] officers engaged in drunken and debauched behaviour while by all accounts the Reds behaved themselves with great restraint. [Moreover, the Reds] accurately and honestly paid [for what they took from] the local population ... The secret of the discipline of the Reds can be explained, parenthetically, very simply. As soon as the Soviet forces fully occupied some region, they began to implement a general requisition, of which the lion's share went to the Red Army. Guaranteed in advance of the 'spoils of war,' [the latter] learned to display revolutionary restraint.[32]

In addition, the Reds seemed better able to adapt their message and their tactics to the village mentality. Their main arguments – that the peasant poor had more in common with industrial workers than either had with kulaks and landlords, and that the White army would take away their possessions and their sons – played to the most common rural fears and suspicions and were close enough to reality to offset Omsk's counter-efforts to focus attention on the excesses of Bolshevism. Initially at least, the Soviet system had the great advantage of representing something new and unknown, while its chief enemies appeared to be virtually a replica, especially as seen from below, of the discredited old order. Moreover, Bolshevik propaganda had the ring of truth about it in precisely the negative tones that have always resonated best in the peasant mind. This was the case even in Siberia, where otherwise the general audience was not receptive to revolutionary appeals.

The Soviet effort was certainly abetted by the fact that throughout Kolchak's vast domain, civil authority increasingly was overshadowed by the military, which often treated local peasants more like the enemy than a population it was ostensibly seeking to defend. The signs and symbols of the Omsk regime, moreover, were by and large suggestive of reaction and restoration. As one close and astute critic observed, almost immediately after the proclamation of Kolchak as supreme ruler many of the old attributes of tsarist pomp and circumstance started to return: the same phrases in official documents, the same imperial tone and manner, even a physical resemblance between the admiral and the last Romanov. "The complete parallel between Kolchak and the [former] autocrat became stronger and stronger."[33] The resemblances went beyond external appearances and several already have been noted in the previous chapter, but at least one more deserves to be mentioned: Kolchak's mystical and errant assumption, so reminiscent of the late emperor, that he had special insight and access to the popular mind.[34] It was therefore unnecessary and unworthy to engage the Bolsheviks or any other "anti-state" groups in vying for the people's affections.

N.V. Ustrialov, the head of the Press-Bureau that was charged with responsibility for propaganda under the supreme ruler, complained that his office was given insufficient funding to do a proper job; even basic items like typewriters and paper were not always available. This contrasted sharply with the Soviet situation where both the Commissariat of Enlightenment and the Political Administration of the Revolutionary-Military Soviet (*Politicheskoe upravlenie revvoensoveta*) were given high priorities for the use of precious resources. The Red military press continued to expand its operations, even when shortages of supplies seriously reduced the production of all other Soviet newspapers. The successful literacy cum political-education campaign in the Red Army was a direct result of this policy.[35] Ustrialov believed that his department's relatively low profile was a reflection of the fact that neither the admiral nor most of his senior advisers regarded dissemination of information, especially in the villages, as a priority.[36] It was also clear that the Omsk government took little interest in local issues. In no case would such petty considerations be permitted to interfere with the larger state priorities as defined by the White leadership. "Our ideology ... was not Siberian, but All-Russian. Here we were not willing to compromise. After all, the very person of Kolchak was a symbol least of all of regionalism or of Siberia."[37]

Because of these and similar assumptions, the Omsk government did very little even to satisfy the needs or secure the loyalties of its fighting men. For instance, there was no White equivalent of the *Sovnarkom* decree that guaranteed special care and provisions for Red Army invalids and their families. Not surprisingly, Ustrialov's propaganda had a minimal effect on the White recruits: "[Men] were supposed to sacrifice their blood at the front ... [but] their salary was pennies, their future – vague, their families – insecure. [They] were told of the villainy of the Bolsheviks. But the speeches were given without enthusiasm, without faith ... The soldier bulged his eyes, listened and responded as before: Yes, Sir! No, Sir! And it was clear that the aristocratic explanations did not fit into his head."[38] It was not until the summer of 1919 that Kolchak finally ordered a bonus of 100 rubles for soldiers serving in the front lines. The measure was long overdue and it might have made a big difference in White fighting morale had it been introduced a year earlier when the idea of a coordinated military opposition to Bolshevism was first being broached in Siberia.[39]

At that early stage, while "the overthrow of Bolshevik power was greeted everywhere with enthusiasm by the most diverse sections of the population," the political momentum in Siberia clearly favoured the Whites. But it was a fleeting and deceptive opportunity. Even allowing for the normal exaggerations of a government press, the mournful tone in Omsk during May 1919 was unmistakable, with officials condemning the "shameful apathy [and] ... indifference" of the Siberian citizenry towards the anti-Bolshevik struggle.[40] This declining support reinforced the hawks around the supreme ruler in their view that the country was still not ready for genuine political pluralism and that civil liberties were somehow unfairly exploited by the Bolsheviks and other enemies of the state to undermine popular support for the White cause.

It was therefore all the more remarkable that Kolchak did not abandon his government's social agenda. Despite his often-stated belief in the priority of military concerns, he seemed to understand that other issues also counted. However, he lacked the political will and the administrative skills to carry through on a social compact with the broad peasant constituency that would have demonstrated the relative narrowness and the vulnerability of Bolshevik support. Moreover, a social compact would have been the most effective way to counter Lenin's argument that the Whites were nothing more than the party of the landlords, while offering a concrete alternative for rebuilding the Russian state (following Stolypin) upon the strong foundation of the small peasant householder. Of course, such policy initiatives required daring, imagination, and time – qualities that were in short supply everywhere in Civil War Russia, and especially in Omsk, where, moreover, they would have risked the alienation of landlord and possibly middle-class support. What is more, even if Kolchak himself understood the necessity of undertaking such programs (though the evidence for this is not conclusive, neither is it negligible), he lacked the power to do so on his own, and might well have been removed from office if he had attempted to go too far in a reformist direction.[41]

Unreservedly brave in formal combat situations, the admiral was not adept at the political infighting that was necessary in order to promote any new policy in Omsk. Nevertheless, he could sound very much like a populist at times: "without a secure, strong and happy peasantry, there is and can be no well-being for the whole Russian state. All the efforts of the supreme ruler are directed toward the creation of a Russian state on such a sound peasant base."[42] The best indication that these were not just pretty words came on 8 April 1919 when Omsk announced a new agrarian policy that seemed to be inspired by an unlikely combination of social welfare and conservative principles. The obvious precedent was Stolypin's plan, with its underlying assumption that security in private land possession and exploitation was the key to making a responsible and patriotic citizen of the peasant-farmer. The idea was to "create strong, small working peasant households based on private property and free of the coercive controls of the *obshchina* [peasant commune]."[43] Skirting the thorny issue of who held legal title to the land, the decree tacitly sanctioned and guaranteed the status quo in the countryside while promising relief for the poor peasantry: "The Government therefore states that everyone who now possesses the land, everyone who sowed it and worked on it, whether he [is] the owner or the renter, has the right to gather in the harvest. Moreover, the Government will take measures to provide in the future for the landless peasants and for those who have little land, utilizing, first of all, the land of private owners and of the state that has already passed into the actual possession of the peasantry."[44]

If taken at face value, this represented a significant shift in emphasis for the Omsk regime away from the principle of the inviolability of private property in all circumstances to a looser usage that allowed at least some "transfer of the land to the tilling peasants."[45] Moreover, according to Kolchak's leading domestic adviser, G.K. Guins, the Council of Ministers gave serious consideration to the redistribution of private estates. Guins's own proposal, which would have allowed the tilling peasants to keep the land with reimbursement to the former owners coming from a special government fund, was just barely defeated by a vote of seven to six.[46]

The delay of several months in addressing the land issue was at least in part a reflection of the fact that only in April 1919 was Kolchak's military position sufficiently strong at the front to allow for social engineering in the rear. In any case, it was no mere coincidence that it was at the apogee of his military success that the supreme ruler moved on the domestic front as well. Finally able to act from a position of strength, he gave some hopeful signs of where he planned to take Russian society. But like Stolypin before him, Kolchak needed time and peace to implement his land reforms, and Lenin's Bolsheviks would give him neither.[47] Even allowing that the April legislation was close to Kolchak's heart, there was never any doubt where his first loyalties and priorities remained. As he never tired of stating, he saw his job as supreme ruler to be principally military, and only success in that sphere gave him the moral authority as well as the political clout to take on the "Omsk camarilla" – to borrow Budberg's apt term again – which was generally indifferent (when not hostile) to specific social reforms.

If as a naval officer Kolchak's qualifications for commanding a major land campaign were questionable, there was also almost nothing in his background to prepare him for political leadership. His failure on both counts was predictable (indeed it was predicted by several contemporaries, including some who were not unsympathetic to him), but it was not inevitable. In the first instance, that failure occurred because of the unstinting efforts of dedicated Red Army men and of anti-Omsk partisans who together turned the military tide in the late spring of 1919. This in turn caused Kolchak to lose confidence in his own judgement and to accept the wild delusions of some of his less scrupulous military and civilian advisers. Following the rightward cabinet shuffle that was meant to appease the disgruntled and alarmed conservatives in Omsk, the admiral's stewardship began to show signs of serious deterioration and opposition on several fronts.[48] Increasingly, his government reverted to the failed formula of previous administrations: an unholy mixture of Great Russian chauvinism, xenophobia, and anti-Semitism. The first and third were intimately related but so volatile and offensive to international public opinion, especially in the United States, that even some of their strongest advocates recognized the potential liabilities. The second, which in this instance sought to depict the Bolsheviks as German agents, was also a double-edged sword – after all there was the little matter of the allies and the Czechs on the White side.

General Janin tried to warn the White leaders that their anti-Semitism was "ultra dangerous in view of [the Jews'] power in the entourage around [President] Wilson."[49] But this only seemed to reinforce their prejudices, if one may judge from statements such as the one made by Captain N.F. Romanoff who spoke on behalf of many Russians, especially Kolchakovite officers: "There is one [main] reason why the Russians are against America. At the American headquarters, the American Red Cross and the American Y.M.C.A., there [are] too many Russian Jews ... The Americans should not forget that the Russian people have a very strong feeling against Jews for centuries."[50] These explanations did little to win over the Americans, although they may have been received more sympathetically in western Europe. In England, for instance, at the end of March 1919 Wickam Steed editorialized in the pages of the *Daily Mail* against any agreement with the Bolsheviks, suggesting that Jewish financial interests "wished above all to bolster up the Jewish Bolshevists in order to secure a field for German and Jewish exploitation of Russia."[51]

It should not be surprising then that Siberia in 1919 also experienced the anti-Semitic blight, despite some half-hearted efforts by official Omsk to discourage the worst offenders. Generally speaking, White officials tended to look the other way during pogromist activities. By contrast, in areas controlled by the Bolsheviks severe punishments were exacted for even spontaneous anti-Semitic outbursts. The comparisons were obvious to all, but especially to the Russian Jews themselves: "Soviet rule ... offered the best chance of survival ... [Only] soviet leaders were willing to fight against pogroms and punish the offenders."[52] While Kolchak himself gave assurances to Jewish business and religious leaders, both at home and abroad, and anti-Semitic excesses in Siberia were notably less widespread and frequent than in such other places as Ukraine and Poland where the Jewish population was much greater, nevertheless they continued throughout his administration. His own military headquarters was the source of some of the most vicious proclamations depicting Jews, along with socialists and certain foreigners, as by nature hostile to Russia's legitimate state aspirations and national character.[53]

In any case, the Jews were always perfect scapegoats. It was no coincidence that the Ekaterinburg pogrom, taking 2,000 Jewish lives, occurred in July 1919 just days after one of the most humiliating White military defeats at the hands of the Red Army of the Jew Bronstein, better known as Trotsky. Unarmed Jewish civilians paid the terrible price of belonging to the same "nationality" as him, even though most of them had nothing else in common. The Jewish issue had always lent itself to manipulation by Russian governments seeking to deflect criticism from their own failures in other areas, and in this sense Kolchak's administration was no different. But the popular response was changing, as public apathy and passive resistance reached new depths. This was evident even in the urban centres of Siberia where growing numbers expressed their true feelings by boycotting the political process, such as it was. Thus, in the spring 1919 the rate of participation in the Novonikolaevsk town duma elections was only 22 per cent.[54]

The breakdown of civil government in Omsk was a major contributor to the general political cynicism. Institutions like Kolchak's State Economic Council seemed to be largely for show, while the real business of government remained as ever the exclusive preserve of the small clique around the supreme ruler, accountable to no one but themselves. A good indication of the problem was the decision to sever trade relations with European Russia which was made without wide consultation and was based on what turned out to be false assumptions about what the allies would do to pick up the slack. When that assistance did not materialize, it was of course ordinary Siberians who suffered most. Soviet sources have suggested that the immediate result was a Siberian "mini-scissors' crisis," with the price of manufactured goods rising much faster than foodstuffs: a Siberian peasant would have to sell twelve pounds of butter in order to be able to buy one pound of iron.[55]

Moreover, Omsk actively encouraged cheap prices for agricultural products and high ones for manufactured goods in order to facilitate the growth of capital investment by the manufacturing-industrial class at the expense of both peasant and cooperative producers. This process has been described as "a market war between the countryside and the towns."[56] It was little consolation to the Siberian peasant that the situation was even worse in the Soviet-controlled areas, according to the economist P.P. Maslov. As compared to 1913, "for every unit of their own products the agricultural population now receives from 2 to 20 times less in industrial products, depending on the nature of the goods. For each pood of flour, for instance, it now receives about 7 times less in manufactured wares, about 2 to 3.7 times less in iron and about 22.5 times less in kerosene than before the War."[57]

MILITARY REVERSALS

By May–June 1919, the tide turned against the Whites in Siberia when first Kolchak's Southern Army, and then his Western Army suffered major reversals. The long anticipated formal recognition from the allies never came despite a flurry of exchanged memoranda and basic agreement between Omsk and the Western capitals on specific terms. At the same time, ironically, the Bolsheviks felt sufficiently vulnerable themselves, especially to the threat of concerted Allied action, that they were fully prepared to make major concessions to their enemies. This was evident in their acceptance of the mediation efforts of an American diplomat, William Bullitt, who proposed relatively unfavourable terms that would have left Soviet Russia only the central portion of the former empire while relegating the larger outlying regions to the Whites.

It was clear to Lenin that he could not afford to continue the struggle on all fronts for very much longer. The combination of forces aligned against the young Soviet state, especially if fully coordinated, would almost certainly mean its destruction. The obvious (and already

tested) way to win time for his cause was to make territorial concessions in the western, non-Russian parts of the old empire where
Marshal Jozef Pilsudski's armies were pushing Polish irredentism eastward. In fact, *Sovnarkom* was willing to go to great lengths to placate
the marshal and his French sponsors. But nothing short of conceding
Ukraine would satisfy Pilsudski's appetite, and not even Lenin found
that acceptable. It would take another full year of war before the Poles
finally agreed to a settlement with Soviet Russia that set boundaries
well to the west of those they could have had in 1919 without the
additional bloodshed.[58]

For London and Paris the Red military successes, rather than any
democratic scruples about the nature of the Kolchak government,
were ultimately the deciding factor against recognizing Omsk. Moreover, despite the best efforts of Churchill and a few other like-minded
Western conservatives, by the middle of 1919 the possibility of additional British and French intervention had become even more remote.
Moscow's prospects were further enhanced by the fact that both imperial Germany and Pilsudski's Poland were in no position to engage
actively in an anti-Soviet campaign: "This was of enormous value to
the Bolsheviks, for without Germany and Poland it would be impossible to launch an attack against Soviet Russia from the west."[59] In the
event, July 1919 saw the White strategic position in the east virtually
collapse when in quick succession Perm and Kungur, Krasnoufimsk,
Zlatoust, and Ekaterinburg all fell to the Reds. By August the White
retreat had turned into a great rout throughout Siberia, even as White
armies in Ukraine and the Baltics were scoring major victories. Minsk
was occupied by the Poles at about the same time that Denikin captured Kiev and Iudenich advanced towards Petrograd. At this point
Trotsky and his commander-in-chief, I.I. Vatsetis, were inclined to halt
the drive in Siberia to concentrate Soviet forces against Denikin in the
south, where, in fact, the largest part of the Red Army already was.
Field commanders in the east objected, however, on the grounds that
this would permit Kolchak to regroup; their view prevailed, and Vatsetis was replaced by S.S. Kamenev.[60]

After the retreats of July and August from advanced positions just
west of the Urals, White troops were re-formed in September into
three new armies east of the Tobol' River under General M.K. Diterikhs (Dieterichs), who finally replaced Lebedev as chief of staff.[61] In
his diary entry for 9 June 1919 Budberg lamented that Kolchak's
unconditional loyalty both to Lebedev and to others in his inner circle,
while personally admirable, served to "exacerbate the break between
the front [line soldiers] and the [Omsk] rear, between the army and
the Admiral."[62] In the new setup under Diterikhs' overall command,

the first army was led by General A.N. Pepeliaev, the second by General A.N. Lokhvitskii, and the third by General K.V. Sakharov.

These changes did little to stabilize the Siberian front. By late September masses of civilian refugees were joining White deserters in fleeing eastward, overcrowding the towns, paralysing the transportation facilities in Western Siberia the Czechs did not control, and overrunning the villages along the way with dispirited and rapacious troops. In the meantime, the Soviet First Army broke through Kolchak's southern flank and linked up with Red units in Turkestan. To make matters even worse, the Czechs kept several de luxe trains at key points along the railway line for exclusive use by themselves and Allied diplomatic and military missions, making it virtually impossible for Kolchak to organize a proper retreat in order to regroup his forces in Irkutsk or to move desperately needed supplies and reinforcements back and forth.[63]

The critical moment of the Civil War came and passed far away from Siberia, however, when in October Denikin in the south and Iudenich in the north-west only just failed to link up their armies, although the former's advance brought him to Orel, a mere 400 kilometres from Moscow. If, at that time, Kolchak's forces had been in a position to play an offensive role in Western Siberia and the Urals similar to what they had done in the spring, the whole Soviet campaign might have collapsed. Instead, the Omsk military command was in such disarray that even the most essential supplies like footwear could not be delivered to the front lines.[64] The moment of crisis passed for the Reds, and the Whites fell back on all fronts.

In the east, by the end of October the Third Red Army recaptured Ishim, Tobol'sk, and Petropavlovsk. Omsk itself fell on 14 November to the Fifth Red Army. Despite all the warning signals, it came as a great shock to residents of the White capital: "We were too inclined to believe in the generals and the military specialists as a whole. They constantly assured us that there was no danger to Omsk, and continued to assert that until virtually the appearance of the Reds at the gates of Omsk."[65] Novonikolaevsk, Tomsk, Taiga Station, and Mariinsk followed in quick succession. The ensuing White retreat involved all segments of the population and was a *débâcle*: roadways were strewn with so many dead bodies that it was difficult to distinguish age or gender, or even whether the corpses were human or animal. A general breakdown in railway services, brought on by workers not getting paid and rolling-stock deteriorating into terrible disrepair, meant that only the military could gain access to the trains and that there was no organized civilian evacuation.[66]

This quick collapse of the White military positions in Siberia demonstrated what many observers, both Russian and foreign, had been saying for some time, that the civil infrastructure was fragile or non-existent and that the government in Omsk rested on a very thin layer of public apathy rather than support. In the estimation of American Consul Eichelberger, as recorded in a report he filed a week before the fall of Omsk, an opinion confirmed by an independent French source,[67] 97 per cent of the people of Siberia today are anti-Kolchak. This alienation he attributed in large part to the fact that "in the name of the Kolchak Government ... Ataman Kalmikoff and Ataman Semenoff have murdered, tortured and robbed in Eastern Siberia, and ... Rozanoff and Annenkoff have murdered in Western Siberia."[68]

The best summary of the situation was made in August 1919 by the U.S. ambassador to Japan, Roland Morris, while on a fact-finding mission in Omsk. His comments, which were consistent with those made earlier by representatives of both the British and the French governments, are worth quoting at some length:

Nothing like civil administration exists ... The Government [has] lost all touch ... with those groups in the population, the Co-operatives, the Zemstvos, the existing party organizations – which know the conditions and might suggest practicable measures. The result has been inaction in every department, and this has offered to the military leaders the opportunity they have sought. On the ground that the only object of the Government was the destruction of Bolshevism by force, they have seized the power in every locality and have wielded it with a ruthlessness which has antagonized the population and with a disregard of vital economic and financial problems which now endanger the success of the whole movement ... The result is now a total collapse – financial, economic and sanitary; the transportation system alone survives under the protection of Czech and Allied troops and the supervision of Allied engineers. But even this arrangement cannot long survive the present financial and economic chaos. To mistakes of military policy must be added an incredible amount of corruption among individual officials which Kolchak has not seriously attempted to correct or punish.[69]

The supreme ruler's inability to maintain order and security in his own backyard was arguably the critical factor in his undoing. Under the very trying circumstances of civil war, people were probably willing to put up with authoritarian government, material hardships, and personal sacrifice. But they had to believe, at the very least, that the man in charge knew what he was doing and could control his own agents and territory. Thus, paradoxically, Kolchak's greatest failure may have been not his violations of civil and political liberties or slowness in implementing economic and social reforms but his inability to impose the minimal standards of governmental authority over the domain under his nominal rule, particularly over his own army and assorted allied or associated brigands.

The military situation in Siberia was also profoundly affected by the growing strength and direct involvement of self-contained, largely autonomous, and strategically located partisan movements. Beginning as early as the summer of 1918, with as few as several hundred men but rapidly gaining in numbers and strength thereafter (perhaps reaching 15,000 by the end of the year in Western Siberia alone), the partisans – or "Greens" – were the independent variable that in many instances shifted the military balance against Omsk. It was, for instance, partisan armies that took Minusinsk and Krasnoiarsk as early as December 1918, Tomsk the following September, and Slavgorod in November.[70] Because of these activities, ever larger areas behind the White lines, especially after April 1919, became insecure and inaccessible to Omsk even if they also remained beyond Moscow's control. In the words of a recent Soviet account, "The partisans diverted onto themselves major resources of the [White] enemy ... They disrupted communications, destroyed existing resources, and interfered with the functioning of Kolchak [government] institutions."[71] A British historian has come to similar conclusions:

Partisan contribution should ... be measured by what they denied to the Whites. All through the campaign the Kolchak forces were short of men, of horses and supplies ... [O]nce the Partisans got going there were large and increasing areas from which no men and no supplies could be obtained, and into which an ever increasing flow of recalcitrant peasants and unwilling recruits could fly for refuge. And above all there was the moral factor. The Partisan movements were a practical alternative to Omsk. They stood for freedom from injustice, from extortion and from interference. They seemed to satisfy that inarticulate longing for a peasant utopia.[72]

That the partisan movement arose against a government in Omsk seen as unresponsive to needs in the Siberian countryside seems undeniable, but that this made it pro-Soviet, much less a formal part of the Red armed forces, is much more contentious. Indeed, by the second half of 1919 it was clear that when the Siberian Greens called for soviet power they had in mind soviets dominated by the peasants rather than by the urban proletariat or the Bolsheviks.[73] Nevertheless, White policies – specifically forced recruiting and requisitioning – did have the effect of driving Reds and partisans into each other's arms. It has been suggested, moreover, that the best recruiting grounds for anti-Kolchak partisans proved to be those places most affected by the dictates of the all-Russian and international market-place and where the local peasant economy suffered the most, such as in the Altai and Eniseisk provinces, with their large numbers of *novosely*.[74]

Among the most active of the partisan bands were those of V.I. Shevelev-Lubkov in Tomsk *guberniia* and I.V. Gromov and E.M. Mamontov in Altai *guberniia*. They and other partisan leaders were all men who violently opposed the Omsk government, although they were not for the most part poor peasants or formally affiliated with the Bolsheviks. Mamontov, for instance, the commander-in-chief of the Altai Peasant Red Army (formed in September 1919 by merging Gromov's and Arkhipov's units with Mamontov's own men, and not to be confused with the Soviet Red Army), was a middle peasant and a *frontovik*. Others, such as Shevelev-Lubkov, Ia.P. Zhigalin, M.A. Ignatov, and I.N. Zinov'ev, came from the village intelligentsia (most often teachers), served as non-commissioned officers in the old imperial army, and remained outside party ranks or leaned in the direction of the Socialist Revolutionaries (SRs). A few exceptions – Gromov, R.P. Zakharov, I.P. Mazdrin, and I.A. Ivanov – were from poor peasant origins or early adherents of Bolshevism or both.[75]

It was inevitable that the partisans would come into greater and more immediate conflict with the Omsk authorities than the Soviets, if for no other reason than because the Whites were the ones trying to impose order in the Siberian villages during 1918–19. An American reporter described how, upon entering a settlement, White forces "would demand the name and residence of every partisan, the location of hostile bands and a guide to lead them in a surprise attack. Failing to secure this information, every house was burned, and in the event that the demands were not complied with, every fifth male was shot regardless of age."[76]

As long as the Omsk government remained a more or less viable operation, most Siberian partisans were not disposed to judge the Bolsheviks too critically, although at least one group fought under the slogan of a free Siberia "without Communists and Kikes [*Zhidy*]."[77] More typical was Mamontov's call to his constituents to join him in actively resisting the Kolchak government with the goal of "founding genuine, popular Soviet authority in Siberia." To sensitive Bolshevik ears, however, this must have sounded alarmingly similar to the position of the Left SRs.[78] By the end of 1919, the Altai Peasant Red Army had a combined strength of more than 16,000 men (with 9,000 rifles, 60 machine-guns and about 90 grenade-launchers), and they were located in a strategically critical part of Kolchak's rear. Overall, partisan groups controlled an area that included over 200 *volosty* with a population of 1.8 million, about 25 per cent of the total for Siberia.[79]

DEMISE OF THE SUPREME RULER

The finale for Kolchak came quickly. By September opposition SRs had formed military organizations in Krasnoiarsk and Irkutsk under Gajda's staff officers. The two centres, along with Vladivostok, renounced the supreme ruler's authority with the encouragement of the Czechoslovak Legion. The latter also took over exclusive control of the railway line between Irkutsk and Krasnoiarsk, which meant that Kolchak's echelons and those of his three main army corps that were retreating eastward could not move without permission from Syrovy. So desperate was the situation that V.N. Pepeliaev tried to convince the admiral to bribe the legionnaires to let the Russians through.[80]

It was the ultimate humiliation for Kolchak personally to become effectively a hostage to the restive and increasingly hostile Czechs, who could wilfully deny him passage eastward through what was, after all, still Russian territory over which he had supreme command. U.S. Vice-Consul T.R. Hansen sent this eyewitness account from the scene: "Admiral Kolchak's train was being detained by the Czechs at Krasno-yarsk as well as all other Russian trains between Taiga and Krasnoyarsk. This was a very complicated situation; no cooperation at all among these parties, the Czechs having the superior armed forces held up both Russian and Polish transportation; Poles having good armed forces held up the Russian and the Russians were powerless as their troops were retreating on foot."[81] Thus, Kolchak's train, with the gold reserve in tow, was sidetracked for several days at a time (in Novoni-kolaevsk, Krasnoiarsk, and finally Nizhneudinsk, 300 miles west of Irkutsk), while echelon after echelon of Czechs, their camp-followers, and their booty were given priority on the main line eastward.[82] It was no wonder that the hot-tempered admiral, who still had plans to regroup his military command and civil government in Irkutsk or even further east, finally lost his composure and good sense. His rash decision to call upon the only force still at his disposal, that of the ever-adaptable Ataman Semenov who belatedly rallied to the defense of the supreme ruler as the symbol of Russian statehood, only made him appear desperate, irresponsible, and even more isolated.[83]

Semenov's men were among the worst criminal elements in Siberia. While they never numbered more than 12,000 and were now down to a fraction of that, they could still do a lot of damage, especially to unarmed civilians.[84] For this particular occasion, they threatened to blow up the tunnels through which the Czech echelons would have to pass after Irkutsk unless the admiral was allowed to proceed without further delay or interference.[85] This was no empty threat, as events over the next month and a half demonstrated.[86] It was, however, also of not much help to Kolchak, who by the middle of November faced insurrection in his rear as he was trying to withdraw what was left of the Siberian White forces in some order from the onrushing Red Army. Former associates, from Irkutsk to Vladivostok, were combining with reinvigorated enemies against him. Only their ineptness salvaged the situation, and then only briefly, for the supreme ruler. For example, his man in Vladivostok, the notorious General S.N. Rozanov, had no difficulty in putting down a bizarre Czech–PSR uprising that barely lasted one day.

Both the irrepressible Gajda and President Iakushev of the Siberian Regional Duma were chameleons with unlimited ability to reinvent themselves,[87] but even by the fantastic standards of Vladivostok's comic-opera politics they achieved new quixotic heights on 17 November 1919. Before the mailed fist of Rozanov could strike, Iakushev managed to issue a statement pointing to the supreme ruler's failure to preserve civil order against the depredations of the lawless atamans ("local satraps, each one acting as a full sovereign") and concluding that "Nine months of the dictatorship of Admiral Kolchak ... have brought Siberia to total ruin and catastrophe ... Cut off from the population, the peasants and the workers, not recognized by the organs of self-government [zemstvos and municipal boards], the Government of Kolchak has shown itself incapable of fulfilling that task which it set itself as the first priority, to organize the defence of the country."[88]

There was no denying either the truth or the irrelevance of this judgement, as the beleaguered admiral played out the last act of his personal drama several hundred miles away. With Eastern Siberia still nominally subject to the supreme ruler and the seat of the White government transferred from Omsk to Irkutsk, officials loyal to Kolchak anxiously awaited his arrival there. On 19 November they issued an appeal to "all healthy public forces" to set aside differences in the name of saving the state from chaos and usurpation by Bolsheviks and their foreign agents, a statement almost identical to one made by the Provisional Government just before its demise, and with similar non-results. Two days later another official announcement from Kolchak's government promised a new and more responsive Supreme Council. In addition, Vologodskii was replaced as prime minister by the more decisive and vigorous V.N. Pepeliaev. Several of the most controversial ministers were relieved of their duties; Mikhailov, Sukin, and Nekliutin were indicted for various acts of malfeasance. The changes made sense, but they too were largely irrelevant. As the ever mordant Baron Budberg observed, "I am sure that 4/5 of the population of Siberia does not even know who Vologodskii is; [and] the 1/5 which does know from newspapers and is interested in politics would be quite happy with any change in the make-up of the government, inasmuch as that would give hope of better times to come."[89]

Pepeliaev sought to broaden the base of popular support by increasing the mandate of the State Economic Conference and by convening a State Zemstvo Conference. At this late stage, however, most of the zemstvos were unwilling to having anything more to do with Kolchak's government in whatever form; the influential one in Irkutsk called for the resignation of both Pepeliaev and the supreme ruler, followed by a full constituent assembly in the form of a *Zemskii sobor* (Zemstvo Convocation). For once, the moderate left found allies among the White military. A meeting of officers in Novonikolaevsk called for "Peace with Soviet Russia" and the convening of a Siberian constituent assembly. Kolchak's loyal General S.N. Voitsekhovskii was able to arrest and execute the leaders of this particular insubordination, but the trend was irreversible. On 9 December, General A.N. Pepeliaev, brother of the new prime minister, echoed the demand for a Siberian Constituent Assembly, and he added that for the sake of the cause Kolchak himself should resign. The two brothers then moved to replace General K.V. Sakharov with the talented V.O. Kappel' as commander-in-chief. These initiatives might still have made some difference a month or two earlier, before Sakharov's ill-conceived and very costly defence of Omsk destroyed what at that time was still a viable army.[90]

Given the consequent disarray as well as the hostility of the Czechs who still controlled the railway, even the withdrawal eastward from Omsk of the vestiges of the White armies was uncertain and unpredictable. There was no telling when they would reach Irkutsk. Nor could Kolchak count on the support of the local garrisons there. In fact, during the evening of 24 December on the left bank of the Angara near the railway station, two battalions of the 53rd Regiment and the garrison of nearby Batareina mutinied. In the absence of a reliable force in Irkutsk to reassert the authority of Omsk's rump Council of Ministers, it simply expired, unlamented and virtually unnoticed. In its place stood the loosely organized Military-Socialist Union, a small paramilitary outfit with left-of-centre sympathies and loyalty to the Irkutsk Political Centre, made up largely of PSR veterans, plus a few Mensheviks and unorthodox Bolsheviks.

The Centre itself had been preceded at the end of September and beginning of October 1919 by an illegal zemstvo-socialist congress that had formed a Political Bureau for all the anti-Kolchak forces in the region to gather around.[91] On 5 January 1920 the Centre announced the formal overthrow of the Kolchak government, restored civil liberties, reaffirmed relations with the allies and the Czechs, and, most significantly, called for immediate peace with the soviets.[92] In acknowledgement of his desperate situation, on 4 January 1920 the admiral had named Denikin as his successor and, in a final act of defiance, appointed Semenov viceroy "with the fulness of both military and civil power" over the Russian Far East.[93] This obvious slap at the Czechs and the PSR, together with the brutal murder of several hostages removed from Irkutsk by the Semenovites and another mutiny by workers at nearby Cheremkhovo, convinced the Irkutsk Political Centre that there was nothing to do but to take power immediately.

Finally, on the night of 14–15 January the supreme ruler's train reached the outskirts of Irkutsk where, despite solemn Allied guarantees for his personal safety, he was surrendered by Syrovy on instructions from Janin to representatives of the Irkutsk Political Centre. This decision was taken in direct contravention of the Allied High Commissioners' promise to take Kolchak "under their protection and ... conduct him to such locality as he might specify."[94] The French general tried to argue that he was in fact following standard procedure and that he had no right "to contradict prior orders and to prescribe an intervention which would put the army in danger." He reassured Syrovy: "Do your best in safeguarding the Czech name. I will support you."[95]

Janin spent several years afterwards defending this decision to sacrifice Kolchak, on the grounds that he had no choice but to accept Syrovy's judgement given that he himself was some 150 miles from the scene and therefore could not determine at firsthand what was going on in Irkutsk. But his true feelings and reasoning come through in an addendum to his apologia pro vita sua:

[Since the Czechs] were under strict orders from [President] Masaryk to remain neutral in Russian internal conflicts ... I had no right to contravene this, much less to put in jeopardy the troops entrusted to [my command] ... In any case, the Czechs would not have obeyed me, and they would have been right. The last acts of Kolchak ... showed him to be their inveterate enemy ... But even if I had the right to give the Czechs the order to protect the Admiral ... at the risk of their own probable peril, in conscience ought I to have done so? Did I have the right to add this disaster to all the rest which the Admiral had caused in Siberia over the past year?[96]

In the event, the Centre was already fading from the scene, under the opposing pressures of the Irkutsk soviet, especially through its military arm, the Irkutsk Military-Revolutionary Committee (*Revkom*), and the approaching White forces. On 22 January Kolchak and V.N. Pepeliaev were handed over to that Committee, which was tantamount to putting them in the hands of the Bolsheviks. The Czechs were anxious to cut a deal with the Bolsheviks and quite prepared to sacrifice Kolchak if necessary.[97] The subsequent interrogation of the supreme ruler and his last prime minister coincided with the approach of the army led by Kappel', which threatened Irkutsk and raised the possibility of their rescue. This was probably why Moscow's plan to bring Kolchak to the Soviet capital for a show trial was jettisoned in favour of a quick execution on the spot.

In contrast to the hysterical Pepeliaev who begged for mercy from his executioners, the admiral's only comment when he was informed of the decision by the Irkutsk Military-Revolutionary Committee, was, "that means there will be no trial?" At five o'clock in the morning of 7 February 1920, in the presence of S. Chudnovskii of the Cheka and I. Bursak, military commander of Irkutsk, Kolchak went to his death with extraordinary dignity.[98] He exchanged pleasantries with his guards and members of the firing-squad, refusing the proferred blindfold but smoking a final cigarette. The two bodies were thrown under the ice of the Angara River.[99] With the end of the Kolchak phase of the Civil War in Siberia, only one chapter – to be played out largely in the Russian Far East – remained.

7 Aftermath and Consolidation of Soviet Power

Early Spring 1920 to Fall 1922

The summary by Roland Morris, U.S. Ambassador to Japan, of the reasons for Kolchak's failure are worth citing in detail:

I submit the following as the chief causes [of] Kolchak's failure to win any substantial popular support: First: Distrust of Cossack leaders who have represented him in Eastern Siberia. Second: Inability of the Russian military and civil officials, trained under the old regime, to realize the change in popular feeling since the war and the revolution ... Third: Absence of constructive measures to meet the serious financial and economic conditions ... Fourth: Resentment, particularly among the peasants, against the system of conscription which has taken more boys from the towns and villages ... Fifth: Suppression of all attempts at local self-government in larger towns and cities.[1]

The demise of the Kolchak government in the region from the Urals to Irkutsk also signalled the end of any pretence of loyalty in the Russian Far East to a central national authority. It meant that local governments in the region would have to deal directly with the Japanese, whose overwhelming military presence would now be felt all the more strongly. During the early months of 1920 what was left of Kolchak's retreating forces began to arrive, adding another destabilizing ingredient to the already volatile mix of forces, especially in Vladivostok. These survivors, veterans of the "Icy March" across the full breadth of Siberia, were the remnants of the army of Kappel' (without their leader who died in transit), still battleworthy under generals S.N. Voitsekhovskii and V.M. Moltchanoff (Molchanov).[2]

Upon their arrival in the Far East they found themselves facing a confusing array of feuding local authorities, from the leftish Maritime Regional Zemstvo Board (*Primorskaia Oblastnaia Zemskaia Uprava*) in Vladivostok under A.S. Medvedev, which in January had replaced the Kolchakovite administration of General S.N. Rozanov, and a similar zemstvo organization in Verkhneudinsk (soon taken over by local Bolsheviks), to the reactionary warlords G.M. Semenov in Chita and I.P. Kalmykov in Khabarovsk. Not far away in Blagoveshchensk there was also the government of M.A. Trilisser, which barely disguised its Communist sympathies.[3]

The most important of the transitional authorities was the Far Eastern Republic, led by the two veteran Communists, A.M. Krasnoshchekov and P.M. Nikiforov, whose headquarters had been moved from Blagovechensk to Chita in November. Founded on 6 April 1920 – that is, within two months of Kolchak's execution in Irkutsk – the Far Eastern Republic was supposed to be an independent state that could act as a buffer between Soviet Russia and the Japanese for an indefinite period of time.[4] It was to be endowed with enormous territory, extending from Lake Baikal to the Pacific Ocean and incorporating the route of the Chinese-Eastern Railway, the Transbaikal, Amur, and Maritime provinces, Sakhalin Island, and Kamchatka peninsula. For Moscow the Far Eastern Republic represented a sort of Treaty of Brest-Litovsk for the east, a temporary exchange of territory for time to recuperate. The main idea was to avoid direct conflict with Tokyo, especially any provocation that would increase or extend Japanese involvement in the Russian Far East. Simultaneously, measures had to be taken to impose central party controls over the remote region precisely in order to prevent local Bolsheviks and other radicals from undertaking revolutionary actions on their own initiative.

Thus, as soon as the Red Army had taken Irkutsk and opened channels of communication eastward, an immediate halt was imposed on further sovietization in order to avoid provoking the Japanese or their Russian clients. Every effort to appease Tokyo also was made by the Bolshevik-backed Maritime Provisional Government in Vladivostok, formed on 31 January 1920 in the vacuum created by Kolchak's defeat and the removal of his local agents, by some Socialist Revolutionaries (SRs) with the support of the departing Czechs. Both the Japanese and the Bolsheviks were suspicious of the Maritime Provisional Government, but Moscow believed it was the safest alternative under the circumstances. The main reason for *Sovnarkom*'s reasonableness was not just the threat but the reality of Tokyo's superior military force in the region. This was made very evident when a minor incident involving the death of a Japanese civilian on the night of 4 April was used to justify attacks on Soviet positions in several Maritime Province locations. After some days of desultory fighting, with hundreds of Russian casualties but no clear-cut decision, both sides agreed to a cease-fire under which the Bolshevik-backed Russian government in Vladivostok continued to function but the Japanese army retained control over the main towns of the province. Indeed, the agreement of 29 April barred Soviet armed forces from a twenty-mile zone around all major railways as well as the borders of China and Korea. From Moscow's standpoint, the benefit of the deal was that it bought a precious respite and reduced the likelihood of further hostilities.[5]

What had really changed the political power balance, however, was the departure of the Americans from Vladivostok on April Fool's Day. Finally, Japan had a free hand to do what it wanted throughout the Transbaikal, Amur, and Maritime provinces. In the weeks following there were several incidents of Japanese military intervention, most notably during the early part of May 1920 at Nikolaevsk-na-Amure where partisans under a man named Triapitsyn had earlier caused some 700, mainly civilian, Japanese casualties. Now the Japanese retaliated with a brutal show of force that claimed between two and three times as many Russian lives.[6] Moscow was obliged to accommodate Tokyo because, although its strategic position was clearly improving, it remained vulnerable at several places thousands of miles apart. As the remotest point from the centre of Soviet power, the Russian Far East was the most expendable and could be sacrificed temporarily, if necessary, to the ministrations of the Japanese, bands of White soldiers, and marauding Cossacks. During the spring of 1920 the focus was elsewhere, as the Red Army swept aside its adversaries from Rostov and Astrakhan to Vladikavkaz, Baku, and Enzeli in convincing fashion. The Polish attack stalled after the dramatic conquest of Kiev by Pilsudski's forces in April, and by June they were thrown back beyond the starting-point of their incursion; there was a real danger that Warsaw itself might fall to the Red counter-offensive.

Because the overall situation was so unstable, however, once again Moscow did not press its advantage and offered to make peace with the Poles on generous terms.[7] Also contributing to this spirit of accommodation was a concern over the presence of the anarchistic and peasant-based Greens in the midst of the turmoil. While more anti-White than anti-Red, these combative rural partisans were a dangerous wild card whose impact on events was highly unpredictable. In the event, it was several more months before the Red Army fully liquidated the Green forces of N.I. Makhno in Ukraine and A.S. Antonov in Tambov province.[8]

These troubles in the south and the west were the main reasons why any further conflict in the Far East with Japan had to be avoided, even at the cost of major territorial and political concessions. Moreover, by contrast to the Treaty of Brest-Litovsk, when Lenin was initially unable to convince the majority of his own Central Committee to accept the onerous terms of the enemy, this time around no one dared challenge his judgement. Going through the charade of the creation of the Far Eastern Republic as well as accepting a limited Japanese presence in the Maritime Province and a long-term Japanese occupation of half of Sakhalin Island were the price that had to be paid for the precious breathing space (*peredyshka*). The critical trade-off was that Red forces could then concentrate on the more urgent business at hand. By mid-August they were successful in repulsing the offensive by General Denikin's successor, Baron Wrangel, in the Crimea and the Caucasus. This, in turn, made it possible by the fall of 1920 to shift the focus back to Siberia and the east.[9]

Under pressure from the Western powers, led by the United States, and because of significant divisions between the civilian and military leadership in Tokyo over the policy to pursue in the Russian Far East, on 21 October Japanese forces began their withdrawal from Khabarovsk.[10] Lenin and the Soviet military command recognized that their best hope of getting the Japanese out of the region altogether was to convince the allies (first of all the Americans) that Moscow was prepared to coexist with an independent and pluralistic buffer state in the Far East, as long as that state was not a direct threat to Soviet Russia. It was in order to reassure the world of its peaceful intentions, as well as to avoid any hint of offence to the Japanese, that Moscow continued to recognize and support the Far Eastern Republic, well after its military forces were in a position to reclaim all the territory for the Soviet state.[11]

The Red Army thus delayed its attack on Chita until after the first Treaty of Riga was signed on 12 October 1920 with Poland and, even more importantly, the Japanese had evacuated the Transbaikal. Towards the end of October, in concert with local partisans, Chita was cleared of Kappel's and Semenov's troops, who retreated to the southeast. Even after this resounding victory, however, Moscow's line continued to be conciliatory. On 29 October the independent and multiparty nature of the Far Eastern Republic was again reaffirmed, along with its capital in Chita and boundaries that corresponded to the entire Far Eastern territory of the former Russian empire. The Vladivostok provisional government, moreover, was not dissolved in order to avoid giving offence to the Japanese, whose military had established relations with it. Under V.G. Antonov, an old Bolshevik with close ties to the centre, its chief function was to mediate between Chita and Tokyo.[12]

But time was on Moscow's side. With each passing day the continuing presence of the Japanese in the Russian Far East served to further isolate Tokyo in international opinion; American displeasure, in particular, was mounting and could not be ignored indefinitely. In terms of domestic public opinion as well, this helped Soviet Russia. Russian patriotism now shifted towards the Bolsheviks and against all those who were seen to be too closely tied with the Japanese. In elections held for the Siberian Constituent Assembly in December 1920, Bolsheviks captured well over half the votes in Vladivostok and elsewhere. Moreover, an influential group of White intellectuals (including former Kolchakovite officials) calling themselves *smenovekhovtsy* (changing eras) to indicate the sea change that had occurred in both the external realities and their own consciousness urged the acceptance of the Soviet victory in the Civil War in the name of Russian national unity and greatness. A recent Russian émigré has aptly termed this phenomenon National Bolshevism to suggest the continuation of the old statist tradition that, under a similarly strong, undivided central authority over the ages, had defended the Russian motherland against foreign and domestic enemies.[13]

If, as it seemed, the tide was running in favour of the Bolsheviks, that was all the more reason for desperate White leaders in the Russian Far East to act sooner rather than later. While the Japanese army still occupied in the southern portion of the Maritime Province and northern Sakhalin Island, there was always the possibility that Tokyo might reverse the process of disengagement. Moreover, strategic access points in Manchuria and Outer Mongolia were occupied by Kappelites, Semenovites, and the notorious Ungern-Sternberg. With the support of the Japanese, S.D. and N.D. Merkulov at the end of May 1921 ousted the Far Eastern Republic authority in Vladivostok and established themselves as the Provisional Priamur Government. A few days later Semenov arrived in Vladivostok and grandly proclaimed himself commander-in-chief and Omsk's viceroy for the Far East, an assertion that was not without some legal standing in light of Kolchak's final orders but that was meaningless in practice because the ataman no longer enjoyed the support of his old Japanese benefactors and thus was unable to do more than cause the local Russians some moments of increased anxiety. Soviet accounts have stressed that the background to these events was a March 1921 meeting in Port Arthur where Japan and France signed a secret treaty that provided for the establishment of a pro-Japanese Merkulov government in Vladivostok as a counterweight to the Far Eastern Republic.[14]

For the next several months the Provisional Priamur Government struggled unsuccessfully to gain support among the fractious yet still viable remnants of the anti-Bolshevik movements in the Russian Far East.[15] But whatever remaining hopes there may have been for preventing a total Soviet victory disappeared with Tokyo's announcement on 24 June 1922 that it was evacuating all its troops from Siberia by the end of October. At the urging of the Japanese, the government of the discredited Merkulov brothers was replaced by martial law. This precipitated the final episode in Vladivostok's theatre of the bizarre in search of political legitimacy. During July the historic institution of the *Zemskii sobor* was revived and it proceeded to install an increasingly eccentric and mystical General M.K. Diterikhs, Kolchak's former chief of staff, as military dictator.

None of this, to be sure, slowed down the advance of the Red Army, which entered Vladivostok on 25 October 1922. Three weeks later the Far Eastern Republic government dissolved itself and transferred all its authority and territory to Soviet Russia. Not until January 1925, however, did Japan finally withdraw her troops from the northern half of Sakhalin Island.[16]

RURAL UNREST AND PARTISAN MOVEMENTS

As the military campaign in the Russian Far East drew to its desultory close, many of the factors that contributed to the defeat of the Whites became more obvious. General Moltchanoff, successor to Kappel' as commander of Kolchak's rump army in the east, came to harsh conclusions about both the White political leadership and the populace: "What we did not have was an ability to lean on the people and get the people's support. Had we been able to come to the people from some direction or other, things might have been different, but we were not able to do this. The Russian people are not just a devout people; they can also be beasts, and with them you have to deal in that fashion."[17] While other White generals also recognized that they could not win a civil war without the support of the rural masses and that they ought to regard them as their natural constituency and allies against the urban-oriented Bolsheviks, no concerted effort was made by the government in Omsk to implement a social policy that would win over the countryside. Small wonder then that popular response to White military and political exhortations was frequently apathetic when not overtly hostile. Moltchanoff conceded that it was quite impossible to win a civil war "where the population is willing to attack you from the rear ... [as] was happening to us in Siberia."[18]

By contrast, as already noted in the two preceding chapters, Soviet relations with the peasantry, even taking into account differences from one region to another, were generally more successful, especially during the early stages of the Civil War. But this had less to do with populism than the political acuity of the Leninist leadership. One of the many ironies of the Russian Civil War was that it showed Bolshevik and Kadet attitudes towards the peasants to have more in common than either party would care to admit publicly. Both mistrusted the rural masses and saw them as politically immature, subject to nihilistic spontaneity (*stikhiinost'*), and unwilling or unable to make the transition *on their own* to modernity, that is to an industrialized society. It may seem a paradox that peasant unrest in Siberia actually increased after the fall of Kolchak.[19] Moreover, Moscow was not quick to pick up the warning signs, despite receiving regular alarming reports, such as the one from its agent in Slavgorod dated 17 October 1920: "After spending four months in Siberia ... I can say that the estrangement of the Siberian peasantry from Soviet construction [*stroitel'stvo*] remains a fact."[20] By far the most powerful expressions of this spontaneous peasant antagonism were the series of partisan movements that, with the subsiding of the White threat, now turned against the Reds.

Soviet historiography has treated the phenomenon of the Siberian partisans with extreme caution and ambivalence. This is not surprising given the origins and the make-up of the movement. By nature a transclass phenomenon that was never fully subject to Moscow's control, it seriously challenged Lenin's neat, if overschematized, social and ideological categories for the peasantry. One close observer has argued that in terms of their economic and social position, most partisans were at the level of the middle peasantry. In any case, "poor peasants were an insignificant number in the[ir] ranks."[21] Even at the height of the military campaign against Kolchak, during which the partisans were so helpful, Lenin and Trotsky had regarded them as a mixed blessing. For one thing, the *partizanshchina* (partisan chaos) involved more than a bit of banditry, pillage, and *stikhiinost'* that could not but gravely alarm the Bolshevik leaders. In addition, Siberian partisans "neither asked for nor expected help from the towns. They were suspicious of anything that came from the towns, including the proletariat. This cut away the ground from under the feet of the Communist Party in attempts to organize and control the movement."[22]

When the partisans got around to addressing questions of purpose and ideology, moreover, they sounded more like Socialist Revolutionaries (SRs) or, even worse, anarchists. A good summary of their views may be seen in the Declaration of the Congress of the Representatives of the Peasant Army issued in 1919 in Minusinsk which, though giving unqualified support to the notion of a Soviet Russia, at the same time echoed many standard populist (and *unBolshevik*) catch-phrases, such as proportional representation in the soviets, guarantees of freedom of speech, press, and meetings for "every individual," and, perhaps most importantly, the formation of an united socialist front. The focus of the declaration was entirely rural, with only passing mention of the urban proletariat.[23] Similar pan-socialist sentiments were expressed in other publications. The organ of the south Eniseisk partisans in October 1919 argued that "Our struggle is not a party matter. We [peasants] are not Bolsheviks or SRs, although in our ranks there are the ones and the others ... Our struggle is purely a class struggle, that is labour against capital."[24]

This catholicity did not recommend itself to Moscow where, as already noted, there was great reluctance to acknowledge a major role for any spontaneous peasant movements behind Kolchak's front lines; forces under E.M. Mamontov, I.V. Gromov, and F.I. Arkhipov were regarded with suspicion for several months. Only in July 1919 had the central party leadership come around to the view that it would be better to co-opt existing partisan detachments in Siberia before they became any more powerful on their own. At about the same time, Moscow also began to increase significantly the subsidies it made to its own Siberian Revolutionary Committee (*Sibrevkom*), reaching 1,347 million rubles in the second half of 1919.[25] Bolshevik control over the partisan movement was never very effective, and remained something of an afterthought even as the Kolchak government crumbled. A recent study by a scholar of Siberia of the connection concluded that "The thesis of Bolshevik direct supervision of the partisan movement is mainly a matter of declaration ... Factual material essential for its validation is not provided by the literature, and theoretical argumentation likewise is lacking. As a consequence of this, there have arisen problems in defining the political character and class essence of the struggle waged by the Siberian partisans."[26]

In other words, far from being pliable instruments of *Sovnarkom* policy the partisans were a force unto themselves and quite possibly represented different political and social interests. To minimize the immediate threat, the West-Siberian Regional Committee of the Bolshevik party tried during the summer to gain direct control over the partisans near the Ob River and to subordinate them to the Red Army, but this met with strong resistance from rank and file partisans who regarded Red commissars from Moscow with deep suspicion.[27] The rapidly growing number of Green partisans in the fall of 1919 raised the possibility of their maintaining separate status as a counterweight to both Reds and Whites, in the manner of Nestor Makhno in Ukraine.

Indeed, spontaneous peasant resistance to Soviet authority in Siberia was evident well before the so-called SR-kulak mutinies of 1921. The two most obvious examples were G.F. Rogov and I.P. Novoselov, popular partisans in the Altai who were killed leading their men against the Bolsheviks only shortly after having helped defeat Kolchak.[28]

The armed force represented by such organized peasant detachments – and their political ideology – could not be taken lightly. Lenin himself warned that "The partisan movement is to be feared like fire, [as is] the wilfulness of individual detachments unwilling to subordinate themselves to the central authority; this leads to ruin, as the Urals, Siberia, and Ukraine all have shown."[29] Nevertheless, the final Soviet military victory in Siberia was facilitated greatly by the *prior* efforts of that movement and its "individual detachments." Even the official Soviet historical encyclopedia was obliged to concede that "about 100,000 Siberian partisans liberated enormous areas [of Siberia] from the White-guardists well before the approach of the Red Army."[30] Other Soviet sources, which were also not disposed to give credit liberally, have indicated that in the Barnaul, Slavgorod, and Semipalatinsk regions there were about 30,000 partisans and that another 40,000 served under A.D. Kravchenko and P.E. Shchetinkin.[31] Estimates of overall strength ranged from 140,000 to 175,000 combatants for Western Siberia alone.[32] In any case, the numbers were sufficient to warrant a special campaign to bring the different Siberian partisan movements to heel through a combination of force, appropriate political re-education, and other incentives.

Still, it was only after considerable additional debates and vacillations in policy that on 19 August 1919 a special decision was reached by the Bolshevik Central Committee concerning the Siberian partisan detachments. This decree ordered that they "must immediately establish among themselves a regular line of communication and coordinate their actions and the transition to a centralized command." Party workers were instructed to take "measures eliminating the negative aspects of the partisan movement."[33] The goal was the absorption of partisan units into the regular structure of the Red Army, but guidelines for that process were slow in coming and not fully worked out until 11 December 1919. These specified stricter military discipline, excluded former partisans from front-line units, and launched a major educational campaign aimed at convincing rank and file members of the advantages of the regular army over their old organizations.[34]

On 26 December 1919 Soviet authorities assigned all partisans in Siberia up to the age of thirty-five to reserve units of the Fifth Red Army, where they were to undergo military and political re-education. The process did not run smoothly. For instance, M.V. Kozyr's Fourth

Peasant Corps, meeting on 15 January 1920 at Ust'-Kamengorsk, voted not to give up their arms and not to subordinate themselves to the Communists.[35] Siberians showed themselves to be quite capable of accepting strict military discipline when it came from their own leaders, as was evident in Mamontov's Altai partisan army in particular.[36] But Soviet agents deplored their tendency to make decisions for themselves: "the partisans' unwillingess to give up their unlimited freedom and to subordinate themselves to the rules and discipline of the Red Army is the basic reason for ... [their] massive desertions."[37] In any case, by February 1920 many Western Siberian partisans had been forcibly disarmed or integrated into reserve units of the Fifth Army or both; the process involved anywhere from 20,000 to 30,000 men, no mean feat under the circumstances.[38]

Nevertheless, this did not prevent the re-emergence of a formidable Green peasant movement in Western Siberia by the end of the year, and by then it was strongly anti-Bolshevik. In the towns there was less evidence of organized opposition, although some leftovers from the Kolchak regime, such as former Finance Minister Mikhailov and his friends, were busy plotting a return to power in Omsk (on a much-reduced bankroll that still, however, amounted to about 1,150 pounds of gold).[39] Beginning in April and May 1920 and growing in strength and numbers with each passing month, mutinies involving from fifty to seven hundred people – peasants, Cossacks, priests, *frontoviki*, and some town folk – occurred in Semipalatinsk, Tiumen', Tomsk, Omsk, Krasnoiarsk, Altai, and Eniseisk *gubernii* amid cries of "death to the Communists."[40] The rebels had a very specific purpose in mind – getting rid of the "Red yoke" with its twin harnesses of *razverstka* and labour and carting conscription (*trudovaia i guzhevaia povinnost'*).[41] According to a local Cheka agent, the situation was very serious and the atmosphere highly dangerous for supporters of the party. "The absence of political education in the countryside [and] the ignorance [*temnota*] of the peasantry has reached the point that the word 'Communist' has become [the object of] hate ... The [kulaks] slaughtered Communists with all their families and small children. In the villages a massive massacre of Communists is occurring."[42]

Considering the fact that this was happening several months after the decisive defeat of the Whites in Western Siberia, it suggests that anti-Soviet feelings were spontaneous, intense, and widespread. Moreover, these outbursts occurred despite Moscow's conscious attempt to move gradually to introduce many of its more controversial social measures. For instance, it nationalized only large industrial and business enterprises at first; not until the end of 1920 did those that employed as few as five workers also become affected. But these measures touched far fewer people and thus mattered much less than the Soviet agrarian program. The July 1920 *Sovnarkom* decree that fixed the grain procurement goal for Siberia at 163,800 tons did more than anything else to fan anti-Soviet sentiments.[43] The requisition was about a quarter of the total state plan and amounted to nearly half the projected Siberian harvest. It meant, among other things, that very little grain would be left over for moonshining (*samogon*), a widespread activity seen as a basic right in Siberia. Local officials were warned that peasants who did not cooperate in the production and delivery of surpluses, as well as all those responsible for supervising the process, would face the severest punishment, including "confiscation of property and imprisonment in concentration camps as traitors to the cause of the worker-peasant revolution."[44]

To enforce these measures, Moscow dispatched over 26,000 militant cadres from the hungriest regions of European Russia where, despite the most vigorous efforts, the total yield in bread grains during 1920–21 was still only about half of what it had been in 1916–17.[45] In addition, as if to punish Siberia for having been White for so long and for being so uncooperative in general, the introduction of the New Economic Policy (NEP) in March 1921, which would allow peasants greater freedom to market their produce, was deliberately delayed in Siberia.[46]

The substitution of the milder tax in kind (*prodnalog*) for requisitioning was put off until August and then was set at a higher rate, 20 to 30 per cent of gross harvest, compared with an average of 12 to 13 per cent in the Russian republic as a whole. Even after the introduction of NEP, these tactics continued: the grain procurement campaign of 1922 assigned an excessively burdensome 27 per cent of the total as Siberia's share. *Prodnalog*, nevertheless, did represent a significant easing of demands on Siberian peasants. The state took only 58 per cent of the amount of grain that had previously been requisitioned under *razverstka*.[47] For reasons of both accessibility and productivity, Altai *guberniia* continued to be hit with the highest impositions, which undoubtedly contributed to the tradition of peasant resistance there. In the middle of March 1922 Siberian peasants were delivering to Soviet authorities 1,260 million pounds of bread, 36 million pounds of meat, and 13 million pounds of butter. Siberia accounted for more than a quarter of all the grain produced in the Russian republic. Even local Bolshevik officials recognized that this excessive burdening of the Siberian peasantry had deeply alienated the mass of the population.[48]

In addition, the central authorities were slow to react in correcting the technical difficulties of transport and distribution. A local official in Omsk had sent a message dated 13 October 1920 that contained the following warning: "Lack of fuel on the Siberian Railway makes it impossible ... to fulfil the transshipment of foodstuffs according to the instructions of the centre." The report went on to urge that strict measures be taken by Moscow to provide emergency coal supplies to the Siberian railway on a level of priority "equal to front-line military transport."[49]

The problem with the Soviet grain policy was not only that the rural masses were unlikely to cooperate voluntarily but also that local party cadres were not provided with the means to enforce the will of the centre. Though the number of Communist cells increased, party work in both town and country remained weakly developed.[50] Under the circumstances, a resort to massive coercion in order to get the food-stuffs necessary to forestall the very real prospect of starving cities in the Russian heartland was predictable, even if paradoxically it was also creating conditions for the unprecedented catastrophe of the famine of 1921–22. The food crisis was a test that confronted each of the succeeding Russian central governments, from the imperial, through the Provisional, to the Soviet and the White. What was striking about the responses was their degree of continuity and similarity, suggesting that certain common and unalterable elements persisted. The impe-rial and Provisional governments introduced most of the coercive techniques that were subsequently adopted by both the soviets and Kolchak.

Nevertheless, while the process was cumulative and the underlying resentments of the peasantry against government controls and expro-priations had been building for generations, a new stage of estrange-ment was reached during the six particularly brutal and exhausting years of war and civil conflict. In 1920, with the removal of all serious White and foreign alternatives to Soviet power in Western Siberia, these popular antipathies had burst forth in a series of spontaneous insurrections in Tiumen', Omsk, and Altai *gubernii*. As even some Soviet officials conceded, the conflict with the Siberian peasantry were brought on principally by the government policies themselves. Because the issue was the survival of the regime, however, there could be no question of Moscow backing off, only how best to take what was needed from the countryside whatever the cost:

We had no choice but to break the alliance between the workers and the peasants, made during the October days ... in order to save the Socialist Revolution ... We know how we took the peasants' last seed materials but we had to do it ... Nobody doubts that all those outrages by the Soviet authorities, that all these mistakes in assessing how much grain to take engendered the hatred of the peasantry towards the Soviet regime, and their hatred was justified; the peasants were right to protest.[51]

In February peasant insurrectionists took control of seven districts in Tiumen' *guberniia*, four in Omsk, and one in Cheliabinsk.[52] Belatedly the message got through to Moscow that something had to be done to mollify the peasants, but the official response continued to be inadequate. Measures like the declaration of 6 March 1920 by *Sibrevkom* on the allotment and use of land, which liquidated all discriminatory tax distinctions among *starozhily*, *pereselentsy*, Cossacks, *inorodtsy*, and other groups, wiped out all tax arrears, and created a land fund for peasants who were landless or who had insufficient holdings from former church and court lands, were not enough to overcome popular aversion to Soviet collectivism.[53] Reliable units of the Red Army had to be brought in force, especially to Novonikolaevsk, to put down the rebellions.[54] The Western Siberian peasant uprisings, along with coincident disturbances in Tambov and Kronstadt, and Moscow's response to these challenges, redefined the nature of the Russian Civil War in this its last stage. If it was ever only or even mainly a conflict of landlords versus peasants and capital versus labour, the terms of reference by mid 1920 had changed significantly. During this phase, with the departure of many of the "former people" and the dispersal of the White officers to places as distant as California and Argentina, it became a struggle between the new Soviet order and all those (from whatever social categories) who refused to go along with the Bolsheviks. Moscow's last remaining adversary was the so-called kulak, a category of peasant defined by Lenin not so much on the basis of economic as of ideological criteria. In this final stage, with no White officers, bourgeoisie, or foreigners on the opposing side, the Red Army had to wage war against the Russian peasantry.

From May through July 1920, major rebellions occurred in Semipalatinsk and Tomsk *gubernii*; in Slavgorod district (*uezd*) alone there were at least 10,000 rebels.[55] By January 1921 popular uprisings were in progress in Kokchetav, Petropavlovsk, Ishim, and Tobol'sk. The participants were well-off, middle, and poor peasants, contrary to Soviet characterizations of their opposition in the countryside as exclusively "kulak-SR."[56] Among the more predictable consequences was a drastic reduction in grain production, as much as half in some places.[57] It was no accident, moreover, that armed opposition took the most serious form in the Altai, home of some of the strongest partisan detachments throughout 1919. Here veteran units under G.F. Rogov and I.P. Novoselov rose up in 1920 against the increasing constraints of the Soviet regimen. Rogov, in particular, enjoyed enormous personal prestige among his men for his bravery and earlier successes against the superior forces of Admiral Kolchak, as well as for his unauthoritarian style of command. In the eyes of the Cheka in Altai this, of course, made Rogov all the more dangerous.[58] He embodied an inflammatory and non-Marxist mixture of peasant populism with anarchism, and echoed an increasingly common theme – soviets free of Communist domination. Indeed, his message was remarkably similar to a declaration issued in Buzuluk on 14 July 1920 by A.P. Sapozhkov, which described the Communist party as unfit to govern and called for the election of free soviets, the abolition of the requisitioning brigades and the Cheka, and the declaration of free trade.[59]

Local Bolsheviks blamed the success of Rogov and Novoselov on fundamental mistakes in a policy that was formulated in Moscow with scant regard for or understanding of conditions in Siberia.[60] A telegram from Barnaul dated 11 April 1920 protested the negligence of *Sibrevkom* in permitting kulak elements to prosper, thus undermining the revolutionary alliance in the village and the authority of the party as the defender of the poor peasantry. "The almost unlimited permission for hiring labour and renting land ... facilitates the transformation of middle peasants into kulaks ... alienates from us the poorest part of the middle peasants and the poor peasants [themselves, and] strengthens the position of the Right SRs."[61] But it is unlikely that the socio-political configuration of Siberian villages could have been affected from Moscow by merely tactical adjustments. Nor were the peasants going to be fooled at this stage by promises of future benefits. They responded as they did to Novoselov and Rogov because they were finding the Red bosses to be no better than their White predecessors. Moreover, the defeat of the latter permitted all the fundamental differences between the partisans and the Bolsheviks to come out into the open.

The movement in the Altai had begun very modestly. At the end of April Rogov gathered about 200 men in his home village some seventy-five miles north-east of Barnaul. Just days later, at a meeting nearby, that number rose to 1,000 men, who then called for the abolition of all state authority. Soviet rule was described as being similar to that of Nicholas II, Kerensky, and Kolchak in its anti-democratic nature. The meeting ended with adoption of a battle cry, "Down with all forms of authority, whatever they may be. Hail anarchy – the mother of order."[62] A Federation of Altai Anarchists, with the explicit purpose of overthrowing Soviet power, had come into being. Fuelled by widespread hunger and by shortages that could be attributed directly to Soviet grain policies, and offering an attractive blend of populist ideology and down-home rhetoric, Rogov's May insurrection burst forth on a wave of popular support. But Moscow was now in a better position to respond, having eliminated Kolchak and, for the time being at least, facing a diminished military threat on the other fronts, which would permit redistributing scarce resources back to Western Siberia.[63] Still, Cheka agent I.P. Pavlunovskii proved to be unduly optimistic when he reported at the end of June that the insurrection "can be considered to be completely liquidated."[64]

Rogov, moreover, was only a small part of the problem. Flash points appeared in dozens of places throughout Siberia during the spring and summer of 1920. Secret intelligence reports serve to illustrate the extent and nature of the opposition: an agent in Irkutsk described continuing SR successes in recruiting both peasants and workers to their cause; from Omsk came word that "the peasants and workers understand poorly the structure of Soviet power"; in Semipalatinsk it was reported that the Kirghiz did not trust Soviet authorities, while Cossacks, kulaks, and the village intelligentsia were openly hostile; in Omsk evangelists and Doukhobors refused to recognize Soviet rule, while minority nationalities were forming new counter-revolutionary organizations. The general atmosphere was summarized by one agent in the following stark terms:

[It] has changed dramatically for the worse ... The attitude of the better-off peasants and the Kirghiz towards Soviet authority ... is universally hostile. In a majority of instances, the Cossacks are also hostile. Among the workers of the urban enterprises, factories, plants, railways and related institutions, the attitude towards Soviet authority is sympathetic, but in part unclear. There is hostility among a significant section of the population, in the towns as well as in the villages, towards the Communists.[65]

Even from radical Barnaul there were reports that peasants were refusing to cooperate with *razverstka* and were plotting to kill any Communists they could find; from Novonikolaevsk that popular opposition was growing because of the absence and expense of foodstuffs and other essentials, and because of the high-handedness of some Soviet officials; from Tomsk and Novonikolaevsk (Novosibirsk) that uprisings were anticipated at the end of September; again from Novonikolaevsk that some Cheka agents participated in the looting of government storehouses, while militia officers and other Soviet officials were engaged in "criminal behaviour ... every step of the way [*na kazhdom shagu*]."[66]

Despite these warnings, which, while not conclusive, were certainly indications of deep-seated popular alienation, the "kulak mutinies" of

1920–21 surprised almost everyone by their intensity, extent, and duration. That neither Moscow nor local Soviet authorities anticipated these developments may be inferred from the *Sibrevkom* resolution of 4 December 1920 that lifted martial law (*voennoe polozhenie*) for all of Siberia with the exception of parts of Irkutsk *guberniia*.[67] It seemed that Moscow was taken in by its own propaganda to believe that with the defeat of Kolchak and the withdrawal of the allies and the Czechs, the military threat to Soviet hegemony was over.

As we have seen, however, it was precisely as the White threat receded that the forces of local opposition "from below" began to organize. Now, under the leadership of the broadly based and strongly anti-Communist Siberian Peasant Union, tens of thousands of peasants rallied to the very same democratic principles the SRs had been unable to promote successfully during their brief time in power. According to Cheka agent Pavlunovskii, Altai *guberniia* was especially receptive to the Siberian Peasant Union recruiters. This may help explain why the Civil War blazed there for two more years after 1920.[68] The rebels called for "peasant dictatorship" and true "peoples' power." Specifically, the Union wanted to convene a Siberian constituent assembly to decide the issues of state power; in the meantime, all the land would be "put back in the hands of the people," which in this instance meant denationalization and an end to the policy of levelling.[69]

In the second half of 1920, local representatives of the Siberian Peasant Union were all over the place, organizing anti-Bolshevik resistance. In the Ishim *uezd* alone, peasant rebels may have numbered as many as 60,000, while smaller and less organized contingents fought against Soviet power in much of the area between Novonikolaevsk and the Urals. At the height of their success, in the first months of 1921, peasant insurgents controlled all or parts of Eniseisk, Tiumen', Omsk, and Cheliabinsk *gubernii*, reaching as far west as Agbasar and Akmolinsk.[70] Apart from their geographic scope, these uprisings were noteworthy for the fact that they brought together different nationalities that had not always cooperated in the past, Russian peasants, Kirghiz tribesmen, and Cossacks.[71]

The Western Siberian peasant insurrection was not an isolated phenomenon in Soviet Russia. A recent study of the Volga region describes similar developments and circumstances at roughly the same time. Peasant uprisings there were brought on by many of the same issues and espoused similar goals and concerns:

an intolerable increase in the tax burden on the rural economy as a result of the civil war; a sharp swing in the urban-rural terms of trade against the peasantry; and a process of political centralization, which undermined the influence of the peasants in the local soviets ... [T]he sabotage of the food requisitionings and the sporadic village riots of 1918–19 developed into the mass peasant wars of 1920–1 as the economic crisis deepened. The appearance of the "peasant armies" in the field awaited the final defeat of the Whites: because they supported the October revolution, the peasants dared not endanger the Bolshevik government until the counter-revolution had been defeated.[72]

From the perspective of Moscow, there was no credit earned for earlier services in defeating the common White enemy. And the present danger was the more serious because it came from below; it had to be liquidated ruthlessly as well as discredited. The Left SR I.N. Steinberg, who served briefly as commissar of justice in *Sovnarkom*, observed that the Bolsheviks resorted to terror in large part because of their sense of isolation in the vast peasant sea. The partisans rebelled against Soviet authority because they valued what the Bolsheviks were trying to take away from them, "the human rights they had just won: the rights to personal liberty, to free, creative labor, to individual responsibility. They sensed that the one-time *barin* [lord] and his knout were returning to the village in a new disguise ... [as] the 'proletarian state.'"[73] Peasants may not have been sure about what they wanted in every instance, but there is little reason to doubt that they were pretty clear about what they wished to avoid and about what constituted at any given time the greatest threat to their well-being. For most of the period between 1917 and 1920 a majority of Russian peasants, even in relatively affluent and remote Siberia, preferred the Reds over the Whites. But by 1921, at the latest, they were starting to change their collective mind.[74]

For the Whites it was, of course, too late. To be sure, among their most able field commanders and politicians some – Kappel' and Guins come to mind – may have understood the importance of appealing to the rural population, and especially of securing the support of the middle peasants with their natural preference for stable property relations and a market economy. But the Omsk leadership had shortsightedly "concerned [itself] almost exclusively with urban problems," where the advantages, both political and geographic, clearly resided with the Bolsheviks. Gajda had tried to convince Kolchak that this was a suicidal course because "no power will be able to do its job if the peasantry regards it as alien, as an authority [not] close to home."[75]

It may be said, however, that Lenin and the Bolsheviks proved Gajda wrong. Lenin was no romantic populist and harboured no illusions about the *narod*.[76] Moreover, he was never squeamish about using whatever force was necessary to neutralize opposition in the countryside and to impose discipline. "One of the last and most determined struggles which we shall conduct," he asserted, "is against the 'petty *bourgeois*' peasantry, because we have not conquered that 'petty *bourgeois*' anarchic element, and upon the victory over it immediately depends the destiny of the revolution in the very near future."[77] Siberian partisans – along with Kronstadt, the insurrections led by A.S. Antonov and N.I. Makhno, and other instances of peasant *stikhiinost'* – fell before that inexorable Leninist logic.

Moscow's response to peasant insurrections provided the first hints that the Bolshevik version of socialism was to be based upon a combination of coercive agricultural collectivization and intensified industrialization – what would come to be known under Stalin as the "Ural-Siberian Method" – and that peasant resistance would be smashed without compunction and with the active support of at least a portion of urban society. It became clear, moreover, that no genuine popular movement would be acceptable to the Bolsheviks. In fact, when in 1921 spontaneous disturbances threatened to spill over from one rural district to another and to involve soldiers or sailors (as in the case of the 15,000 armed men of Kronstadt), the Bolshevik response was not just mass repression but also a campaign of organized defamation and terror. Least of all was Lenin willing to tolerate challenges to his claim to represent the true proletarian and peasant democracy such as those that were evident in the Petropavlovsk Resolution adopted by the men of the battleship *Petropavlovsk* in Kronstadt on 28 February 1921. Among its demands were free elections to the soviets in order to ensure the representation of the will of the workers and the peasants; organizational freedom for all socialist parties as well as elimination of the Bolshevik political monopoly; trade unions and peasant unions operating without interference or dictates from above; political amnesty for all imprisoned socialists, workers, peasants, soldiers, and sailors; and full peasant control of the land and its produce, free from arbitrary government confiscations.[78]

For the Bolshevik winners, arguably the most important lessons of the Civil War experience were the utility of "mass terror as a means of socialist transformation in the countryside" and the applicability of military techniques to civilian life.[79] The specific cost of the five years of turmoil between 1917 and 1922 would be very difficult to measure even if the data about loss of property and life were fully available and reliable. According to standard Soviet sources, the Civil War in Siberia caused a total destruction of 24,724 peasant households, with another 36,724 partly damaged, and left 27,200 children orphaned.[80] For Russia as a whole those numbers must be multiplied many times over; and in the process over 12 million people died, roughly 8 per cent of the country's pre-revolutionary population.[81] Beyond the concrete losses, the principles of liberalism and regionalism suffered a total eclipse from which they have only begun to emerge after seven and a half decades.

PEASANT CHARACTERISTICS AND RED VICTORY

The scholarly convention, for both Western and Soviet historiography, has been to treat peasant wars and rebellions in general as negative, apolitical, and ephemeral, although recent nationalist and populist historiography in Russia has taken a much more sympathetic, indeed ardent, approach.[82] Among Western students of Russia, the anti-peasant prejudice has been especially strong, both because of Euro-centric terms of reference and because the Russian muzhiks, with their myriad superstitions and antediluvian ways, have done little to alter the worst of their misgivings. Of course, the key has been the nature and limits of the sources of information available in the West.

While Slavophile elements within the Russian intelligentsia have always tended to romanticize the common folk, Westernizers "looked upon the peasant as a first-class scoundrel, a thorough cheat, idler and drunkard, who would 'eat his own father in his porridge.'"[83] For them the muzhik's least endearing trait was a combination of petty materialism and reluctance to assume responsibility for his own situation. This in turn led him to resent even the slightest advantages enjoyed by his neighbour, but also prevented him from actively seeking ways to improve his own lot. His attitude toward authority was therefore ambiguous: he wanted it to do things for him, but not for others. Most of his energy was expended in deflecting attention from his own failings and building resentment against those he imagined to be better off than himself, including all outsiders, but especially Jews, Mongols, and other Orientals. One of novelist Ivan Bunin's characters suggests that these qualities went beyond the peasantry and were typically Russian: "[We] blame our neighbours instead of ourselves! The Tatars oppressed us, you see! We're a young nation, you see! Just as if, over there in Europe, all sorts of Mongols didn't oppress folks a lot, too! As if the Germans were any older than we are!"[84]

This refusal to assume responsibility for the situation in which one finds oneself was, of course, not unique to the Russians, but it may help explain why the Reds won the Civil War. If the Whites were too far removed from the peasants, and the Greens were too close, only the Reds combined an appealing vision of the future with coercive discipline in the present: they treated the peasants like children (in truth, the same could be said of the proletariat) and promised them security in return for complete subordination. It worked, if only in the short-term, because unlike the Whites they had no illusions about the muzhik's patriotism or loyalty, and unlike the partisans, they were not populists bound by democratic scruples.

Just as the Democratic Counter-Revolution may be seen to have degenerated into the Kolchak dictatorship by the fall of 1918, so too the partisan movement can be disparaged as a form of *atamanshchina*, especially after 1920. A more sympathetic – and balanced – picture, however, must reflect the spontaneous and democratic nature of a phenomenon which expressed the deep-rooted peasant belief that the Reds, Whites, and parties in between, neither really understood nor cared about their interests. A recent study has suggested that the major contenders in the Civil War "represented national politics [while] the peasants represented the pre-national identity and regional allegiance."[85]

The Bolsheviks, at least, made a point of avoiding the tired rhetoric of God and country that every peasant knew to be code words for the *status quo ante*. Instead they offered a vision of a brave new world that, while somewhat alien (especially for Siberia) and not widely understood, had the negative virtue of being untested. Its biggest selling point was in the contrast with White governments, which often appeared to take pride in the absence of any social policy and a staunch refusal even to address issues of primary importance for the countryside. The latter attitude was clearly reflected in the words of Ivan Mikhailov: "We don't have a program, and see no need for one. We do from day to day whatever is necessary."[86]

If the peasants generally accepted Soviet power only under extreme duress and never in its entirety, there were other former opponents who rallied to Moscow with genuine enthusiasm.[87] Several prominent White leaders from both civilian and military life came to the conclusion that it was their patriotic duty to accept the new political reality because a great Soviet Russia was better than a dismembered and fatally weakened country. Here was the ultimate irony: the Bolsheviks became the heirs of the Russian statist tradition that had always been the hallmark of their most intransigent enemies. Even some right-wing Russian intellectuals turned to Lenin at the end of the Civil War as a bulwark against the breakup of the state and the inchoate nihilism of the twentieth-century *pugachevshchina* that they believed threatened the Russian nation.[88]

Bolshevism's essentially urban, statist, centralist, and anti-peasant nature made the transition easier. The Soviet government emerged as the institution that could best co-opt the wild muzhik and resurrect the great Russian nation.[89] But the process itself, as Maxim Gorky predicted, might spell the end of civil society: "All that is finest in art and culture in Russia, all that has been built up with such pain and sacrifice, will ultimately be killed. The peasant is angry and revengeful for the wrongs he believes the city and city leaders have done against him and he would destroy the very life of the cities. He will revolt and throw the whole country into anarchy."[90] Indeed he did, and it is still not certain that Russia will ever fully recover.

Conclusion

What, if anything, could have changed the outcome of the Civil War in Siberia and Russia? Concerted Allied intervention in support of the Whites as advocated by Winston Churchill certainly was a necessary precondition, both for morale and *matériel*. As it was, virtually all the bullets fired by Kolchak's troops came from abroad (mainly from Britain), and the same was true for the rest of their ordnance and even for their uniforms.[1] It would also have required a more far-sighted leadership in Omsk, one that had a clearer understanding of the relationship between social policy and success in civil war and that was capable of acting decisively in the former arena no less than the latter to win support from the general population. The key prior condition was to recognize the revolutionary land transfers of 1917–18 in the countryside; otherwise the Whites could never hope to broaden their appeal and compete on an equal footing with the Reds. Lenin was prepared to make (if only temporarily) this non-Marxist concession to the peasantry, but the Whites vacillated and thus missed their historic opportunity.

A.V. Kolchak's ultimate failure as supreme ruler was more political than military. He never succeeded in getting his vision of a resurrected Great Russian state across to a sufficiently wide constituency. He believed incorrectly that it would be enough to stigmatize the Bolsheviks as unpatriotic for public support to rally to his banners. Kolchak, and the White leadership generally, did not take into account adequately the underdeveloped nature of political culture in Russia and the Bolshevik capacity to co-opt the resentment, anger, and anarchism of the "dark" masses. In addition, the admiral's inability and unwillingness to appreciate the regional distinctions of Siberia or of its people dissipated the significant initial political advantage that he enjoyed in the fall of 1918; whether that advantage could have been translated into a broadly-based anti-Bolshevik alliance of all the contending forces in the region is less clear, but his government never made a consistent attempt to do so. Instead, the supreme ruler mistook rhetoric and symbols for substance, an illusion the Siberian peasants rejected. Kolchak's idea of leadership too often consisted of little more than repeating the tired and discredited God-and-Country slogans of the imperial past while ascribing all that was wrong to his enemies on the left.

Even if all or most of the internal political and administrative problems could have been resolved by superior leadership in Omsk, however, the Whites still would have had to overcome several objective advantages of the enemy. Among these was the fact that the Reds occupied the densely populated geographic centre, the old Muscovite state that included the main industrial and agricultural zones of the country, while the Whites were spread around the periphery in lands that were either thinly populated and remote (like Siberia) or non-Russian (as in the south and parts of the north-west). Given the obvious demographic disadvantages of his location, Kolchak's initial successes were all the more impressive.[2] They were a testament to the relatively small number of effective and skilled combatants on both sides during the first year of the Russian Civil War.[3] In the early goings, as the Czechoslovak Legion demonstrated, a few thousand veteran soldiers could dominate the vast eastern reaches of the country. Indeed, even as late as the middle of 1919, when the Red Army had swollen, on paper at least, to more than two million men, disease and mass desertions so riddled their ranks that the difference between defeat and victory might have been a few tough and well-placed regiments around Kazan.[4] If the spring 1919 offensive of the Whites from Siberia had been delayed or extended to coincide better with the fall campaigns of Denikin and Iudenich, the month of October might well have witnessed a three-pronged (instead of just two, from the south and north-west) and decisive assault on the Soviet heartland.

As we have seen, numerical superiority by itself or even in combination with ethnic homogeneity was no guarantee of military success. In Siberia, by contrast to central Russia, the comparative number of combatants until mid 1919 generally favoured the Whites; thus, at the time of the critical April campaign there were only 80,000 Soviet troops facing a considerably larger White force.[5] Other factors, notably morale and supplies, seemed to favour the Red Army, however. This was the judgement of several independent observers, including U.S. Ambassador Morris, who added that he could "personally confirm the fact that captured Bolshevik soldiers are well fed and on the whole well clothed; they are arrogant in their confidence and profess their communistic faith with almost religious zeal."[6]

It is commonplace to recognize that the Bolshevik organization was closer in many ways to a military machine than to a conventional political party, and thus that it enjoyed a distinct advantage over an *ancien régime* or a parliamentary democratic government in making war, whether external or internal. Lenin's determined leadership provided the direction, dedication, and discipline that were so manifestly absent from both White military and civil ranks. M.V. Frunze did not overstate the case: "If you take the whole life of the Red Army from its beginning ... you will see that an outstanding role has been played by our political organs. This was and is the factor sharply differentiating the Red Army from the [other] armies."[7] By contrast, the divisions and often competing nature of civil authority on the scattered White territories constituted major impediments to the unity of the anti-Soviet forces and virtually guaranteed the demise of the Democratic Counter-Revolution of 1918 in favour of military dictatorship as the only realistic response to the Red threat. This development lent support to the Bolshevik depiction of the White cause, which, in fact, always encompassed a broad range of political philosophies, as a façade for restoring the old order. The credibility of the White movement increasingly depended on military success, which in turn required total mobilization of both society and the economy; this was understood too late, if ever, by the ruling camarilla in Omsk.

On the subject of Kolchak's leadership, G.M. Semenov may have been closer to the truth than the admiral's critics from the left, however, when he argued that the major reason for the failure of the supreme ruler was a lack, rather than an excess, of dictatorial capacity. Far from being a right-wing version of Lenin and Trotsky, Kolchak was "very soft and subject to the influence of surrounding conditions and personalities."[8] In their more candid moments, even an Omsk official like Minister of Lands N.I. Petrov came to a similar conclusion: "There [among the Reds] all elements are subordinated to one dominant idea, one will. Here everyone acts on the basis of his own desire and at his own risk."[9]

In Trotsky and Lenin the Reds had leaders who understood that victory in the Civil War necessitated not only strict and ruthless military discipline, flexibility in adapting to changing conditions and exigencies (including a selective use of officers from the old imperial forces), and a regular mass army, but also a political program that met the chief demands of the workers and poor peasants. The latter meant temporary concessions in the countryside to reassure the "rural proletariat" that under Red rule they would be permitted to keep the land they had recently appropriated, as well as massive propaganda depicting the Whites as restorers of the property rights of landlords. It also helped that the Bolsheviks (unlike the Mensheviks) were not unduly burdened by prior ideological strictures that otherwise might have prevented them from baldly co-opting the (recently) reviled land program of the populist Socialist Revolutionaries.

Even at the very end of the Civil War, however, the difference between victory and defeat was very small. Armed resistance continued in several parts of Siberia until the mid-1920s – long after the dispersal of the White forces – and the peasantry as a whole was even then not reconciled to Soviet power. But the Red Army did finally establish effective control over Siberia as part of its general campaign of sustained aggression against the recalcitrant Russian countryside.[10] Victory came at unprecedented cost – both immediately in the form of the calamitous famine of 1921 and in the long-term in the retardation of the development of a pluralistic political culture. It remains a moot point whether, after centuries of autocracy, the numerous factions of the Constituent Assembly could have set aside their differences in order to create a viable constitution, even if Lenin had not cut short their proceedings as he did in January 1918. The failure to achieve parliamentary democracy and a stable market economy in the years immediately following 1917 makes the task at the end of the twentieth century all the more formidable.

As recently as a decade ago almost no one imagined that A.V. Kolchak would become a hero in Russia itself.[11] The land-locked admiral who lost Siberia to the Reds has been the subject recently of several hagiographic reviews, especially in the popular conservative-nationalist press.[12] Nothing could be a better indication of the total reversal in values and judgements since 1985 than that Kolchak, portrayed for decades as the worst of the White bandits, is now depicted as the gallant and chivalrous knight who died a martyr-patriot, fulfilling his officer's oath to a great and restored *rodina* (homeland). The truth, once again, lies somewhere between the two extremes.

Notes

1 These include Bubnov et al., *Grazhdanskaia voina 1918–1921*; Piontov-skii, *Grazhdanskaia voina v Rossii*; and Maksakov and Turunov, *Khronika grazhdanskoi voiny v Sibiri*.
2 For a summary, see my "Soviet Historiography of the Civil War in Siberia," 38–51.
3 The notorious exchange of insults and recriminations between A.F. Kerensky and P.N. Miliukov is merely the best known of many similar incidents.
4 In this regard, see *Sibirskie ogni* (Novosibirsk) and the new serial, *Russkoe proshloe* (St Petersburg).
5 White, *The Siberian Intervention*; Carley, *Revolution and Intervention*; Morley, *The Japanese Thrust into Siberia*; Ullman, *Britain and the Russian Civil War*; Unterberger, *American Intervention in the Siberian Civil War*; Bradley, *Allied Intervention in Russia*; Kettle, *The Road to Intervention, March–November 1918*; and MacLaren, *Canadians in Russia, 1918–1919*.
6 Koenker et al., *Party, State, and Society in the Russian Civil War*; Pipes, *The Russian Revolution*; and Debo, *Survival and Consolidation*. An important exception to the centralist focus is Raleigh's *Revolution on the Volga*.
7 A good example is Snow, *The Bolsheviks in Siberia*.
8 Connaughton's book on Admiral Kolchak, *The Republic of the Ushakova*, is particularly superficial and derivative in nature. Bobrick, *East of the Sun* is a broad popular history of Siberia which makes extensive use of recent scholarship in English; chapter 15 is a survey of the Civil War

period. Collins and Smele, *Kolchak i Sibir'*, contains important original documents with solid scholarly annotations and background materials, but it is not a monographic study.

9 Recent British contributions include Collins, *Siberia and the Soviet Far East*; Mawdsley, *The Russian Civil War*; and Wood, *The History of Siberia*. Footman's earlier works were *Civil War in Russia*; *Siberian Partisans in the Civil War*; *The Last Days of Kolchak*; and *The Red Army on the Eastern Front*. Among the Americans, the most important volumes are the two by Kenez, *Civil War in South Russia, 1918* and *Civil War in South Russia, 1919–1920*. Lincoln's *Red Victory* provides an excellent overview.

10 One of the most readable and reliable of the émigré memoirs is Dotsenko, *The Struggle for a Democracy in Siberia*.

11 V. Brovkin, D. Foglesong, Y. Kotsonis, J. Long, M. Melancon, D. Raleigh, J. Smele, and M. Von Hagen are among those doing the most interesting new work.

12 See especially V.I. Shishkin on Siberia during the period of the Civil War and V.G. Bortnevskii on the White movement generally.

13 Brovkin "Identity, Allegiance and Participation in the Russian Civil War," 541–67.

14 The term soviet refers simultaneously to the councils of workers, soldiers, and, later, peasants that appeared during the 1905 Revolution and really became important after February 1917, as well as to the hierarchy of elected government bodies in Soviet Russia. After 1917 the term was often also used interchangeably (if not always accurately) with the Communist party and the Bolsheviks.

CHAPTER ONE

1 In some accounts the Russian Far East is not considered to be a part of Siberia, but the more comprehensive definition here follows the useage in *Entsiklopedicheskii slovar'*, 58:748–814.

2 This physical description of Siberia is taken in large part from Gibson, "Paradoxical Perceptions of Siberia," 67–93.

3 The Cossacks were a warrior caste of free Russian and Ukrainian rural residents who won privileges and land along the frontiers of the expanding Russian empire in exchange for military service. Unlike the peasants, they never experienced serfdom, and even to the extent that they were part of the communal land tenure system they were not subject to quit-rent (*obrok*), corvée (*barshchina*), or land redemption payments. Most importantly, Cossacks were exempt from the *podushnaia podat'* (soul tax or capitation). This was widely seen as a fundamental distinction between the quasi-bourgeois Cossacks and the poor peasants. See McNeal, *Tsar and Cossack, 1855–1914*, 7ff.

4 Iadrintsev, *Sibirskie inorodtsy, ikh byt' i sovremennoe polozhenie.*

5 Forsyth, "The Siberian native peoples before and after the Russian conquest," 71. Also Turchaninov, "Naselenie aziatskoi Rossii," 64–92.

6 Gibson, "Paradoxical Perceptions of Siberia," 85.

7 Okladnikov and Shunkov, *Istoriia Sibiri,* 2:127–31.

8 Raeff, *Michael Speransky.*

9 Mohrenschildt, *Toward a United States of Russia,* 90.

10 Treadgold, *The Great Siberian Migration.* Also Marks, *Road to Power.*

11 Poppe, "The Economic and Cultural Development of Siberia," 141.

12 Okladnikov and Shunkov, *Istoriia Sibiri,* 3:173–211.

13 Macey, *Government and Peasant in Russia, 1861–1906,* 87–9. Also Goryushkin, "Migration, settlement and the rural economy of Siberia, 1861–1914," 140–57.

14 Golovachev, "Chastnoe zemlevladenie v Sibiri," 134. There may have been another 140,000 peasants living on imperial or crown lands.

15 Kerner, *The Urge to the Sea.*

16 Levin and Potapov, *The Peoples of Siberia,* 139; Kaufman, *Pereselenie i kolonizatsiia,* 183; and Alferov, *Krest'ianstvo Sibiri v 1917 godu,* 3.

17 This had been foreseen by S.S. Shashkov (1841–82) who believed that the main issue in Siberian history was the struggle between the Russians and the *inorodtsy,* with the latter doomed to absorption and extinction. Mirzoev, *Istoriografiia Sibiri,* 334–5.

18 Poppe, "The Economic and Cultural Development of Siberia," 144–5.

19 In Canada over the same period the rise was roughly comparable to Siberia and also mainly due to immigration.

20 Poppe, "The Economic and Cultural Development of Siberia," 145. Also Serebrennikov, "Eastern Siberia."

21 1 *desiatina* equals 2.7 acres. Gushchin, *Sibirskaia derevnia na puti k sotsializmu,* 29. Also Goriushkin, *Sibirskoe krest'ianstvo na rubezhe dvukh vekov,* 272.

22 Herzen, *Childhood, Youth and Exile,* 222.

23 Goriushkin, *Agrarnye otnosheniia v Sibiri perioda imperializma (1900–1917 gg.).*

24 HIA, Serebrennikov, "Eastern Siberia."

25 Goriushkin, *Sotsial'no-ekonomicheskie predposylki sotsialisticheskoi revoliutsii v sibirskoi derevne,* 56.

26 Tiukavkin, *Sibirskaia derevnia nakanune oktiabria,* 365, 378.

27 *Osobennosti agrarnogo stroia Rossii v period imperializma,* 175.

28 HIA, Serebrennikov, "Eastern Siberia."

29 Baikalov, "Siberia since 1894," 338.

30 Snow, *The Bolsheviks in Siberia, 1917–1918,* 24–5.

31 El'sukova, "Krest'ianskie vosstaniia v zapadnoi Sibiri osen'iu 1918 goda," 48. Also Baikalov, "Siberia since 1894," 332–3.

32 Glink, *Aziatskaia Rossiia*, 1:258; Tiukavkin, *Sibirskaia derevnia*, 340.

33 Quoted in Aristov, "Zhizn' Athanasiia Prokof'evicha Shchapova," 310.

34 Iadrintsev, *Sibir' kak koloniia v geograficheskom, etnograficheskom, i istoricheskom otnoshenii*. Also Svatikov, *Rossiia i Sibir'*, 51–3.

35 Poppe, "The Economic and Cultural Development of Siberia," 140–2, puts the percentages even higher.

36 Okladnikov and Shunkov, *Istoriia Sibiri*, 3:219.

37 Nikolai Mikhailovich Iadrintsev was an accomplished archaeologist and ethnographer. He was arrested in 1865 for his regionalist agitations and writings and spent nine years in jail and exile. Subsequently he became Siberia's leading populist muckraker through the newspaper *Vostochnoe obozrenie* (*Eastern Review*), in which he criticized the Russian central government's policies towards Siberia, especially its one-sided, colonial exploitation of the region's land and resources. Another leading journal of the regionalists was *Sibirskaia gazeta* (*Siberian Newspaper*) in Tomsk.

Grigorii Nikolaevich Potanin was an explorer, ethnographer, and folklorist who dedicated his long life to the study of Siberia and central Asia. He attended a military secondary school in Omsk, followed by five years of active duty in provincial Siberia. During 1859–61 he was enrolled at St Petersburg University, where he was very active in student political life. Potanin's studies were interrupted by his arrest for participation in revolutionary activity and consequent exile to Siberia. Not until 1874 was he again free to resume his normal life and career. During the next few years Potanin visited several remote and little-known parts of Siberia where he gathered valuable information about the flora and fauna of the region. He also made significant contributions to the knowledge of the Turkic- and Mongol-speaking peoples of Siberia, and of others in central Asia. He was among the first Russians to acknowledge the latter as positive influences upon Russian culture. In later life Potanin became a universally respected elder statesman who was seen by many as the greatest living symbol of Siberia's struggle for recognition and respect.

38 Just the opposite view, however, prevailed in some radical circles. For instance, Gertsen [Herzen], *Sobranie sochinenii*, 8:256–7, believed that "the Siberian People are healthy, well-formed, intelligent, and extremely positive."

39 Quoted in Gibson, "Paradoxical Perceptions of Siberia," 69.

40 Lemke, *Nikolai Mikhailovich Iadrintsev*, 34–5.

41 Quoted in Mohrenschildt, *Toward a United States of Russia*, 95. Bassin, "A Russian Mississippi?," 186, confirms "the close affinity which developed in Russia in the [mid-nineteenth century] ... toward the United States."

42 Kropotkin, *Memoirs of a Revolutionist*, 184.

43 According to Lemke, *Iadrintsev*, 53–5, Iadrintsev was among those who saw the futures of Siberia and North America as linked.

44 Even Iadrintsev was in his own way a Russian nationalist, as was evident in his views on the desirability of proselytizing for Russian Orthodoxy in Mongolia and Central Asia. See Glinskii, "Nikolai Mikhailovich Iadrintsev," 447.

45 Treadgold, *The Great Siberian Migration*, 21.

46 Nevertheles, Sesiunina, *G.N. Potanin i N.M. Iadrintsev – ideologi sibirskogo oblastnichestva*, 40–1, argues that both the authorities and subsequent scholarship have exaggerated the radicalism of the demands made by the Siberian regionalists.

47 Quoted in Mohrenschildt, *Toward a United States of Russia*, 104.

48 See Wood, "Administrative Exile and the Criminals' Commune in Siberia," 395–414.

49 Mirzoev, *Istoriografiia Sibiri*, 298.

50 Quoted in Mohrenschildt, *Toward a United States of Russia*, 85.

51 Quoted in Shilovskii, *Sibirskie oblastniki v obshchestvenno-politicheskom dvizhenii v kontse 50kh–60kh godakh XIX veka*, 78. This statement and others made by leading regionalists may have been influenced by Old Believers' communities in Siberia. The latter were models of local self-determination, numbered among the most independent and prosperous in Siberia and the north, did the most to retain traditional Russian folk-ways, and had higher educational and cultural levels than other Russian peasant communities. They also steadfastly stood apart from the political dialogue and had their own reasons for being hostile to the central government.

52 Orshanskii, *Issledovaniia po russkomu pravu obychnomu i brachnomu*, 129, commented that "every peasant looks upon himself primarily and before all else as a member of the *mir* [peasant commune], and [only] then as an independent person." Also Channon, "Regional Variation in the Commune: The Case of Siberia," 66–85.

53 According to Mohrenschildt, *Toward a United States of Russia*, 97, many of these ideas orginated with A.P. Shchapov.

54 BAR, Golovachev, "Rapport du Professeur Golovatchoff." Also Potanin, *Oblastnicheskaia tendentsiia v Sibiri*, 11. Iadrintsev was of a similar mind in stressing "the idea of conscious service [by the Siberian intelligentsia] to the region." Quoted in Lemke, *Iadrintsev*, 34.

55 Shanin, *Russia as a "Developing Society"*, 2:203, suggests that "ethnic divisions have often proven in Russia as significant as class conflict, or more so, in the defining of political camps."

56 As Potanin put it, "The basis of the Siberian idea is purely territorial." Potanin, "Nikolai Mikhailovich Iadrintsev. Nekrolog," 171.

57 Serebrennikov "The Siberian Autonomous Movement and its Future," 406; Sesiunina, "K voprosu ob evoliutsii sibirskogo oblastnichestva (70-e – nachalo 90-kh godov XIX v.)," 99.

58 In 1875 Siberia's first important regional newspaper was founded in Irkutsk by V.I. Vagin and M.V. Zagoskin under the title *Sibir'* with about 600 subscribers. In its very first issue, the editorial staff identified regional economic development as the top priority. See *Sibir'*, no. 1 (1875); also Potanin, "Iz istorii provintsial'noi pressy," 31. Iadrintsev wrote over a dozen articles that appeared on its pages over the next five years, mostly on the topics of exile, social conditions, and Siberian autonomy and self-sufficiency.

59 The admiration among Siberians for entrepreneurial achievement was evidently well established. "Merchants, in particular, seem to be more esteemed here. For while they are regarded as nothing in Russia, where everyone is judged according to military rank ... they are valued in Siberia all the more as there are here fewer people of military station and of rank, and one sees people esteemed more according to the size of their real estate and capital than according to their character, rank, and title." From *The Journey of Hans Jakob Fries, 1774–1776*, as quoted in Gibson, "Paradoxical Perceptions of Siberia," 88.

60 Iadrintsev, "K moei avtobiografii," 166.

61 While many of the political deportees subsequently made significant contributions to raising the region's cultural level, that was not generally the case for the others who only added to the large number of brigands and sociopaths wandering about rural Siberia. Not until the legislation of 10 June 1900 would the routine exiling of criminals to Siberia be terminated. See Wood, "Russia's 'Wild East': Exile, Vagrancy and Crime in Nineteenth-Century Siberia," 118–20.

62 A more centralist and statist orientation reasserted itself shortly after *Vostochnoe obozrenie* moved its base of operation to Irkutsk in 1888. This paradox can be explained by the fact that in St Petersburg the Iadrintsevs and other regionalists were actually more influential on the editorial board, while in Irkutsk the paper was run by younger men who were more Eurocentric.

63 As Quoted in Lemke, *Iadrintsev*, 134.

64 Quoted in Svatikov, *Rossiia i Sibir'*, 89.

65 Iadrintsev, "Nachalo pechati v Sibiri," 380. This was also the conclusion of Potanin, "Goroda Sibiri," 234.

66 Guins, "Impressions of the Russian Imperial Government," 91–2. Guins was a professor of Law at Tomsk University, a moderate regionalist, and a major player in all the White Siberian administrations. He also wrote several books, most importantly *Sibir', soiuzniki, i Kolchak*.

67 *Sibir'* (1877), nos. 20–21:2.

68 Iadrintsev, *Sibir' kak koloniia*, 64–5. Similar observations had been made earlier by the Decembrists, Herzen, Bakunin, and other members of the radical Russian intelligentsia.

69 Gushchin, *Sibirskaia derevnia*, 62–4.

70 USNARS, RG 165, MID 164–313, "Report from the Military Attache of the French Embassy to Japan" (20 May 1919): 25.

71 Baikalov, "Siberia since 1894," 335–6; Snow, *The Bolsheviks in Siberia*, 27–8.

72 Pares, *My Russian Memoirs*, 522. Also see his "Political Conditions in Western Siberia."

73 Ackerman, *Trailing the Bolsheviki*, 270.

74 Wood, "Russia's 'Wild East,'" 129–30: "It was the exile system itself which contributed more than anything else to the lawlessness from which Siberia suffered and which helped to create the territory's 'Wild East' image."

75 Iurasova, *Omsk: ocherki istorii goroda*, 110–13.

76 Snow, *Bolsheviks in Siberia*, 23; Levin and Potapov, *Peoples*, 193–4.

77 Svatikov, *Rossiia i Sibir'*, 115–16.

78 Figes, *Peasant Russia, Civil War*, 23.

CHAPTER TWO

1 The Second Irkutsk Provincial Peasant Congress met in August and took this position. Maksakov and Turunov, *Khronika grazhdanskoi voiny v Sibiri (1917–1918)*, 43.

2 Golovachev, "Siberian Movement and Communism," 93.

3 The Russian Social Democratic Workers' Party – in Russian the initials are RSDRP – split at its Second Congress in 1903 into two wings, the Majoritists (Bolsheviks) and Minoritists (Mensheviks). Each of the two factions had subgroups, although these were much less prominent within the former, especially after 1917. From the beginning, the dominant figure among the Bolsheviks was V.I. Lenin, whose singular political style, which combined a quasi-military chain of command and organizational discipline with total dedication to revolutionary politics, set his faction apart from not only the more moderate and parliamentary Mensheviks (who in many ways resembled the German Social Democratic Party) but also every other political party in existence. Schapiro, *The Origin of the Communist Autocracy*, 77–9.

4 "Soveshchanie predstavitelei sotsial-demokraticheskikh organizatsii gorodov zapadnoi Sibiri" (25 March 1917) in Cherniak, *Politicheskie partii v Sibiri*, 13. This was modified somewhat in the following month at a meeting in Krasnoiarsk (presumably under the influence of radical local Bolsheviks) to the effect that cooperation with the PSR was only

possible if the latter accepted the *RSDRP*'s definition of a minimal program. See "Soveshchanie predstavitelei pravdistskikh grupp *RSDRP* eniseiskoi gubernii" (10–13 April 1917) in ibid., 29.

5 In some parts of Eastern Siberia they also included Kadets. Morley, "The Russian Revolution in the Amur Basin," 454.

6 Keep, *The Russian Revolution*, 91. Also Snow, *The Bolsheviks in Siberia, 1917–1918*, 127–9, shows that many of the same people were active in both the public safety committees and the soviets.

7 Goriushkin et al., *Krest'ianskoe dvizhenie v Sibiri 1914–1917*, 132.

8 Kosykh, *S"ezdy, konferentsii i soveshchaniia*, 126. Also Goriushkin et al., *Krest'ianskoe dvizhenie v Sibiri 1914–1917*, 156–60.

9 Raleigh, *Revolution on the Volga*, 266–7, shows that in Saratov the soviet was consistently more Bolshevik than its Petrograd counterpart, and completely overshadowed the local municipal equivalent of the Provisional Government after February. The closest parallel in Siberia was Krasnoiarsk, but even it was less revolutionary.

10 This was entirely consistent with the position of the *PSR* which continued to call for "All Power to the Constituent Assembly." See "Soveshchanie Eserov tomskoi gubernii" (14 January 1918) in Cherniak, *Politicheskie partii*, 125.

11 Soviet studies such as Shornikov, *Bol'sheviki Sibiri v bor'be za pobedu oktiabr'skoi revoliutsii*, tend to exaggerate the general importance of the Bolsheviks in Krasnoiarsk, and in particular the Siberian Regional Bureau of the *RSDRP*(b) which was formed at the end of March 1917. The reality was that many Siberian Bolsheviks ignored the militant Leninist strictures of this body.

12 Snow, *Bolsheviks in Siberia*, 74.

13 Kadet or *KD* are transliterations of Russian acronyms for the Constitutional Democratic Party, also known as the Party of the People's Freedom.

14 Iurasova, *Omsk: ocherki istorii goroda*, 120–7.

15 For a statement of Siberian Menshevik "defencism," see "Rasshirennoe sobranie Sotsial-Demokratov Chity i Dal'nego Vostoka" (3–4 April 1917) in Cherniak, *Politicheskie partii*, 15–6.

16 For the Siberian *SR* position on Zimmerwaldism, see "Novonikolaevskaia gorodskaia konferentsiia Partii Sotsialistov-Revoliutsionerov" (14 May 1917) in ibid., 37.

17 Raleigh, *Revolution on the Volga*, 116, notes that before the Revolution in Saratov, "local Bolsheviks stood very close to other socialists on most tactical matters." But cooperation broke down immediately after March 1917, while in Siberia it lasted several months longer. In the Caucasus the pattern resembled Siberia's. According to King, "Sergei Kirov and the Struggle for Soviet Power in the Terek Region, 1917–1918," 197,

the Vladikavkaz Bolsheviks continued to follow a "tactically cautious revolutionary policy well after the Bolshevik seizure of power in Petrograd." No less a figure than S.M. Kirov had supported the idea of "a united Social Democratic Party in Vladikavkaz until October 1917, when the First Caucasus Regional Congress of Bolsheviks ordered all local organizations to split with the Mensheviks" (ibid., 259). Also Kuchiev, *Oktiabr' i sovety na Tereke (1917–1918 gg.)*, 96–7.

18 Quoted in Gill, *Peasants and Government in the Russian Revolution*, 49.

19 Keep, *The Russian Revolution*, 257.

20 "Obshchesibirskii s"ezd partii 'Narodnoi Svobody'" (30 April-2 May 1917) in Cherniak, *Politicheskie partii*, 34–5.

21 HIA, Serebrennikov, "The Siberian Autonomous Movement and its Future," 9.

22 Ibid., 14. In its contemporary Russian usage the term democracy embraced the idea of Western parliamentary systems and assumed the participation of centre-left parties that accepted due process of law and political pluralism, thereby generally excluding the Bolsheviks on the left and everyone from the Kadets rightward.

23 *Vol'naia Sibir'*, no. 1 (14 January 1918): 1.

24 Spirin, *Klassy i partii v grazhdanskoi voine v Rossii*, 93–6.

25 Maksakov and Turunov, *Khronika*, 45.

26 Raleigh, *Revolution on the Volga*, 120.

27 Figes, *Peasant Russia, Civil War*, 35. Also Polner, *Russian Local Government*, 289–90.

28 Keep, "October in the Provinces," 191. For comparison see Rabinowitch, *The Bolsheviks Come to Power*.

29 Quoted in Gill, *Peasants*, 89. Raleigh, *Revolution on the Volga*, 182–3, makes it clear that peasants in Saratov were not so easily satisfied. They prevailed upon a provincial soviet congress to redistribute land immediately, before the convocation of the Constituent Assembly. Keep, *The Russian Revolution*, 176, notes that the 25 May Petrograd resolution had the secret support of Chernov.

30 Gill, *Peasants*, 159. Also see Figes, *Peasant Russia, Civil War*, 46–7.

31 For comparisons see Raleigh, *Revolution on the Volga*, 189–90.

32 Goriushkin et al., *Krest'ianskoe dvizhenie v Sibiri 1914–1917*, 82–91.

33 Rosenberg, *Liberals in the Russian Revolution*, 384.

34 Quoted in Radkey, *The Sickle under the Hammer*, 93.

35 BAR, Golovachev, "Siberian Movement and Communism," 96.

36 Dumova, *Kadetskaia kontrrevoliutsiia i ee razgrom*, 25.

37 Mawdsley, *The Russian Civil War*, 62–3.

38 Radkey, *The Sickle under the Hammer*, 469.

39 Vladimirova, *God sluzhby 'sotsialistov' kapitalistam*, 95.

40 Guins, *Sibir'*, 1:55, noted the close ties between the veterans and the Bolsheviks. A factor which contributed to the radicalizing of the soldiers in particular, beginning early in the spring of 1917 and culminating with the June offensive, was the threat of being sent back to the front.

41 Alferov, *Krest'ianstvo Sibiri v 1917 godu*, 32–4.

42 "Chastnoe soveshchanie Bol'shevikov-Pravdistov g. Krasnoiarska" (26 May 1917) in Cherniak, *Politicheskie partii*, 43.

43 "Irkutskaia gubernskaia konferentsiia RSDRP" (20–21 July 1917) in ibid., 55–6. Also Zykova, *S"ezdy, konferentsii i soveshchaniia*, 64.

44 "I-ia zabaikal'skaia oblastnaia konferentsiia RSDRP" (11–13 July 1917) in Cherniak, *Politicheskie partii*, 49.

45 "Sobranie aktiva Bol'shevistkikh grupp irkutskoi gubernii" (8 October 1917) in ibid., 112.

46 Shumiatskii, *Sibir' na putiakh k oktiabriu*, 77–9; also Maksakov and Turunov, *Khronika*, 4–6, 46.

47 Keep, "October in the Provinces," 189.

48 Snow, *Bolsheviks in Siberia 1917–1918*, 34.

49 Vegman, *Profsoiuzy Sibiri v bor'be za vlast' sovetov*, 22.

50 Quoted in Bunyan and Fisher, *The Bolshevik Revolution, 1917–1918*, 670.

51 Tyrkova-Williams, *From Liberty to Brest-Litovsk*, 295.

52 Ouspensky, *Letters from Russia, 1919*, 37.

53 Quoted in Goriushkin et al., *Krest'ianskoe dvizhenie v Sibiri 1914–1917*, 211–12.

54 Vilenskii-Sibiriakov, *Bor'ba za sovetskuiu Sibir'*, 3–4.

55 *Tsentrosibir'* should not be confused with the similar sounding All-Siberian Executive Bureau of the RSDRP(b) cited earlier in this chapter. See Maksakov and Turunov, *Khronika*, 46–7.

56 Vegman, "Kak i pochemu pala v 1918 g. Sovetskaia vlast' v Tomske," 128. Also *Sibirskaia zhizn'*, no. 217 (6 October 1917): 2.

57 Dedenev, "Bol'shevistskie organizatsii Sibiri," 38, states that in the general population of Siberia, the Bolsheviks only got 10 per cent of the vote to Constituent Assembly, but they did somewhat better than that among the poor peasantry.

58 Radkey, *The Elections to the Russian Constituent Assembly of 1917*, 42ff.

59 This prophetic statement was made on 6 January 1918. Lenin, *Polnoe sobranie sochinenii*, 35: 240–2.

60 Leikina, "Oktiabr' po Rossii," 217–29.

61 Maksakov and Turunov, *Khronika*, 57. Also Sokolov, "Oktiabr' za Baikalom," 389–91; and Snow, "The Russian Revolution of 1917–1918 in Transbaikalia," 208–12.

62 Reikhberg, "Bol'sheviki Dal'nego Vostoka," 77–8. At the end of December in Khabarovsk the Third Congress of Far Eastern Soviets proclaimed

Dalsovnarkom (Far Eastern Council of People's Commissars) as the government of the entire Russian Far East. See Stephan, *The Russian Far East*, 114–15.

63 Keep, "October in the Provinces," 211, noted that "the anti-Bolshevik forces in particular seemed to suffer from a curious paralysis of the will."

64 Iurasova, *Omsk*, 130–2.

65 The point here is that nationalization implied that the land was not being given permanently to the peasantry for their individual exploitation and tenure, as many peasants believed and as advocated by the PSR.

66 Bunyan, *The Bolshevik Revolution, 1917–1918*, 377–8; and Pershin, *Agrarnaia revoliutsiia v Rossii*, 2:36–9. Macey, *Government and Peasant in Russia*, 195, notes that as early as 1906, populists were calling for the expropriation of all private, state, and church lands that were not being personally cultivated into a national fund for peasants who would work it with their own labour; compensation to the landowners was to be paid by the state, not the peasantry.

67 Spirin, *Klassy i partii*, 77. These figures and their significance have been challenged by Bernshtam, "Storony v grazhdanskoi voine 1917–1922 gg.," 281ff.

68 Gushchin, *Sibirskaia derevnia na puti k sotsializmu*, 26–8.

69 Dedenev, "Bol'shevistskie organizatsii Sibiri," 36.

70 Equally negative sentiments appear to have prevailed in other parts of provincial Russia such as the Caucasus. On 30 October 1917 a congress of the Union of Towns of the Terek Region voted against recognizing *Sovnarkom*, and ordered all local governments to take appropriate measures to forestall Bolshevik seizure of power. See Dolunts, *Kirov na severnom Kavkaze*, 145.

71 *Zemlia i volia*, no. 1 (9 January 1918): 2.

72 Quoted in *Golos svobody*, no. 175 (2 November 1917): 1.

73 According to Maxim Gorky, "On the Russian Peasantry," 17: "The peasants in Siberia dug pits and lowered Red[s] ... into them upside down, leaving their legs to the knees above the ground; then they gradually filled in the pit with soil, watching by the convulsions of the legs which of the victims was more resistant, livelier, and which would be the last to die."

74 Poole, *The Village: Russian Impressions*, 97.

75 The Popular Socialists (*Narodnye Sotsialisty*) were a small but influential party which formed an essential part of the democratic coalition under the old Provisional Government. Their brand of moderate populism occupied a place on the political spectrum between the PSR (on their immediate left) and the Kadets (on their immediate right).

76 On the Siberian srs' attitude towards regionalism, see "ii Tomskii gubernskii s"ezd chlenov Partii Sotsialistov-Revoliutsionerov" (22–28 September 1917), in Cherniak, *Politicheskie partii*, 99.

77 *Zemskaia gazeta*, no. 8 (28 January 1918): 1.

78 Snow, *Bolsheviks in Siberia*, 220–1.

CHAPTER THREE

1 Kenez, *Civil War in South Russia, 1918*, 14ff.

2 Guins, *Sibir'*, 1:29ff; and Safronov, *Oktiabr' v Sibiri*, 97ff. Dacy, "The White Russian Movement," 198, has suggested that "in so far as the Whites had any claim to be a people's movement, the Cossacks were that people. There was no one else ... The Cossack component of the White armies made up perhaps 50% of the total."

3 The term "census society" meant roughly the same group as the propertied classes; it probably derived from usage in the official pre-revolutionary government censuses.

4 This exclusiveness was the explicit basis for the opposition of the Kadets. See *Sibirskaia rech'*, no. 171 (20 December 1917): 1.

5 hia, "Morozov Memorandum" in Mel'gunov (Melgounov) Collection, (12 September 1918): 2.

6 Serebrennikov, *Moi vospominaniia*, 1:213.

7 In addition to Derber, pgas included P.V. Vologodskii, V.M. Krutovskii, A.A. Krakovetskii, A.E. Novoselov, I.A. Mikhailov, I.I. Serebrennikov, G.B. Patushinskii, D. Ripchino, M.A. Kolobov, L.A. Ustrugov, I.S. Iudin, V.T. Tiber-Petrov, N.E. Zherniakov, V.I. Moravskii, M.B. Shatilov, S.A. Kudravtsev, E.V. Zakharov, G.Sh. Neometullov, and someone named simply Sulim. I.A. Iakushev was elected president of the Siberian Regional Duma. See Guins, *Sibir'*, 1:76–9.

8 *garf/TsGAOR*, fond 130, opis 2, ed.khr. 133:128.

9 Quoted in *Zaria*, no. 24 (11 July 1918): 2.

10 *Zemlia i volia*, no. 3 (22 January 1918): 1.

11 Cherniak, *S"ezdy, konferentsii i soveshchaniia*, part 2:159–60.

12 Ataman roughly translates as headman (from which it may have derived) or chieftain, and was the title used initially among the Don Cossacks and subsequently among all the other *voiska* of Russia and Siberia. See *Entsiklopedicheskii slovar'*, 3:411–12.

13 Morley, *The Japanese Thrust into Siberia, 1918*, 173, notes that the Japanese were very sensitive to the charge that they had territorial ambitions in Siberia. This "suspicion would undoubtedly arouse the hostility of the Americans ... and would destroy the understanding which the empire was laboring so hard to build." The dominant faction in Tokyo's Advisory Council on Foreign Relations only supported intervention if it had

the public support of the United States, if Japan was put in supreme command of the Allied expeditionary forces, and if the intervention did not go beyond eastern Siberia; the British and the French were prepared to give the Japanese a much freer hand. Ibid., 229.

14 GARF/TsGAOR, fond 130, opis 2, ed.khr. 600:2.

15 Khorvat is sometimes transliterated as Horvat or Horvath. In any case, the general never went beyond Grodekovo, the last town in Russian territory on the railway line between Vladivostok and Harbin.

16 Kolchak was not exactly enamoured of his colleagues in Harbin. "At Harbin ... I never met two people who would speak well of each other ... It was an atmosphere of such deep disintegration that to build up anything was unthinkable. This was one of the reasons why I considered Horvath's government so skeptically: it consisted of men who lived in that Harbin gutter." Varneck and Fisher, *The Testimony of Admiral Kolchak*, 143.

17 Mel'gunov, *Tragediia Admirala Kolchaka*, part 1:148.

18 For an outline of Khorvat's moderately conservative program, see Challener, *United States Military Intelligence, 1917–1927*, 4:17–18.

19 Morley, *The Japanese Thrust into Siberia, 1918*, 161.

20 See the report on Derber's denunciation of Khorvat as a traitor and counter-revolutionary in the *Manchester Guardian* of 19 July 1918.

21 Budberg, "Dnevnik," 13:208 .

22 White, *The Siberian Intervention*, 104. On the indifference towards PGAS of the Cossacks in particular, see the telegram dated 15 August 1918 from an agent named Fet in HIA, Russia: "Vremennoe Sibirskoe Pravitel'stvo."

23 Budberg, "Dnevnik," 13:234.

24 Klante, *Von der Wolga zum Amur*, 77ff. Also Stephan, *The Russian Far East*, 124.

25 Bunyan, *Intervention, Civil War and Communism in Russia*, 322.

26 *Papers relating to the Foreign Relations of the United States (Russia)*, 2:261. Also SSEES, Pares Papers, box 23, Pares, "Siberian Diary," 28, refers to the government as "a number of nobodies headed by a Jew, Derber." For a detailed report of the positions taken by the Derber government, see ibid., 100–3.

27 Budberg, "Dnevnik," 13:199.

28 See the report from A. Pedashenko in Chita to P.V. Vologodskii in Omsk, GARF/TsGAOR, fond 176, opis 3, ed.khr 21:4, where it was noted that though a powerful force against the Bolsheviks throughout the Transbaikal, Semenov "systematically plundered the public purse, in the most varied forms."

29 See the petition, dated 12 December 1918, of a refugee named Ia. Egoshkin to Kolchak in GARF/TsGAOR, fond 176, opis 4, ed.khr. 9:70,

which described the bestiality of Ataman Annenkov's men who behaved as though they were "in a conquered country." Egoshkin appealed to Kolchak to stop the depredations of these Cossack units which nominally served his government.

30 GARF/TsGAOR, fond 176, opis 1, ed.khr. 2:23-ob., 26, 26-ob.

31 Ibid., 1.

32 HIA, Andrushkevich, "Posledniaia Rossiia," 7.

33 In the Russian Far East, the Cossack *voiska*, concentrated along the Trans-Siberian Railway, included the Transbaikal (1916 population: 265,000), the Amur (49,000), and the Ussuri (34,000). See Smith, "Atamanshchina in the Russian Far East," 58. While many of the atamans were known for their anti-Semitism, Semenov's very influential and strong-willed mistress was in fact Jewish; moreover, his immediate entourage included not only Russians, but also Chinese, Koreans, Buriats, and other nationalities. Indeed he saw himself as a champion of these ethnic groups, especially of the Mongols and Buriats, whose languages he spoke fluently. See letter from A. Ivanova in GARF/TsGAOR, fond 193, opis 1, ed.khr. 3:3 (Lichnyi fond P.V. Vologodskogo).

34 Novikov, "Omsk v period kapitalizma (1861–1917 gg.)," 116–18. Also Gibson, "Paradoxical Perceptions of Siberia," 88.

35 Kennan, *Siberia and the Exile System*, 1:140–1.

36 Potanin, "Nuzhdy Sibiri," 250.

37 Budberg, "Dnevnik," 13:197 (10 April 1918): "[M]oney pours like water, nightclubs and speakeasies [*shantany*] are overcrowded; prices are going up on everything."

38 HIA, Pares, "Political Conditions in Western Siberia," 4–5 (20 June 1919). Also SSEES, Pares Papers, box 44.

39 Iurasova, *Omsk: ocherki istorii goroda*, 115: "Omsk was literally overrun with recently arrived speculators. The dominant role was played by Moscovite, Petersburg, and Nizhegorod entrepreneurs, [and by] representatives of foreign power[s] ... [all] making additional profits from Siberian bread, meat, [and] butter."

40 Dubarbier, "Omsk under Kolchak," 168: "Every evening the fashionable restaurants ... were crowded to the doors."

41 Kenez, *Civil War in South Russia, 1918*, 18.

42 GARF/TsGAOR, fond 131, op. 1. ed.khr. 87:1: "The main task of the Provisional Siberian Government is the liberation of Siberia from Bolshevik bondage and the transformation of Siberia through the Siberian Constituent Assembly (elected on the basis of universal, equal, secret and direct suffrage) to full statehood."

43 Quoted in GARF/TsGAOR, fond 1561, opis 1, ed.khr. 156:30 ("Iz donesenii s mest o nastroenii krest'ian v krasnoiarskom uezde.").

44 *GARF/TsGAOR*, fond 1561, opis 1, ed.khr. 68:2–4 (Fond NKVD SSSR).

45 *GARF/TsGAOR*, fond 131, opis 1, ed.khr. 2:1-ob ("Iz sobraniia postanovlenii i rasporiazhenii Zapadno-Sibirskago Komissariata Sibirskago Vremennago Pravitel'stva.").

46 Ibid., 21.

47 The parallels with the moderate SR government in northern Russia were striking. See Kotsonis, "Arkhangel'sk, 18," 526–44.

48 Nikolaev, "Politika 'Komucha'," 118.

49 See the WSC decree (*postanovlenie*) of 28 June 1918 denationalizing businesses and ordering them to be restored to their former owners. *GARF/TsGAOR*, fond 131, opis 1, ed.khr. 2:10-ob.

50 Mel'gunov, *Tragediia Admirala Kolchaka*, part 1:71.

51 Kenez, *Civil War in South Russia, 1918*, 65, dates the beginning of the Civil War in the south to this time, when Ataman Kaledin attacked and occupied Rostov on the Don.

52 PRO, FO 4098, "Memorandum on Siberia," 11 (20 December 1919) gives the Czechoslovak strength at the beginning as 42,500 men but this figure appears to have increased to 60,000 in transit. Also Skácel, *Československá armáda v Rusku a Kolčak*, 92–5; and Papoushek, "Prichiny Chekhoslovatskogo vystupleniia v 1918 godu," 287–350.

53 IOR, *The War: Eastern Reports*, L/P&S/10/587, no. 75 (3 July 1918). In the south the Germans had a similar impact. Kenez, *Civil War in South Russia, 1918*, 127: "The arrival of the Germans radically changed the course of the Civil War in South Russia in favor of the Whites. In overthrowing Bolshevik rule the Germans enabled the Whites to organize at a time when, if left on their own, they could not have survived."

54 Fic, *The Bolsheviks and the Czechoslovak Legion*, 29; and Thunig-Nittner, *Die Tschechoslowakische Legion in Russland*, 78.

55 The Czechoslovak nationalist dream was, in fact, accomplished without the Legion when on 20 October 1918 the Czech national government was formed in Paris. See Masaryk, *The Making of a State*, 82–5.

56 MAE, série E, carton 127, dossier 3 (1918–22), 1:8–13.

57 Carley, "The Origins of the French Intervention," 438, observes that "the French were the first of the Allies to move toward a rapprochement with the Bolsheviks, and then the first to veer away. In late January [1918] the French general staff initiated the period of detente; in late March the Quai d'Orsay acted to end it."

58 Debo, *Revolution and Survival*, 272.

59 Kennan, "The Czechoslovak Legion," 16:3–16 and 17:11–28.

60 Klante, *Von der Wolga zum Amur*, 157.

61 Naida and Naumov, *Sovetskaia istoriografiia grazhdanskoi voiny*. According to Carley, "The Origins of the French Intervention," 437, "The uprising

of the Czech Legion in late May 1918 furnished the French with the necessary pretext to draw their British and American allies into a position of unambiguous hostility toward the Soviet regime."

62 Bradley, "The Allies and the Czech Revolt against the Bolsheviks in 1918," 292.

63 Bradley, *The Czechoslovak Legion in Russia*, 95–6.

64 Safronov, *Oktiabr' v Sibiri*, 600. Dotsenko, *The Struggle for a Democracy in Siberia*, 17, argues that these foreign forces were crucial in the establishment of Soviet authority in most Siberian cities. According to Trotsky, *How the Revolution Armed*, 1:276, about 50,000 former German and Austro-Hungarian prisoners of war eventually served in the Red Army.

65 GARF/TsGAOR, fond 130, opis 2, ed.khr. 124-b:40.

66 Erickson, *The Soviet High Command*, 31.

67 Boldyrev, *Direktoriia, Kolchak, Interventy*, 28.

68 Fomin, "Kooperatsiia i perevorot v Sibiri," 1–9.

69 Rosenberg, *Liberals in the Russian Revolution*, 287–8.

70 Dolgorukov, *Natsional'naia politika i Partiia Narodnoi Svobody*, 9. Also Krol', *Za tri goda*, 28.

71 *Zariia*, no. 47 (8 August 1918): 1–2 ("Adres biuro omskago otdela Soiuz vozrozhdeniia Rossii"). Also BAR, Astrov, "Moskovskie organizatsii 1917–1918 g.," 8–11.

72 A poster dated 20 July 1918 announced the formation of the Omsk Branch of the Union of Regeneration and invited those of "Statist-Patriotic" point of view to join. Its aims were very close to those of the main branch. See SSEES, Pares Papers, box 28.

73 USNARS, RG 395, E-6011, box 40 (from *Dal'nevostochnoe obozrenie*, 8 August 1919). Also BAR, Panina, "Civil War – Kadets (in general)"; also Dumova, *Kadetskaia kontrrevoliutsiia*, 120–1, 149.

74 BAR, Astrov, "Moskovskie organizatsii 1917–1918 g.," 8–9.

75 Bunyan and Fisher, *The Bolshevik Revolution, 1917–1918*, 359–66.

76 Vladimirova, *God sluzhby 'sotsialistov' kapitalistam*, 196–7.

77 Spirin, *Klassy i partii v grazhdanskoi voine v Rossii*, 137.

78 For a discussion of the relationship between the SRs and the Mensheviks, as well as the political resurgence of the latter in the spring of 1918, see Brovkin, "The Mensheviks' Political Comeback," 1–50; and his *The Mensheviks after October*. There was also renewed support among the workers of Moscow, Petrograd, and elsewhere for both the majority SRs and the Left SRs, as well as for smaller groups such as the Revolutionary Communists (*Revoliutsionnye Kommunisty*) and the Popular Communists (*Narodniki-Kommunisty*). See Raleigh's forthcoming *Civil War on the Volga*, and Fel'shtinskii, *Bol'sheviki i Levye Esery*.

79 Babikova, "Bor'ba s kontrrevoliutsionnym zemstvom v tomskoi gubernii," 201. Also Spirin et al., *Neproletarskie partii Rossii*, 391.

80 GARF/TsGAOR, fond 9550, opis 2, ed.khr 59:1. "On a large part of the
territory of Siberia ... the local population is completely disenchanted
with zemstvo institutions." A similar conclusion is reached in Kotsonis,
"Arkhangel'sk, 18," 538.

81 GARF/TsGAOR, fond 1561, opis 1, ed.khr. 68:8–9 ob. (Fond NKVD
SSSR), report from Alekseevskoe sel'skoe obshchestvo; also ibid., 32
("Doklad Instruktora Peremilovskogo o rabote 1–31 avgusta 1918 g.").

82 Maiskii, Demokraticheskaia kontrrevoliutsiia, 175–8. This freedom did not
apply to the Bolsheviks or even to the newspaper of the Menshevik-
Internationalist.

83 Bunyan, Intervention, Civil War and Communism in Russia, 284.

84 GARF/TsGAOR, fond 1561, opis 1, ed.khr. 156:30 ("Iz donesenii s mest o
nastroenii krest'ian v krasnoiarskom uezde"): "In the whole district
there is not a single zemstvo office that has adequate personnel ... In
many cases, there was no one other than a caretaker. There was no
administrator, nor even any secretaries, and what happened to them
no one knows."

85 GARF/TsGAOR, fond 1561, opis 1, ed.khr. 82:25 (report of P.L. Barsuk).

86 Spirin, Klassy, 266–7. Also Maiskii, Demokraticheskaia kontrrevoliutsiia, 82.

87 Lenin and Trotsky, after careful consideration, declined the offer
because they feared that the Whites would not be satisfied for long
with holding the line in Siberia and would soon try to roll back the
soviets west of the Urals as well. GARF/TsGAOR, fond 130, opis 2, ed.khr.
785:41–2.

88 On the weakness of the "People's Army," see HIA, Vyrypaev, "Vladimir
Oskarovich Kappel,'" 4–7.

89 Dotsenko, The Struggle for a Democracy in Siberia, 37. There is confirmation of this account in HIA, Vologodskii, "Diary," 4. Also Delo Sibiri, no.
35 (2 July 1918): 1.

90 Sobranie uzakonenii i rasporiazhenii Vremennago Sibirskago Pravitel'stva, no.
1 (5 July 1918): 2. Kotsonis, "Arkhangel'sk, 18," 542, observes that in
the north of Russia, as in Siberia, the moderate socialists started calling themselves sotsialisty gosudarstvenniki – "those who understood the
exigencies of statehood if the electorate did not."

91 Guins, Sibir', 1:120.

92 Maiskii, Demokraticheskaia kontrrevoliutsiia, 145.

93 Spirin, Klassy i partii v grazhdanskoi voine v Rossii, 258.

94 Vladimir Oskarovich Kappel' was by far the most effective and the
most popular commander in the People's Army. He believed that the
only antidote to Bolshevism was to "give [the people] what they
needed, in order to satisfy their just hopes." Quoted in HIA, Vyrypaev,
"Vladimir Oskarovich Kappel,'" 12.

95 Budberg, "Dnevnik," 13:249.

96 Quoted in Varneck, *Testimony of Admiral Kolchak*, 267.

97 *GARF/TsGAOR*, fond 9550, opis 2, ed.khr. 103:1.

98 *GARF/TsGAOR*, fond 1561, opis 1, ed.khr. 128:72.

99 For an example of the strongly anti-*Komuch* attitude prevalent in Omsk, see "Konferentsiia Kadetskikh organizatsii Urala i Sibiri," (20–24 August 1918) in Cherniak, *Politicheskie partii v Sibiri*, 168.

100 Quoted in HIA, Vyrypaev, "Vladimir Oskarovich Kappel,'" 28–9.

101 Quoted in Morley, *The Japanese Thrust into Siberia*, 290.

102 Quoted in HIA, Harris, "Conditions in Chita." Emphasis added.

103 HIA, Vologodskii, "Diary," 3.

104 Statement of 17 July 1918 in *Russian Series*, 2:288–9.

105 USNARS, RG 165 (MID), 2376–87.

106 Schmid, *Churchills privater Krieg*, 46–8.

107 Graves, *America's Siberian Adventure*, 72–4.

108 PRO, Foreign Office memorandum to Eliot in Vladivostok (8 December 1918), WO 106/1224.

109 Carley, *Revolution and Intervention*, 37–48.

110 According to Soviet sources, up to 10,000 Bolsheviks, Red Army men, and Red Guards were arrested and jailed almost immediately. *GARF/TsGAOR*, fond 130, opis 2, ed.khr. 559:11.

111 Dotsenko, *The Struggle for a Democracy in Siberia*, 38–9.

112 Quoted from "Deklaratsiia Vremennago Sibirskago Pravitel'stva," in *Delo Sibiri*, no. 40 (7 July 1918): 1. Emphasis added.

113 *GARF/TsGAOR*, fond 131, opis 1, ed.khr. 2:21-ob.-22 ("Ob annulirovanii dekretov sovetskoi vlasti"). Despite the closing of the soviets, the right of professional organizations that "are not pursuing political agendas" was confirmed.

114 *GARF/TsGAOR*, fond 1561, opis 1, delo 156:31 ("Doklad gospod. zaved. informatsionno-agitatsionnym otdelom srednei Sibiri – MVD Vremennago Sibirskago Pravitel'stva, Eniseiskii gubernskii instruktor").

115 Vologodskii, *Deklaratsiia Vremennago [Sibirskago] Pravitel'stva*, 17. Also *Sobranie uzakonenii i rasporiazhenii Vremennago Sibirskago Pravitel'stva*, no. 2:10–39.

116 *GARF/TsGAOR*, fond 130, opis 2, ed.khr. 559:12.

117 Kadeikin, "Antirabochaia politika Vremennago Sibirskago Pravitel'stva," 154.

118 *Novosti zhizni* (22 October 1918).

119 Kal'nin, "Trud pri belykh," 134–40; and *Sibirskoe biuro RKP(b), 1918–1920: sbornik dokumentov*, 139. Kadeikin, "Antirabochaia politika Vremennogo Sibirskogo Pravitel'stva," 151, argues that "in terms of the trade unions the Provisional Siberian Government took a more reactionary position than had the government of Kerensky." Espe, *God v*

tsarstve Kolchaka, 20, also sees the Omsk government's strongly pro-management policies as responsible for the work stoppages and strikes.

120 HIA, "Sibirskaia Oblastnaia Duma" in Nikolaevsky Collection, no. 145, box 1, file no. 1.

121 Quoted in Dumova, *Kadetskaia kontrrevoliutsiia,* 195. See also Rosenberg, *Liberals in the Russian Revolution,* 384–8.

122 *Sibirskii vestnik* (2 August 1918): 1–2.

123 Guins, *Sibir',* 1:287.

124 Dotsenko, *The Struggle for a Democracy in Siberia,* 46–51.

125 HIA, Andrushkevich, "Posledniaia Rossiia," 9.

126 Mel'gunov, *Tragediia Admirala Kolchaka,* part 2:96.

127 "Obshchesibirskaia konferentsiia Sotsial-Demokratov" (19–24 August 1918) in Cherniak, *Politicheskie partii v Sibiri,* 161.

128 HIA, Ustrialov, "Belyi Omsk," 52–3. Both Mikhailov and Vologodskii began their political careers as SRs and never formally renounced those affiliations.

129 Radkey, *The Elections to the Russian Constituent Assembly of 1917,* 42ff.

130 Mel'gunov, *Grazhdanskaia voina v osveshchenii P.N. Miliukova,* 41.

131 Solov'ev, "O roli vnutrennei kontrrevoliutsii v razviazyvanii interventsii," 407–8.

132 Freeze, "The Soslovie (Estate) Paradigm and Russian Social History," 11–36.

133 Burbank, *Intelligentsia and Revolution,* 122. Also Dumova, *Kadetskaia kontrrevoliutsiia,* 36–53, confirms this general picture of Kadet dominance over the PSR.

134 GARF/TsGAOR, fond 176, opis 3, delo 23:97 ob. Report dated 23 January 1919.

135 Guins, *Sibir',* 1:48.

136 Brovkin, "Identity, Allegiance and Participation in the Russian Civil War," 553.

137 Radkey, *The Sickle Under the Hammer,* 2. Despite their extreme volatility and subsequent violent quarrels with the Bolsheviks, the Left SRs regarded themselves as ardent supporters of Soviet power and adamant opponents of the White counter-revolution in all its forms. Their position was in sharp contrast to that of the PSR majority. Vladimirova, *God sluzhby,* 200–1, noted that both the majority SRs and the Kadets preferred the umbrella of the *Soiuz vozrozhdeniia* to a formal alliance along party lines.

138 Spirin, *Neproletarskie partii Rossii,* 391–5. At the end of May in Moscow, there was also a major Menshevik conference that called for the replacement of "Soviet power by an authority which unites the forces of all the democracy," but the Mensheviks remained reluctant to join *Soiuz vozrozhdeniia.*

139 Kotsonis, "Arkhangel'sk, 18," comes to similar conclusions about events in the north.

140 White, *The Siberian Intervention*, 106.

141 Krol', "Sibirskoe pravitel'stvo i avgustovskaia sessiia sibirskoi oblastnoi dumy," 73.

142 *Sibirskaia kooperatsiia*, no. 9–10 (1918): 1.

CHAPTER FOUR

1 Berk, "The Democratic Counterrevolution," 443–59.

2 In the beginning of August 1918 an Ural Government formed under the Kadets P.V. Ivanov and L.A. Krol', with some participation of moderate socialists. Its program was therefore a mixture of free enterprise and some government sponsored social welfare – much closer to Omsk than to Samara ideologically. Guins, *Sibir'*, 1:134–5. Also Dumova, *Kadetskaia kontrrevoliutsiia i ee razgrom*, 161–3.

3 Lenin, *Polnoe sobranie sochinenii*, 28:302–3.

4 GARF/TsGAOR, fond 1561, opis 1, ed.khr. 68:5 (Fond NKVD SSSR), "Otchetnye materialy o rabote instruktorsko-informatsionnogo otdela MVD Vremennago Sibirskago Pravitel'stva." (8 August 1918).

5 Lih, "Bread and Authority in Russia," 264, identifies the period from January to July 1918 as the critical time during which People's Commissar A.D. Tsiurupa and his colleagues set up the food-supply dictatorship and a centralized apparatus to run it under a system of state capitalism. Lih argues that this initiative predated the outbreak of the Civil War and would have occurred even without its imminent threat.

6 Shikanov, "K voprosu o khronologicheskikh ramkakh 'demokraticheskoi' kontrrevoliutsii v Sibiri," 62–7.

7 Quoted in Maiskii, *Demokraticheskaia kontrrevoliutsiia*, 84.

8 Daniels, *The Conscience of the Revolution*, 85–6.

9 Kolosov, *Sibir pri Kolchake*, 27. Figes, *Peasant Russia, Civil War*, 214: "Bolshevism … took root in the countryside among beardless peasant sons educated during the decade prior to 1914 and radicalized in the Imperial or the Red Army."

10 GARF/TsGAOR, fond 130, opis 2, ed.khr. 124-b:68. Dotsenko, *The Struggle for a Democracy in Siberia*, 12.

11 This mutual urban-rural antipathy has already been noted, but it is worth adding that the Marxists were not alone in having a low opinion of the Russian peasantry. One of the least flattering characterizations may be seen in Engel'gardt, *Iz derevni. 11 pisem*, 430: "Envy, mistrust of each other, intrigue against each other, the humiliation of the weak before the strong, forceful arrogance, worship of wealth – all of this is highly developed in the peasant culture … Every peasant … will be

the most excellent example of an exploiter of anyone else, be he lord or peasant, to squeeze the juices out of him, to exploit his needs."

12 Quoted in Steinberg, *In the Workshop of the Revolution*, 154.

13 A *pud* equals 36 pounds or about 16 kilograms. See the report in *Svoboda Rossii*, no. 7 (19 April 1918): 5. According to Shumiatskii, *Sibir' na putiakh k Oktiabriu*, 34, over six million *poods* of grain were shipped from Western Siberia to the capital cities between December 1917 and March 1918.

14 Spirin, *Klassy i partii v grazhdanskoi voine*, 247.

15 Ibid., 145, provides this proportional breakdown of the peasant population of Siberia.

16 Yaney, *The Urge to Mobilize*, 472.

17 Figes, *Peasant Russia, Civil War*, 126: "The Volga peasantry gained a relatively large amount of land as a result of the revolution, compared with the other regions of European Russia." At the other extreme was Siberia where the peasants acquired very little from Soviet legislation.

18 GARF/TsGAOR, fond 1561, opis 1, ed.khr. 68:32-ob., "Doklad Instruktora Peremilovskogo o rabote 1–31 avgusta 1918 g.," for evidence of the hostility of Siberian peasants towards what they saw to be the privileges of both Cossack and Kirghiz. They did not have much more use for each other, however, according to Bunin, *The Village*, 106: "But with us, all are enemies of one another, every one envies and slanders every one else, goes to see acquaintances once a year, sits apart, each in his kennel; all bustle about like madmen when any one drops in for a visit, and dash around to put the rooms in order. But what's the truth of the matter? They begrudge the guest a spoonful of preserves! The guest will not drink a second cup of tea without being specially invited. Ygh, you slant-eyed Kirghizi! You yellow-haired Mordvinians! You savages!"

19 Meijer, "Town and Country in the Civil War," 259. Figes, *Peasant Russia, Civil War*, 192, argues that "the natural-patriarchal bonds of the peasant farmers in the village were still very much stronger than the socio-economic divisions between them."

20 GARF/TsGAOR, fond 130, opis 2, ed.khr. 430:35.

21 Quoted in Tyrkova-Williams, *Why Soviet Russia is Starving?*, 13.

22 GARF/TsGAOR, fond 130, opis 2, ed.khr. 675:78.

23 Ibid., 117. Emphasis added.

24 Von Hagen, *Soldiers in the Proletarian Dictatorship*, 123–4. By contrast, the White government failed to provide its own officers with adequate salaries, which drove many of them to take what they needed from the civilian population; one can only imagine how much worse the situation of the ordinary soldier must have been.

25 This hostility was reciprocated by the Russian peasants who, according to Bernshtam, "Storony v grazhdanskoi voine," 295–6, were "always

completely conservative and profoundly religious" and had nothing in common with even the Kadets, much less any of the socialist parties.

26 Quoted in GARF/TsGAOR, fond 1561, opis 1, ed.khr. 69:15, "MVD Vremennago Sibirskago Pravitel'stva, informatsionno-agitatsionnyi otdel."

27 "O nashikh putiakh," *Znamia truda*, no. 155 (16 March 1918): 1.

28 14 May 1918: 1.

29 Haefner, "The Assassination of Count Mirbach," 324–44, argues convincingly that the Left SRs never intended a military uprising or to overturn the government; they assassinated the German ambassador because they wanted to disrupt the Brest-Litovsk peace process and to poison relations with the Germans.

30 Kakurin, *Kak srazhalas' revoliutsiia*, 1:236.

31 Petrov, *Rokovye gody (1914–1920)*, 104–10.

32 Quoted in Debo, *Revolution and Survival*, 325.

33 There were pockets of support, to be sure. At the Second Congress of Peasant Deputies of Altai *Guberniia*, 27 January–3 February 1918, in Barnaul, with 98 delegates present, a resolution was adopted by vote of 58 to 10 and 14 abstentions that read: "Power must belong exclusively to the class of the workers and exploited, that is, workers, peasants, and soldiers; there is no place for the class of the exploiters, and all power, at the centre as well as locally, must be in the hands of the soviets of peasants', workers', and soldiers' deputies." Cherniak, *S"ezdy, konferentsii i soveshchaniia*, 85.

34 See the newspaper *Tsentrosibir'*, no. 21 (1 August 1918).

35 Debo, *Revolution and Survival*, 366–7.

36 PRO, WO 106/1232 (21 November 1918).

37 Livshits, *Imperialisticheskaia interventsiia v Sibiri*, 54–6.

38 Carley, *Revolution and Intervention*, 87. Also Kolz, "British Economic Interests in Siberia," 483–91.

39 Krol', *Za tri goda*, 62.

40 HIA, Nikolaevsky Collection, "Czech Diary," no. 189. Krol', *Za tri goda*, 68, adds that Samara also threatened to cut off the supply of fuel.

41 Dotsenko, *The Struggle for a Democracy*, 51–2.

42 Quoted in Bunyan, *Intervention, Civil War and Communism in Russia*, 349.

43 Spirin, *Neproletarskie partii Rossii*, 259.

44 Dotsenko, *The Struggle for a Democracy*, 43.

45 Quoted in Maksakov and Turunov, *Khronika grazhdanskoi voiny v Sibiri*, 240.

46 Budberg, "Dnevnik," 13:262. Also HIA, Serebrennikov, "K istorii sibirskago pravitel'stva," 2–3.

47 GARF/TsGAOR, fond 131, op. 1, ed.khr. 3:55-ob. ("Vysshii sovet snabzheniia Kolchakovskoi armii. Sobranie prikazov i zakonopolozhenii"). The

members of the Administrative Council were Professor V.V. Sapozhnikov (popular enlightenment), A.N. Grishin-Almazov (military), Stepanenko (communication and transport); Prof. P.P. Gudkov (trade and industry); Assistant Professor N.I. Petrov (land and resources), S.S. Starynkevich (interior), N.S. Zefirov (food production), L.I. Shumilovskii (labour), A.P. Morozov (justice), M.P. Golovachev (foreign affairs), Buianovskii (finance), and G.K. Guins (administration and liaison with the Council of Ministers). See Guins, *Sibir'*, 1:185–6, and HIA, Vologodskii, "Diary," 25–6 (entries for 29 and 30 September 1918).

48 Guins, *Sibir'*, 1:195. Another indication was the decree of the Administrative Council of 24 October 1918 that allowed bread prices in the Cheliabinsk region to rise up to a maximum of 20 per cent.

49 The story was recounted to me by Paul Dotsenko during an interview that took place in Stanford, Calif., in October, 1987. HIA, Harris, "Political Situation in the Omsk District covering Period from May 1918 to Date" (10 November 1918), box 2:10, confirms that Grishin-Almazov was removed after having offended Allied officers in Omsk.

50 HIA, Ovchinnikov Collection, "Outlines of My Reminiscences," 6–9.

51 Guins, *Sibir'*, 1: 233–4. Maiskii, *Demokraticheskaia kontrrevoliutsiia*, 252–3, blames the PSG for precipitating the conflict when its agents prevented the Siberian Regional Duma from sending a delegation to the Far East to counter Vologodskii's mission, but the conflict was inevitable in any case. The same incident, but from the opposite point of view, is recounted in HIA, Vologodskii, "Diary," 25.

52 G.N. Potanin, A.V. Adrianov, N. Novomberskii, and V.M. Popov, "O konflikte Sibirskoi Oblastnoi Dumy s Vremennym Sibirskim Pravitel'stvom," *Sibirskii vestnik*, no. 53 (26 October 1918): 2–3, assert that both the tragic incident and the proroguing of the Siberian Regional Duma were "an inevitable consequence of the obstinate struggle for power carried out by the SR party from the beginning of the February Revolution to the present day." Bernard Pares came to a similar conclusion about the "proto-Bolshevism" of the PSR. See SSEES, Pares Papers, box 48.

53 If Serebrennikov is to be believed, however, the circumstances surrounding the death of Novoselov so mortified him and his colleagues in the Omsk delegation that they agreed to a compromise at Ufa that they otherwise would have resisted. See HIA, Serebrennikov, "K istorii sibirskago pravitel'stva," 10.

54 Bradley, *Allied Intervention in Russia*, 103.

55 Quoted in Gutman, *Rossia i bolshevizm*, 279–80.

56 Guins, *Sibir'*, 1:261.

57 Maiskii, *Demokraticheskaia kontrrevoliutsiia*, 320–2. Also Brovkin, "The Mensheviks' Political Comeback," 14ff.

58 Shikanov, "K voprosu o khronologicheskikh ramkakh 'demokrat-icheskoi' kontrrevoliutsii v Sibiri," 64–5.

59 *GARF/TsGAOR*, fond 180, opis 3, ed.khr. 11:1 (Fond Vremennago Vse-rossiiskago Pravitel'stva): Vologodskii, president of the Council of Minis-ters and minister of foreign affairs; Serebrennikov, minister of supplies; Mikhailov, minister of finance; Sapozhnikov, national enlight-enment; Starynkevich, interior; Stepanenko, transport and communica-tions; Petrov, lands and colonization; Zefirov, food provisions; Shumilovskii, labour; Surin, war; Morozov, justice; Shchukin, com-merce and industry; Nikolaev, president of the Provisional Council of State Control; Guins, administrator for the Council of Ministers. See also Bunyan, *Intervention, Civil War and Communism in Russia,* 369–71.

60 *GARF/TsGAOR*, fond 180, opis 1, ed.khr. 1:6–7 (Fond Vremennago Vse-rossiiskago Pravitel'stva, delo I-go otdeleniia).

61 Ibid., 16.

62 The original document, "O peredache verkhovnoi vlasti na territorii Sibiri Vremennomu Vserossiiskomu Pravitel'stvu," was dated 3 Novem-ber 1918 and may be seen in *GARF/TsGAOR*, fond 131, opis 1, ed.khr. 2:207-ob. Also quoted in HIA, Serebrennikov, "The Siberian Autono-mous Movement and its Future," 20, and in Piontovskii, *Grazhdanskaia voina v Rossii,* 275–6.

63 Miliukov, "Admiral Kolchak," 73.

64 Quoted in HIA, Nikolaevsky Collection, no. 145, box 1, file no. 2: "Pro-tokoly komiteta Sibirskoi Oblastnoi Dumy" (29 September 1918).

65 See the telegram of 13 November 1918 to Zenzinov announcing that in the name of "the greater interests of the motherland and the achievements of the revolution which require the complete unification of all the diverse parts of the country around one state centre, the Siberian Regional Duma is taking the decision to terminate its work as the organ of regional [self-]government." *GARF/TsGAOR*, fond 180, opis 1, ed.khr. 1:42.

66 Argunov, "Omskie dni v 1918 godu," 198. Also Rosenberg, *Liberals in the Russian Revolution,* 395.

67 *GARF/TsGAOR*, fond 180, opis 1, ed.khr. 5:53.

68 *GARF/TsGAOR*, fond 9550, opis 2, ed.khr. 119:1 and 1-ob.

69 HIA, "Russia: Posol'stvo (United States)," box 9.

70 Quoted in Bunyan, *Intervention, Civil War and Communism in Russia,* 355. This was in contrast with the Bolsheviks' land and fiscal policies which, according to Guins, *Sibir',* 1:48, "unmercifully stole from the SRs." Mints, *God 1918i,* 252, however, argues that "there should be no confusion of the Bolshevik and SR positions on the land question, despite superficial similarities, since the Bolsheviks saw the key to be the "social exploitation of the land, whereas the SRs believed in … the

socialization of the land, that is the withdrawal of the land from commercial transactions and the equalizing of holdings among peasant households."

71 Varneck and Fisher, *The Testimony of Admiral Kolchak*, 247. Also Boldyrev, *Direktoriia, Kolchak, Interventy*, 94.

72 Chernov, *Pered burei*, 376.

73 *Papers Relating to the Foreign Relations of the United States (Russia)*, 2:421.

74 Garmiza, "Bankrotstvo politiki 'tret'ego puti' v revoliutsii," 12. On 18 October 1918 the Czechoslovak National Council in Paris proclaimed the independence of its country. As soon as the news reached them, the Czechs in Siberia lost all interest in continuing to fight.

75 Zenzinov, *Gosudarstvennyi perevorot Admirala Kolchaka*, 191.

76 Ibid., 77–86.

77 Mel'gunov, *Tragediia Admirala Kolchaka*, part 1:235.

78 Quoted in "Vserossiiskii torgovo-promyshlennyi s"ezd," *Golos rabochago* (10 September 1918): 1–2.

79 Guins, *Sibir'*, 1:284.

80 Ibid., 287.

81 Il'in, "Omsk, Direktoriia, Kolchak," no. 72, 204–5. Also Dotsenko, *The Struggle for a Democracy in Siberia*, 53.

82 Ibid., 63. Also Bourne and Watt, *British Documents on Foreign Affairs*, part 2, series A, 2:37–9.

83 Parfenov, *Uroki proshlogo*, 82; also Janin, *Ma mission en Sibérie*, 84–6.

84 Quoted in Dotsenko, *The Struggle for a Democracy in Siberia*, 63. A.V. Kolchak was born in 1873 in St Petersburg into a well-placed military family. He attended the Sixth Classical Gymnasium in the capital city, and then the Naval College from which he graduated second in his class at age 19. In 1900–2 he became involved in a major scientific exploratory expedition to the Taimyr Peninsula and the New Siberian Islands in the Arctic Ocean. There followed a tour as instructor at the Naval Academy in St Petersburg, but after several months he returned to his research interests. In 1908 he volunteered to participate in an expedition to establish a sea route connecting the Atlantic and Pacific oceans through the northern reaches of Siberia, and he spent most of the next two years working in oceanography and hydrology. From 1910 to 1912 Kolchak was reassigned to a prestigious post at the Naval General Staff. In 1912 he received his first command of a ship, a destroyer in the Baltic Fleet and by 1916 had risen to the rank of vice-admiral of the Russian Black Sea Fleet. In the late summer of 1917 he resigned this command by ostentatiously throwing his sword overboard after denying to the assembled crew that either he or his officers were counter-revolutionary. Varneck, *Testimony of Admiral Kolchak*, 81. Also Egorov, *Kolchak Aleksandr Vasil'evich*, 64–88.

85 *Pravitel'stvennyi vestnik*, no. 26 (26 January 1919): 1.
86 Quoted in Maiskii, *Demokraticheskaia kontrrevoliutsiia*, 337.

CHAPTER FIVE

1 Knox, "General Janin's Siberian Diary," 724. Janin, *Ma mission en Sibé-rie*, 31. Mel'gunov, *Tragediia Admirala Kolchaka*, part 2, 1:104–13, suggested that Grishin-Almazov, Rudolf Gajda, Colonel Ward, and General Knox were all involved to varying degrees.
2 *Papers Relating to the Foreign Relations of the United States (Russia)*, 2:313.
3 The French view was expressed in MAE (21 August–15 October 1919), book 12:3: "The partiality of the Americans in favour of Bolshevism is undeniable, [as] is their manifest hostility towards the Russians."
4 Quoted in PRO, FO 4110 (2 March 1919), memorandum entitled "Attitude of Americans in Siberia."
5 Stewart, *The White Armies of Russia*, 153. Chamberlin, *The Russian Revolution*, 2:152; and Dacy, "The White Russian Movement," 222–3.
6 The Council of Ministers' decision, at Mikhailov's urging, to order the expulsion of the two arrested SR Directors might well have been preliminary to their physical elimination as well. The pair only barely escaped across the Chinese frontier with their lives, thanks to the protection of an Allied escort. "Supreme State Authority" had been delegated to Kolchak with the title of *Verkhovnyi Pravitel'* by an order of the Council of Ministers dated 18 November 1918. GARF/TsGAOR, fond 9550, opis 2, ed.khr. 134:1. It is worth adding that the original initiative for Kolchak's appointment to that ministry came from the PSR and not, as one might have expected, from the right. See Mel'gunov, *Tragediia Admirala Kolchaka*, part 2, 1:51.
7 GARF/TsGAOR, *Kollektsia TsGAOR*, "Pis'mo A.L. Syromiatnikova Ivanu Aleksandrovichu [Mikhailovu]" (14 April 1919): 1–2.
8 Varneck and Fisher, *The Testimony of Admiral Kolchak*, 175–6. Kolchak admitted to learning the identity of the chief coup makers after the fact, and added with his characteristic, if misguided, sense of dignity that "I never returned to this question and never spoke of it with any of the ministers," presumably because he did not want to know the details or be involved any more than absolutely necessary.
9 Guins, *Sibir'*, 1:306–7.
10 Ibid., 1:310.
11 Varneck and Fisher, *The Testimony of Admiral Kolchak*, 271.
12 The story of Kolchak's relationship with Semenov was not a happy one. It dated back to the former's brief involvement, during his stay in Harbin, with the board of Horvath's Chinese-Eastern Railway in the early months of 1918. The admiral was appalled by Semenov's total

disregard for higher Russian authority and his arrogant flirtation with the Japanese. Matters came to an ugly denouement when Semenov's men raided a store and robbed it of much of its contents. Kolchak responded violently: "This adventure made me boil, as this constituted an invasion of the territory directly subordinate to me. I immediately gathered a detachment of about forty men under command of two officers and sent them by special train to that station in order to have that gang arrested and to restore the seized property. The gang was arrested and brought to Harbin, and everything was returned to the store." Semenov, and even more important, his Japanese backers, felt that they had been publicly humiliated. Kolchak, moreover, disregarded the sound advice of the Russian ambassador to Tokyo: "You have assumed from the beginning too independent a position with regard to Japan, and they have understood it. You allow yourself to speak to them in a too imperative and independent tone – this was a mistake on your part. You ought to have smoothed it over. They have come to regard you as an enemy of theirs who is going to oppose anything they initiate, the whole work; therefore, naturally, they not only will not help you but will oppose your work." Quoted in Varneck and Fisher, *The Testimony of Admiral Kolchak*, 126–8. From Semenov's perspective, Kolchak had been hostile and uncooperative from the time they first met, when the admiral prevented his troops from getting needed arms and supplies from Harbin. See GARF/TsGAOR, fond 193, opis 1, ed.khr. 3:8 (Lichnyi fond P.V. Vologodskogo).

13 SSEES, Pares Papers, box 43, "Siberian Diary," 48. Pares observed that Kolchak "meant well but was surrounded by quite inferior instruments. Men who had neither his patriotism nor his honesty."

14 According to Zenzinov, *Gosudarstvennyi perevorot Admirala Kolchaka*, 192–4, Mikhailov could count on the support of a clear majority within the Council, including Sukin, Smirnov, Tel'berg, Gattenberger, Petrov, Zefirov, and Guins.

15 Guins, *Sibir'*, 2:34–5. Specifically, the Bloc at this time comprised representatives from: the Council of All-Siberian Cooperative Congresses, A. Sazonov; the Omsk Section of the Union of Regeneration (*Soiuz vozrozhdeniia*), V. Kulikov; the All-Russian Council of Congresses of Trade and Industry, D. Kargalov; the Omsk Committee of the Labour Popular Socialist Party, A. Novikov; four Cossack hosts: E. Berezovskii from Siberia, I. Lapshakov from Transbaikal, S. Shendrikov from Semireche, and S. Melent'ev from Irkutsk; the Omsk Group of the SRs (*Volia naroda*), I. Stroganov; the Eastern Section of the Central Committee of the Party of the People's Freedom (Kadets), V. Zhardetskii; the Central-Military-Industrial Committee, N. Dvinarenko; the Akmolinskii Regional Section of the All-Russian National Union, G. Riazhskii; the Russian

Social Democratic Worker's Party (*Edinstvo*), I. Rubankov; and the Bloc of Political and Social Unity (*Ob"edinenii*), A. Balakshin.

16 *Struggling Russia*, 1:319.

17 BAR, Panina Collection, box 13, "Kadet Conferences in Omsk, November 1918 & May 1919" (quoted in the entry for 21 May 1919).

18 GARF/TSGAOR, fond 9550, opis 2, ed.khr. 125:1 ("K naseleniiu Rossii," 18-xi-1918).

19 Budberg, "Dnevnik," 13:267. Egorov, *Kolchak Aleksandr Vasil'evich*, 4, describes Kolchak as "a Russian to the marrow of his bones. He loved Russia more than anything else on earth."

20 Quoted in Guins, *Sibir'*, 2:94.

21 GARF/TSGAOR, fond 5844, opis 1, delo 3a:76, 85 ("Dnevnik A.V. Kolchaka," 22/ii/1917–29/iv/1918.)

22 Guins, *Sibir'*, 2:32.

23 Varneck and Fisher, *The Testimony of Admiral Kolchak*, 46–8.

24 Ibid., 71.

25 HIA, Vologodskii, "Diary," part 2:13–14: "The principal nest of the monarchists centers around the new editorial office of the newspaper *Russkaia armiia* ... This group advances for the future monarch ... a rurikovich by descent ... Prince A.A. Kropotkin."

26 *New York Times* (1 June 1919): 3. Emphasis added.

27 HIA, Ustrialov, "Belyi Omsk," 52–3. The entry for 20 May 1919 in BAR, Panina Collection, "Kadet Conferences in Omsk," reads: "The Civil War and bolshevism have pushed Russian political thought towards two magnetic poles, at one are the bolsheviks and their socialist ideology, while at the other are we Kadets with our ideology."

28 HIA, Elachich, "Obryvki vospominanii," 67–9.

29 In a letter dated 8 December 1918 to his ambassador to the United States, Kolchak wrote: "I suspended [Ataman G.M.] Semenov from his command and all his posts, and ordered my troops to force him ... to curtail [his] wild arbitrariness and anarchy. But there are objections in this regard from Japan which is Semenov's protector." The admiral ordered his emissary to complain to the Americans that the Japanese were interfering in Russian internal affairs in so flagrant a manner that it constituted "de facto occupation of Russian territory." GARF/TSGAOR, fond 200, opis 1, ed.khr. 407:13. Semenov continued to exact heavy and arbitrary payments from railway passengers who traversed his territory and he did not stop this practice even after his relations with Omsk improved. See GARF/TSGAOR, fond 176, opis 3, ed.khr 21:64.

30 USNARS, RG 45 (NRC), WA-6, box 611 (from Peking, 20 January 1919, quoting Captain George W. Williams).

31 McCord, "The Emergence of Modern Chinese Warlordism," 2:37ff.

32 See the telegram from an agent named Klemm (17 June 1919) in GARF/TsGAOR, fond 200, opis 1, ed.khr. 405:165, which reported on the negative impression upon the allies of Kolchak's *rapprochement* with Semenov. Klemm warned that it might affect the chances of Allied recognition of the Omsk government.

33 See the report to Kolchak (11 March 1919) in GARF/TsGAOR, fond 176, opis 7, ed.khr. 30:2.

34 GARF/TsGAOR, fond 193, opis 1, ed.khr. 3:18 (Lichnyi fond P.V. Vologodskogo). When Tomsk merchant A.I. Reshetskii complained through official channels to Omsk about the way in which Ataman Annenkov's men had barged in on a private card-playing party and confiscated all the money in the house, he got a sympathetic hearing from chairman of the Council of Ministers, Vologodskii. But when the latter called upon Annenkov to explain his behavior, the ataman did not even bother to reply and nothing more could be done about it. GARF/TsGAOR, fond 176, opis 2, ed.khr. 86:8.

35 Silverlight, *The Victors' Dilemma*, 215.

36 *Pravitel'stvennyi vestnik* (14 December 1918): 1.

37 HIA, Ustrialov, "Belyi Omsk," 55.

38 *New York Times* (2 August 1919): 2.

39 Despite the obvious political differences, there were some striking similarities between the positions of the Provisional Government and the Omsk government. See Kakurin, *Kak srazhalas' revoliutsiia*, 1:67.

40 Quoted in Mel'gunov, *Tragediia Admirala Kolchaka*, part 3, 1:245. Kolchak's program and rhetoric in Siberia, down to the specific words used, bore a striking resemblance to those of Denikin in the south despite the fact that there was very little communication or coordination between the two. Many of the White leaders in the south were also Kadets, in fact if not always in name. See Kenez, *Civil War in South Russia, 1918*, 80.

41 Budberg, "Dnevnik," 15:273. Here again, the similarity between Kolchak's position and Denikin's is striking. See Kenez, *Civil War in South Russia, 1918*, 179, for a description of the latter's very negative attitude toward the role of an independent Kuban army.

42 Guins, *Sibir'*, 2:22–3.

43 There were in fact more foreigners fighting on the side of the Bolsheviks than with their enemies. Danilov, *Istoriia otechestva*, 56: "The number of internationalists in the Red Army (250–300,000) far outnumbered the number of [pro-White] interventionists."

44 Bourne and Watt, *British Documents on Foreign Affairs*, part 2, series A, 2:37. Also Lenin, *Polnoe sobranie sochinenii*, 29:67–8.

45 HIA, Ustrialov, "Belyi Omsk," 90. Also Stewart, *The White Armies of Russia*, 276–7.

46 MAE (21 August–15 October 1919), book 12:252. "The suppression of
   Zaria produced the worst impression on all of the population of Sibe-
   ria and of Omsk in particular." Also Adrianov, *Periodicheskaia pechat' v
   Sibiri*, 18–19; and Mel'gunov, *Tragediia Admirala Kolchaka*, part 3, 1:268.

47 Shanin, *The Awkward Class*, 145, argues for basic continuity by contrast
   to the standard Soviet view that in the first stage of the revolution
   (1917–18) the property of the upper classes was divided up by the
   peasants but that there was also a second stage (from late 1918
   onwards), when the land of the rich peasants and kulaks was taken by
   the village poor in a levelling second revolution. Bernshtam goes
   much further in "Storony v grazhdanskoi voine," 281–3, and argues
   that, contrary to the Soviet view (broadly accepted in the West) of the
   peasantry receiving an additional 375 million acres of land as a result
   of the land settlement after October 1917, they actually lost land. He
   asserts that prior to October 1917 the peasants already owned 316 million acres, or over 77 per cent of all arable land (the gentry share was
   under 17 per cent), but that by the end of 1918, because of confiscations and the reversal of Stolypin's private ownership policies, *personal*
   peasant land holdings actually declined by 78 million acres.

48 Plotnikov, *Bol'shevistskoe podpol'e v Sibiri*, 45, gives the following breakdown: in 1917 poor peasants in the Siberian countryside constituted
   less than 50 per cent of all peasant households, middle peasants were
   another 30 to 35 per cent, and the remainder were well off or kulaks.
   Also Zhurov, *Eniseiskoe krest'ianstvo*, 40. For parallels with the Ukrainian
   peasantry, see Adams, *Bolsheviks in the Ukraine*, 386–404.

49 Okinskii, *Dva goda sredi krest'ian*, 101, 217, 265. Tambov province provides a good example of these perceptions at work. In the beginning
   of April 1919 there were constant rumours that any surplus grain
   would be requisitioned by force. This followed the successful harvests
   of the previous summer when peasants had been able to set aside
   enough grain to engage in a profitable trade with the bagmen and
   also to produce *samogon* (home-brewed illegal vodka) to make up for
   the absence of state-monopoly vodka. These developments confirmed
   the Bolshevik authorities in their view that the peasants could not be
   trusted and had to be kept under strict control and surveillance, at
   the same time convincing the peasants that the Bolsheviks wanted to
   take away their possessions.

50 According to Danilov, *Rural Russia under the New Regime*, 84: "The egalitarian use of land ... [introduced by] the October Revolution ... satisfied the peasants' mood and aspirations, while they sought to expand
   their smallholding family farm economy." Poliakov, *Sovetskaia strana
   posle okonchaniia grazhdanskoi voiny*, 220, concludes that thanks to
   Soviet policy there was "a dramatic decline by 1920 in the number of

landless households." Frenkin, *Tragediia krest'ianskikh vosstanii*, 21, concedes that the peasants of European Russia got significant amounts of
additional land for their use: average holdings for the *bedniak* (poor
peasant) went from five acres in 1917 to slightly over six acres in
1920. According to Andreev, "Prodrazverstka i krest'ianstvo," 43, from
1917 to 1920 poor peasants increased their landholdings by 150 per
cent, while kulaks saw theirs diminish by 54 per cent.

51 The single law of greatest importance for the land tenure system
during this period had been enacted in 1904. It gave Siberian peasants the right to demand the partitioning of their own lands from that
of the commune. See Glink, *Aziatskaia Rossiia*, 2: 562. Whereas
Stolypin's liquidation of the commune in European Russia was based
on the ukase of 9 November 1906, and later on the laws of 14 June
1910 and 29 May 1911, these measures did not apply initially to Siberia. Shanin, *Awkward Class*, 192–5, argues that the commune was the
key socio-economic levelling force in the rural revolution throughout
Russia, but that it was also often at odds with the proletarian dictatorship of the Communist party.

52 Gushchin, *Sibirskaia derevnia na puti k sotsializmu*, 77–81.

53 Golovachev, "Chastnoe zemlevladenie v Sibiri," 133–4.

54 Orlovsky, "State Building in the Civil War Era," 180–209.

55 GARF/TsGAOR, fond 1561, opis 1, ed.khr. 68:32 (fond NKVD SSSR),
"Doklad Instruktora Peremilovskogo o rabote 1–31 avgusta 1918 g." –
"The people want free trade all over the country, without fixed prices
on food items."

56 Quoted in Maksakov and Turunov, *Partizanskoe dvizhenie v Sibiri*, 1:166.

57 Quoted in Nikitin, *Dokumental'nye istochniki*, 62.

58 Mel'gunov, *Grazhdanskaia voina v osveshchenii P.N. Miliukova*, 46. There
were uncoordinated peasant insurrections simultaneously in Akmolinsk,
Mariinsk, Minusinsk, and Slavgorod.

59 Romanenko, "Slavgorodskoe vosstanie," 61–72.

60 Gorky, "On the Russian Peasantry," 24.

61 Guins, *Sibir'*, 2:245–6.

62 GARF/TsGAOR, fond 1235, opis 54, ed.khr. 2:14.

63 Ibid., 3.

64 Agurskii, "L'Aspect millénariste de la Révolution bolchévique," 505,
makes the suggestive assertion that "Old Believer peasants supported
the Bolsheviks, especially in the peripheries of the country, notably in
the Far East."

65 Alferov, *Krest'ianstvo Sibiri v 1917 godu*, 3.

66 Guins, *Sibir'*, 2:20.

67 Serebrennikov, *Moi vospominaniia*, 1:243. Also Mel'gunov, *Tragediia
Admirala Kolchaka*, part 3, 1:41.

68 Adelman, "The Development of the Soviet Party Apparat in the Civil War," 99. General Rozanov was particularly notorious for his bloody reprisals. According to HIA, Andrushkevich, "Posledniaia Rossiia," 11, he ordered his troops to have no pity for the populations sympathetic to the Bolsheviks.

69 Mel'gunov (Melgounov), *The Bolshevik Seizure of Power*, 181.

70 Spirin, *Klassy i partii v grazhdanskoi voine*, 300.

71 Serebrennikov, *Moi vospominaniia*, 216–17.

72 Varneck and Fisher, *The Testimony of Admiral Kolchak*, 107.

73 Cumming and Pettit, *Russian-American Relations*, 299–300. Emphasis added.

74 Ullman, *Britain and the Russian Civil War*, 139.

75 In order to avoid precisely this kind of conflict, the Allied plan had Janin in charge of the front and Knox of the rear. Also HIA, Vologodskii, "Diary," part 2:2.

76 BAR, Abrikosov, "Memoirs," 29.

77 Moltchanoff, "The Last White General," 96.

78 Janin, *Ma mission en Sibérie*, 212.

79 Carley, *Revolution and Intervention*, 184.

80 BAR, Pokrovskii, "Printed Materials – Civil War Broadsides."

81 Bradley, *Allied Intervention in Russia*, 114.

82 USNARS, RG 164, no. 289, Eugene Trupp, "Leaflets from the History of the Civil War in Russia," 3:9.

83 Debo, *Survival and Consolidation*, 25.

84 Stewart, *The White Armies of Russia*, 254–5. Also Chamberlin, *The Russian Revolution*, 2:189.

85 Dacy, "The White Russian Movement," 63.

86 The strategically important city of Ufa was captured in March. For details of what some considered the turning point of the military campaign in the east, see Kakurin, *Kak srazhalas' revoliutsiia*, 2:239.

87 Dacy, "The White Russian Movement," 61–2.

88 Ibid., 199.

89 Spirin, *Klassy i partii*, 290. Also Kakurin, *Kak srazhalas' revoliutsiia*, 2:130; and PRO, FO 4098, "Memorandum on Siberia" (20 December 1919): 1–2.

90 Overall the Red Army in May 1918 had only about 300,000 men, but by September it was 550,000, and at year's end, 800,000. Another two million were called up in the course of 1919. By 1920 there were more than five million soldiers; of these 77 per cent were peasants, 15 per cent were blue-collar workers, and 8 per cent were white-collar workers. Spirin, "Iz istorii PKP(b) v gody grazhdanskoi voiny i interventsii," 37. Also Azovtsev, *Grazdanskaia voina v SSSR*, 2:76–89.

91 Budberg, "Dnevnik," 14:227. See Mel'gunov, *Tragediia Admirala Kolchaka*, part 3, 5:144–45. This combination of bad judgement and wilful arbitrariness, as well as fierce personal loyalty to those who served him, were among the many traits in Kolchak which resembled those in Nicholas II.

92 Vologodskii, "Diary," part 2:31.

93 At the Interior Ministry, V.N. Pepeliaev took A.N. Gattenberger's place; at Justice, S.S. Starynkevich was replaced by G.G. Tel'berg; at Trade and Industry, N.N. Shchukin gave way to Mikhailov; the sole Menshevik, Labour Minister Shumilovskii, lost his job to L.I. Shundevskii; and at Education, P.I. Preobrezhinskii succeeded Professor V.V. Sapozhnikov.

94 HIA, Harris, Assorted Papers, box 2, "Memo of A.R. Thomson."

95 Guins, *Sibir'*, 2:183–6. Also Brovkin, *Behind the Front Lines*, 201.

CHAPTER SIX

1 Graves, *America's Siberian Adventure*, 201ff.

2 Dacy, "The White Russian Movement," 74–5.

3 Varneck and Fisher, *The Testimony of Admiral Kolchak*, 291–2.

4 HIA, Ovchinnikov Collection, "Outlines of my Reminiscences," 12–13.

5 GARF/TsGAOR, fond 130, opis 2, ed.khr. 575:100.

6 Kadeikin, *Sibir' nepokorennaia*, 418.

7 Trotskii, *How the Revolution Armed*, 1:455.

8 Piontovskii, *Grazhdanskaia voina v Rossii*, 248.

9 Quoted in Shanin, *The Awkward Class*, 149.

10 Logvinov, *V bor'be s kolchakovshchinoi*, 89. Also *Vos'moi s"ezd RKP(b)*, 402–6. The change in policy towards the rural population was reflected in the influx of peasants into the party; according to Figes, *Peasant Russia, Civil War*, 227, by 1921 the peasantry represented nearly one-third of the Bolshevik party membership in the Volga region.

11 USNARS, RG 165 (MID), 2327-A-18 (Memorandum of a conversation with an Allied army officer).

12 Stewart, *The White Armies of Russia*, 273–5, notes that a very large proportion of other supplies also failed to reach the front altogether.

13 USNARS, RG 165 (MID), AEF Siberia (10 July 1919), "Report from R.L. Eichelberger," 164–75.

14 Gorky, "On the Russian Peasantry," 22.

15 The railway was the largest of the three major recipients of subsidies from Omsk; the other two were the banks and private businesses. See *Struggling Russia*, 1: 293.

16 HIA, Pogrebetskii, "Currency Difficulties under the Kolchak Government," 4–6.

17 White, *The Siberian Intervention*, 303–4. Budberg, "Dnevnik," 13:306, refers to Mikhailov's currency reform as a disaster reflecting his "financial illiteracy and state cretinism."

18 According to Bourne and Watt, *British Documents on Foreign Affairs*, part 2, series A, 2:261, in the four months between December 1918 and April 1919 the value of the ruble in relation to pounds sterling fell by 42 per cent.

19 The Kolchak government was especially active in this regard during March and April of 1919; in those two months alone, it issued nearly three billion new rubles. The relative value and popular confidence in Omsk's currency plunged accordingly. Even friendly foreign banks in Siberia refused to accept the government's script. See Shikanova, "Denezhnaia reforma Kolchaka," 151.

20 HIA, Pogrebetskii, "Currency Difficulties under the Kolchak Government," 2.

21 USNARS, RG 45 (NRC), WA-6, box 611.

22 Shikanova, "Denezhnaia reforma Kolchaka," 154, estimates the consequent increase in the price of food and consumer goods to have been between 100 and 150 per cent.

23 Guins, *Sibir'*, 2:118, 404.

24 SSEES, Pares Papers, box 41: "They are for the most part landowners, small or great, and for that reason are opposed to Bolshevism."

25 Dacy, "The White Russian Movement," 290–1. In Eastern Siberia at about the same time, Semenov was threatening to help set up an independent Mongol state with the support of Japan, which would have liked nothing more than to "have the Mongols under its exclusive influence." See the telegram from Klemm (2 April 1919) in GARF/TsGAOR, fond 200, opis 1, ed.khr. 405:119. Two months earlier Semenov had helped organize a Mongol conference in Chita that proposed the formation of an independent state to include Mongolia, Tibet, and a large part of Transbaikal Russia bordering on Manchuria. See *Doklad predsedatelia chrezvychainoi sledstvennoi komissii po delu polkovnika Semenova* (25 March 1919) in GARF/TsGAOR, fond 200, opis 1, ed.khr. 404:49.

26 Gajda specifically warned of this danger in his report to Admiral Kolchak at the end of May 1919. See GARF/TsGAOR, fond 176, opis 3, delo 45:1.

27 Spirin, *Razgrom armii Kolchaka*, 114.

28 PRO, WO 32/5707 (10 December 1919) "Report on the Work of the British Military Mission to Siberia, 1918–1919," 12–13.

29 Quoted in Guins, *Sibir'*, 2:191.

30 Raleigh, *A Russian Civil War Diary*, 65, notes that there was "much discontent among soldiers who have recently returned from the front, shabbily dressed and shod and underfed, with the refusal of the Bolsheviks to furnish them necessary clothing."

31 Quoted in Piontovskii, *Grazhdanskaia voina*, 98–9.

32 Guins, *Sibir'*, 2:420.

33 HIA, Mel'gunov Collection, box 13, "Prestupleniia Kolchaka," 12.

34 To be sure, there were also important differences, notably in the realm of marital and family relations. Unlike the devoted tsar, the supreme ruler was far from an ideal husband and father. He maintained a mistress in Omsk while his wife and son were kept at a safe distance hundreds of miles away. Nevertheless, the former's portrait of Kolchak in her reminiscences is very romantic and flattering. Kniper, "Fragmenty vospominanii," 99–190.

35 Berezhnoi, *K istorii partiino-sovetskoi pechati*, 5–7.

36 Kenez, *Civil War in South Russia, 1919–1920*, 77, observes that "the very notion of propaganda went contrary to the White leaders' conception of the Civil War."

37 HIA, Ustrialov, "Belyi Omsk," 73, 85.

38 HIA, Andrushkevich, "Posledniaia Rossiia," 33–4.

39 Budberg, "Dnevnik," 14:332.

40 GARF/TsGAOR, fond 176, opis 3, delo 45:1-ob.

41 Guins, *Sibir'*, 2:196–7.

42 Bonch-Osmolovskii, *Gramota Verkhovnago Pravitelia o zemle*, 8.

43 GARF/TsGAOR, fond 193, opis 1, ed.khr. 42:22 – P.V. Vologodskii's testimony in "Zapiska o napravlenii agrarnoi politiki pravitel'stva, March–April 1919."

44 Piontovskii, *Grazhdanskaia voina*, 301–2. Another version, slightly modified to appeal to Western opinion, may be found in *Struggling Russia*, 1:183–4. Also see BAR, Pokrovskii, "Printed Materials – Civil War Broadsides." The declaration, however, also included a statement noting that the final resolution of the land question would have to await the "National [as distinct from the previous Constituent] Assembly," and that in the meantime no more spontaneous grabbing of land would be tolerated. It was signed by Kolchak and his Council of Ministers.

45 Quoted in Aver'ev, "Agrarnaia politika kolchakovshchiny," 6:30. Nevertheless, Aver'ev sees Kolchak's agrarian program, especially the idea of creating a state land fund out of alienated lands, as essentially Kadet and conservative. He also makes the point that it was better suited to conditions in European Russian (with which Kolchak was both more familiar and more concerned) than those in Siberia. Mel'gunov, *Tragediia Admirala Kolchaka*, part 3, 1:262–3, however, believed that Kolchak himself favoured transferring state and crown lands to needy peasants.

46 Guins, *Sibir'*, 2:151–8.

47 Smele, "'What Kolchak Wants!,'" 52–110.

48 Guins, *Sibir'*, 2:201ff.

49 Janin, *Ma mission en Sibérie*, 105. Also see MAE, Série E, carton 127, dossier 3, book 1:59 (Janin's note to the French Minister of War, 27 November 1919).

50 HIA, *Russia Posol'stvo* (United States), box 18, "Report of Captain N.F. Romanoff," 8. The sentiment was widespread and at least to some degree it was encouraged by the government in Omsk (if not personally by Kolchak). Propaganda pamphlets and posters released by the Russian Press Bureau frequently drew attention to Trotsky's very Jewish sounding family name and to the alleged connections between international Jewry, Communism, and imperial Germany. See GARF/TsGAOR, fond 9550, opis 2, ed.khr. 145:1, especially the pamphlet labelled "Lenin-Trotsky/Bronshtein, The Federated Soviet Monarchy."

51 Quoted in Silverlight, *The Victors' Dilemma*, 162.

52 Kenez, *Civil War in South Russia, 1919–1920*, 170. Gorky, "On the Russian Peasantry," 18, captured the popular anti-Semitic animus: "[No one] … enjoined the terrorist hundreds taking part in the pogroms to cut off the breasts of Jewish women, beat their children, drive nails into Jewish skulls – all these bloody abominations must be seen as 'manifestations of the personal initiative of the masses.'"

53 SSEES, Pares Papers, box 43, "Siberian Diary," 114.

54 Gimpel'son, "Vybory v sel'skie sovety v 1919 g.," 414–32.

55 Spirin, *Klassy i partii v grazhdanskoi voine*, 350.

56 Aver'ev, "Agrarnaia politika kolchakovshchiny," 8:42.

57 *Struggling Russia*, 1:293.

58 Debo, *Survival and Consolidation*, 403.

59 Ibid., 70.

60 Chamberlin, *The Russian Revolution*, 2:41.

61 During the early fall of 1919 Diterikhs attempted to recoup the fading fortunes with a counter-attack at Cheliabinsk. He issued orders to Siberian Ataman Ivanov-Rinov to effect a vital flanking movement, but the orders were rebuffed. When Diterikhs discharged the insubordinate ataman, the governing council of the Siberian Cossacks reinstated their leader at the head of his troops. See Dacy, "The White Russian Movement," 90.

62 Budberg, "Dnevnik," 14: 283. Also ibid., 285: "When it comes to matters relating to the front, the Admiral only listens to Stavka." Lebedev lasted as long as he did because he not only enjoyed the personal confidence of the supreme ruler but had also made effective political alliances with Mikhailov's clique.

63 Stewart, *The White Armies of Russia*, 293–4.

64 Ataman Dutov complained that his men were inadequately supplied, especially because of the total absence of any clothing. How, he asked, were his men to fight in mud and snow when they had no boots or

even *valenki* (peasant felt boots). Dutov pleaded for Kolchak's personal intercession to provide his men with "the basic necessities." GARF/ TsGAOR, fond 5873, opis 1, ed.khr. 8, "Dnevnik I.I. Serebrennikova," 142 (31 October 1919).

65 Quoted in Serebrennikov, *Moi vospominaniia*, 1:263.

66 HIA, Mel'gunov Collection, box 13, "Reziume doklada Iu.V. Kliuchnikova," 8 (2 June 1919).

67 MAE, Série E, carton 127, dossier 3 (1 July–20 August 1919), book 11:59. A French diplomat made this observation after visiting the front: "The name of Admiral Kolchak is little known at the front and ... his popularity has hardly penetrated there."

68 American Consul Eichelberger's report of 7 November 1919 in USNARS, RG 395, E6011, box 53:1. Similar conclusions are drawn by Pares; see SSEES, Pares Papers, box 43, "Siberian Diary," 79.

69 *Papers Relating to the Foreign Relations of the United States (Russia)*, 3:404. Also MAE, Série E, carton 127, dossier 3 (25 May–30 June, 1919), book 10:114: "What is most striking to the foreigner arriving in the 'Russia of Order' [Kolchakia] is the disorganization which prevails everywhere – in the transportation, monetary, army, and command [structures]." And PRO, FO 4098, "Memorandum on Siberia," 8 (20 December 1919): "Nor in the purely political realm has anything ever been done to remedy the genuine grievances of the civilian population or to take any account of their political aspirations. In particular, Kolchak's disregard of the zemstvos led to the greatest estrangement of political opinion."

70 Maksakov and Turunov, *Partizanskoe dvizhenie v Sibiri*, 1: 29. Seliunin, "Istoki,"166, argues that already in 1918 it was a three-way struggle among Reds, Whites, and Greens.

71 Logvinov, *V bor'be s kolchakovshchinoi*, 94.

72 Footman, *Siberian Partisans in the Civil War*, 6–7.

73 Nikitin, *Dokumental'nye istochniki*, 66–7, 85.

74 Aver'ev, "Agrarnaia politika kolchakovshchiny," 8:43.

75 Stishov, *Bol'shevistskoe podpol'e i partizanskoe dvizhenie*, 316–7.

76 Graves, "The Truth about Kolchak," 671.

77 Quoted in Mel'gunov, *Tragediia Admirala Kolchaka*, part 3, 1:207. At roughly the same time, very similar slogans circulated widely in Kazan' *guberniia* and Ukraine. See Litvin, *Kazan': vremia grazhdanskoi voiny*, 159; and Adams, *Bolsheviks in the Ukraine*, 297.

78 Quoted in Seleznev, *Partizanskoe dvizhenie v zapadnoi Sibiri*, 67–8.

79 Gushchin and Il'inykh, *Klassovaia bor'ba v sibirskoi derevne*, 45. Also Erickson, *The Soviet High Command*, 65.

80 Bradley, *The Czechoslovak Legion in Russia*, 144.

81 Quoted in HIA, Harris, Assorted Papers, box 1.

82 Of course, it was common knowledge that Kolchak's officers routinely abused their privileges by taking onto their convoys "not only family members but even acquaintances" at a time when desperately needed military supplies were left standing by the wayside at depots. GARF/ TsGAOR, fond 5873, opis 1, ed.khr. 8:60.

83 Actually Semenov had recognized Kolchak as supreme ruler in late May and promised his "disinterested [beskorystnoe] service" for the sake of the motherland. See the telegram from Semenov to Kolchak (27 May 1919) in GARF/TsGAOR, fond 200, opis 1, ed.khr. 405:153. However, Semenov did not make his move until after Kolchak had rescinded decree no. 60 against the Ataman and restored him to his previous duties, with a promotion to lieutenant general. Semenov had insisted all along that the admiral would have to make the first gesture of reconciliation. See ibid., 100, 124.

84 In the spring of 1919 sources in Irkutsk put the number of men under Semenov's command at about 4,000, "including Chinese and Mongols." See ibid., 102.

85 Bourne and Watt, British Documents on Foreign Affairs, part 2, series A, 2:123.

86 Svetachev, Imperialisticheskaia interventsiia v Sibiri, 194–5.

87 After returning home, Gajda became in due course a leader of the Czechoslovak Nazis. Khromov, Grazhdanskaia voina i voennaia interventsiia v SSSR, 139

88 Quoted in HIA, Nikolaevsky Collection, no. 145, box 1, file 7, "Gramota I. Iakusheva," 1–2.

89 Budberg, "Dnevnik," 15:333–4.

90 Sakharov, Belaia Sibir', 76ff.

91 Kolosov, Sibir pri Kolchake, 27.

92 The Irkutsk Political Centre was not acting in total isolation from the central party leadership. At the Ninth Council of the PSR in June 1919 in Moscow, several pro-Soviet resolutions were passed.

93 See Kolchak's decree of 4 January 1920 from Nizhne-Udinsk in GARF/ TsGAOR, fond 200, opis 1, ed.khr. 405:229.

94 Quoted in Krol', Za tri goda, 207. This "betrayal" by the agents of the allies has long been the subject of bitter recriminations among émigré admirers of the admiral. Recently the cause has been taken up in Russia as part of the rehabilitation of Kolchak in particular and of the Whites in general; both are now being portrayed as true Russian patriots and nationalists. See Egorov, Kolchak Aleksandr Vasil'evich, 4, where the admiral is described glowingly as "a Russian to the marrow of his bones. He loved Russia more than anything else on earth."

95 Janin, Mission, 261.

96 Ibid.

97 Bradley, Czechoslovak Legion, 149.

98 Egorov, *Kolchak Aleksandr Vasil'evich*, 56.
99 Varneck and Fisher, *The Testimony of Admiral Kolchak*, 222.

CHAPTER SEVEN

1 USNARS, RG 164 (MID), 164–223 (26 July 1919): 1–3.
2 Moltchanoff, "The Last White General," 92–5.
3 Smith, *Vladivostok under Red and White Rule*, xiii.
4 Parfenov, *The Intervention in Siberia*, 51, concedes that the Far Eastern Republic "was formed on the initiative of the Soviet Republic as a temporary measure to avoid friction with the Japanese, who were still ensconced in the Maritime Region."
5 Debo, *Survival and Consolidation*, 380–4.
6 Subbotovskii, *Soiuzniki, russkie reaktsionery i interventsiia*, 176.
7 Debo, *Survival and Consolidation*, 212–18.
8 Adams, *Bolsheviks in the Ukraine*, 280.
9 An additional incentive was the surplus grain in Siberia at this time. GARF/TsGAOR, fond 130, opis 4, ed.khr. 345:191.
10 Smith, *Vladivostok under Red and White Rule*, 62.
11 Norton, *The Far Eastern Republic of Siberia*, 79.
12 Debo, *Survival and Consolidation*, 388.
13 Agurskii, *Ideologiia natsional-bol'shevizma*.
14 Parfenov, *The Intervention in Siberia*, 52–4.
15 Moltchanoff occupied Khabarovsk as late as December 1921. Stephan, *The Russian Far East*, 150.
16 Balakshin, *Final v Kitae*, 1:98; and Smith, *Vladivostok under Red and White Rule*, 152–65.
17 Moltchanoff, "The Last White General," 130.
18 Ibid., 131. See Kenez, *Civil War in South Russia, 1919–1920*, xiii, for similarities.
19 GARF/TsGAOR, fond 1561, opis 1, ed.khr. 69:14 ("MVD Vremennago Sibirskago Pravitel'stva, Informatsionno-Agitatsionnyi Otdel").
20 GARF/TsGAOR, fond 130, opis 4, ed.khr. 602:416.
21 El'tsin, "Krest'ianskoe dvizhenie v Sibiri v period Kolchaka," 3:59.
22 Ibid., 80.
23 Quoted from the Declaration in Nikitin, *Dokumental'nye istochniki*, 82: "The freedoms of speech and the press are the most essential conditions for the development of the human being."
24 *Sokha i molot*, 18 October 1919, as quoted in Nikitin, "Gazeta *Sokha i molot* kak istochnik," 160–1.
25 GARF/TsGAOR, fond 130, opis 3, ed.khr. 885:1-ob. Also Mirzoev, *Partizanskoe dvizhenie v zapadnoi Sibiri*, 23–4.
26 Shishkin, "Bol'sheviki i partizanskoe dvizhenie v Sibiri v osveshchenii," 73–4.

27 Shishkin, "Kozyrevshchina i ee likvidatsiia," 67–70.

28 Kanev, *Oktiabr'skaia revoliutsiia i krakh anarkhizma*, 99ff.

29 Quoted in Gromov, *Partizanskoe dvizhenie v zapadnoi Sibiri*, 128.

30 *Sovetskaia istoricheskaia entsiklopediia*, 10:884. Parfenov, *Grazhdanskaia voina v Sibiri*, 91, puts the figure at closer to 120,000.

31 According to HIA, Andrushkevich, "Posledniaia Rossiia," 21, Shchetinkin repeated this tale, except that in his confused version, "in the Far East the [Grand] Prince Mikhail Aleksandrovich was appointed a minister by Trotsky and Lenin; and that only one thing remained, to defeat Kolchak."

32 Golub, *Revoliutsiia zashchishchaetsiia*, 255.

33 Stishov, *Bol'shevitskoe podpol'e i partizanskoe dvizhenie*, 198–9. Also Mirzoev, *Partizanskoe dvizhenie v zapadnoi Sibiri*, 122–4.

34 Nenarokov, *Vostochnyi front 1918*, 154–7.

35 Shishkin, "Bor'ba bol'shevikov za ob"edinenie sibirskikh partizan," 89–90.

36 Seleznev, *Partizanskoe dvizhenie v zapadnoi Sibiri*, 134.

37 Zhigalin, *Partizanskie otriady zanimali goroda*, 97.

38 Shishkin, "Bor'ba bol'shevikov za ob"edinenie sibirskikh partizan," 100–1.

39 GARF/TsGAOR, fond 130, opis 3, delo 414:34–6. The Cheka responded by intervening actively and arresting hundreds of suspects. See ibid., 59-ob., 60.

40 The clergy were especially fearful for their properties and privileges, and were among the most outspoken critics of the new regime. See GARF/TsGAOR, fond 130, opis 3, delo 414:27-ob.

41 Ibid., 57.

42 Ibid., 57, 59.

43 GARF/TsGAOR, fond 130, opis 4, ed.khr. 345:222.

44 *Dekrety sovetskoi vlasti*, 10:239–40.

45 Kabanov, *Krest'ianskoe khoziastvo*, 183. And GARF/TsGAOR, fond 130, opis 4, ed.khr. 345:191.

46 It was no mere coincidence that in these first months of 1921 the entire Menshevik leadership (about 2,000 individuals) were arrested or sent into exile. According to Schapiro, *1917: The Russian Revolutions*, 190, this marked "the virtual end of the party."

47 GARF/TsGAOR, fond 130, opis 4, ed.khr. 599:124-a, indicates that as of August 1920 local *razverstka* was completed to the following extent in these *gubernii*: Omsk–58 per cent, Tomsk–23 per cent, Altai–29 per cent, Semipalatinsk–43 per cent, Eniseisk–28 per cent, and Irkutsk–56 per cent.

48 Gushchin, *Sibirskaia derevnia na puti k sotsializmu*, 61–6. This was, of course, not a pattern peculiar to Siberia. Figes, *Peasant Russia, Civil War*, 270, points out that there was great resentment in many places

because "the peasants lost a part of their basic food and seed stores as a result of the 1919–20 procurement campaign."

49 *GARF/TsGAOR*, fond 130, opis 4, ed.khr. 599:131-ob.

50 *GARF/TsGAOR*, fond 130, opis 3, delo 414:28.

51 Quoted in Figes, *Peasant Russia, Civil War*, 273.

52 Shishkin, "Prodovol'stvennaia kampaniia 1920–21 goda v Sibiri," 136.

53 Goriushkin, "Ob izuchenii istorii krest'ianstva Sibiri," 102.

54 *GARF/TsGAOR*, fond 130, opis 3, delo 414:59-ob.

55 Gushchin and Il'inykh, *Klassovaia bor'ba v sibirskoi derevne*, 64.

56 Shanin, *The Awkward Class*, 161, suggests that common village interests were paramount, especially in response to an "increase in the external pressures from the state." Even "the so-called kulak rebellions [of 1919–21] seem nearly always to have been general peasant uprisings, in which no class distinction can be traced … All strata of the peasantry seem to have risen by localities with remarkable unity and with no trace of internal class division." Ibid., 147.

57 Stishov, *Bol'shevistskoe podpol'e*, 192–4.

58 *GARF/TsGAOR*, fond 130, opis 3, delo 414:43-ob. On Novoselov's anti-Soviet activity in Krasnoiarsk *guberniia*, see ibid., 60, 60-ob.

59 Figes, *Peasant Russia, Civil War*, 339. Also Trotskii, *How the Revolution Armed*, 2:137; Kenez, *Civil War in South Russia, 1919–1920*, 162–5; and Pietsch, *Revolution und Staat*, 27–9.

60 *GARF/TsGAOR*, fond 130, opis 3, delo 414:60-ob.

61 Ibid., opis 4, ed.khr. 981:94–5.

62 Quoted in Shishkin, "Iz istorii bor'by kommunisticheskoi partii i sovetskoi vlasti protiv anarkhizma," 22.

63 *GARF/TsGAOR*, fond 130, opis 3, delo 414:23.

64 Pavlunovskii, *Obzor banditskogo dvizheniia po Sibiri*, 27.

65 *GARF/TsGAOR*, fond 393, opis 22, ed.khr. 219:18.

66 *GARF/TsGAOR*, fond 130, opis 3, ed.khr. 414:76–101.

67 *GARF/TsGAOR*, fond 130, opis 4, ed.khr. 345:394.

68 Pavlunovskii, "Sibirskii krest'ianskii soiuz," 123.

69 Ibid. Also Bogdanov, *Razgrom zapadno-sibirskogo kulatsko-eserovskogo miatezha*, 12–19; *GARF/TsGAOR*, fond 130, opis 3, ed.khr. 414:68.

70 Kakurin, *Kak srazhalas' revoliutsiia*, 2:136–8.

71 Frenkin, *Tragediia krest'ianskikh vosstanii*, 124.

72 Figes, *Peasant Russia, Civil War*, 322.

73 Steinberg, *In the Workshop of the Revolution*, 265–6.

74 Vladimir Brovkin is rather more critical of the peasantry: "Survival of the Bolshevik dictatorship out of the ordeal of the Civil War [was] not … a manifestation of popular support but … the pre-national consciousness and backwardness of the Russian peasantry, the majority of the nation. And the brutality of the new regime was partly a manifestation

of the crassness and brutality of those peasant upstarts who strove to be the new masters." Brovkin, "Identity, Allegiance and Participation," 563.

75 Report of Lieutenant General Gajda to Admiral Kolchak (May 1919) in *GARF/TsGAOR*, fond 176, opis 3, delo 45:2-ob.

76 For a thoughtful analysis of Lenin's mentality, see Scheibert, *Lenin an der Macht.*

77 Quoted in Owen, *The Russian Peasant Movement*, 247.

78 Avrich, *Kronstadt 1921*, 72–4.

79 Figes, *Peasant Russia, Civil War,* 355. The overlap of Marxist and militarist values is a main thesis of Von Hagen, *Soldiers in the Proletarian Dictatorship.*

80 *Sibir' v proshlom i nastoiashchem*, 25.

81 Bernshtam, "Storony v grazhdanskoi voine," 325–6. Moroever, Bernshtam asserts that of these, 10.5 million disappeared as a direct result of revolutionary violence rather than of hunger, disease, or emigration, and 80 per cent of them were civilian bystanders.

82 Kolchak, "Ia znal bor'bu," 87–96. Another exception may be seen in the words of Left SR leader Maria Spiridonova (quoted in Steinberg, *In the Workshop of the Revolution,* 246), during her own incarceration under the Soviet government in Butyrki prison, that "Everybody knows that the resistance of peasants acting in self-defense is not counter-revolution, that counter-revolution is rather in the acts that are responsible for these uprisings and in their brutal suppression."

83 Dineo, "The Russian Peasant–What Is He," *The New Russia,* 2:265.

84 Bunin, *The Village,* 63.

85 Brovkin, "Identity, Allegiance and Participation," 562, concludes: "One of the reasons the peasant movement did not win militarily, despite its magnitude and scope, was that each province or area of several provinces had its own political dynamics, out of tune with the rest of the country." Alroy, *The Involvement of Peasants,* 26, observes that the conduct of civil war is "actually premised on advantage flowing from the victimization of peasants."

86 Quoted in Krol', *Za tri goda,* 190.

87 There were small pockets of armed anti-Soviet resistance well into the 1920s in remote areas of Siberia like Kolyma and along the Mongolian frontier. See Krotov, "Bor'ba s kontrrevoliutsiei v severo-vostochnoi Iakutii," 66–102. And Spence, "White against Red in Uriankhai," 97–120.

88 In the *Far Eastern Review* (5 February 1920): 3, Kolchak's former propaganda chief, N.V. Ustrialov, wrote that the chief reason for the Bolsheviks' triumph was that they came to represent the Russian nation. The White "anti-governments tied themselves too closely with foreigners, and this is what made the Bolsheviki [appear] ... as defenders of the national cause."

89 For many patriotic anti-Communists the choice was clear and irresist-
ible. Professor Ustrialov expressed it best (as quoted in Serebrennikov,
Moi vospominaniia, 1:272): "I am now completely at peace about Russia: she once again is gathering herself into an unified whole." To be
sure, most Whites did not reconcile with the new masters of the Russian state and many emigrated eastward instead. In the middle of the
1920s, in Harbin alone, with an overall population of half a million
people, about 150,000 were Russians. Among the many prominent
anti-Communists in the Manchurian city were professionals (like the
Russian-Jewish leader I.A. Kaufman), academics (G.K. Guins and V.N.
Riasanovsky), journalists, businessmen, and former civil servants. Some
helped organize political groups, such as the Russian Fascist Party with
its emphasis upon Orthodoxy and nationalism; it, along with the Toil-
ing Peasants' Party and the Brotherhood of the Russian Truth,
believed in the viability of armed struggle and continued to finance
forays into the Soviet borderlands for several years after the end of the
Civil War. See Balakshin, *Final v Kitae*, 1:105ff.
90 *Struggling Russia*, 2:433.

CONCLUSION

1 The French estimate was that it would take 100,000 Allied expeditionary
troops to turn the tide of battle in favour of the Whites in Siberia. MAE,
Série E, carton 128, dossier 1 (1 June 1918–31 July 1918), book 2:88.
2 Mawdsley, *The Russian Civil War*, 213–14, estimates the population of
the Red-controlled central regions to have been on average (taking
into account constantly shifting fronts) more than twice the combined
total of the territories under Kolchak and Denikin.
3 Figes, "The Red Army and Mass Mobilization," 184: "Given its enormous social and political significance, the Russian civil war was actually
fought between miniscule armies (the forces deployed by either side
on a given front rarely exceeded 100,000)."
4 Degtiarev, "O sotsial'noi strukture krasnoi armii," 55; Movchin, "Komplektovanie krasnoi armii," 2: 75–90; Olikov, *Dezertirstvo v krasnoi armii*,
27–33; and Molodtsygin, *Raboche-krest'ianskii soiuz*, 138–9.
5 Spirin, *Klassy i partii v grazhdanskoi voine*, 290, states that in the spring
of 1919 Kolchak had brought military strength up to about 400,000
men, with fully a third of them at the front. According to Pipes, *Russia
under the Bolshevik Regime*, 78, however, Lenin's decision to concentrate
all manpower on the eastern front meant that by June it was the Reds
who enjoyed a numerical advantage of 20,000 to 30,000 men.
6 *Papers Relating to the Foreign Relations of the United States (Russia)*, 3:211.
In fact, desertions and inadequate supplies for the men were serious

problems for both sides, with the Whites having an obvious advantage only in terms of food. Rations in the Red Army declined significantly from the norm set in February 1919 at approximately one pound of bread per day, which itself was lower than what the tsar's army received during most of World War I. See Figes, "The Red Army and Mass Mobilization," 191. Brovkin, *Behind the Front Lines*, 192, argues that the triumph of the Reds over the Whites should be seen as "a victory of one weak and unpopular regime over another weak and unpopular regime."

7 Frunze, *Sobranie sochinenii*, 2:175.

8 Semenov, *O sebe*, 127.

9 Guins, *Sibir'*, 2:272.

10 Pipes, *Russia under the Bolshevik Regime*, 373, however, goes too far when he asserts that by "1920–21, except for its own cadres, the Bolshevik regime had the whole country against it."

11 On the question of Western misreading of the final crisis of the Soviet Union, see Malia, *The Soviet Tragedy*.

12 A more scholarly but still sympathetic approach may be seen in recent volumes of *Russkoe proshloe* and in major journals like *Voprosy istorii* (Drokov, "Aleksandr Vasil'evich Kolchak.").

Bibliography

ARCHIVES

ARCHIVES DU QUAI D'ORSAY, Paris
Ministère des Affaires étrangères (MAE), Russie d'Asie. Direction des Affaires politiques et commerciales. (1918–22).

BAKHMETEFF ARCHIVES (BAR), Columbia University, New York
Abrikosov, D.I. "Memoirs."
Akintievskii, K.K. "K istorii grazhdanskoi voiny v Sibiri i na Dal'nem Vostoke 1818–1922 gg." (1955).
Astrov, N.I. "1918 god." S.V. Panina Collection, box 13.
– "Moskovskie organizatsii 1917–1918 g." S.V. Panina Collection, box 10.
Denikin, A.I. Collection. (1918), box 56.
Fedotov [Fedotoff] White, D. N. "Untitled Autobiography," folders 7–15.
Golitsyn, A.D. "Vospominaniia."
Golovachev, M.P. "Perevorot Admirala Kolchaka." (1918).
– "Programma sibirskoi narodnoi partii." (1918).
– "Rapport du Professeur Golovatchoff." (1918), box 2.
– "Siberian Movement and Communism." (1918), box 1.
– "Territoriia Rossii." (1918).
Martynov, N.A. "Civil War Memoirs."
Mikhailov, V.A. "Memoirs on Russian Revolution & Civil War."
Miliukov, P.N. "Diary of Paul N. Miliukov (1918–1920)."
– "The First Step in Russian Regeneration." (1919).
– "Kadet Party in Civil War."

Panina S.V. Collection, "Civil War – Kadets (in general)," box 13.
Pokrovskii, V.L. & B.L. "Printed Materials – Civil War Broadsides." (1919).
Reitzel, G.B. "Shifting Scenes in Siberia." (1920). Paul B. Anderson Collection.
S.R. Party Collection. "Siberia." (1919).
Zenzinov, V.M. "Collection." (1919).

GOSUDARSTVENNYI ARKHIV ROSSIISKOI FEDERATSII [formerly Tsentral'nyi gosudarstvennyi arkhiv oktiabrskoi revoliutsii] (GARF/TsGAOR), Moscow
Fondy 130, 131, 176, 180, 193, 200, 393, 1235, 1561, 5844, 5873, 9550.

HOOVER INSTITUTION ARCHIVES (HIA), Stanford, California
Andrushkevich, N.A. "Posledniaia Rossiia."
Anichkov, V.P. "Vospominaniia."
Ceska Druzhina. *The Operations of the Czechoslovak Army in Russia in the Years 1917–1920.*
Elachich, S.A. "Obryvki vospominanii."
Fedichkin, D.I. "Izhevskoe vosstanie, ot 8 avgusta po 15 oktiabria 1918 goda."
Guins (Gins), G.K. "Collection."
Harris, E.L. "Assorted Papers." (1918–21), boxes 1–3.
Kolobov, M.V. "Bor'ba s bol'shevikami na Dal'nem Vostoke (Khorvat, Kolchak, Semenov, Merkulovy, Diterikhs): vospominaniia uchastnika."
Kriukov, B.A. "Collection." (1919).
Markov, A. "Encyclopedia of the White Movement." 4 vols.
Mathews, S.E. "Siberia." (1918–20).
Maklakov, V.A. "Papers." (1917–1956), boxes 1–22.
Mel'gunov (Melgounov), S.P. "Collection." box 13.
Moravsky, V.I. "Collection." (1917–34).
Nikolaevsky, B.I. "Collection." (1918–19), boxes 1–2.
Ostroukhov, P. "Collection." (1918).
Ovchinnikov, A.Z. "Collection." (1920).
Pares, B. "Political Conditions in Western Siberia." (1919), box 1.
Pogrebetskii, A.I. "Currency Difficulties under the Kolchak Government."
Puchkov, F.A. "The Icy March." (1921–22).
Russia: "Posol'stvo (United States)." (1914–33), boxes 9, 18.
Russia: "Vremennoe Sibirskoe Pravitel'stvo." (1918–20).
Semenov, G.M. "Istorii moei bor'by s bol'shevikami." (1918).
Serebrennikov, I.I. "Eastern Siberia," box 9.
– "K istorii sibirskago pravitel'stva," box 9.
– "Pamiatka sibiriaka."
– "Poslednyi put' Admirala Kolchaka."
– "The Siberian Autonomous Movement and its Future," box 11.
– "Sibirskoe tsarstvo."
– "Vospominaniia ob A.V. Kolchake."

Sychev, E. "Vosstanie v Irkutske." (1919–20).
Tibbar, W. "Revolutionary Odyssey of the White Rabbit."
United States Army. "American Expeditionary Force–Siberia." (1919).
Upovalov, I. "How We Lost Our Liberty." (1918–19).
Ustrialov, N.V. Collection. "Belyi Omsk." (1920–34), box 1.
Varneck, E. "The Revolution and Civil War in Siberia and the Russian Far East."
Volkov, B. "About Ungern." (1921–31).
Vologodskii, P.V. (Varneck, E. trans.). "Diary." (1918), box 1.
– "Otchet po poezdke na pervyi obshchesibirskii s'ezd'" (1918–25).
Vyrypaev, V.I. (Varneck, E. trans.). "Vladimir Oskarovich Kappel': vospominaniia uchastnika beloi bor'by." (1918), box 1.

INDIA OFFICE RECORDS (IOR), London
The War: Eastern Reports. L/P&S/10/587. (1917–19).

PUBLIC RECORDS OFFICE (PRO), London and Kew
British Cabinet Papers. "Memorandum on the Japanese Role in the Intervention in Siberia & Notes on the Intervention of Japan in Siberia." (1918).
Foreign Office Files (FO), 4098, 4110.
War Office Files (WO), 32, 106.

RUSSIAN MUSEUM, San Francisco
Fedulenko (Fedoulenko), V.V. "Rol' byvshikh soiuznikov Rossii po otnosheniiu k belomu dvizheniiu v Sibiri." (1961).

SCHOOL OF SLAVONIC AND EAST EUROPEAN STUDIES, UNIVERSITY OF LONDON (SSEES), London
Pares Papers, boxes 28, 41, 42, 43, 44, 46 and 48.

UNITED STATES NATIONAL ARCHIVES AND RECORDS SERVICE (USNARS), Washington, D.C.
Military Intelligence Division (MID).
Naval Records Collection (NRC).
Record Groups (RG) 45, 164, 165, 395.

NEWSPAPERS

Dalekaia okraina (1918–19).
Delo Sibiri (1918).
Delo svobody (1918).
Far Eastern Review (1920).
Golos Altaia (1918).

Golos rabochago (1918).

Golos svobody (1917).

Izvestiia (1918–20).

Kooperativnoe slovo (1918).

Manchester Guardian (1918–20).

Nasha derevnia (1918–19).

New York Times (1918–20).

Novosti zhizni (1918).

Pravitel'stvennyi vestnik (1918–19).

Sibir' (1875, 1877).

Sibiriak-Krest'ianin (1918).

Sibirskaia kooperatsiia (1918).

Sibirskaia rech' (1917).

Sibirskaia zhizn' (1917).

Sibirskii vestnik (1918).

Sotsialist-Revoliutsioner (1918).

Soviet Russia (1920).

Svoboda Rossii (1918).

Times (London) (1918–19).

Vol'naia Sibir' (1918).

Vol'nyi Kazak (1918).

Volia (1918).

Vozrozhdenie (1919).

Zapadnaia Sibir' (1918).

Zaria (1918).

Zemlia i volia (1918).

Zemskaia gazeta (1918).

Znamia truda (1918).

MONOGRAPHIC AND PERIODICAL LITERATURE

Abov, A. "Oktiabr' v vostochnoi Sibiri." *Sibirskie ogni*, no. 4 (1924): 107–21.

Abrams, R. "The Local Soviets of the RSFSR, 1918–1921." Columbia University: PH D dissertation 1966.

Ackerman, C.W. *Trailing the Bolsheviki; Twelve Thousand Miles with the Allies in Siberia.* New York: Charles Scribner's Sons 1919.

Adams, A.E. *Bolsheviks in the Ukraine, 1918–19.* New York: Kennilcat Press 1973.

Adelman, J.R. "The Development of the Soviet Party Apparat in the Civil War: Center, Localities, and Nationality Areas." *Russian History*, no. 9 (1982): 86–110.

Adrianov, A.V. *Periodicheskaia pechat' v Sibiri.* Tomsk: Tipo-Litografiia tomsk. zhel.-dorogoi 1919.

Agalakov, V.T. "Bol'shevistskoe rukovodstvo v sovetakh Sibiri v kontse 1917–1918 gg." *Sibirskii istoricheskii sbornik*, no. 2 (1974): 101–28.

– *Podvig tsentrosibiri.* Irkutsk: Vostochno-Sibirskoe kn. izd. 1968.

– *Sovety Sibiri (1917–1918).* Novosibirsk: Nauka 1978.

Agurskii, M. "L'Aspect millénariste de la Révolution bolchévique." *Cahiers du Monde russe et soviétique* 29, no. 3–4 (1988): 487–514.

– *Ideologiia natsional-bol'shevizma.* Paris: YMCA-Press 1980.

Alekseev, S.A., ed. *Grazhdanskaia voina v Sibiri i severnoi oblasti.* 6 vols. Moscow-Leningrad: Gosizd. 1926–30.

Alekseev, V.V., ed. *Velikii oktiabr' i sotsialistichekie preobrazovaniia v Sibiri.* Novosibirsk: Nauka 1980.

Alferov, M.S. *Krest'ianstvo Sibiri v 1917 godu.* Novosibirsk: Nauka 1958.

Alroy, G.C. *The Involvement of Peasants in Internal Wars.* Princeton, N.J.: Princeton University Press 1966.

Amfiteatrov, A.V. *Sibirskie etiudy.* St Petersburg: Obshchestvo Pol'za 1904.

Andreev, L., ed. "K istorii razgroma vooruzhennykh sil Kolchaka." *Krasnyi arkhiv* 6(49) (1931): 55–91.

Andreev, V.M. "Prodrazverstka i krest'ianstvo." *Istoricheskie zapiski* 97 (1976): 5–49.

Andrushkevich, N.A. "Posledniaia Rossiia." *Beloe delo* 4 (1928): 108–45.

Anishev, A. *Ocherki istorii grazhdanskoi voiny 1917–1920 gg.* Leningrad: Gosizd. 1925.

Antsiferov, A.N., A.D. Bilimovich, et al. *Russian Agriculture during the War.* New Haven: Yale University Press 1930.

Arans, D. *How We Lost the Civil War. Bibliography of Russian Emigre Memoirs on the Russian Revolution, 1917–1921.* Newtonville, Mass.: Oriental Research Partners 1988.

Argunov, A.A. "Omskie dni v 1918 godu." *Sibirskii arkhiv,* no. 5 (1935): 191–208.

Aristov, N.Ia. "Zhizn' Athanasiia Prokof'evicha Shchapova," *Istoricheskii vestnik,* no. 10 (1882): 307–14.

Arnoldov, L.V. *Zhizn' i revoliutsiia.* Shanghaii: Zaria 1935.

Astrov, N.I. "Priznanie Gen. Denikinym Admirala Kolchaka." *Golos minuvshago na chuzhoi storone,* no. 1(14) (1926): 201–22.

Atkinson, R.O. "Traveling through Siberian Chaos." *Harper's Magazine* (November 1918): 813–27.

Aver'ev, V.N. "Agrarnaia politika kolchakovshchiny." *Na agrarnom fronte,* no. 6 (1929): 24–45; no. 8 (1929): 23–44.

Avrich, P. *Kronstadt 1921.* Princeton: Princeton University Press 1970.

Azadovskii, M.K., et al., eds. *Sibirskaia sovetskaia entsiklopediia.* 3 vols. Novosibirsk: Sibirskoe kraevoe izd. 1929–32.

Azovtsev, N.N., et al., eds. *Grazhdanskaia voina v SSSR.* 2 vols. Moscow: Voenizd. 1980–86.

Bibliography

- *V boiakh rozhdennaia, 1918–1920: boevoi put' 5 armii.* Irkutsk: Vostochno-Sibirskoe knizhnoe izd. 1985.

Babikova, E.N. "Bor'ba s kontrrevoliutsionnym zemstvom v tomskoi gubernii (1917–aprel' 1918 gg.)." *Voprosy istorii Sibiri,* vyp. 4 (1969): 189–202.

Baikalov, A.V. "Siberia since 1894." *Slavonic and East European Review* 11, no. 32 (1933): 328–40.

Balakshin, P. *Final v Kitae.* 2 vols. San Francisco: Sirius 1958.

Bartlett, R., ed. *Land Commune and Peasant Community in Russia. Communal Forms in Imperial and Early Soviet Society.* London: SSEES/Macmillan 1990.

Bassin, M. "A Russian Mississippi? A Political-Geographical Inquiry into the Vision of Russia on the Pacific 1840–1865." University of California, Berkeley: PH D dissertation 1983.

Batalov, A.N. *Bor'ba bol'shevikov za armiiu v Sibiri 1916-fevral' 1918.* Novosibirsk: Nauka 1978.

Baturin, V. "Eshelon smerti. (Vospominaniia rabochego)." *Sibirskie ogni,* no. 6 (1929): 129–39.

Belikova, L.I. *Kommunisty Primor'ia v bor'be za vlast' sovetov na Dal'nem Vostoke (primorskaia organizatsiia RKP(b) v 1917–1922 gg.).* Khabarovsk: Khabarovskoe knizh. izd. 1967.

Beling, A.B. "The Question of Allied Recognition of the Kolchak Government." Columbia University: MA thesis 1949.

Berezhnoi, A.F. *K istorii partiino-sovetskoi pechati.* Leningrad: Izd. leningrad. gos. universitet 1956.

Berk, S.M. "The 'Class-Tragedy' of Izhevsk: Working-Class Opposition to Bolshevism in 1918." *Russian History* 2, no. 2 (1975): 176–90.

- "The Coup D'Etat of Admiral Kolchak: The Counterrevolution in Siberia and East Russia 1917–1918." Columbia University: PH D dissertation 1971.

- "The Democratic Counterrevolution: Komuch and the Civil War on the Volga." *Canadian-American Slavic Studies* 7, no. 4 (1973): 443–59.

Bernshtam, M.S. "Storony v grazhdanskoi voine 1917–1922 gg." *Vestnik russkogo khristianskogo dvizheniia,* no. 128 (1979): 252–357.

-, ed. *Ural i Prikam'e noiabr' 1917–ianvar' 1919.* Paris: YMCA-Press 1982.

Bobrick, B. *East of the Sun.* New York: Poseidon Press 1992.

Bogdanov, M.A. *Razgrom zapadno-sibirskogo kulatsko-eserovskogo miatezha 1921 g.* Tiumen': Tiumenskoe knizhnoe izd. 1961.

Boldyrev, V.G. *Direktoriia, Kolchak, Interventy.* Novonikolaevsk: Sibkraiizd. 1925.

- "Vospominaniia byvshego glavkoverkha Ufimskoi Direktorii (s predisloviem i primechaniiami V. Vegmana)." *Sibirskie ogni,* no. 5–6 (1923): 105–26.

Bol'tin, E.A. *Kontrnastuplenie iuzhnoi gruppy vostochnogo fronta i razgrom Kolchaka (1919).* Moscow: Voenizd. 1949.

Bonch-Osmolovskii, A., ed. *Gramota Verkhovnago Pravitelia o zemle.* Omsk: Russkoe biuro pechati 1919.

Bondarenko, A.A. "Levye Esery Sibiri v nachal'nyi period grazhdanskoi voiny." In *Oktiabr' i grazhdanskaia voina v Sibiri. Istoriia. Istoriografiia. Istochnikovedenie,* 86–101. Tomsk: Izd. tomsk. universiteta 1985.

Borman, A. "My Meetings with White Generals." *Russian Review,* no. 27(2) (1968): 215–24.

Borrero, M. "Hunger and Society in Civil War Moscow." Indiana University: PH D dissertation 1992.

Bortnevskii, V.G., et al., eds. *Russkoe proshloe.* St Petersburg: Svelen 1991– .

Bourne, K., and D.C. Watt, eds. *British Documents on Foreign Affairs: Reports and Papers from the Foreign Office Confidential Print.* Frederick, Maryland: University Publications of America 1984.

Bradley, J.F.N. *Allied Intervention in Russia.* London: Weidenfeld and Nicolson 1968.

– "The Allies and the Czech Revolt against the Bolsheviks in 1918." *Slavonic and East European Review* 43, no. 6 (1965): 275–92.

– *Civil War in Russia, 1917–1920.* London: B. T. Batsford 1975.

– *The Czechoslovak Legion in Russia, 1914–1920.* Boulder, Colorado: East European Monographs 1991.

British Foreign Office Historical Section. "Eastern Siberia." London: H.M. Stationery Office 1920.

Brovkin, V.M. *Behind the Front Lines of the Civil War.* Princeton, New Jersey: Princeton University Press 1994.

– "Identity, Allegiance and Participation in the Russian Civil War." *European History* 22, no. 4 (1992): 541–67.

– *The Mensheviks after October: Socialist Opposition and the Rise of the Bolshevik Dictatorship.* Ithaca, N.Y.: Cornell University Press 1987.

– "The Mensheviks' Political Comeback: The Elections to the Provincial City Soviets in Spring 1918." *Russian Review* 42, no. 1 (1983): 1–50.

– "The Mensheviks under Attack: The Transformation of Soviet Politics, June-September 1918." *Jahrbücher für Geschichte Osteuropas* 32 (1984): 378–91.

Bubnov, A.S., S.S. Kamenev, and R.P. Eideman, eds. *Grazhdanskaia voina 1918–1921.* 3 vols. Moscow: Gosizd. 1928–30.

Budberg, A. P. "Dnevnik." *Arkhiv russkoi revoliutsii* (1923–24), 12:197–290, 13:197–313, 14:225–341, 15:254–345.

Bunin, I. *The Village.* Translated by I. Hapgood. London: Martin Secker 1934.

Bunyan, J., ed. *Intervention, Civil War and Communism in Russia, April-December 1918: Documents and Materials.* New York: Octagon Books 1976.

– and H.H. Fisher, eds. *The Bolshevik Revolution, 1917–1918. Documents and Materials.* Stanford: Stanford University Press 1961.

Burbank, J. *Intelligentsia and Revolution: Russian Views of Bolshevism, 1917–1922.* New York: Oxford University Press 1986.

Bystrianskii, B. *Raboche-Krest'ianskaia revoliutsiia v Rossii v otsenke burzhuaznoi publitsistiki.* Petrograd: Izd. petrograd. soveta 1919.

Carley, M.J. "The Origins of the French Intervention in the Russian Civil War, January-May 1918: A Reappraisal." *Journal of Modern History* 48, no. 3 (1976): 413–39.

– *Revolution and Intervention: The French Government and the Russian Civil War, 1917–1919.* Kingston and Montreal: McGill-Queen's University Press 1983.

Challener, R.D., ed. *U.S. Military Intelligence, 1917–1927: Weekly Summaries.* 5 vols. New York and London: Garland Publishing 1978–79.

Chamberlin, W. H. *The Russian Revolution.* 2 vols. New York: Grosset & Dunlap 1965.

Channon, J. "Regional Variation in the Commune: The Case of Siberia." In R. Bartlett, ed., *Land Commune and Peasant Community in Russia. Communal Forms in Imperial and Early Soviet Society,* 66–85. London: SSEES/Macmillan 1990.

– "'White' Agrarian Policy: A Research Commentary and Documentary Material." *Sbornik,* no. 12 (1986): 108–17.

Chase, W.J. *Workers, Society, and the Soviet State. Labor and Life in Moscow, 1918–1929.* Urbana and Chicago: University of Illinois Press 1987.

Chechek, S. "Ot Penzy Do Urala." *Voliia Rossii* 8–9 (1928): 246–65.

Cherniak, E.I. *Eserovskie organizatsii v Sibiri v 1917–nachale 1918 gg.* Tomsk: Izd. tomsk. universiteta 1987.

–, ed. *Politicheskie partii v Sibiri (mart 1917–noiabr' 1918 gg.).* Tomsk: Izd. tomsk. universiteta 1993.

– "Razgrom kontrrevoliutsii na vostoke strany i formirovanie osnovnykh elementov ideologii 'smenovekhovstva.'" In *Iz istorii interventsii i grazhdanskoi voiny v Sibiri i na Dal'nem Vostoke, 1917–1922 gg.,* 194–9. Novosibirsk: Nauka 1985.

–, ed. *S"ezdy, konferentsii i soveshchaniia sotsial'no-klassovykh, politicheskikh, religioznykh, natsional'nykh organizatsii v Tomskoi gubernii (mart–noiabr' 1918 gg.).* 2 parts. Tomsk: Izd. tomsk. universiteta 1992.

Chernov, V.M. *Pered burei. Vospominaniia.* New York: Izd. im. Chekova 1953.

Coleman, F. *Japan Moved North. The Inside Story of the Struggle for Siberia.* London: Cassell and Co. Ltd. 1918.

Collins, D., ed. *Siberia and the Soviet Far East.* Oxford: Clio Press 1991.

– and J. Smele, eds. *Kolchak i Sibir': dokumenty i issledovaniia, 1919–1926.* New York: Kraus International 1988.

Colton, T.J. "Military Councils and Military Politics in the Russian Civil War." *Canadian Slavonic Papers* 8, no. 1 (1976): 36–57.

Congressional Record–House 58. Washington, D.C.: United States Congress 1919.

Connaugton, R. *The Republic of the Ushakova.* London: Routledge 1990.

Cumming, C.K., and W.W. Pettit. *Russian-American Relations, March 1917–March 1920, Documents and Papers.* New York: Harcourt, Brace and Howe 1920.

Dacy, D. "The White Russian Movement." University of Texas: PH D dissertation 1972.

Dallin, D. "The Outbreak of the Civil War." In L.H. Haimson, ed., *The Mensheviks*, 156–90. Chicago: University of Chicago Press 1971.

Daniels, R.V. *The Conscience of the Revolution.* New York: Simon & Schuster 1969.

Danilov, A.A. et al., eds. *Istoriia otechestva* vyp. 1. Moscow: Obshchestvo 'Znanie' rossiiskoi federatsii 1992.

Danilov, V.P., ed. *Kooperativno-kolkhoznoe stroitel'stvo v SSSR, 1917–1922.* Moscow: Nauka 1990.

– *Rural Russia under the New Regime.* Bloomington, Ind.: Indiana University Press 1988.

Debo, R.K. *Revolution and Survival: The Foreign Policy of Soviet Russia, 1917–1918.* Liverpool: Liverpool University Press 1979.

– *Survival and Consolidation: The Foreign Policy of Soviet Russia, 1918–1921.* Montreal and Kingston: McGill-Queen's University Press 1992.

Dedenev, L.S., "Bol'shevistskie organizatsii Sibiri v izbiratel'noi kampanii po vyboram v uchreditel'noe sobranie (iun'-dekabr' 1917 g.)." In *Sbornik rabot aspirantov kafedry istorii KPSS*, 22–40. Tomsk: Izd. tomsk. universiteta 1971.

Degras, J., ed. *Soviet Documents on Foreign Policy.* 2 vols. London: Oxford University Press 1953.

Degtiarev. "O sotsial'noi strukture krasnoi armii." *Politrabotnik*, no. 2 (1922): 55–62.

Dekrety sovetskoi vlasti. 10 vols. Moscow: Izd. pol. lit. 1986.

Demidov, V.A. et al., eds. *Bol'sheviki Sibiri v trekh revoliutsiiakh.* Novosibirsk: Novosibirsk. gos. universitet 1981.

– *Partiinye organizatsii Sibiri i Dal'nego Vostoka v period oktiabr'skoi revoliutsii i grazhdanskoi voiny (1917–1922 gg.).* Novosibirsk: Novosibirsk. gos. universitet 1978.

Dineo. "The Russian Peasant – What Is He?" *The New Russia* 2 (1920): 264–9.

Dolgorukov, P.D. *Natsional'naia politika i Partiia Narodnoi Svobody.* Rostov-na-donu: Svobodnaia rech' 1919.

Dolinin (Moravskii), E.Z. *V vikhre revoliutsii.* Detroit: Izd. Drug 1954.

Dolunts, G.K. *Kirov na severnom Kavkaze.* Moscow: Politizdat. 1973.

Dotsenko, P. *The Struggle for a Democracy in Siberia 1917–1920.* Stanford, California: Hoover Institution Press 1983.

– "The Struggle for the Liberation of Siberia, 1918–1921." Interviewed by R.A. Pierce. *California-Russian Emigre Series.* Berkeley, California: Regional Oral History Office 1960.

Drokov, S.V. "Aleksandr Vasil'evich Kolchak." *Voprosy istorii*, no. 1: 50–67.

Dubarbier, G. "Omsk under Kolchak." *The Living Age* 322, no. 4179 (1924): 167–72.

Dubrovskii, K.V. *V tsarstve nagaiki i viselitsy. Sibirskaia kontrrevoliutsiia 1918–1919 godov.* Moscow-Leningrad: Gosizd. 1929.

Dubrovskii, S.M. *Krest'ianstvo v 1917 godu.* Moscow-Leningrad: Gosizd. 1927.

Dugarm, D. "Hunger and Duty: Food Supply in Rural Russia, 1914–21." Stanford University: PH D dissertation 1992.

Dumova, N.G. *Kadetskaia kontrrevoliutsiia i ee razgrom (oktiabr' 1917–1920 gg.).* Moscow: Nauka 1982.

– *Kadetskaia partiia v period pervoi mirovoi voiny i fevral'skoi revoliutsii.* Moscow: Nauka 1988.

Dvorianov, N. and V. *V tylu Kolchaka.* Moscow: Mysl' 1963.

Dzhon. "Dva generala." *Golos minuvshago na chuzhoi storone,* no. 1/14 (1926): 189–99.

Efimov, A.G. "Pamiati Admirala Kolchaka." *Voennaia byl',* no. 66 (1964): 2–10.

Efremov, M.P., et al., eds. *Nezabyvaemoe.* Moscow: Voenizd. 1961.

Egorov, G.V., ed. *Kolchak Aleksandr Vasil'evich–poslednie dni zhizni.* Barnaul: Altaiskoe knizhnoe izd. 1991.

Eikhe, G.Kh. *Oprokinutyi tyl'.* Moscow: Voenizd. 1966.

– *Ufimskaia avantiura Kolchaka (mart–aprel' 1919 g.).* Moscow: Voenizd. 1960.

Elagin, V., ed. "Iz istorii semenovshchiny v 1919 g." *Krasnyi arkhiv* 6(67) (1934): 131–46.

El'sukova, Z.M. "Krest'ianskie vosstaniia v zapadnoi Sibiri osen'iu 1918 goda." In *Novosibirskii elektrotekhnicheskii institut, trudy kafedr obshchestvennykh nauk* vyp. 1 (1960): 44–52.

El'tsin, B. "Krest'ianskoe dvizhenie v Sibiri v period Kolchaka." *Proletarskaia revoliutsiia,* no. 2(49) (1926): 5–48; no. 3(50) (1926): 51–82.

Engel'gardt, A.N. *Iz derevni. 11 pisem.* Moscow: Mysl' 1987.

Entsiklopedicheskii slovar'. 86 vols. St. Petersburg: F.A. Brokgauz and I.A. Efron 1900.

Erickson, J. *The Soviet High Command.* Boulder, Colorado: Westview Press 1962.

Espe. *God v tsarstve Kolchaka. Materialy po istorii rabochego dvizheniia v Sibiri s iiulia 1918 g. do iiulia 1919 g.* Kazan: Izd. vneshkol'nogo 1920.

Eudin, X.J. "Soviet National Minority Policies, 1918–1921." *American Slavic and East European Review* 21 (1943): 31–55.

Fedotov [Fedotoff] White, D.N. *The Growth of the Russian Army.* Princeton, N.J.: Princeton University Press 1944.

Fedulenko (Fedoulenko), V.V. "Russian Emigre Life in Shanghai." Interviewed by B. Raymond. *California-Russian Emigre Series.* Berkeley, California: Regional Oral History Office 1967.

Fel'shtinskii, G. *Bol'sheviki i Levye Esery, oktiabr' 1917-iiul' 1918: na puti k odnopartiinoi diktature.* Paris: YMCA-Press 1985.

Fic, V.M. *The Bolsheviks and the Czechoslovak Legion: The Origins of their Conflict, March–May 1918.* New Delhi: Abhinar Publishers 1978.

Figes, O. *Peasant Russia, Civil War, the Volga Countryside in Revolution.* Oxford: Clarendon Press 1989.

- "The Red Army and Mass Mobilization during the Russian Civil War, 1918–1920." *Past and Present*, no. 129 (1990): 168–211.
- "The Russian Peasant Community in the Agrarian Revolution, 1917–18." In R. Bartlett, ed., *Land Commune and Peasant Community in Russia: Communal Forms in Imperial and Early Soviet Society*, 237–53. New York: St. Martin's Press 1990.

Filat'ev, D.V. *Katastrofa belogo dvizheniia v Sibiri*. Paris: YMCA-Press 1985.

Filimonov, B.B. *Na putiakh k Uralu. Pokhod stepnykh polkov leto 1918 goda*. Shanghai: T.S. Filimonovoi 1934.

Fitzpatrick, S. "The Civil War as a Formative Experience." In *Bolshevik Culture*, 57–76. Bloomington, Ind.: Indiana University Press 1985.

Fleming, P. *The Fate of Admiral Kolchak*. London: Hart-Davis 1963.

Foglesong, D.S. "America's Secret War against Bolshevism: US Intervention in the Russian Civil War, 1917–20." Rutgers University: PH D dissertation 1991.

Fomin, N. "Kooperatsiia i perevorot v Sibiri." *Sibirskaia kooperatsiia*, no. 6–8 (1918): 1–9.

Fominykh, S.F. *K istorii interventsii i grazhdanskoi voiny v Sibiri i na Dal'nem Vostoke. Kriticheskii analiz amerikanskoi diplomaticheskoi perepiski kak istoricheskogo istochnika*. Tomsk: Izd. tomsk. universiteta 1988.

Footman, D. *Civil War in Russia*. London: Faber and Faber 1961.
- *The Last Days of Kolchak*. Oxford: Oxford University Press 1953.
- *The Red Army On The Eastern Front*. Oxford: Oxford University Press 1955.
- *Siberian Partisans in the Civil War*. Oxford: Oxford University Press 1954.

Forsyth, J. *A History of the Peoples of Siberia: Russia's North Asian Colony, 1581–1990*. New York: Cambridge University Press 1992.
- "The Siberian Native Peoples before and after the Russian Conquest." In A. Wood, ed. *The History of Siberia*, 69–91. London: Routledge 1991.

Foster, G.M. "Peasant Society and the Image of Limited Good." *American Anthropologist* 67, no. 2 (1965): 293–315.

Freeze, G.L. "The Soslovie (Estate) Paradigm and Russian Social History." *American Historical Review* 91, no. 1 (1986): 11–36.

Frenkin, M. *Tragediia krest'ianskikh vosstanii v Rossii 1918–1921 gg*. Jerusalem: Leksikon 1987.

Frierson, C. "From Narod to Kulak: Peasant Images in Russia, 1870–1885." Harvard University: PH D dissertation 1985.

Frunze, M.V. *Sobranie sochinenii*. 3 vols., ed. A.S. Bubnov. Moscow: Gosizd. 1927–9.

Furmanov, D. "Kratkii obzor literatury (neperiodicheskoi) o grazhdanskoi voine (1918–1920)." *Proletarskaia revolutiutsiia*, no. 5 (1923): 321–41.

Furshchik, M. "K voprosu o vozrozhdenii burzhuaznoi ideologii." *Sibirskie ogni*, no. 5 (1922): 84–101.

Gardner, L.C. *Safe for Democracy: The Anglo-American Response to Revolution, 1913–1923.* New York: Oxford University Press 1984.

Garmiza, V.V. "Bankrotstvo politiki 'tret'ego puti' v revoliutsii (ufimskoe gosudarstvennoe soveshchanie 1918 g.)." *Istoriia SSSR,* no. 6 (1965): 3–25.

– "Direktoria i Kolchak." *Voprosy istorii,* no. 10 (1976): 16–32.

– "Iz istorii bor'by rabochikh Sibiri protiv 'Demokraticheskoi kontrrevoliutsii.'" *Istoriia SSSR,* no. 4 (1975): 120–32.

– *Krushenie eserovskikh pravitel'stu.* Moscow: Mysl' 1970.

Gavrilov, D.V., ed. *Istoriia Urala v period kapitalizma.* Moscow: Nauka 1990.

Gerasimiuk, V.R. "Uravnitel'noe raspredelenie zemel' v evropeiskoi chasti rossiiskoi federatsii v 1918 g." *Istoriia SSSR,* no. 1 (1965): 94–103.

Gertsen [Herzen], A.I. *Childhood, Youth and Exile.* Oxford: Oxford University Press 1980.

– *Sobranie sochinenii.* Moscow: Izd. AN SSSR 1954–65.

Gessen, I.V., ed. *Arkhiv russkoi revoliutsii.* 6 vols. Berlin: Slowo-Verlag 1922.

Getzler, I. *Kronstadt 1917–1921: The Fate of a Soviet Democracy.* Cambridge: Cambridge University Press 1983.

Gibson, J.R. "The Significance of Siberia to Tsarist Russia." *Canadian Slavonic Papers,* no. 14 (1972): 442–53.

– "Paradoxical Perceptions of Siberia: Patrician and Plebian Images up to the Mid-1800s." In G. Diment and Y. Slezkine, eds., *Between Heaven and Hell,* 67–93. New York: St. Martin's 1993.

Gill, G.J. *Peasants and Government in the Russian Revolution.* London: The Macmillan Press 1979.

Gimpel'son, E.G. *Rabochii klass v upravlenii sovetskim gosudarstvom noiabr' 1917–1920 gg.* Moscow: Nauka 1982.

– *"Voennyi Kommunizm": politika, praktika, ideologiia.* Moscow: Mysl' 1973.

– "Vybory v sel'skie sovety v 1919 g." In *Oktiabr' i grazhdanskaia voina v SSSR,* 414–32. Moscow: Nauka 1966.

Glink, G.V., ed. *Aziatskaia Rossiia.* 2 vols. Cambridge, Mass.: Oriental Research Partners 1974.

Glinskii, B.B. "Nikolai Mikhailovich Iadrintsev," *Istoricheskii vestnik,* no. 8 (1894): 422–58.

Glukharev, V. "Kontr-revoliutsiia v Sibiri." *Krasnaia letopis',* no. 5 (1923): 356–70.

Golinkov, D.L. *Krushenie antisovetskogo podpol'ia v SSSR.* 2 vols. Moscow: Izd. polit. literatury 1980.

– "Razgrom ochagov vnutrennei kontrrevoliutsii v sovetskoi Rossii." *Voprosy istorii,* no. 12 (1967): 131–44; no. 1 (1968): 133–49.

Golovachev, L.M. "Chastnoe zemlevladenie v Sibiri," *Sibirskie voprosy,* 1 (1905): 129–43.

Golovin, N.N. *Alphabetical Index of Books and Periodicals in Russian Dealing with the History of the World War, Russian Revolution and Civil War.* N.p. 1929.

Golub, P.A. *Revoliutsiia zashchishchaetsiia.* Moscow: Izd. polit. lit. 1982.

Gordeev, A.A. *Istoriia Kazakov. Velikaia voina 1914–1918 gg. Otrechenie gosudaria. Vremennoe pravitel'stvo i anarkhiia. Grazhdanskaia voina.* Moscow: Strastnoi bul'var 1993.

Gordon, A. *The Russian Civil War.* London: Cassell 1937.

Gorenskaia, V.G. "Rol' gazety 'Bednota' v politicheskom prosveshchenii krest'ianstva v gody grazhdanskoi voiny i inostrannoi voennoi interventsii (1918–1920 gg.)." In *Voprosy istorii partiinykh organizatsii Sibiri, vyp.* 2:37–42. Krasnoiarsk: Izd. Krasnoiarsk. gos. universiteta 1973.

Goriushkin (Goryushkin), L.M. *Agrarnye otnosheniia v Sibiri perioda imperializma (1900–1917 gg.).* Novosibirsk: Nauka 1976.

–, ed. *Istochniki po istorii osvoenia Sibiri v period kapitalizma.* Novosibirsk: Nauka 1989.

– "Migration, settlement and the rural economy of Siberia, 1861–1914." In A. Wood, ed., *The History of Siberia,* 140–157. London: Routledge 1991.

– "Ob izuchenii istorii krest'ianstva Sibiri v period oktiabr'skoi revoliutsii i grazhdanskoi voiny." In *Problemy istorii sovetskogo obshchestva Sibiri,* 94–106. Novosibirsk: SOAN SSSR 1970

– *Politicheskaia ssylka v Sibiri XIX-nachalo XX v.* Novosibirsk: Nauka 1987.

– *Revoliutsionnoe i obshchestvennoe dvizhenie v Sibiri v kontse XIX–nachalo XX v.* Novosibirsk: Nauka 1986.

– *Sibirskoe krest'ianstvo na rubezhe dvukh vekov.* Novosibirsk: Nauka 1979.

– *Sotsial'no-ekonomicheskie otnosheniia i klassovaia bor'ba v Sibiri dooktiabr'skogo perioda.* Novosibirsk: Nauka 1987.

– *Sotsial'no-ekonomicheskie predposylki sotsialisticheskoi revoliutsii v sibirskoi derevne.* Novosibirsk: Nauka 1962.

– *Ssylka i obshchestvenno-politicheskaia zhizn' v Sibiri.* Novosibirsk: Nauka 1978.

–, G.A. Nozdrin and A.N. Sagaidachnyi. *Krest'ianskoe dvizhenie v Sibiri 1914–1917 gg. Khronika i istoriografiia* Novosibirsk: Nauka 1987.

Gorky, M. "On the Russian Peasantry." In R.E.F. Smith, ed., *The Russian Peasant 1920 and 1984.* London: Frank Cass & Co. Ltd. 1977.

Gorniaki Sibiri, 1917–1927 gg. Novosibirsk: Izd. TsK. sibkraikoma 1928.

Graves, S.C. "The Truth about Kolchak." *New York Times Current History Magazine* (July 1921): 668–71.

Graves, W.S. *America's Siberian Adventure, 1918–1920.* New York: Cape and Smith 1941.

Gromov, I.V. *Za vlast' sovetskuiu.* Barnaul: Altaiskoe knizh. izd. 1966.

–, et al., eds. *Partizanskoe dvizhenie v zapadnoi Sibiri (1918–1920 gg.).* Novosibirsk: Nauka 1959.

Grondijs, L.H. *La guerre en Russie et en Sibérie.* Paris: Éditions Bossard 1922.

– *Le Cas-Koltchak.* Leiden: A.W. Sijthoff 1939.

Gronsky, P.P., and N.J. Astrov. *The War and the Russian Government.* New York: Howard Fertig 1973.

Grushin, I. "Bor'ba s kolchakovshchinoi v Kustanae." *Proletarskaia Revoliutsiia*, no. 9(56) (1926): 150–92.
Guins (Gins), G.K. "Impressions of the Russian Imperial Government." Interviewed by R.A. Pierce. *California-Russian Emigre Series*. Berkeley, California: Regional Oral History Office 1971.
– "Professor and Government Official: Russia, China, and California." Interviewed by B. Raymond. *California-Russian Emigre Series*. Berkeley, California: Regional Oral History Office 1966.
– "The Siberian Intervention, 1918–1919." *The Russian Review* 28, no. 4 (1969): 428–40.
– *Sibir', soiuzniki, i Kolchak.* 2 vols. Peking: Izd. obshchestvo vozrozhdeniia Rossii 1921.
Gul', R. *Ia unes Rossiiu.* 3 vols. New York: Most 1989.
Gurevich, B. "The End of Ataman Annenkov." *Far Eastern Affairs*, no. 6 (1990): 92–103.
Gusev, K.V., ed. *Bol'sheviki v bor'be s neproletarskimi partiiami, gruppami i techeniiami. Materialy konferentsii.* Kalinin: Kalinin. gos. universiteta 1983.
– *Partiia eserov: ot melkoburzhuaznogo revoliutsionarizma k kontrrevoliutsii.* Moscow: Mysl' 1975.
Gushchin, N.Ia. *Istoriografiia sovetskoi Sibiri (1917–1945 gg.).* Novosibirsk: Nauka 1968.
– *Sibirskaia derevnia na puti k sotsializmu.* Novosibirsk: Nauka 1973.
–, and V.A. Il'inykh. *Klassovaia bor'ba v sibirskoi derevne 1920-e – seredina 1930-kh gg.* Novosibirsk: Nauka 1987.
Gutman, A. (Anatolii Gan). *Rossia i bol'shevizm: materialy po istorii revoliutsii i bor'by s bol'shevizmom 1914–1920.* Shanghai: Russkago tov. 1921.
Haefner, L. "The Assassination of Count Mirbach and the 'July Uprising' of the Left Socialist Revolutionaries in Moscow, 1918." *Russian Review*, no. 3 (1991): 324–44.
Haimson, L., ed. *The Mensheviks.* Chicago: University of Chicago Press 1974.
– "The Mensheviks after the October Revolution, Part II: The Extraordinary Party Congress." *Russian Review* 39, no. 2 (April 1980): 181–207.
– "The Problem of Social Identities in Early Twentieth Century Russia." *Slavic Review* 47, no. 1 (spring 1988): 1–20.
Halpern, M. "The Morality and Politics of Intervention." In *International Aspects of Civil Strife*, 249–88. Princeton, N.J.: Princeton University Press 1964.
Hard, W. *Raymond Robins' Own Story.* New York: Harper 1920.
Heald, E.T. *Witness to Revolution.* Ohio: Kent State University Press 1972.
Hobsbawm, E.J. "Peasants and Politics." *Journal of Peasant Studies* 1, no. 1 (1973): 3–22.
Hughes, J. *Stalin, Siberia and the Crisis of the New Economic Policy.* Cambridge: Cambridge University Press 1991.

Iadrintsev, N.M. "K moei avtobiografii." *Russkaia mysl'*, no. 6 (1904): 161–8.
- "Nachalo pechati v Sibiri." In *Literaturnyi sbornik. Izdanie redaktsii 'Vostochnago obozreniia'*. St Petersburg: Tipografiia I.N. Skorokhodova 1885.
- *Sibir' kak koloniia v geograficheskom, etnograficheskom, i istoricheskom otnoshenii.* St Petersburg: Izd. I. M. Sibiriakova 1882–92.
- *Sibirskie inorodtsy, ikh byt' i sovremennoe polozhenie.* St Petersburg: Izd. I. M. Sibiriakova 1891.
Iakushev, I.A. "Fevral'skaia revoliutsiia i sibirskie oblastnye s"ezdy." *Vol'naia Sibir'*, no. 2 (1927): 13–40.
- "Manifesto of the President of the Regional Duma of Siberia." *Contemporary Review*, no. 117 (1920): 253–5.
- "Ocherki oblastnogo dvizheniia v Sibiri." *Vol'naia Sibir'*, no. 3 (1928): 9–27; no. 4 (1928): 100–13; nos. 6–7 (1928): 88–103.
Iaroslavskii, E. "Bol'sheviki v fevral'sko-martovskie dni." *Proletarskaia revoliutsiia*, no. 2–3 (1927): 36–60.
- "Po Sibiri." *Sibirskie ogni*, no. 3 (1922): 132–45.
- "Zarodishi kommunizma v sibirskoi derevne – ogni Sibiri." *Sibirskie ogni*, no. 1 (1922): 100–4.
Il'in, I.S. "Omsk, Direktoriia, Kolchak." *Novyi zhurnal*, no. 72 (1963): 198–217; no. 73 (1963): 216–43.
Inostrantsev, M.A. "Pervoe poruchenie Admirala Kolchaka." *Beloe delo*, no. 1 (1927): 95–108.
Ioffe, G.Z. "Iz istorii kadetsko-monarkhicheskoi kontrrevoliutsii v Rossii." In *Iz istorii interventsii i grazhdanskoi voiny v Sibiri i na Dal'nem Vostoke, 1917–1922 gg.*, 161–9. Novosibirsk: Nauka 1985.
- *Kolchakovskaia avantiura i ee krakh.* Moscow: Mysl' 1983.
- "Ot kontrrevoliutsii 'demokraticheskoi' k burzhuazno-pomeshchich'ei diktature. (Omskii perevorot)." *Istoriia SSSR*, no. 1 (1982): 108–19.
Iroshnikov, M.P. *Rozhdenie Oktiabria.* Leningrad: Nauka 1987.
Istoriia krest'ianstva v Sibiri. 4 vols. Novosibirsk: Nauka 1982–85.
Istoriia Sibiri. Informatsionno-bibliografisheskii biulleten'. 4 vols. Novosibirsk 1970.
Istoriografiia krestianstva sovetskoi Sibiri. Novosibirsk: Nauka 1976.
Iurasova, M.K. *Omsk: ocherki istorii goroda.* Omsk: Zapadno-Sibirskoe knizhnoe izd. 1972.
Iurkov, I.A. "Financial Policies of the Soviet Government and Monetary Trade Relations during the Civil War (1918–1920)." *Soviet Studies in History* 23, no. 2 (fall 1984): 62–89.
Ivanov, M. "Oktiabr' v Sibiri." *Proletarskaia revoliutsiia*, no. 10(81) (1928): 362–88.
Ivanov, V.N. *V grazhdanskoi voine. Iz zapiska omskogo zhurnalista.* Harbin: Zaria 1921.
Iz istorii sotsial'no-ekonomicheskoi i politicheskoi zhizni Sibiri. Tomsk: Izd. tomsk. universiteta 1976.

Iz istorii sovetskogo Omska (1917–iun' 1941 gg.). Omsk: Zapadno-Sibirskoe knizhnoe izd. 1975.

Janin, P.T.C.M. *Ma Mission en Sibérie*. Paris: Payot 1933.

K.V. "Oblastnoe obozrenie." *Sibirskie zapiski*, no. 3 (1919): 84–93; nos. 4–5 (1919): 96–109.

Kabanov, P.I. *Obshchestvenno-politicheskie i istorichskie vzgliady A.P. Shchapova*. Moscow: Gos. ucheb.-pedagog. izd. 1954.

Kabanov, V.V. *Krest'ianskoe khoziastvo v usloviakh 'voennogo kommunizma'*. Moscow: Nauka 1988.

Kadeikin, V.A. "Antirabochaia politika vremennogo sibirskogo pravitel'stva." In *Voprosy istorii Sibiri*, vyp. 4:148–61. Tomsk: Izd. tomsk. universiteta 1969.

– "Grazhdanskaia voina v Sibiri." In *Istoriografiia sovetskoi Sibiri (1917–1945 gg.)*, 32–72. Novosibirsk: Nauka, 1968.

– *Sibir' nepokorennaia. Kemerovo: Kemerovskoe knizh. izd.* 1968.

Kakurin, N. *Kak srazhalas' revoliutsiia*. 2 vols. Moscow-Leningrad: Gosizd. 1925.

– *Strategicheskii ocherk grazhdanskoi voiny*. Moscow-Leningrad: Gosizd. 1926.

Kal'nin, Ia. "Trud pri belykh." *Sibirskie ogni*, no. 3 (1929): 134–42.

Kaminskii, S.B., and A.I. Romanenko. "Istoriografiia partiinogo prosveshcheniia v Sibiri v 1917–1937 gg." In *Istoriografiia kultury i intelligentsii sovetskoi Sibiri*, 98–118. Novosibirsk: Nauka 1978.

Kanev, S.N. *Oktiabr'skaia revoliutsiia i krakh anarkhizma*. Moscow: Mysl' 1974.

Katkov, N.F. *Agitatsionno-propagandistskaia rabota bol'shevikov v voiskakh i tylu belogvardeitsev v period 1918–1920 gg.* Leningrad: Izd. Leningrad. universiteta 1977.

Kaufman, A.A. *Krest'ianskaia obshchina v Sibiri*. St Petersburg: Tipografiia P.P. Soikina 1897.

– *Pereselenie i kolonizatsiia*. St Petersburg: Tipografiia obshchestvennaia pol'za 1905.

Kayden, E.M., and A.N. Antisiferov. *The Cooperative Movement in Russia during the War*. New Haven: Yale University Press 1929.

Kazmer, D.R. "The Agricultural Development of Siberia, 1890–1917." MIT: PH D dissertation 1973.

Keep, J.L.H. *The Russian Revolution: A Study in Mass Mobilization*. New York: Norton 1976.

–, ed. *The Debate on Soviet Power: Minutes of the All-Russian Central Executive Committee of Soviets, Second Convocation, October 1917-January 1918*. Oxford: Clarendon Press 1979.

– "October in the Provinces." In R. Pipes, ed., *Revolutionary Russia: A Symposium*, 229–75. New York: Doubleday 1969.

Kenez, P. *The Birth of the Propaganda State*. Cambridge: Cambridge University Press 1985.

– *Civil War in South Russia, 1918*. Berkeley and Los Angeles: University of California Press 1971.

- *Civil War in South Russia, 1919–1920*. Berkeley and Los Angeles: University of California Press 1977.
- "The Ideology of the White Movement." *Soviet Studies* 32, no. 1 (1980): 58–83.

Kennan, G. *Siberia and the Exile System*. 2 vols. New York: The Century 1891.
- *Siberia: Natural Scenery*. New York: The New York Public Library 1935.

Kennan, G.F. "The Czechoslovak Legion." *Russian Review* 16, no. 4 (1957): 3–16; 17, no. 1 (1958): 11–28.
- *The Decision to Intervene*. Princeton, N.J.: Princeton University Press 1958.
- *Russia Leaves the War*. Princeton, N.J.: Princeton University Press 1956.

Kerner, R.J. *The Urge to the Sea: The Course of Russian History*. Berkeley, California: University of California Press 1942.

Kesarev, S.P., A.N. Korolev, and S.G. Pichugov. *Osobaia brigada*. Moscow: Voenizd. 1962.

Kettle, M. *The Road to Intervention, March–November 1918*. New York: Routledge 1988.

Khromov, S.S., et al., eds. *Grazhdanskaia voina i voennaia interventsiia v SSSR. Entsiklopediia*. Moscow: Sovetskaia entsiklopediia 1983.

King, R.D. "Sergei Kirov and the Struggle for Soviet Power in the Terek Region, 1917–1918." University of Illinois: PH D dissertation 1983.

Kirilov, A.A. "Sibirskaia armiia v bor'be za osvobozhdenie." *Vol'naia Sibir'*, no. 4 (1928): 36–68.

Klante, M. *Von der Wolga zum Amur. Die tschechische Legion und der russische Bürgerkrieg*. Berlin: Ost-Europa verlag 1931.

Klarov, Iu. "Fakty svidetel'stvuiut." In *Perepiska na istoricheskie temy*, 266–307. Moscow: Izd. Politicheskoi Literatury 1989.

Kniper, A.V. "Fragmenty vospominanii." *Minuvshee*, no. 1 (1986): 99–190.

Knox, A. "General Janin's Siberian Diary." *Slavonic Review* 3, no. 9 (1925): 724.

Kochan, L. "Kadet Policy in 1917 and the Constituent Assembly." *Slavonic and East European Review* 14 (1967): 183–92.

Koenker, D., W.G. Rosenberg, and R.G. Suny, eds. *Party, State, and Society in the Russian Civil War*. Bloomington and Indianapolis: Indiana University Press 1989.

Kolchak, A.V. "Ia znal bor'bu, no ne znal schast'ia pobedy." *Morskoi sbornik*, no. 10 (1990): 87–96.
- "Pis'mo verkhovnago pravitelia." *Belyi arkhiv* 1 (1926): 136–7.

Kolchak, R. "Admiral Kolchak, ego rod i sem'ia." *Voenno-istoricheskii vestnik*, no. 16 (1960): 14–20.

"Kolchak's Methods in Siberia." *New York Times Current History Magazine*. (January 1920): 95–8.

Kolosov, E.E. "Krest'ianskoe dvizhenie pri Kolchake." *Byloe*, no. 20 (1920): 223–67.
- *Sibiri pri Kolchake*. Petrograd: Izd. Byloe 1923.

Kolz, A.W.F. "British Economic Interests in Siberia during the Russian Civil War, 1918–1920." *Journal of Modern History*, no. 48(3) (1976): 483–91.

Komu zemlia? Omsk: Izd. Novaia Rossiia 1919.

Konstantinov, M.M. *Poslednie dni kolchakovshchiny. Sbornik dokumentov.* Moscow-Leningrad: Gosizd. 1926.

Korablev, Iu.I. "Grazhdanskaia voina 1918–1920 godov: novye podkhody." In *Stranitsy istorii sovetskogo obshchestva*, 56–87. Moscow: Izd. politicheskoi literatury 1989.

– and V.I. Shishkin, eds. *Iz istorii interventsii i grazhdanskoi voiny v Sibiri i na Dal'nem Vostoke, 1917–1922 gg.* Novosibirsk: Nauka 1985.

Kosykh, E.N. *Periodicheskaia pechat' Sibiri.* Tomsk: Izd. tomsk. universiteta 1989.

– *S"ezdy, konferentsii i soveshchaniia sotsial'no-klassovykh, politicheskikh, religioznykh, natsional'nykh organizatsii v eniseiskoi gubernii (mart-noiabr' 1918 gg.).* Tomsk: Izd. tomsk. universiteta 1991

Kotsonis, Y. "Arkhangel'sk, 18: Regionalism and Populism in the Russian Civil War." *Russian Review* 51 (1992): 526–44.

Krol', L.A. *Za tri goda.* Vladivostok: Svobodnaia Rossiia 1921.

Krol', M.A. "Sibirskoe pravitel'stvo i avgustovskaia sessiia sibirskoi oblastnoi dumy." *Vol'naia Sibir'*, no. 4 (1928): 69–82.

– "Stranitsa iz sibirskoi obshchestvennosti." *Sibirskii arkhiv* 3 (1930): 105–20.

Kropotkin, P. *Memoirs of a Revolutionist.* New York: Dover Publications 1971.

Krotov, M. "Bor'ba s kontrrevoliutsiei v severo-vostochnoi Iakutii." *Proletarskaia revoliutsiia* no. 5 (1928): 66–102.

Krusser, G.V. *Kolchakovshchina.* Novosibirsk: Sibkraiizdat 1927.

Kubanin, M.I. "Anti-sovetskoe krest'ianskoe dvizhenie v gody grazhdanskoi voiny (voennogo kommunizma)." *Na agrarnom fronte*, no. 2 (1926): 36–45.

Kuchiev, V.D. *Oktiabr' i sovety na Tereke (1917–1918 gg.).* Ordzhonikidze: Izd. Ir 1979.

Kudriavtsev, R.A., and G.A. Bendrikh. *Irkutsk. Ocherki po istorii goroda.* Irkutsk: Irkutskoe kn. izd. 1958.

Kulikowski, M. "A Neglected Source: The Bibliography of Russian Emigre Publications since 1917." *Solanus* 3 (1989): 89–102.

Kurlov, P.G. *Gibel' imperatorskoi Rossii.* Moscow: Sovremmenik 1992.

Kuz'min, G.V. *Razgrom interventov i belogvardeitsev v 1917–1922 gg.* Moscow: Voenizd. 1977.

Lampe, A.A., ed. *Beloe delo.* 7 vols. Berlin: Mednyi vsadnik 1926–33.

The Lansing Papers, 1914–1920: Papers Relating to the Foreign Relations of the United States. Washington, D.C.: United States Department of State 1940.

Lasch, C. "American Intervention in Siberia: A Reinterpretation." *Political Science Quarterly* 77, no. 2 (June 1962): 205–23.

Leadenham, C.A. *Guide to the Collection in the Hoover Institution Archives relating to Imperial Russia, the Russian Revolutions and Civil War, and the First Emigration.* Stanford, California: Hoover Institution Press 1986.

239 Monographic and Periodical Literature

Lebedev, V.I. "Armiia poslednei russkoi reaktsii." *Volia Rossii* 2 (1925): 183–91; 4 (1925): 167–81.

– *Bor'ba russkoi demokratii protiv bol'shevikov.* New York: First Russian Publishing Corporation 1919.

Leggett, G. *The Cheka: Lenin's Political Police.* Oxford: Clarendon Press 1981.

Lehovich, D.V. *White against Red: The Life of General Anton Denikin.* New York: Norton 1974.

Leikina, V. "Oktiabr' po Rossii." *Proletarskaia revoliutsiia,* no. 49 (1926): 217–29.

Lemke, M.K. *Nikolai Mikhailovich Iadrintsev: biograficheskii ocherk, k desiatiletiiu so dnia konchiny.* St Petersburg: Izd. red. gazety "Vostochnoe obozrenie" 1904.

Lenin, V.I. *Polnoe sobranie sochinenii,* 5th ed. 56 vols. Moscow: Gospolitizd. 1958–66.

Levin, M.G., and L.P. Potapov. *The Peoples of Siberia.* Chicago: University of Chicago Press 1964.

Levinson, A. "Poezdka iz Peterburga v Sibir' v ianvare 1920 g." *Arkhiv russkoi revoliutsii* 1 (1922): 190–209.

Lih, L.T. "Bolshevik Razverstka and War Communism." *Slavic Review* 45, no. 4 (1986): 673–88.

– "Bread and Authority in Russia: Food Supply and Revolutionary Politics, 1914–1921." Princeton University: PH D dissertation 1984.

Lincoln, W.B. *The Conquest of a Continent: Siberia and the Russians.* London: Random House 1994.

– *Red Victory.* New York: Simon and Schuster 1989.

Lipkina, A.G. *1919 God v Sibiri.* Moscow: Voenizd. 1962.

Lisovoi, Ia.M., ed. *Belyi arkhiv.* 3 vols. Paris: 1926–8.

Litvin, A.L. *Kazan': vremia grazhdanskoi voiny.* Kazan': Tatarskoe knizhnoe izd. 1991.

Livshits, S.G. *Imperialisticheskaia interventsiia v Sibiri v 1918–1920 gg.* Barnaul: Altaiskoe knizhnoe izd. 1979.

Logvinov, V.K. *V bor'be s kolchakovshchinoi. Ocherki o krasnoiarskom bol'shevistskom podpol'e i partizanskom dvizhenii v eniseiskoi gubernii, 1918–1920 gody.* Krasnoiarsk: Krasnoiarskoe knizhnoe izd. 1980.

Luckett, R. *The White Generals.* London: Longman 1971.

Lunacharskii, A.V. *Byvshie liudi.* Moscow: Gosizd. 1922.

McCord, E.A. "The Emergence of Modern Chinese Warlordism: Military Power and Politics in Hunan and Hubei." 2 vols. University of Michigan: PH D dissertation 1985.

Macey, D.A.J. *Government and Peasant in Russia, 1861–1906.* Dekalb, Ill.: Northern Illinois University Press 1987.

MacLaren, R. *Canadians in Russia, 1918–1919.* Toronto: University of Toronto Press 1976.

McNeal, R.H. *Tsar and Cossack, 1855–1914.* New York: St. Martin's Press 1987.

Maiskii, I.M. *Demokraticheskaia kontrrevoliutsiia.* Moscow-Petrograd: Gosizd. 1923.

Maksakov, V.V., and A.N. Turunov, eds. *Khronika grazhdanskoi voiny v Sibiri (1917–1918).* Moscow: Gosizd. 1926.

– *Partizanskoe dvizhenie v Sibiri.* Moscow-Leningrad: Gosizd. 1925.

Malia, M. *The Soviet Tragedy.* New York: The Free Press 1994.

Malle, S. *The Economic Organization of War Communism, 1918–1921.* Cambridge: Cambridge University Press 1985.

Manning, C.A. *The Siberian Fiasco.* New York: Library Publishers 1952.

Marks, S.G. *Road to Power: The Trans-Siberian Railroad and the Colonization of Asian Russia, 1850–1917.* Ithaca, N.Y.: Cornell University Press 1991.

Masaryk, T.G. *The Making of a State.* London: George Allen & Unwin 1927.

Mawdsley, E. *The Russian Civil War.* Boston: Allen & Unwin 1987.

Medvedev, R.A. *The October Revolution.* New York: Columbia University Press 1979.

Meijer, J.M. "Town and Country in the Civil War." In R. Pipes, ed., *Revolutionary Russia.* New York: Anchor 1969.

Mel'gunov (Melgounov), S.P. *The Bolshevik Seizure of Power.* Santa Barbara: ABC-CLIO 1972.

– *Grazhdanskaia voina v osveshchenii P.N. Miliukova.* Paris: Rapid-Imprimerie 1929.

– *Nikolai Vasil'evich Chaikovskii v gody grazhdanskoi voiny.* Paris: Rodnik 1929.

– *The Red Terror in Russia.* London: J.M. Dent & Sons 1926.

– *Tragediia Admirala Kolchaka.* 3 vols. Belgrade: Russkaia tip. 1930–31.

– *Vospominanii i dnevniki.* 2 vols. Paris: Les Éditeurs Réunis 1964.

Melnik, I.S., ed. *Sibir': ee sovremennoe sostoianie i ee nuzhdy.* St Petersburg: Izd. A.F. Devrena 1908.

Miliukov, P.N. "Admiral Kolchak." In *The New Russia,* 1:73. London: The Russian Liberation Committee 1920.

Mints, I.I. *God 1918i.* Moscow: Nauka 1982.

– *Istoriia velikogo oktiabria.* 3 vols. Moscow: Nauka 1977–79.

–, et al., eds. *Iz istorii grazhdanskoi voiny i interventsii 1917–1922 gg.* Moscow: Nauka, 1974.

Miroshnichenko, P., ed. "Iz istorii kolchakovshchiny." *Krasnyi arkhiv* 3(28) (1928): 225–8.

Mirzoev, V.G. *Istoriografiia Sibiri.* Moscow: Izd. Mysl' 1970.

– *Partizanskoe dvizhenie v zapadnoi Sibiri (1918–1919 gg.).* Kemerovo: Kemerovskoe kn. izd. 1957.

Mohrenschildt, D.V. *Toward a United States of Russia: Plans and Projects of Federal Reconstruction of Russia in the 19th Century.* Rutherford, N.J.: Farleigh Dickinson University Press 1981.

Molodtsygin, M.A. *Raboche-krest'ianskii soiuz, 1918–1920.* Moscow: Nauka 1987.

Moltchanoff, V.M. "The Last White General." Interviewed by B. Raymond. *California-Russian Emigre Series*. Berkeley, California: Regional Oral History Office 1972.

Montandon, G. *Deux ans chez Koltchak et chez les Bolchéviques pour la Croix-Rouge de Genève (1919–1921)*. Paris: Lib. Félix Alcan 1923.

Morley, J.W. *The Japanese Thrust into Siberia, 1918*. New York: Columbia University Press 1957.

– "The Russian Revolution in the Amur Basin." *American Slavic and East European Review*, no. 16 (December 1957): 450–72.

Morokhovets, E.A. *Agrarnye programmy rossiiskikh partii v 1917 godu*. Leningrad: Priboi 1929.

Mote, V.L. "The Cheliabinsk Grain Tariff and the Rise of the Siberian Butter Industry." *Slavic Review* 35, no. 2 (1976): 304–17.

Movchin, N. "Komplektovanie krasnoi armii v 1918–1920 gg." In A.S. Bubnov, S.S. Kamenev, and R.P. Eideman, eds., *Grazhdanskaia Voina 1918–1921*, 2:75–90. Moscow: Gosizd. 1928–30.

Murby, R.N. "The Canadian Economic Commission to Siberia." *Canadian Slavonic Papers* 11, no. 3 (1969): 374–93.

N. [Gen. V. Flug]. "Otchet o komandirovke iz dobrovol'cheskoi armii v Sibir' v 1918 godu." *Arkhiv russkoi revoliutsii* 9 (1923): 243–304.

N. [P.D. Iakovlev]. "Poslednie dni kolchakovshchiny." *Sibirskie ogni*, no. 2 (1922): 76–95.

N.N. "Zapiski belogvardeitsa." *Arkhiv russkoi revoliutsii* 10 (1923): 56–113.

Naida, S.F., and V.P. Naumov, *Sovetskaia istoriografiia grazhdanskoi voiny i inostrannoi interventsii v SSSR*. Moscow: Izd. moskovskogo gos. universiteta 1966.

Nelidov, N., ed. "Kolchak i Finlandiia." *Krasnyi arkhiv* 2(33) (1929): 82–144.

Nenarokov, A.P. *Vostochnyi front 1918*. Moscow: Nauka 1969.

–, ed. *Pervoe sovetskoe pravitel'stvo (oktiabr' 1917-iul' 1918)*. Moscow: Izd. polit. literatury 1991.

Newman, H.W. "Siberia Under Kolchak's Dictatorship." *New York Times Current History Magazine* (May 1920): 300–9.

The New Russia. 2 vols. London: The Russian Liberation Committee 1920.

Nezhdanov, L. "Pokhod na Rossiiu." *Minuvshie dni*, no. 3 (1927): 39–66.

Nikitin, A.N. *Dokumental'nye istochniki po istorii grazhdanskoi voiny v Sibiri*. Tomsk: Izd.tomsk.universiteta 1994.

– "Gazeta *Sokha i molot* kak istochnik po istorii partizanskogo dvizheniia na iuge eniseiskoi gubernii." In *Voprosy istorii obshchestvenno-politicheskoi zhizni Sibiri perioda oktiabria i grazhdanskoi voiny*, 154–73. Tomsk: Izd. tomsk. universiteta 1982.

Nikolaev, S.N. "Politika 'Komucha'" In *Grazhdanskaia voina na Volge v 1918 g.*, 103–64. Prague: Izd. obshchestvo uchastnikov volzhskogo dvizheniia 1930.

Norton, H.K. *The Far Eastern Republic of Siberia*. London: G. Allen & Unwin 1923.

Novikov, I.N. "Omsk v period kapitalizma (1861–1917 gg.)." In *Iz istorii Omska (1716–1917 gg.)*, 112–40. Omsk: Zapadno-Sibirskoe knizhnoe izd. 1967.

Oganovskii, N.P. *Zakupsbyt i soiuzy*. Novonikolaevsk: Izd. sekret. zakupsbyta 1919.

Okinskii, A. *Dva goda sredi krest'ian*. Riga: M. Didkovska izd. N.d.

Okladnikov, A.P., ed. *Krest'ianstvo Sibiri v epokhu kapitalizma*. Novosibirsk: Nauka 1983.

– *Krest'ianstvo Sibiri v period stroitel'stva sotsializma (1917–1937)*. Novosibirsk: Nauka 1983.

– *Ocherki russkoi literatury Sibiri*. 2 vols. Novosibirsk: Nauka 1982.

–, and V.I. Shunkov, eds. *Istoriia Sibiri*. 5 vols. Leningrad: Nauka 1968.

Olikov, S. *Dezertirstvo v krasnoi armii i bor'ba s nim*. Leningrad: Gosizd. 1926.

Orlovsky, D.T. "State Building in the Civil War Era." In D. Koenker, W.G. Rosenberg and R.G. Suny, eds., *Party, State, and Society in the Russian Civil War*. Bloomington and Indianapolis: Indiana University Press 1989.

Orshanskii, I.G. *Issledovaniia po russkomu pravu obychnomu i brachnomu*. St Petersburg: A.E. Landau 1879.

Osobennosti agrarnogo stroia Rossii v period imperializma. Moscow: Nauka 1962.

Ouspensky, P.D. *Letters from Russia, 1919*. London: Routledge & Kegan Paul 1978.

Owen, L.A. *The Russian Peasant Movement, 1906–1917*. London: Russell & Russell 1963.

Packard, L.B. "'Over There' in Siberia." *Social Studies for Teachers and Administrators* 10 (1919): 481–5.

Papers Relating to the Foreign Relations of the United States, 1918–19 (Russia). 4 vols. Washington, D.C.: United States Department of State 1931–37.

Papin, L.M. *Krakh kolchakovshchiny i obrazovanie Dal'nevostochnoi Respubliki*. Moscow: Izd. moskovskogo universiteta 1957.

Papoushek, Ia. "Prichiny Chekhoslovatskogo vystupleniia v 1918 godu." *Voliia Rossii* 8–9 (1928): 287–350.

Pares, B. "Dopros Kolchaka." *Slavonic Review* 8, no. 22 (1929): 225–30.

– *My Russian Memoirs*. London: Jonathan Cape 1931.

Parfenov, P.S. *Grazhdanskaia voina v Sibiri, 1918–1920*. Moscow: Gosizd. 1924.

– "Sibirskie es-ery i rasstrel slavgorodskikh krest'ian v avguste 1918 g." *Proletarskaia revoliutsiia*, no. 7 (1922): 59–71.

– *Uroki proshlogo: grazhdanskaia voina v Sibiri 1918, 1919 gg*. Harbin: Izd. Pravda 1921.

Parfenov, V. *The Intervention in Siberia, 1918–1922*. New York: Workers Library Publishers 1941.

Partiia Sotsialistov-Revoliutsionerov. *Chto dali bol'sheviki narodu*. N.p.: Izd. PSR 1921.

Pavlov, G. "Kolchak nastupal." *Sibirski ogni*, no. 6 (1929): 109–16.

Pavlunovskii, I.P. "Sibirskii krest'ianskii soiuz." *Sibirskie ogni*, no. 2 (1922): 124–31.

– *Obzor banditskogo dvizheniia po Sibiri s dekabria 1920 g. po ian'varia 1922 g.* Novonikolaevsk: 1922.

Pepeliaev, V.N. "Dnevnik." *Krasnye zori*, no. 4 (1923): 75–90; no. 5 (1923): 32–50.

– "Razval kolchakovshchiny." *Krasnyi arkhiv* 31 (1928): 51–80.

Pereira, N.G.O. "The 'Democratic Counter-Revolution' in Siberia during 1918." *Nationalities Papers*, no. 1 (1988): 71–93.

– "The Idea of Siberian Regionalism In Late Imperial and Revolutionary Russia." *Russian History* 20, nos. 1–4 (1993): 163–78.

– "Lenin and the Siberian Peasant Insurrections." In G. Diment and Y. Slezkine, eds., *Between Heaven and Hell*, 133–50. New York: St. Martin's Press 1993.

– "The Partisan Movement in Western Siberia, 1918–1920." *Jahrbücher für Geschichte Ost europas* 38, no. 1 (1990): 87–97.

– "Regional Consciousness in Siberia before and after 1917." *Canadian Slavonic Papers*, no. 1 (1988): 113–33.

– "Soviet Historiography of the Civil War in Siberia." *Revolutionary Russia* 4, no. 1 (1991): 38–51.

– "White Power during the Civil War in Siberia (1918–1920): Dilemmas Of Kolchak's 'War Anti-Communism.'" *Canadian Slavonic Papers*, no. 1 (1987): 45–62.

Pershin, P.N. *Agrarnaia revoliutsiia v Rossii.* 2 vols. Moscow: Nauka 1966.

Petrov, M.N. "The Rise and Fall of the Minority Party Socialist Revolutionaries." *Soviet Studies in History* 23, no. 2 (1984): 12–33.

Petrov, P.P. *Ot Volgi do tikhogo okeana v riadakh belykh (1918–1922).* Riga: Izd. M. Didkovskago 1930.

– *Rokovye gody (1914–1920).* California: Possev-Verlag 1965.

Pichon, Colonel. "Le Coup d'état de l'Amiral Koltchak." *Le Monde Slave*, no. 1 (1925): 1–26; no. 2 (1925): 248–70.

Pietsch, W. *Revolution und Staat: Institutionen als Träger der Macht in Sowjetrussland 1917–1922.* Cologne: Verlag Wissenschaft und Politik 1969.

Piontovskii, S.A., ed. *Grazhdanskaia voina v Rossii (1918–1921 gg.)* Khrestomatiia. Moscow: Gosizd. 1925.

– *Khrestomatiia po istorii oktiabr'skoi revoliutsii.* Moscow: Gosizd. 1926.

– "Kontrrevoliutsiia v Sibiri. Doklad podpolkovnika Glukhareva." *Krasnaia letopis'*, no. 5 (1923): 356–70.

– "Materialy po istorii kontrrevoliutsii." *Proletarskaia revoliutsiia*, no. 1 (1921): 114–46.

– "Ufimskoe soveshchanie i vremennoe sibirskoe pravitel'stvo." *Krasnyi arkhiv* 6 (61) (1933): 58–81.

Pipes, R., *Russia under the Bolshevik Regime*. New York: Alfred A. Knopf 1993.
– *The Russian Revolution*. New York: Alfred A. Knopf 1990.
Plotnikov, I.F. *Bol'shevistskoe podpol'e v Sibiri v period inostrannoi voennoi interventsii i grazhdanskoi voiny (1918–1920 gg.)*. Sverdlovsk: Sverdlovskii gornyi institut 1966.
– *Vo glave revoliutsionnoi bor'by v tylu kolchakovskikh voisk: sibirskoe (uralo-sibirskoe) biuro TsK RKP(b) v 1918–1920 gg.* Sverdlovsk: Izd. uralskogo universiteta 1989.
Plotnikova, M.E. "K istorii eserovskoi kontrrevoliutsii v Sibiri v 1918 g." *Voprosy istorii Sibiri*, no. 4 (1969): 172–88.
– "Kolchak i eserovskaia 'oppozitsiia.'" *Voprosy istorii Sibiri* 190, no. 3 (1967): 168–81.
– "Rol' 'vremennogo sibirskogo pravitel'stva' v podgotovke kolchakovskogo perevorota v Sibiri." In *Sbornik nauchnykh rabot istoricheskikh kafedr. Trudy tomskogo gos. univ*, 167: 51–67. Tomsk: Izd. tomsk. universiteta 1964.
– *Sovetskaia istoriografiia grazhdanskoi voiny v Sibiri*. Tomsk: Izd. tomsk. universiteta 1974.
–, et al., eds. *Oktiabr' i grazhdanskaia voina v Sibiri. Istoriia. Istoriografiia. Istochnikovedenie*. Tomsk: Izd. tomsk. universiteta 1985.
Poliakov, Iu.A. *Sovetskaia strana posle okonchaniia grazhdanskoi voiny*. Moscow: Nauka 1986.
–, ed. *Velikii oktiabr': problemy istorii*. Moscow: Nauka 1987.
Polikarpov, V.D., ed. *Velikaia oktiabr'skaia sotsialistiskaia revoliutsiia. Khronika sobitii*. Moscow: Nauka 1986.
Polner, T.J. *Russian Local Government during the War and the Union of Zemstvos*. New Haven: Yale University Press 1930.
Poltoratskii, N.P. "'Za Rossiiu i svobodu …': ideino-politicheskaia platforma belogo dvizheniia." *Russkoe proshloe*, no. 1 (1991): 280–308.
Poole, E. *"The Dark People": Russia's Crisis*. New York: The Macmillan Company 1918.
– *The Village: Russian Impressions*. New York: The Macmillan Company 1918.
Poppe, N. "The Economic and Cultural Development of Siberia." In G. Katkov, et al., eds., *Russia Enters the Twentieth Century, 1894–1913*, 138–51. London: Methuen 1971.
Potanin, G.N. "Goroda Sibiri." In I.S. Mel'nik ed., *Sibir': ee sovremennoe sostoianie i ee nuzhdy*. St Petersburg: Izd. A.F. Devrena 1908.
– "Iz istorii provintsial'noi pressy," *Otechestvenniia zapiski* 260, no. 3 (1881): 27–36.
– "Nikolai Mikhailovich Iadrintsev. Nekrolog." *Etnograficheskoe obozrenie* 4 (1894): 171–2.
– "Nuzhdy Sibiri." In I.S. Mel'nik, ed., *Sibir': ee sovremennve sostoianie i ee nuzhdy*. St Petersburg: Izd. A.F. Devrena 1908.

- *Oblastnicheskaia tendentsiia v Sibiri.* Tomsk: Sibirskoe t-vo pechatn. dela 1907.
Rabinowitch, A. *The Bolsheviks Come to Power: The Revolution of 1917 in Petrograd.* New York: W.W. Norton 1976.
- *Prelude to Revolution. The Petrograd Bolsheviks and the July 1917 Uprising.* Bloomington, Indiana: Indiana University Press 1968.
Radkey, O.H. *The Agrarian Foes of Bolshevism.* New York: Columbia University Press 1958.
- *The Elections to the Russian Constituent Assembly of 1917.* Cambridge, Mass.: Harvard University Press 1950.
- *The Sickle under the Hammer: The Russian Socialist Revolutionaries in the Early Months of Soviet Rule.* New York: Columbia University Press 1963.
- *The Unknown Civil War in South Russia: A Study of the Green Movement in the Tambov Region, 1920–21.* Stanford: Stanford University Press 1976.
Raeff, M. *Michael Speransky: Statesman of Imperial Russia, 1772–1839.* The Hague: Mouton 1957.
Rakov, D.F. *V zastenkakh Kolchaka. Golos iz Sibiri.* Paris: Pour la Russie 1920.
Raleigh, D.R. *A Russian Civil War Diary.* Durham, N.C.: Duke University Press 1988.
- *Civil War on the Volga: Saratov Province, 1918–22.* Forthcoming.
- *Revolution on the Volga.* Ithaca, N.Y.: Cornell University Press 1986.
- "Revolutionary Politics in Provincial Russia: The Tsaritsyn 'Republic' in 1917." *Slavic Review* 40, no. 2 (1981): 194–209.
Razgon, I.M., and L.M. Goriushkin, eds. *Oktiabr' v Sibiri Khronika sobytii.* Novosibirsk: Nauka 1987.
-, et al., eds. *Pobeda velikogo oktiabria v Sibiri.* 2 vols. Tomsk: Izd. tomsk. universiteta 1987.
Reikhberg, G.E. "Bol'sheviki Dal'nego Vostoka." *Proletarskaia revoliutsiia* 3 (1939): 72–81.
Rieber, A.J. "Landed Property, State Authority, and Civil War." *Slavic Review* 47, no. 1 (1988): 29–38.
Rodney, W. "Siberia in 1919: A Canadian Banker's Impressions." *Queens' Quarterly* 79, no. 3 (1972): 324–35.
Romanenko, I.I. "Slavgorodskoe vosstanie." In *Nezabyvaemoe,* 61–72. Barnaul: Altaiskoe knizhnoe izd. 1960.
Rosenau, J.N. "Internal War as an International Event." In *International Aspects of Civil Strife,* 45–91. Princeton, N.J.: Princeton University Press 1964.
Rosenberg, W.G. *Liberals in the Russian Revolution.* Princeton, N.J.: Princeton University Press 1974.
- "Russian Labor and Bolshevik Power after October." *Slavic Review* 44, no. 2 (1985): 213–38.
Rozwene, E.C., ed. *American Intervention in the Russian Civil War.* Lexington, Mass.: D.C. Heath 1969.

Russian Series: Records Relating to Internal Affairs of Russia and the Soviet Union. 5 vols. Washington, D.C.: United States Department of State 1910–29.

Safronov, V.P. *Oktiabr' v Sibiri.* Krasnoiarsk: Krasnoiarskoe knizhnoe izd. 1962.

Sakharov, K.V. *Belaia Sibir'.* Munich: H. Graf 1923.

Sakwa, R. *Soviet Communists in Power: A Study of Moscow During the Civil War, 1918–1921.* London: Macmillan 1988.

Schapiro, L. *The Communist Party of the Soviet Union.* New York: Vintage 1971.

– *1917: The Russian Revolutions and the Origins of Present-Day Communism.* Hounslow: Maurice Temple Smith 1984.

– *The Origin of the Communist Autocracy: Political Opposition in the Soviet State, First Phase, 1917–1922.* London: G. Bell And Sons 1978.

Scheibert, P. *Lenin an der Macht: Das russische Volk in der Revolution 1918–1922.* Weinheim: VCH 1984.

Schmid, A.P. *Churchills privater Krieg: Intervention und Konterrevolution im russischen Bürgerkrieg, November 1918-Marz 1920.* Zurich: Atlantis 1974.

Scott, J.C. *The Moral Economy of the Peasant.* New Haven: Yale University Press 1976.

Seleznev, K., ed. *Partizanskoe dvizhenie v zapadnoi Sibiri v 1918–1919 gg.* Novosibirsk: zapadno-sibirsksoe kraevoe izd. 1936.

Seliunin, V. "Istoki." *Novyi mir,* no. 5 (1988): 162–90.

Sellen, R.W. "The British Intervention in Russia, 1917–1920." *Dalhousie Review* 40 (1960–61): 360–71, 520–31.

Semenov, G.M. *O sebe. Vospominaniia, mysli i vyvody.* Harbin: Zaria 1938.

Serebrennikov, I.I. "Iz istorii sibirskago pravitel'stva." *Sibirskii arkhiv,* no. 1 (1929): 5–22.

– *Moi vospominaniia.* 2 vols. Tientsin: Star Press 1937–40.

– "The Siberian Autonomous Movement and its Future." *Pacific Historical Review* 3 (1934): 400–15.

– *Velikii otkhod 1919–1923.* Harbin: Izd. M.V. Zaitseva 1936.

Service, R. *The Bolshevik Party in Revolution: A Study in Organizational Change, 1917–1924.* London: Macmillan 1979.

–, ed. *Society and Politics in the Russian Revolution.* London: Macmillan 1990.

Sesiunina, M.G. "Delo sibirskogo separatizma." In *Politicheskaia ssylka v Sibiri XIX–nachalo XX v.,* 39–48. Novosibirsk: Nauka 1987.

– *G.N. Potanin i N.M. Iadrintsev – ideologi sibirskogo oblastnichestva.* Tomsk: Izd. tomsk. universiteta 1974.

– "K voprosu ob evoliutsii sibirskogo oblastnichestva (70-e – nachalo 90-kh godov XIX v.)." In *Trudy tomskogo universiteta* 190 (1967): 89–100.

Shanin, T. *The Awkward Class: Political Sociology of Peasantry in a Developing Society: Russia 1910–1925.* Oxford: Clarendon Press 1972.

– *Russia as a "Developing Society."* 2 vols. New Haven: Yale University Press 1986.

Shchetinkin, P.E. *Bor'ba s kolchakovshchinoi. Ocherk partizanskoi bor'by na minusinskom fronte.* Novosibirsk: Sibkraiizdat 1929.

Shchetinov, Iu.A. *Krushenie melkoburzhuaznoi kontrrevoliutsii v Sovetskoi Rossii (konets 1920–1921 g.).* Moscow: Izd. moskovskogo universiteta 1984.

Shebeko, B. "Russian Civil War, 1918–1922 and Emigration." Interviewed by R.A. Pierce. *California-Russian Emigre Series.* Berkeley, California: Regional Oral History Office 1961.

Shereshevskii, B.M. *V bitvakh za Dal'nii Vostok (1920–1922 gg.).* Novosibirsk: Nauka 1974.

Sherman, I.L. *Sovetskaia istoriografiia grazhdanskoi voiny v SSSR (1920–1931).* Kharkov: Izd. kharkov. universiteta 1964.

Shikanov, L.A. "K voprosu o khronologicheskikh ramkakh 'demokraticheskoi' kontrrevoliutsii v Sibiri." In *Iz istorii interventsii i grazhdanskoi voiny v Sibiri i na Dal'nem Vostoke, 1917–1922 gg.,* 62–7. Novosibirsk: Nauka 1985.

Shikanova, I.S. "Denezhnaia reforma Kolchaka." In *Numizmatika, bonistika, faleristika.,* 148–66. Moscow: Trudy GIM 1992.

Shilovskii, M.V. *Sibirskie oblastniki v obshchestvenno-politicheskom dvizhenii v kontse 50kh-60kh godakh XIX veka.* Novosibirsk: Izd. novosibirskogo universiteta 1989.

– "Sibirskoe oblastnichestvo i kontrrevoliutsiia: k probleme vzaimootnoshe-niia." In *Iz istorii interventsii i grazhdanskoi voiny v Sibiri i na Dal'nem Vostoke, 1917–1922 gg.,* 169–75. Novosibirsk: Nauka 1985.

Shiriamov, A.A. "Irkutskoe vosstanie i rasstrel Kolchaka." *Sibirskie ogni,* no. 4 (1924): 122–39.

Shishkin, V.I., ed. *Aktual'nye problemy istorii sovetskoi Sibiri.* Novosibirsk: Nauka 1990.

– "Bol'sheviki i partizanskoe dvizhenie v Sibiri v osveshchenii sovetskoi literatury 20-nachala 30-x gg." In *Bol'sheviki Sibiri v bor'be za pobedu velikoi oktiabr'skoi sotsialisticheskoi revoliutsii,* 57–77. Novosibirsk: Novosibirskii gos. universiteta 1987.

– "Bor'ba bol'shevikov za ob"edinenie sibirskikh partizan s krasnoi armiei (dekabr' 1919-aprel' 1920 g.)." In *Bol'sheviki vo glave trudiashchikhsia mass Sibiri v trekh rossiiskikh revoliutsiakh,* 81–105. Novosibirsk: Novosibirskii gos. universiteta 1986.

– "Diskussionnye problemy istorii partizanskogo dvizheniia v Sibiri v sovetskoi istoriografii 20-kh-nachala 30-kh godov." In *Sotsial'naia aktivnost' trudiash-chikhsia sovetskoi sibirskoi derevni,* 6–29. Novosibirsk: Nauka 1988.

– "Iz istorii bor'by kommunisticheskoi partii i sovetskoi vlasti protiv anarkhizma v zapadnoi Sibiri v 1919–1920 gg." In *Klassovaia bor'ba v sibirskoi derevne v period postroeniia sotsializma,* 3–38. Novosibirsk: Nauka 1978.

– "Kolybanskii miatezh." *Sibirskie ogni,* no. 10 (1990): 132–48.

– "Kozyrevshchina i ee likvidatsiia." In *Klassovaia bor'ba v sibirskoi derevne v period postroeniia sotsializma,* 52–77. Novosibirsk: Nauka 1978.

–, ed. *Pervye istoriki oktiabr'skoi revoliutsii i grazhdanskoi voiny v Sibiri.* Novosibirsk: Nauka, 1988.

– "Politicheskie pozitsii sibirskikh eserov v period kolchakovshchiny." In *Izvestiia sibirskogo otdeleniia Akademii Nauk SSSR*, 8–14. Novosibirsk: Nauka, 1984.

– "Prodovol'stvennaia kampaniia 1920–21 goda v Sibiri." In *Problemy istorii sovetskogo obshchestva Sibiri*, 124–40. Novosibirsk: Nauka 1970.

– "Rabochie prodovol'stvennye otriady tsentral'noi Rossii v bor'be za zagotovku khleba v zapadnoi Sibiri." *Istoriia SSSR*, no. 3 (1981): 147–57.

– *Revoliutsionnye komitety Sibiri v gody grazhdanskoi voiny (avgust 1919-mart 1921 g.).* Novosibirsk: Nauka 1978.

– *Sotsialisticheskoe stroitel'stvo v sibirskoi derevne.* Novosibirsk: Nauka 1985.

Shornikov, M.M. *Bol'sheviki Sibiri v bor'be za pobedu oktiabr'skoi revoliutsii.* Novosibirsk: Nauka 1963.

Shumiatskii, B.Z. *Sibir' na putiakh k Oktiabriu.* Moscow: Gosizd. 1927.

Sibiriakov, N.S. "Konets zabaikal'skogo kazach'ego voiska." *Minuvshee*, no. 1 (1986): 193–254.

Sibirskoe biuro RKP(b), 1918–1920: sbornik dokumentov. Novosibirsk: Nauka 1978.

Sibir' v proshlom i nastoiashchem. Novosibirsk: Novosibirskoe oblastnoe izd. 1937.

Silverlight, J. *The Victors' Dilemma: Allied Intervention in the Russian Civil War.* London: Barrie & Jenkins Ltd. 1970.

Skácel, J. *Československá armáda v Rusku a Kolčak.* Prague: Pamatnik Odboje 1926.

Slonim, M. "Metamorfozy natsional liberalizma." *Volia Rossii*, no. 2 (1928): 14–16.

Smele, J.D. "An Attempt to Utilize the Northern Sea Route to Siberia in 1919." *Sibirica*, no. 4 (1988): 28–39.

– "Labour Conditions and the Collapse of the Siberian Economy under Kolchak, 1918–1919." *Study Group On The Russian Revolution Sbornik*, no. 13 (1987): 31–59.

– "'What Kolchak Wants!': Military versus polity in White Siberia, 1918–20." *Revolutionary Russia* 4, no. 1 (1991): 52–110.

– "White Siberia: The Anti-Bolshevik Government of Admiral Kolchak, 1918–20." University of Wales (Swansea): PH D dissertation 1992.

Smirnov, I.N., et al., eds. *Bor'ba za Ural i Sibir'. Vospominaniia i stati uchastnikov bor'by s uchredilovskoi i kolchakovskoi kontrrevoliutsiei.* Moscow-Leningrad: Gosizd. 1926.

Smirnov, M.I. *Admiral Aleksandr Vasil'evich Kolchak.* Paris: Izd. voenno-morskogo soiuza 1930.

– "Admiral Kolchak." *Slavonic and East European Review* 11, no. 32 (1933): 373–87.

Smith, C.F. "Atamanshchina in the Russian Far East." *Russian History* 6, no. 1 (1979): 57–67.

– *Vladivostok under Red and White Rule.* Seattle, Washington: University of Washington Press 1975.

Smith, C.H. "Four Years of Mistakes in Siberia." *Asia* 22 (June 1922): 479–83.
– "What Happened in Siberia." *Asia* 22 (May 1922): 373–8; 402–3.
Smith, G. "Canada and the Siberian Intervention, 1918–1919." *American Historical Review* 64 (July 1959): 866–77.
Smith, R.E.F., ed. *The Russian Peasant.* London: Frank Cass & Co. 1977.
Smolin, A.V. *Krushenie "severo-zapadnoi" kontrrevoliutsii 1918–1920 gg. (nachalo bor'by).* Leningrad: GPU im. A.I. Gertsena 1990.
Smolka, M.P. "Arctic Siberia." *Slavonic and East European Review* 16, no. 46 (1937): 60–70.
Smyshliaev, V.A., et al., eds. *Bor'ba kommunisticheskoi partii protiv neproletarskikh partii, grupp i techenii.* Leningrad: Izd. leningrad. universiteta 1982.
Snow, R.E. *The Bolsheviks in Siberia, 1917–1918.* Rutherford, N.J.: Farleigh Dickinson University Press 1977.
– "The Russian Revolution of 1917–1918 in Transbaikalia." *Soviet Studies* 23, no. 2 (1971): 201–15.
Sobranie uzakonenii i rasporiazhenii Vremennago Sibirskago Pravitel'stva. Omsk: Tipografiia akmolinskogo oblast. upravleniia 1918.
Sobranie uzakonenii i razporazhenii pravitel'stva, izdavaemoe pri pravitel'stvuiushchem senate. Omsk: Tipografiia akmolinskogo oblast. upravleniia 1919.
Sokolov, S.N. "Oktiabr' za Baikalom (ianvar'–fevral' 1918 g.)." *Proletarskaia revoliutsiia*, no. 10 (1922): 389–97.
Solodiankin, A.G., et al., eds. *Gody ognevye, gody boevye. Sbornik vospominanii.* Irkutsk: Irkutskoe kn. izd. 1961.
Solov'ev, O.F. "O roli vnutrennei kontrrevoliutsii v razviazyvanii interventsii antanty letom 1918 g." In *Oktiabr' i grazhdanskaia voina v SSSR*, 400–13. Moscow: Nauka 1966.
Soskin, V.L. *Istoriografiia kul'tury i intelligentsii sovetskoi Sibiri.* Novosibirsk: Nauka 1978.
– *Ocherki istorii kul'tury Sibiri v gody revoliutsii i grazhdanskoi voiny (konets 1917-nachalo 1921 gg.).* Novosibirsk: Nauka 1965.
Sovetskaia istoricheskaia entsiklopediia, 16 vols. Moscow: Sovetskaia entsiklopediia 1967.
Spence, R.B. "White against Red in Uriankhai: Revolution and Civil War on Russia's Asiatic Frontier, 1918–1921." *Revolutionary Russia* 6, no. 1 (1993): 97–120.
Spirin, L.M. "Iz istorii PKP(b) v gody grazhdanskoi voiny i interventsii." *Voprosy istorii KPSS*, no. 1 (1989): 36–52.
– *Klassy i partii v grazhdanskoi voine v Rossii (1917–1920 gg).* Moscow: Mysl' 1968.
– *Razgrom armii Kolchaka.* Moscow: Izd. polit. literatury 1957.
–, ed. *Razgrom Kolchaka. Sbornik vospominanii.* Moscow: Voenizd. 1969.
– *Rossiia 1917 god.* Moscow: Mysl' 1987.
–, et al., eds. *Neproletarskie partii Rossii.* Moscow: Mysl' 1984.

–, and A.L. Litvin *Na zashchite revoliutsii. V. I. Lenin,* RKP(b) *v gody grazhdanskoi voiny.* Leningrad: Lenizdat. 1985.

Steinberg, I.N. *In the Workshop of the Revolution.* New York: Rinehart 1953.

– *Ot fevralia po oktiabr' 1917 g.* Berlin: Skify 1919.

Stephan, J.J. *The Russian Far East.* Stanford: Stanford University Press 1994.

Stewart, G. *The White Armies of Russia.* New York: MacMillan 1933.

Stishov, M.I. *Bol'shevistskoe podpol'e i partizanskoe dvizhenie v Sibiri v gody grazhdanskoi voiny (1918–1920 gg.).* Moscow: Izd. moskov. univ. 1962.

Strod, I. "Ungerovshchina i semenovshchina." *Proletarskaia revoliutsiia,* no. 9(56) (1926): 98–149.

Struggling Russia. 2 vols. New York: Russian Information Bureau in the U.S. 1919–20.

Subbotovskii, I. *Soiuzniki, russkie reaktsionery i interventsiia.* Leningrad: Vest. leningrad. soveta 1926.

Svatikov, S.G. *Rossiia i Sibir'.* Prague: Izd. obshchestva sibiriakov 1929.

Sverdlov, Ia.M. *Izbrannye proizvedeniia.* 3 vols. Moscow: Gospolitizdat. 1957–60.

Svetachev, M.I. *Imperialisticheskaia interventsiia v Sibiri i na Dal'nem Vostoke (1918–1922 gg.).* Novosibirsk: Nauka 1983.

Taylor, R. "A Medium for the Masses: Agitation in the Soviet Civil War." *Soviet Studies* 22 (April 1971): 562–74.

Thompson, J.M. "Allied and American Intervention in Russia, 1918–1921." In C.E. Black, ed., *Rewriting Russian History,* 334–400. New York: Praeger 1956.

– "Lenin's Analysis of Intervention." *American Slavic and East European Review* 17 (April 1958): 151–60.

– *Russia, Bolshevism and the Versailles Peace.* Princeton, N.J.: Princeton University Press 1966.

Thunig-Nittner, G. *Die Tschechoslowakische Legion in Russland.* Wiesbaden: Harrassowitz 1970.

Titov, V.Ia., et al. "K istorii partizanskogo dvizheniia v Sibiri." *Istoriia* SSSR, no. 4 (1988): 159–70.

Tiukavkin, V.G. *Sibirskaia derevnia nakanune oktiabria.* Novosibirsk: Nauka 1966.

Trani, E.P. "Woodrow Wilson and the Decision to Intervene in Russia: A Reconsideration." *Journal of Modern History* 48, no. 3 (1976): 440–61.

Treadgold, D.W. *The Great Siberian Migration: Government and Peasant in Resettlement from Emancipation to the First World War.* Princeton, N.J.: Princeton University Press 1957.

Trotskii (Trotsky), L.D. *How the Revolution Armed.* 3 vols. London: New Park Publications 1979.

Tumarkin, D. "Kontrrevoliutsiia v Sibiri." *Sibirskie ogni,* no. 1 (1922): 87–99.

– "Ot partii sotsializma k partii kapitalizma." *Sibirskie ogni,* no. 5 (1922): 123–34.

Turchaninov, N.V. "Naselenie aziatskoi Rossii." In G.V. Glink, ed., *Aziatskaia Rossiia,* 1:64–92. Cambridge, Mass.: Oriental Research Partners 1974.

Turunov, A.N., and V.D. Vegman. *Revoliutsiia i grazhdanskaia voina v Sibiri.* *Ukazatel' knig i zhurnal'nykh statei.* Novosibirsk: Sibraiizdat. 1928.

Turunov, A.N., ed. "Razval kolchakovshchiny. (Iz dnevnika V.N. Pepeliaeva)." *Krasnyi arkhiv* 6(31) (1928): 51–80.

Tyrkova-Williams, A. *From Liberty to Brest-Litovsk: The First Year of the Russian Revolution.* London: Macmillan 1919.

– *Why Soviet Russia Is Starving?* London: Russian Liberation Committee 1919.

Ullman, R.H. *Britain and the Russian Civil War.* Princeton, N.J.: Princeton University Press 1968.

– *Intervention and the War.* Princeton, N.J.: Princeton University Press 1961.

Umnov, A.S. *Grazhdanskaia voina i srednee krest'ianstvo (1918–1920 gg.).* Moscow: Voenizd. 1959.

United States War Office. *Siberia and Eastern Russia.* 3 vols. Washington, D.C. 1918.

Unterberger, B.M. *American Intervention in the Siberian Civil War.* Boston: D.C. Heath and Company 1969.

– *The United States, Revolutionary Russia, and the Rise of Czechoslovakia.* Chapel Hill, N.C.: University of North Carolina Press 1989.

Usatykh, V.S., ed. *V bor'be i trevoge.* Barnaul: Altaiskoe knizh, izd. 1977.

Ustrialov, N.V. *V bor'be za Rossiiu.* Harbin: "Okno" 1920.

Varneck, E. "Siberian Native Peoples after the February Revolution." *Slavonic and East European Review* 21 (1943): 70–88.

–, and H.H. Fisher. *The Testimony of Admiral Kolchak and Other Siberian Materials.* Stanford, Calif.: Stanford University Press 1935.

Vegman, V.D. "Kak i pochemu pala v 1918 g. Sovetskaia vlast' v Tomske." *Sibirskie ogni,* no. 1–2 (1923): 127–47.

– "Oblastnicheskie illiuzii i vozrozhdennie kolchakovshchiny." *Sibirskie ogni,* no. 5–6 (1923): 140–62.

– "Oblastnicheskie illiuzii, rasseiannye revoliutsiei." *Sibirskie ogni,* no. 3 (1923): 89–116.

–, ed. *Profsoiuzy Sibiri v bor'be za vlast' sovetov, 1917–1919 gg.* Novosibirsk: Sibraiizdat 1928.

– "Sibirskie kontrrevoliutsionnye organizatsii 1918 g." *Sibirskie ogni,* no. 1 (1928): 135–46.

– "Sibolduma." *Sibirskie ogni,* no. 4 (1923): 89–111.

Vel'man, V. "Fevral'skaia revoliutsiia v Sibiri." *Proletarskaia revoliutsiia,* no. 10 (1922): 167–200.

Vermenichev, I. "Agrarnoe dvizhenie v 1917 godu." *Na agrarnom fronte,* no. 3 (1926): 46–61.

Vilenskii-Sibiriakov, V.D. *Bor'ba za sovetskuiu Sibir'.* Moscow: Mospoligraf 1926.

– *Tsarstvo Kolchaka.* Moscow: Izd. federatsiia 1931.

Vitol'dova-Liutyk, S. *Na vostok ... vospominaniia vremen kolchakovskoi epopei v Sibiri v 1919–1920 gg.* Riga: Izd, "Orient" 1928.

Vladimirova, V. *God sluzhby 'sotsialistov' kapitalistam.* Moscow-Leningrad: Gosizd. 1927.

– *Iz nedavnego proshlogo.* Moscow-Leningrad: Molodaia gvardiia 1924.

Vologodskii, P.V. *Deklaratsiia Vremennago [Sibirskago] Pravitel'stva. Tomsk: 1918.*

Von Hagen, M. Soldiers in the Proletarian Dictatorship; the Red Army and the Soviet Socialist State, 1917–1930. Ithaca, New York: Cornell University Press 1992.

Vos'moi s"ezd RKP(b) (mart, 1918), protokoly. Moscow: Gosizd. 1959.

Wade, R.A. "Irakli Tsereteli and Siberian Zimmerwaldism." *Journal of Modern History* 39 (December 1967): 425–31.

Ward, J. *With the "Die-Hards" in Siberia.* London: Cassell 1920.

Watrous, S.D. "Russia's 'Land of the Future'; Regionalism and the Awakening of Siberia, 1819–1894." University of Washington: PH D dissertation 1970.

"What Happened at Omsk." *Independent,* no. 97 (8 February 1919): 175–6.

White, J.A. *The Siberian Intervention.* New York: Greenwood Press 1969.

Wilgress, D. "From Siberia to Kuibyshev." *International Journal* 22 (summer 1967): 364–75.

Wood, A. "Administrative Exile and the Criminals' Commune in Siberia." In R. Bartlett, ed., *Land Commune and Peasant Community in Russia. Communal Forms in Imperial and Early Soviet Society,* 395–414. New York: St. Martin's Press 1990.

– "Russia's 'Wild East': Exile, Vagrancy and Crime in Nineteenth-Century Siberia." In A. Wood, ed., *The History of Siberia,* 117–37. London: Routledge 1991.

Woodward, D.R. "The British Government and Japanese Intervention in Russia during World War I." *Journal of Modern History* 46 (1974): 663–85.

Woodward, E.L., and R. Butler, eds. *Documents on British Foreign Policy, 1919–1939.* First series, 2 vols. London: H.M. Stationery Office 1948.

Yaney, G. *The Urge to Mobilize: Agrarian Reform in Russia, 1861–1930.* Urbana, Ill.: University of Illinois Press 1982.

Zeman, Z.A.B. *Germany and the Revolution in Russia, 1915–1918: Documents from the Archives of the Foreign Ministry.* London: Oxford University Press 1958.

Zenzinov, V.M., ed. *Gosudarstvennyi perevorot Admirala Kolchaka v Omske 18 noiabria 1918 g.* Paris: Tip. I. Rirakhovskago 1919.

Zhigalin, Ia.P. *Partizanskie otriady zanimali goroda.* Irkutsk: Vostochno-Sibirskoe knizhnoe izd. 1980.

– "Partizanskoe dvizhenie v zapadnoi Sibiri." *Proletarskaia revoliutsiia,* no. 11 (1930): 98–112.

Zhurov, Iu.V. *Eniseiskoe krest'ianstvo v gody grazhdanskoi voiny.* Krasnoiarsk: Krasnoiarskii gos. ped. institut 1972.

– *Grazhdanskaia voina v sibirskoi derevne.* Krasnoiarsk: Krasnoiarskii gos. ped. institut 1986.

– et al., eds. *Bor'ba bol'shevikov Sibiri za narodnye massy v gody revoliutsii i grazh-danskoi voiny.* Krasnoiarsk: Krasnoiarskii gos. ped. institut 1983.

Zykova, V.G. *S"ezdy, konferentsii i soveshchaniia sotsial'no-klassovykh, politicheskikh, religioznykh, natsional'nykh organizatsii v irkutskoi gubernii (mart–noiabr' 1918 gg.).* Tomsk: Izd. tomsk. universiteta 1991.

Index